nce

Microsoft® Office 2004 for Mac

Richard Baker

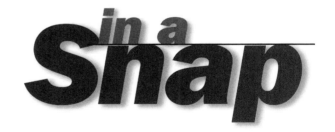

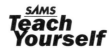
Sams
**Teach
Yourself**

Sams Publishing, 800 East 96th Street, Indianapolis, Indiana 46240 USA

Microsoft® Office 2004 for Mac in a Snap

International Standard Book Number: 0672-32-669-8

Library of Congress Catalog Card Number: 2003099241

Printed in the United States of America

First Printing: August 2004

07   06   05   4   3   2

Trademarks

All terms mentioned in this book that are known to be trademarks or service marks have been appropriately capitalized. Sams Publishing cannot attest to the accuracy of this information. Use of a term in this book should not be regarded as affecting the validity of any trademark or service mark.

Warning and Disclaimer

Every effort has been made to make this book as complete and as accurate as possible, but no warranty or fitness is implied. The information provided is on an "as is" basis. The author and the publisher shall have neither liability nor responsibility to any person or entity with respect to any loss or damages arising from the information contained in this book.

Bulk Sales

Sams Publishing offers excellent discounts on this book when ordered in quantity for bulk purchases or special sales. For more information, please contact

U.S. Corporate and Government Sales

1-800-382-3419

corpsales@pearsontechgroup.com

For sales outside of the United States, please contact

International Sales

international@pearsoned.com

Acquisitions Editor
Betsy Brown

Development Editor
Alice Martina Smith

Managing Editor
Charlotte Clapp

Project Editor
Matt Purcell

Indexer
Mandie Frank

Proofreader
Linda Seifert

Technical Editor
John Traenkenschuh

Publishing Coordinator
Vanessa Evans

Designer
Gary Adair

About the Author

Richard Baker has written 20 or so computer-related books—he has lost the exact count. He also spent more than a decade as editorial director of a PC training development group, writing with, about, and sometimes around the many manifestations of Microsoft Office. In a previous life he was a newspaper reporter and editorial writer. He now lives and works on what are temporarily the outskirts of Houston, Texas, with his wife Beverly, a Border Collie, two PCs, a Mac, and an Osborne 1.

Dedication

To the memory of Professor Floyd Arpan, one of those great teachers every-one should have in their past.

Acknowledgments

I'm hardly the first writer to give credit to a forbearing spouse, but after 40 years of marriage, Bev's reward was to endure the gestation of this book. She deserves extra credit.

Credit is also due the editorial staff that helped make this book what it is. These people infuriated me often. That means they were doing their jobs well.

Tell Us What You Think!

As the reader of this book, *you* are our most important critic and commentator. We value your opinion and want to know what we're doing right, what we could do better, what areas you'd like to see us publish in, and any other words of wisdom you're willing to pass our way.

You can email or write me directly to let me know what you did or didn't like about this book—as well as what we can do to make our books stronger.

Please note that I cannot help you with technical problems related to the topic of this book, and that due to the high volume of mail I receive, I might not be able to reply to every message.

When you write, please be sure to include this book's title and author as well as your name and phone or email address. I will carefully review your comments and share them with the author and editors who worked on the book.

Email: consumer@samspublishing.com

Mail: Mark Taber
         Sams Publishing
         800 East 96th Street
         Indianapolis, IN 46240 USA

Reader Services

For more information about this book or others from Sams Publishing, visit our Web site at **www.samspublishing.com**. Type the ISBN of the book (excluding hyphens) or the title of the book you're looking for in the Search box.

PART I

The Office Package

IN THIS PART:

1

✔ Start Here

You plan to run Microsoft Office on a Mac? What are you *thinking*!?!?

After all, Microsoft Office and Microsoft Windows truly seem to belong together. Few combinations are as inseparable as this one. Across this great land, thousands of cubicle denizens work with Office and Windows on their politically correct PCs. But Macintosh people are different, aren't they? Photoshop. Dreamweaver. iTunes. *Those* are the kinds of applications that belong on a Mac.

Yet here it is: Microsoft Office 2004 for the Mac. Deep within the Microsoft empire is a Macintosh Business Unit whose members for some years now have been putting out versions of Office for the Mac. Successive versions have been tweaked to take advantage of the Mac's unique approach to computing. With the 2004 version, they've put out a product many Windows people would envy. Now they must convince Mac users this product belongs on their computers.

There's a good chance it does belong. Almost by definition, Mac users are creative professionals or have similar pursuits. Many are self-employed, which means they run small businesses. Others work in small departments where they might be responsible for management and budgeting. Many in businesses of all sizes spend their time developing proposals and seeing them through. Although these Mac people might prefer to spend their time in creative pursuits, they have to spend significant amounts of time crunching numbers, processing words, communicating with clients, and dealing with meeting schedules.

Office 2004 for the Mac does this stuff. It can help you write a proposal, submit a bid, keep track of expenses, communicate with clients, and keep track of your schedule. And it does it all on your favorite computer.

What Is Office 2004?

NOTE

Lotus developed a separate version of Symphony for the Mac; it was called Jazz.

Back in the 1980s, most personal computers were single-purpose machines that could run only one program at a time. So, a few software developers set out to create single programs that did many things. Programs such as Ashton-Tate Framework and Lotus Symphony combined word processors, spreadsheets, databases, graphics, and communication functions all in so-called *integrated programs*. They ran on the green-screen operating systems of the day.

These integrated programs had limited success at best, and eventually they disappeared. One reason was that in trying to do everything, they did nothing really well. Another was that the computers of the day were not quite up to attempting more than one thing at a time. Both developers became better known for other products: Ashton-Tate's dBASE line of database managers and the Lotus 1-2-3 spreadsheet, a predecessor of Excel. Neither company now exists in its original form.

Meanwhile, single-purpose products such as Word and Excel were getting better. Furthermore, the Mac and Windows operating systems made it possible to run multiple programs at the same time—and even to exchange information with each other. That meant you could use separate applications together in a new kind of integrated program. This time, the combination works. For example, if you're writing a report in Word, you can readily work in an Excel table that shows the numbers you're talking about.

TIP

For even the most dedicated Mac user, Office can be an essential companion to what are considered the computer's more creative tools.

For some time now, Microsoft Office has been the leader of that pack. Microsoft has variously called it the Office Suite and the Office System. Others have called it things that won't be repeated here. In truth, legions of workers use the Windows version of Office not because they chose it but because their IT departments chose it for them. Be that as it may, Office occupies a throne that has few serious contenders.

What's in Office 2004?

Office 2004 combines four major applications: the Word word processing program; the Excel spreadsheet; the PowerPoint presentation system; and an email, address book, and calendar program called Entourage.

Excel is the tool number crunchers use to crunch numbers. Built like an accountant's worksheet but much larger, this program's forte is to take a bunch of numbers and add them, average them, or make any of a vast number of other computations and analysis. Excel also has the power to present its results in the form of a graph, or as the Excel folks call it, a *chart*.

Consider the process of figuring a bid for a design project. You might bill by the hour or day; the job might also include allowances for expenses. You can use Excel to total items, calculate markups, and arrive at a total bid.

Word is to text as Excel is to numbers. Write up that proposal and explain why you're the best for the job. Pop the bid numbers from Excel into a proposal letter if you want.

Do you think PowerPoint is just for business presentations? If you're an artist, consider a self-running presentation at an art show—one that showcases more of your work, explains your philosophy, and shows your location.

Entourage is a Mac interpretation of Outlook in the Windows version of Office. Outlook has been criticized as an overweight corporate tool, designed for use with a server database of people, projects, and endless meetings. Mac people will find Entourage a more personal tool. Although its emphasis is on communication and group interaction, it is built more for small groups of creative professionals. If you're part of a creative team, you can use Entourage to exchange email and keep the project on schedule. Use the address book to maintain contact with important internal or external clients. In its Office 2004 incarnation, Entourage is also a useful project management tool.

New in This Version

Group interaction is at the center of the changes introduced in Office 2004. In Microsoft's words, this version of Office is designed to help users "better manage their information, create documents with confidence, and share their ideas."

There is now a newly designed **Project Center**. It provides a coordinated way to look at a single project. That project might be made up of files, email messages, contacts, meetings, and tasks to be done. Instead of moving diverse files into a single folder, you can associate them with the project.

NOTE

The Professional Edition of Office 2004 also includes Virtual PC, an application that installs a copy of Windows on your Mac. You can use it to run Windows applications—albeit slowly—in a separate window of your Mac screen.

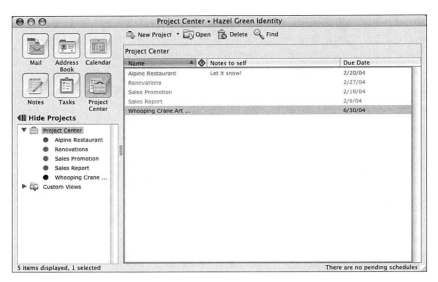

The ***Project Center*** *unites the diverse resources devoted to a single project.*

An entire team can share the project, helping individual members plan and coordinate their activities and providing a running view of the group's progress.

 TIP

Because some project information might originate on Windows or other non-Mac platforms, Office 2004 also provides for **Compatibility Reports**. Mac users can share information and ideas with nearly anyone, regardless of the make of their computer. That's nothing new, but the compatibility feature now examines these reports and flags any items that might cause problems on other platforms—or in other versions of Office.

A wizard helps you set up the project, incorporating existing resources and even selecting a color scheme. You can set the rules by which new information is added. Team members can add their own information, including files from Photoshop and other non-Office programs.

On a more personal level, you can assemble resources for your own use in a **Scrapbook**. This is a repository for text, illustrations, and other resources you might need for a particular job. You can store just about anything you want in a Scrapbook, and once it's there, you can use a search feature to find it again.

Word and Excel each give you a new way of looking at the world. Word now includes a **Notebook Layout** view, which, as its name suggests, is a place to take notes. You can make your notes on a screen that looks like a ruled sheet of paper. Or, you can record your own audio notes. As with the Scrapbook, the **Notebook Layout** view has a search function to help you find what you entered.

A weakness of Excel has always been the reluctance of well-ordered calculations to fit into the confines of well-ordered printed pages. Now, an

Excel **Page Layout** view lets you see, and if necessary adjust, what you'll see on paper, including headers, footers, and a page count.

For Windows Refugees

If you are coming to Office 2004 from a Windows version of Office, you'll find many things that are familiar and a few things that are not.

When you first look for help in an Office 2004 application, expect to be greeted by an old "friend." This is the **Office Assistant** that pops up when you open the help file. Quite a few years ago, Microsoft developed the idea of a cartoon character to liven up the search for help. Uncounted numbers of users found the figure more annoying than useful.

The Office Assistant in a Mac looks like...a Mac.

Nevertheless, the Assistant is still around. In the Mac versions of Office, it takes the form of a cartoon rendition of the original Macintosh. If it remains onscreen for more than a few minutes, the Assistant apparently gets bored and starts twisting itself in Rubik's Cube fashion.

Microsoft's main concession to user complaints has been to make turning off the Assistant easier. Open the **Help** menu, and you will find a checklist option to use it or hide it.

What you won't see in the Mac version of Office, initially at least, are as many toolbars as you might be accustomed to seeing in Windows. The Windows versions of Office applications initially display **Standard** and **Formatting** toolbars and offer options to display many more. Mac versions of Office have varied in the toolbars they initially display; Office 2004 starts you off with only the **Standard** toolbar onscreen. Many more toolbars are still available; select **View**, **Toolbars** and select those you want to display.

The Windows Task Pai...excuse me, Task Pane is gone in Office 2004. Instead, the Mac version has a **Formatting Palette** that sits next to the program's main window. You'll find options there to do things such as change the typeface, add borders and shading, or display the tab and

 TIP

Before you dispatch the Office Assistant, **Ctrl**-click the figure and select **Animate** from the context menu. The figure goes through a few extra comedy acts that are entertaining, if not useful. Repeat the process to see additional variations.

NOTE

Some toolbars do open of their own volition during specialized operations. For example, during some graphics tasks, the **Drawing** or **Picture** toolbar automatically opens.

paragraph marks in a document. The palette appears in sections with arrows you can click to expand or collapse the categories of options.

The **Formatting Palette** is unique to the Mac. It is also adaptable. If the cursor is in a text area, the palette shows text formatting options. If you select a graphic or an Excel chart, the palette displays graphic formatting options instead.

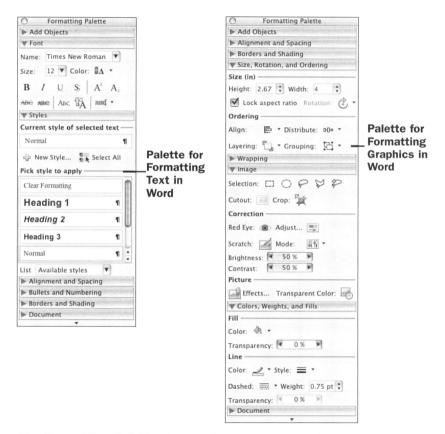

Palette for Formatting Text in Word

Palette for Formatting Graphics in Word

*The **Formatting Palette** changes from text to graphic tools, depending on what you're working with.*

Another Mac-only feature is the **toolbox**, which, as its name suggests, places several utilities in a separate palette. These include the **Scrapbook**, a **Compatibility Check** to ensure compatibility with other Office versions, and a window into the **Project Gallery**. (See Chapter 2,

"Project Management and Scrapbooking.") The Word toolbox also provides reference tools such as a dictionary and thesaurus.

With these few exceptions, Windows veterans should find Office 2004 familiar. At heart, the Windows and Mac versions of the programs are the same. The main changes are adaptations to the Mac interface—or more broadly to the Mac way of thinking. Otherwise, the screens should be familiar, and you'll find most of the menu options in most of the same places. Making the switch from Windows to Mac should take only a little getting used to.

Basic Office Tasks

Because the four Office programs are stable mates, they are all pretty much alike in the way they open, save, and print documents. They also usually have multiple ways to do the same jobs. For example, to start a program you have a choice of these methods:

- Click the program's icon in the **Dock**.

- Open the **Office 2004** folder. Depending on the installation, it might be in the **Macintosh HD** folder or in the **Applications** folder. Wherever it is, open the folder, and a new window displays the Office applications. Select the application you want to use.

- In the **Finder** window, double-click the filename of an Office document. The selected document opens in the application that was initially used to create it.

What's on the Screen

If you have any amount of computer experience, many elements of Office 2004 will seem familiar. For you, what's to come in this section might seem elementary. Then again, some of you might not have made it all the way around the block yet. Others might be experienced Mac users who could use some familiarization with the ways in which Office does things.

The authors of Office 2004 have done a fairly thorough job adapting what was originally a Windows suite of programs to the Mac operating system and interface. At the same time, the core elements—the things that make Office behave like Office—are pretty much the same on both platforms.

One of the first things a Windows user might notice about the Mac interface is that there is no **Start** menu. The **Finder** serves that function instead.

After you install Office 2004, its folder appears in the Mac **Finder**. Depending on the installation, it might be in the **Macintosh HD** folder or in the **Applications** folder. Wherever it is, open the **Office 2004** folder, and a new window displays the Office applications. Select the application you want to use.

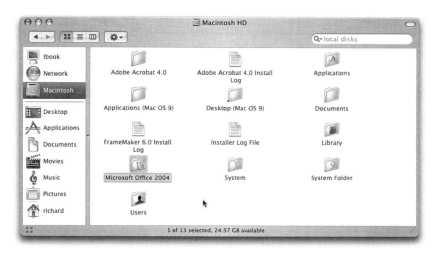

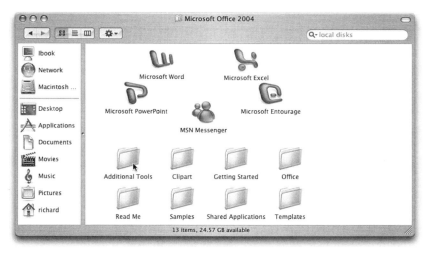

*The **Office 2004** folder appears in the **Macintosh HD** folder in the Finder; open that folder to see the Office applications.*

Opening a Document

When you open a program, the first screen is the **Project Gallery**. To open a blank document, you can select **Blank Document** in the **Groups** list on the left. Alternatively, you can explore the document *templates* available in other groups. Start with **15 Use a Template to Design a Document** for more information about templates.

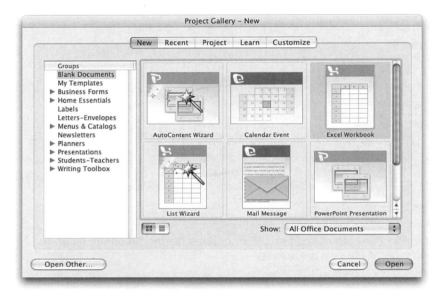

The **Project Gallery** *gives you options for opening a file.*

To open an existing document, look for it on the **Recent** tab of the **Project Gallery**. If you have organized files in a **Project**, they also appear on that page (see **1 Display the Project Center** for more information about projects). If the **Project Gallery** is not open, use the application's main menu and select **File**, **Open**.

Saving a Document

To save a document from any application, select **File**, **Save**. The first time you save a document, the **Save As** dialog box opens. You can use it to name the file, select a folder in which to save it, and specify its format. This dialog box also opens when you select **File**, **Save As**. In this case, you can specify a different filename, folder, or format.

TIP

If you're an experienced Office user, you might find that the **Project Gallery** offers too much help. If so, click the **Cancel** button to close it. If you want to avoid the gallery completely, open the application menu (the one that says **Word**, **Excel**, or **PowerPoint**) and select **Preferences**. Depending on the application, either the **General** or **View** tab of the **Preferences** dialog box has an option to **Show Project Gallery at startup**. Disable the check box for that option.

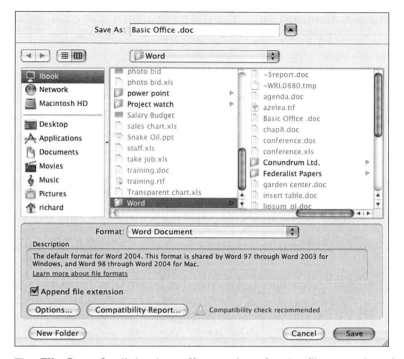

The **File Save As** dialog box offers options for the filename, location, and type of file you are saving.

NOTE

The compatibility section at the bottom of the **Save As** dialog box helps ensure that different versions of the same file will be compatible. You can click the **Compatibility Report** button to see whether any changes would be needed to improve compatibility.

TIP

If you choose a combination of printer settings you would like to use again, you can save it as a preset. Select the desired options, open the **Presets** list, select **Save as**, and give your preset a name. You can retrieve your named preset later from this list.

Going to Print

In all Office programs, printing a file begins with the menu selection **File**, **Print**. The **Print** dialog box has three drop-down lists. If the correct printer is not displayed, use the **Printer** list to make a different selection. The **Presets** box offers a selection of preset printer settings. The list initially labeled **Copies & Pages** offers a menu of printer settings.

Common Features in Office Applications

The computer industry once saw a major lawsuit over whether one product had illegally duplicated another's "look and feel." Because the components of Office are pieces of the same overall product, they can duplicate a look and feel without fear of litigation.

When an Office application opens, it displays several common elements that vary only a little from application to application.

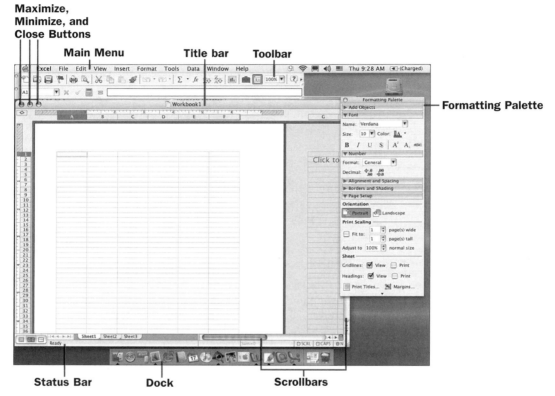

The Office applications have many elements in common.

The standard screen elements include

- **Title bar**—At the top of the document window, the title bar displays the current document's name. If the document has not yet been saved, the program assigns a number.

- **Menu bar**—This displays the main menu categories for the program. Each main menu item opens a pull-down menu of subordinate selections. Although the menu selections vary with each program, many such as **File**, **Edit**, and **View** are consistent from application to application.

- **Toolbars**—Each program displays one or more toolbars, which are collections of buttons that execute common tasks such as copying or setting up tables.

- **Minimize, Maximize, and Close buttons**—The **Maximize** button expands the application window to cover the full screen; the **Minimize** button stores it in the **Dock**, a graphic the Mac operating system places at the bottom of the screen. The **Close** button closes the document.

- **Scrollbars**—When a document is larger (longer or wider) than the window, use the scrollbars to move the document or up and down within the window.

- **Status bar**—This bar at the bottom of the screen displays a variety of information depending on the program in use. For example, in Word it displays the current page number and your position on the page. In Excel it shows the results of formulas.

Displaying Toolbars

KEY TERMS

Icon—A graphic label intended to describe the purpose of a toolbar button.

ToolTip—A text label that pops up to define an icon.

If you choose to display toolbars, or if the program does it for you, their rows of buttons provide clickable shortcuts to various program operations. Each button is labeled with a graphic *icon* that is supposed to describe what the button does. Sometimes the icon is successful at picturing its function; sometimes it isn't.

Icons were invented some years ago in the belief that they would be an improvement on text labels. That hasn't proven to be the case. Some of the little graphics are quite descriptive, but others are completely obscure. That's why the development of icons was followed closely by the development of *ToolTips*. Place the mouse pointer over the icon, take a deep breath or two, and a text label appears to tell you what the icon stands for.

Entourage has only a single toolbar. The remaining Office applications have an assortment, including two basic toolbars: **Standard** and **Formatting**. Although these toolbars vary among applications, the **Standard** toolbar has buttons for file-handling functions such as opening and closing files plus the cut-copy-paste combination. The **Formatting** toolbar provides options such as selecting a typeface and style. For the most part, the **Formatting** toolbar duplicates options available in the **Formatting Palette**.

Excel has a special toolbar called the **Formula bar**. Its main feature is a large window on the right end, where you can write and edit the entries in a selected worksheet cell.

Standard Toolbar

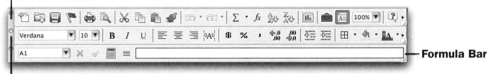

Formula Bar

Formatting Toolbar

*The **Standard** toolbar provides tools for program operation, the **Formatting** toolbar helps set a worksheet's appearance, and the **Formula bar** provides tools for entering and calculating formulas.*

Selecting, Cutting, and Pasting

All Office applications have some way of *selecting* items in a document so that you can copy, delete, edit, or otherwise manipulate them. Selecting can include any action that results in a *selection*. In addition to document contents, a selection can include things such as menu items and the buttons in dialog boxes.

If you select some of the contents of a document or worksheet, you can cut (delete) it from its current position or copy it, leaving the original selection in place. Either way, the selection is stored on a *clipboard*.

You can then paste the selection somewhere else, including another open document. As it often does, the application provides multiple ways of doing this. You can select the **Paste** command from the **Edit** menu or click the **Paste** button from the **Standard** toolbar. Alternatively, you can use the keyboard combinations ⌘-**X** to cut, ⌘-**C** to copy, and ⌘-**V** to paste.

A Word About Word

When you open either a new or existing Word document, the window displays many of the standard Office features such as a main menu, toolbars, and scrollbars. Word also can display your work in varying *views*.

You can open the **View** menu to select a view, or you can click one of the **View** buttons in the lower-left corner of the screen.

KEY TERMS

Select—To make a *selection*, usually by clicking or dragging. A selection can be a block of text, a range of worksheet cells, a button, or a menu item.

Clipboard—A temporary storage place for items that have been cut or copied for pasting in another location.

KEY TERM

View—One of several ways to display a document.

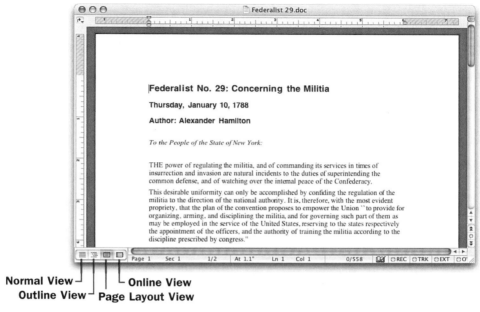

Normal View ⌐
Outline View ⌐ ⌐ Online View
Page Layout View

*The Word screen includes standard Office elements plus unique items such as the **View** buttons in the lower-left corner.*

You can display a Word document in any of these views:

- **Normal**—This is the view you use for fast text entry. It doesn't display graphics or page layouts.

- **Online**—This view shows how the document would look as a World Wide Web page.

- **Page Layout**—This view displays the layout of a printed page.

- **Outline**—Use this view to display the document's structure and to organize and reorganize it.

- **Notebook**—New to Word 2004, this view makes taking notes while you work easier. It's explained more fully in **55** **Set Up a Notebook**.

 TIP

Also new to Word 2004 is a *Navigation pane*. Select **View, Navigation Pane**, and thumbnails of each page appear along the left side of the document window. Click any thumbnail to proceed to that page.

Once upon a time, every elementary instruction manual for Word started with the concept of word wrap. Liberated typists were shown that when text reached the end of a line, it "miraculously" flowed onto the

next line. To most, that's now a familiar concept. As you type in Word, the text flows from one line to the next, in the format and style you choose, within the margins you have specified.

As you work, you might see wavy red or green lines under the text. A red line indicates the word might be misspelled; a green line indicates it might violate a rule of grammar. **Ctrl**-click the word to see possible corrections.

Looking at Excel

As with other Office applications, the Excel window observes typical Office conventions. At the same time, some elements are unique to Excel.

Excel files are organized as **workbooks**; each workbook contains one or more **worksheets**. When you open a workbook, each worksheet is represented by a series of worksheet tabs at the bottom of the window.

> **NOTE**
>
> The wavy lines indicate a *possible* error. The spelling and grammar checkers are useful but not infallible. Don't rely on them absolutely; think of them as cues to check further.

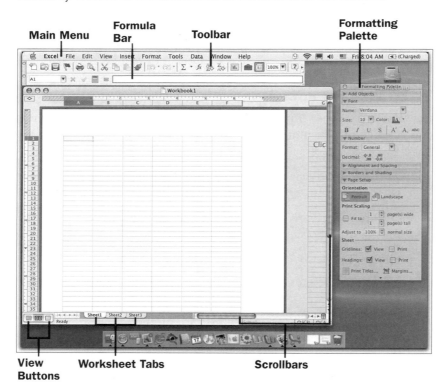

An Excel workbook is made up of worksheets, which are represented by tabs at the bottom of the window.

Unique to Excel is a **Formula** bar that shares space with the toolbars at the top of the window. The large window displays any values or *formulas* that have been entered in the currently selected cell. At the left end of the **Formula** bar is a **Name** window that identifies the current cell.

When you open Excel, it displays a blank document in **Page Layout** view, a new feature that displays the way the worksheet appears on a printed page. You can select other views by opening the **View** menu or by clicking a **View** button in the lower-left corner of the window.

 TIP

When you click a single cell, you also select it. You can select a range of multiple cells by dragging across them. You might do this to apply a different number format or type style to the selected cells.

A worksheet is made up of *cells* arranged in columns and rows. You can activate a cell by clicking it; then you can enter numbers, text, or a formula. You also can make an entry in an active cell by typing in the **Formula** bar. Each cell is identified by its column and row. For example, the cell at the intersection of column C and row 4 is cell **C4**. When you select the cell, its reference appears in the **Name** box of the **Formula** bar.

If you expect to refer often to this range, you can give the range of cells a name. For example, if you create a range of cells that contains income items on a balance sheet, you can name the range **Income**. To find the range later, select it from the **Name** drop-down list box.

Varied Views of PowerPoint

Compared with other Office 2004 applications, the onscreen appearance of a PowerPoint presentation depends greatly on the view you select. These are your choices:

- **Normal**—This view provides an overall picture. You can use it to work directly on the slide, in the outline, and on the notes page.

- **Outline**—This view lets you concentrate on the presentation's text and organization.

- **Slide**—This view lets you work directly on the slide.

- **Slide Sorter**—This view provides another way to organize the presentation.

- **Slide Show**—This view previews the presentation.

Each PowerPoint presentation is a series of slides. Each slide acts as a container for text, illustrations, and other types of information. You can use layout tools to give the slides a consistent look and to lay out slides for different combinations of text and artwork.

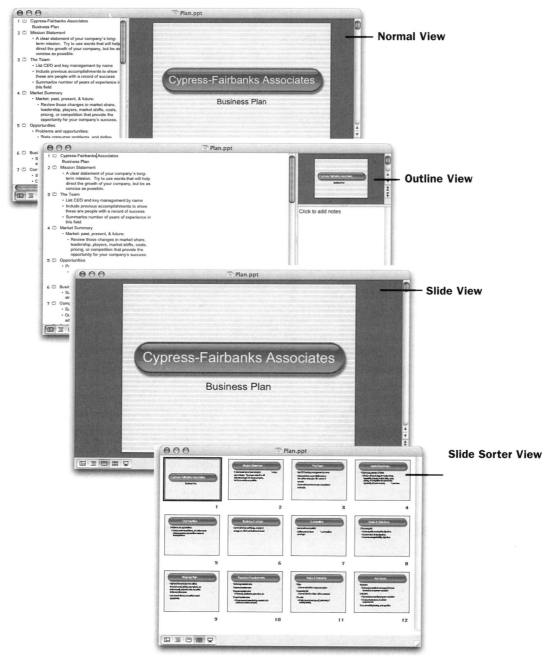

Different views of a PowerPoint presentation give you different ways to work with it.

Communicating with Entourage

Entourage is a multipurpose program that includes email, an address book, calendar scheduling, notes and tasks, and a new **Project Center**.

The initial screen displays navigation buttons in the upper-left corner. Click one of these buttons to use that function.

Navigation Buttons   **Toolbar**   **Office Notification**

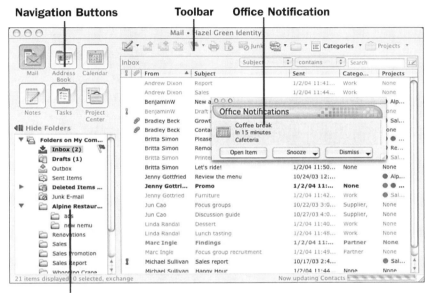

Folder List

Navigation buttons lead the way to Entourage functions.

Entourage is a close cousin to Outlook in the Windows version of Office and displays many of the same items. You can make selections from a list of folders on the left; you also can hide or redisplay this folders list.

 TIP

When you schedule calendar items and ask to be notified in advance, Entourage generates an **Office Notification**. It appears over any other open application.

When you select a function, such as **Mail** or **Address Book**, the contents are displayed in the main window. This information usually is arranged in columns. Click any item to see more details. Use the **New** button in the toolbar to add a new item. To sort the list, click a column heading. To reverse the sort order, click the heading again.

2

Project Management and Scrapbooking

IN THIS CHAPTER:

According to Microsoft, "up to 80% of Mac users work on projects on a daily basis."

You can ponder what "up to" might mean in this context, but it's clear that the *Project Center* is the centerpiece of the Office 2004 upgrade. It brings together all the resources you need to complete a particular project. These resources might include email messages, Word documents, Excel spreadsheets, contact names, and non-Office files such as Photoshop images. The **Project Center** puts these all together in one central resource.

1 Display the Project Center

See Also

→ **2** Set Up a Project

→ **3** Add Project Resources

→ **4** Share Project Resources

→ **6** Keep a Scrapbook

The main access to the *Project Center* is through Entourage, where it appears as an option along with more conventional Entourage operations such as **Mail**, **Calendar**, and **Address Book**.

You can use the **Project Center** to set up new projects and bring together the files, contact information, and other resources the project entails. Then, you can display and work with this project through the **toolbox** in the other Office applications.

1 Open Entourage

Open a Finder window and go to the **Office 2004** application folder. Depending on how Office was installed, this folder might be inside the **Applications** or **Macintosh HD** folder.

Open the **Office 2004** folder and select **Microsoft Entourage**. Entourage opens and displays **Project Center** among the function buttons in the upper-left corner of the screen.

2 Display the Project Center

Click the **Project Center** button. The **Project Center** opens and displays a list of current projects. Actually, it displays two project lists: one in the **Navigation Pane** on the left and one in the main **Project Center** window.

Each project is color-coded, and the color is carried throughout operations that involve that project. You can use the **Hide Projects** arrow to conceal the project list on the left side of the screen. When this list is hidden, a companion button reopens the list.

1 Open Entourage

2 Display the Project Center

3 Display a Project

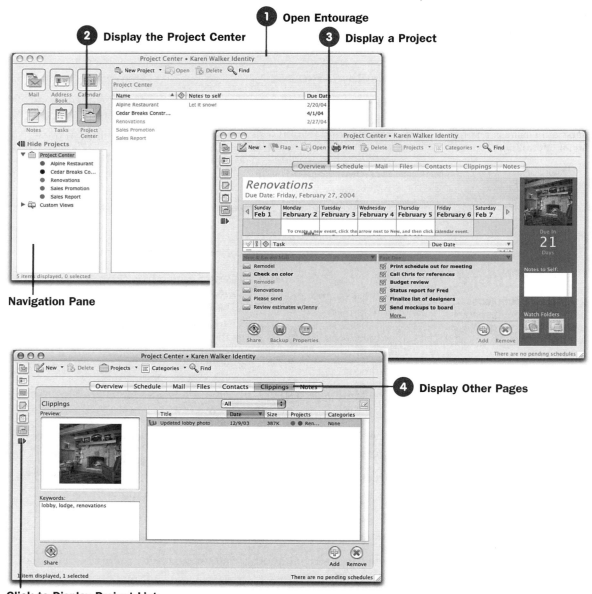

Navigation Pane

4 Display Other Pages

Click to Display Project List

NOTE

The **Custom Views** option (at the bottom of the project list on the left side of the screen) is an Entourage feature that lets you sort messages into categories. You could use this option, for example, to maintain separate business and personal information.

From this screen, you can open a new project, delete an existing one, search your Entourage files, or work on an existing application.

3 **Display a Project**

In the project list column on the left side of the screen, click one of the projects. Alternatively, select the project name in the **Project Center** window and click the **Open** button in the upper toolbar.

A dialog box displays the status of the chosen project. Select the **Overview** page if it is not already open. The display summarizes the project calendar, displays recent mail messages, shows the status of various tasks, and gives a large reminder of when the project is due.

4 **Display Other Pages**

Other pages in the **Project Center** dialog box display details of the project components. Click each tab to display the *items* on the various pages.

KEY TERM

Item—In Entourage, an email message, a contact, a calendar entry, a note, or a task.

The **Schedule** page displays the Entourage calendar with meetings, deadlines, and other key dates and times associated with the project.

The **Mail** page displays any email messages related to the project, no matter where the messages are stored.

The **Files** page provides a view of the files associated with a project.

The **Contacts** page again emulates the Entourage display but limits its contents to contacts who are involved in the project.

The **Clippings** page is a free-form place to store other project materials, such as illustrations, from the **Scrapbook** in Word.

NOTE

A **Share** button gives you the opportunity to share your work with co-workers. You can designate which items you do and do not want to share. Some items, such as the **Clippings** page, also provide for keywords you can use in a search. This feature requires that you and your co-workers have network access with security provided by the file sharing technology. As the owner of the project, you have to configure access for each person on the network you want to access your project. See the online help system for details.

The **Notes** page is another Entourage display tailored to the specific project.

For details on how to manage these pages, see **2** Set Up a Project, **3** Add Project Resources, and **4** Share Project Resources.

To return to the **Project Center**, open the project list in the left pane if necessary and select **Project Center**.

2 Set Up a Project

Sure, you can open and work with information in Word, Excel, and PowerPoint. But if you use materials from multiple sources in a single project, the *Project Center* is the place to bring them together. If this is a new project, you can take preliminary steps to put all these resources in place. Then, as new documents, meetings, and activities are added, you can include them in the existing structure.

1 Open the New Project Wizard

In Entourage, open the **Project Center**. In the main toolbar at the top of the window, click the **New Project** button. The **New Project Wizard** opens the first page of an untitled project.

2 Name the Project

In the **Name** text box, type a name for the project. It can be anything you choose; the main requirement is that you and others understand what it refers to.

If the project has a due date, enable the **Due Date** check box and enter the deadline. Type the date in the text box, or click the calendar icon to the right of the text box to select a date.

The **Notes to Self** text box is a free-form resource. Enter anything here you might want to recall in the future.

If you have a picture you want to use to identify the project, you can drag it from its current position in a Finder folder, on a network, or on the Web to the **Drag and drop image here** window.

When you're finished specifying the basics of the project, click the right-facing arrow at the bottom of the page. You move to Page 2 of the wizard.

3 Set Up Watch Folders

The **Project Center** uses a pair of *watch folders* to hold key information for each project. Each bears the project's name. One appears along with other mail folders in the **Navigation Pane** of the Entourage Mail window. If you move a message to that folder, it becomes part of the project.

Before You Begin

✔ 1 Display the Project Center

See Also

→ 3 Add Project Resources

→ 4 Share Project Resources

TIP

You can use color coding to identify a project wherever it might appear in Office. On the first wizard page, click the **Color** box and select a color from the list that opens. The selected color appears throughout the displays associated with this project.

1 Open the New Project Wizard

3 Set Up Watch Folders

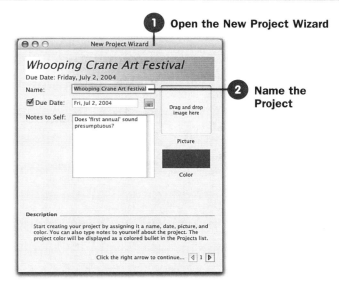

2 Name the Project

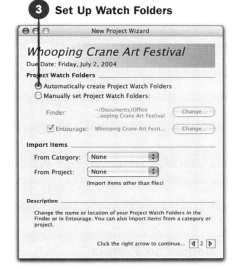

4 Write Email Rules

5 Create the Project

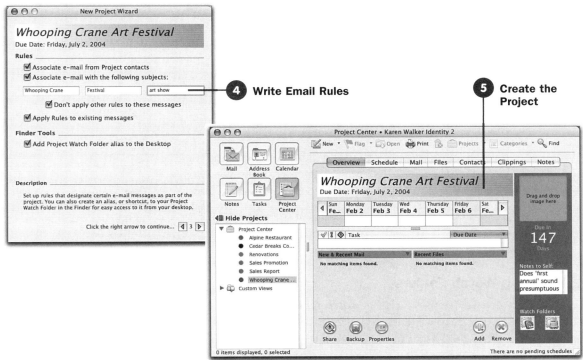

On the wizard's Page 2, you set the location of a watch folder that is created within the Finder structure. It contains information about the files you add to the project. When you add a file, an *alias* that points to the file is added to this folder. You also can add files to a project by directly dragging them to this watch folder.

If you allow the program to automatically create the folder, it will do so within Entourage. If you prefer, you can select **Manually set Project Watch Folders** and specify your own location, either within Entourage or in the Finder. The watch folder is named to match its project's name. Don't try to move or rename it.

From Page 2 of the wizard, you also can import existing Entourage *items*—messages, contacts, events, notes, and tasks—into the project. You can select from items that have been grouped into Entourage categories or that are already parts of other projects. If you want to incorporate selected contacts and their messages, create a new group for the purpose and add the contacts to that group. Their future email messages also will be attached to the project.

When finished, click the right-facing arrow at the bottom right of the screen. You move to Page 3 of the wizard.

4 Write Email Rules

If you're a typical email user, you probably receive a lot of messages everyday. Some messages are associated with the project, but most probably are not. You can manually sort through the daily load of spam to find the project-related messages, or you can let Entourage sort them out for you.

In Page 3 of the **New Project Wizard**, you can set up rules by which an email message can be automatically included in the project. Enable the check boxes for those options you prefer. The **Associate e-mail with the following subjects** choice provides room to enter three words or phrases associated with the project. When any of these terms appears in the subject line of an email message, the message is included in the project.

On this page, you also can decide whether to add an alias (a shortcut icon) for the project's Finder watch folder to the desktop. If so, enable the **Add Project Watch Folder alias to the Desktop** check box.

KEY TERM

Watch folders—Folders set up to contain key information about a project and its resources.

NOTE

You cannot add files to the project at this point. After the project is set up, you can open the project and import files through the **Files** page.

When you've finished making your choices, click the right arrow at the bottom right of the screen. You move to Page 4 of the wizard.

NOTE

On any page of the **Project Center** dialog box, you can click the **Add** button at the bottom of the page to add new Entourage items to the project and the **Remove** button to remove them.

5 Create the Project

Page 4 of the wizard displays a summary of your choices. If you want to make any changes, click the left arrow at the bottom right of the page to return to previous wizard pages. When you're satisfied with the project summary, click the right arrow to create the project and open its window.

 Add Project Resources

Before You Begin

✔ **2** Set Up a Project

See Also

➜ **4** Share Project Resources

The **Project Center** is not an application that generates new information in its own right; it is an organizer that helps you assemble the resources associated with a particular project.

Most of these resources are Entourage items: email messages, Calendar events, Address Book contacts, and the like. Adding these items to a project is no more complicated than the familiar magic wand technique: Wave the wand and say, "You're in." (The vocalization is optional.) Adding clips from the **Scrapbook** is much the same.

Adding a related file is a bit more complicated. When you add a file to a project, an alias or shortcut to the file is added to the project's *watch folder* (you can view the watch folder's contents in the Finder).

TIPS

You can press the ⌘ or **Shift** key as you click contacts to make multiple selections and add them all at once.

Use this same technique to add items to other Project Center windows, including Schedule, Mail, and Notes. If you want to add a clip from the Notebook, the **Add** button displays a list of clips from which you can select.

1 Add a Contact

You can add an Entourage item from any Entourage window, including the **Project Center**. If your project is to stage an art show, you no doubt have several assistants. You want to add their names and email addresses to the project so you can address messages to them.

Display the **Contacts** page in the **Project Center**. Click the **Add** button in the lower-right corner. The names in your Address Book appear in the **Add Contact** dialog box. Select the contact you want to include and click **Add**. The contact is immediately associated with the project.

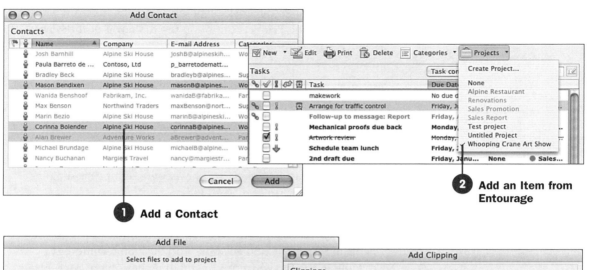

1 Add a Contact

2 Add an Item from Entourage

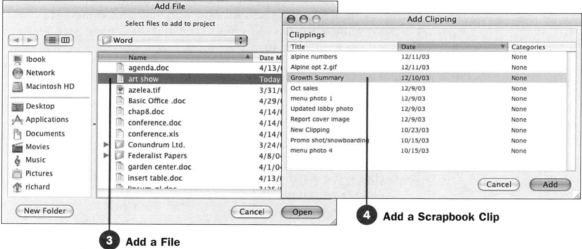

3 Add a File

4 Add a Scrapbook Clip

2 Add an Item from Entourage

You also can add items to a project from any other Entourage window: Mail, Address Book, Calendar, Notes, or Tasks.

Many individual tasks are surely involved in putting on an art show. You can add them to the project as well. The **Project Center** has no specific window for Notes items from Entourage, but you can add them to the **Notes** page in your project.

In Entourage, open the **Tasks** window. Select the task you want to add and click the **Projects** button in the toolbar. Select the project to which you want to add the selected task from the list that displays.

You also can use this technique to add items from other Entourage windows.

③ Add a File

If you're fortunate, your predecessor as art show manager left some notes about how previous shows were set up. These notes might be in the form of a Word file.

Because this probably is valuable information, you want to add the file to your current project so you can gain ready access to it. Open the **Files** page and click the **Add** button. A Finder list opens. Navigate to the file you want to add and click **Open**. An alias to the file is added to the Finder watch folder.

④ Add a Scrapbook Clip

Although the **Scrapbook** is a component of Word, not Entourage, you can link scrapbook items to a project much as you link Entourage items.

In the **Clippings** page, click the **Add** button. A list of **Scrapbook** clips is displayed. Select one or more and click **Add**. The clips become part of the project.

4 Share Project Resources

Before You Begin

✔ **2** Set Up a Project

See Also

→ **3** Add Project Resources

KEY TERM

Share—In an Office project, to make resources available over a network to other participants in the project.

A project is seldom a one-person activity. After all, it probably includes contact names and email messages to and from other people. If you and your colleagues are linked by a network, you can use that network to *share* project resources.

① Open the Project Sharing Assistant

From the main menu of any **Project Center** window, select **File**, **Share a Project**. Alternatively, click the **Share** button at the bottom of any project display and select **Start sharing project**.

① **Open the Project Sharing Assistant**

③ **Choose a Location**

② **Select the Project to Share**

⑤ **Invite Others to Share**

④ **Identify Items for Sharing**

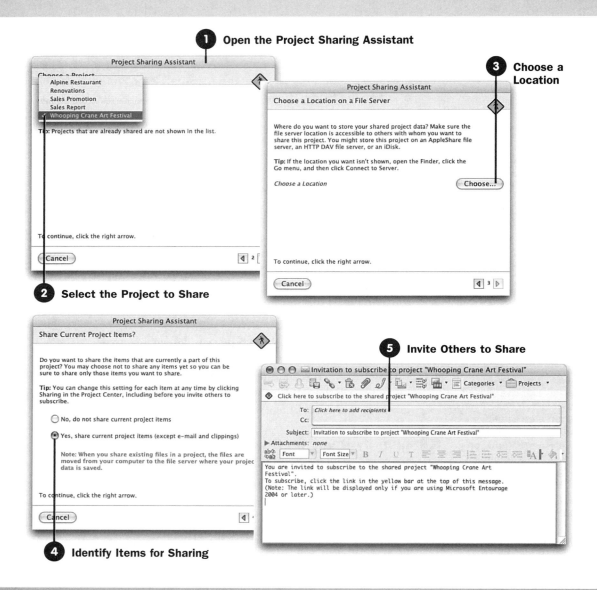

The **Project Sharing Assistant** opens with a description of the process.

② **Select the Project to Share**

Click the right arrow in the bottom-right corner of the window to advance through the pages of the Assistant. Page 2 of the Assistant asks you to identify the project you want to share. Open the drop-down list and make a selection. Click the right arrow to advance to the next page of the Assistant.

③ **Choose a Location**

You are asked to select a network location for the shared project resources. You can use the established project *watch folder*, or you can choose or create another folder. The main requirement is that it be accessible by people over the network. If you want to share a folder on your own system, open the **System Preferences** dialog box. Set the **Sharing** options to ensure that the **Personal File Sharing** option is enabled; check the online help system for assistance in doing this. If the folder is to be on a network server, the network administrator must allow access to it.

Click the **Choose** button. A **Finder** window opens. Select the folder you want to make the shared folder for this project and click **Choose** again. The volume and path of the server location are displayed. Click the right arrow at the bottom of the screen to advance to the next page of the Assistant.

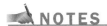

NOTES

When you share files in a project, the files are moved to the network location you selected in step 3; they do not remain on your computer. Entourage items, on the other hand, remain in their original locations.

In a network location, you can share a file only with those who have been granted access by the network administrator. If the file remains on your computer, you can control access by Ctrl-clicking the file name, selecting **Get Info**, and opening the **Ownership and Permissions** and **Details** lists. As the network's creator, you have the authority to initiate sharing. Others cannot "sublet" the permissions you grant.

④ **Identify Items for Sharing**

Page 4 of the Assistant asks whether you want to share the items that currently are part of the project. If you select **Yes**, you grant blanket permission for project colleagues to share all project resources. If you select **No**, you reserve the right to later make individual choices about which resources to share. On any page of the project window, you can select an item and click a **Share** button to control who, if anyone, is entitled to share the item.

Make a choice and click the right arrow to move to the next page of the Assistant. A second project sharing page asks how you want to handle the sharing of new items. This option specifies only an initial setting: to share new items or not to do so. When you add a new item to the project, the choice you make here is the default setting; you can change it if you want for individual items. Make a choice and click the right arrow again.

The program reports that the shared project has been created at the network location. Click **Close**.

Close the project window. Entourage displays the **Project Center**.

5 Invite Others to Share

At the bottom of the **Project Center** window for the current project, click the **Share** button and select **Invite people to join project**. When asked to verify the choice, select **Create E-Mail Invitation**.

An email message is created. In the **To** box, add the email addresses of colleagues with whom you want to share the project resources. They can *subscribe* by clicking the link in the message or by selecting **File**, **Subscribe to a Project** in the Entourage main menu.

KEY TERM

Subscribe—At the invitation of a project manager, to add your name to the list of contacts associated with the project. Subscribing gives you access to shared project resources.

5 Archive a Project

Congratulations. Your project is a success. The art show was so successful there will definitely be a second annual show next year. So relax—for a minute.

There's an old adage that says, "The job is never finished until the paperwork is done." That's also true of the electronic paperwork involved in a project. Particularly if things went well, you should save a record of what you did right, and perhaps of things you could do better. This will be an invaluable resource to you or anyone else who has to run this project next year.

To save this information, you can *archive* the project. Archiving takes the project off the active projects list and moves it into a new archive file on your hard disk, network, or some other location you select. If you need to do so later, you can retrieve the information from the archive file.

Before You Begin

✔ **2** Set Up a Project

KEY TERM

Archive—To maintain a record of a completed project for future reference.

1 Select Export Options

With the **Project Center** open, select the project to be archived. Select **File**, **Export** from the main menu. An **Export** dialog box opens asking you to select export options.

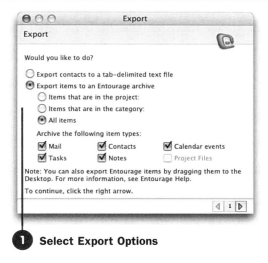

1 Select Export Options

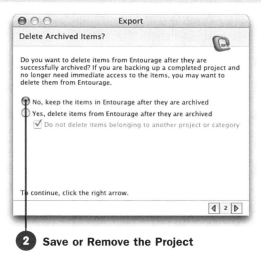

2 Save or Remove the Project

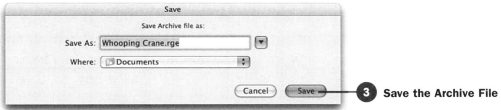

3 Save the Archive File

NOTE

Normally, you will want to export everything connected with the project. If you have some reason not to export a particular type of resource, you can disable the check box for that item type. The **Export contacts to a tab-delimited text file** option calls for an entirely different type of export. It prepares contact information from your Address Book for export to a Windows system.

Select the **Export items to an Entourage archive** option. Also select the **All items** option and enable the check boxes for all the item types.

Make your selections from the **Export** dialog box; then click the right arrow in the lower-left corner of the window to advance to the second page of the **Export** dialog box.

2 **Save or Remove the Project**

The second page of the **Export** dialog box asks whether you want to remove the exported items from the **Project Center**. If you are exporting a completed project, you probably will want to delete them from the **Project Center**. If you think you'll need quick access to the project after you archive it, keep the items in the **Project Center** after they are archived.

Choose whether you want to keep or delete the items in the project in the **Project Center** and click the right-facing arrow to advance to the **Save** dialog box.

3 Save the Archive File

In the **Save** dialog box, type a filename for the archive file you are creating. In the **Where** box, select a folder in which to store the file. Make it one you can remember; the system will leave you no clues.

Click **Save**. A dialog box reports on the progress of the export as individual resources are exported. When the export is finished, click **Done**.

You can retrieve the project later by opening the **Project Center** and selecting **File, Import**. Navigate to the archive file and select it. If it's on a CD or other removable media, you must of course insert the media first.

6 Keep a Scrapbook

Think of the Office 2004 **Scrapbook** feature as kind of a long-term *clipboard*. When you select, say, a passage from a Word document and copy it to the clipboard, it's there until you paste it somewhere else. When you add an item to the **Scrapbook**, on the other hand, it's there until you decide you don't need it any longer.

You can use the **Scrapbook** to store multiple items called *clips* from all Office programs and from external files. Let's say you are collecting items for a research report. As you find source material on the Web, you can create clips and store them in the **Scrapbook**. One clip might be a passage from another research report; another might be a picture or an Excel chart.

After you add a clip to the **Scrapbook**, the clip remains there until you remove it, even if you close the application and shut down the computer. If you want, you can organize the clips by assigning them to projects or categories. You also can assign keywords to help find the clips later.

See Also

→ **7** Organize the Scrapbook

→ **8** Search for Clips

NOTE

The **Scrapbook** is a new feature in Word 2004 and works in conjunction with another new feature—the **Project Center**. Both features are unique to the Mac, at least initially.

KEY TERM

Clip—A text or graphic selection stored in the Office **Scrapbook**. A clip can be pasted into a document much like a selection from the clipboard.

1 Open the Scrapbook

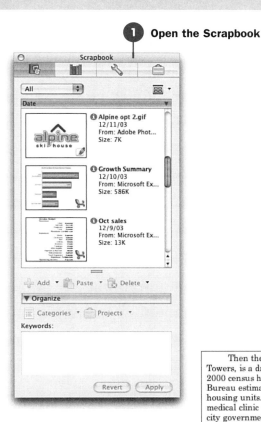

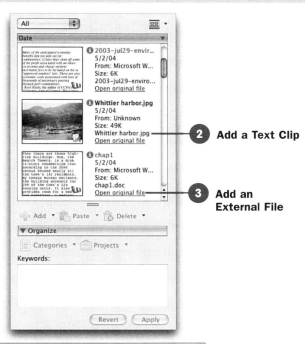

2 Add a Text Clip

3 Add an
External File

Then there are those high-rise buildings. One, the Begich Towers, is a drab 14-story condominium that according to the 2000 census housed nearly all the town's 300 residents. By Census Bureau estimate, the building accounts for 208 of the town's 224 housing units. It also provides room for a bed and breakfast, a medical clinic where the doctor visits once a week, the offices of city government, a post office, a couple of stores and a coin

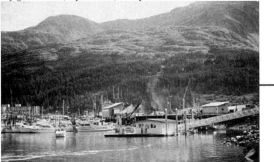

4 Paste the
Clips

laundry. Tunnels connect this building with other worthwhile destinations like the 36-student school and the seaport/railroad terminal that is the reason for Whittier's existence. The second high-rise, the Buckner Building, is abandoned -- occupied, it is said, by bears and lethal quantities of asbestos.

① Open the Scrapbook

In the main menu of any Office application, select **Tools**, **Scrapbook**. Alternatively, in the **Standard** toolbar for any Office application, click the **Toolbox** button and then select the **Scrapbook** icon.

② Add a Text Clip

Open the source document (for example, a Word document or an Excel workbook) and select the text you want to clip. Drag the selection into the **Scrapbook** or click the **Add** button near the bottom of the **Scrapbook** window.

The selection is added to the **Scrapbook**. You can later paste it into your report or into any other Word document.

③ Add an External File

In addition to clips from Office applications, you can add external files such as pictures or other graphics to the **Scrapbook**.

Click the arrow next to the **Add** button. From the menu that opens, select **Add File**. A **Finder** window opens so that you can locate the file you want to add to the **Scrapbook**. Select the file and click **Choose**. The file is added to the **Scrapbook**.

The **Add** menu also gives you the option of adding a clip from the clipboard. Foregoing the **Always Add Copy** selection keeps you from overdoing it. When the **Always Add Copy** option is selected, anything copied onto the clipboard while the **Scrapbook** is open also is added to the **Scrapbook**. Unless you want to quickly add a large collection of clips, you will probably want to turn off this option.

④ Paste the Clips

Open the document into which you want to paste one or more clips from the **Scrapbook**. This might be the document that will become your report. Select a clip from the **Scrapbook** and drag it into the document. Alternatively, place the insertion point in the

When you paste something from the **Scrapbook**, you have the option of opening the original file. In this way, you could clip a small part of a long document and use the clip in the **Scrapbook** as a key to the larger file.

The **Scrapbook** accepts only a limited selection of graphic file types. These types include the GIF and JPEG formats common in Web pages, but not the TIFF format preferred for print publication.

TIP

When you paste contents from outside sources into your documents, be sure to include proper attribution. The rules of plagiarism are becoming more strict, and the means of detecting it more sophisticated.

document where you want the clip to appear. In the **Scrapbook**, select the clip and then click the **Paste** button.

The clips are added to the document. In practice, you probably will want to reformat pasted text and change the sizes and positions of pasted graphics. Pasting does not remove a clip from the **Scrapbook**. To remove a clip from the **Scrapbook**, select it and click the **Delete** button.

7 Organize the Scrapbook

Before You Begin

✔ **2** Set Up a Project

✔ **5** Keep a Scrapbook

See Also

→ **8** Search for Clips

→ **123** Organize Your Email

Whether it's the traditional kind or the Microsoft Office version, a scrapbook can easily become a disorganized collection of miscellaneous information. Things can get lost there. That is, unless you use the organizational tools Microsoft has placed at your disposal.

These tools include assigning a clip to a project, placing the clip in a category, and adding keywords so you can search for the item later. After you have established these keywords, you can use them to search the **Scrapbook** for relevant items.

In this task, the **Scrapbook** is filled with clips for research projects on two distinctly different subjects: personal privacy and the environment of Alaska's Prince William Sound. You need some means to distinguish between these clips. You also want to be able to identify subtopics such as the privacy implications of pay-TV services and the economic and environmental effects of cruise ships. Using the features of the **Scrapbook**, organizing your clips is easy.

1 Assign a Clip to a Project

You can link a clip to an existing project. If you have created separate environment and privacy projects, for example, you can easily assign a clip to either of these projects.

For example, you might have a clip that is a bibliographic reference to a report on the environmental impact of Alaskan cruise ships. You need to include it in your Prince William Sound project.

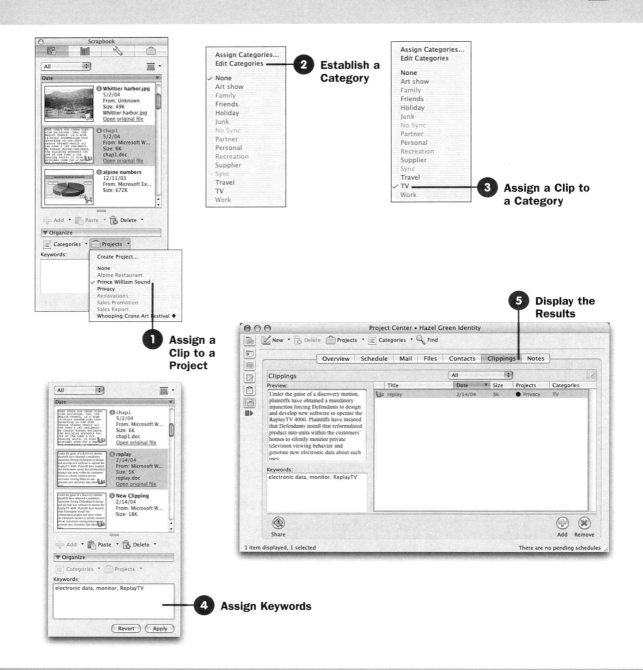

2 Establish a Category

3 Assign a Clip to a Category

5 Display the Results

1 Assign a Clip to a Project

4 Assign Keywords

TIP

If you have not yet created an appropriate project, the **Projects** menu includes a **Create Project** option. Selecting that option opens the **New Project Wizard**. See ❷ **Set Up a Project** for instructions on creating a new project.

If the **Scrapbook** is not open, in the host application—Word, Excel, Entourage, or PowerPoint—select **Tools**, **Scrapbook**. The **Scrapbook** palette opens. Select the clip in the **Scrapbook**. Then open the **Organize** section of the palette and click the **Projects** button. From the menu that opens, select the project to which you want to assign the selected clip. The clip is assigned to that project.

If you start in Entourage, you can find all the clips listed on the **Clippings** page.

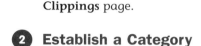 ❷ **Establish a Category**

Entourage maintains a list of categories to help organize your email, meetings, and other resources. You can use these categories to organize your **Scrapbook** clips as well, but you might want to create categories of your own.

TIP

Entourage supplies an initial list of categories you can use, but you might not find them very useful for organizing a research project. The initial categories run along the lines of separating email into business and personal messages.

In the **Scrapbook**, click the arrow next to the **Categories** button. From the menu that opens, select **Edit Categories**. The **Categories** dialog box displays a list of existing categories. Click the **Add Category** button at the top of the dialog box. The program creates a new category to which you can apply your own name.

For example, if you want to categorize a clip in the **Privacy** category under the issue of monitoring TV viewing, you could add a category called **TV**. For categories to be used in the Alaskan project, you might want to create categories such as **Cruise ships**, **Wildlife**, or **Exxon Valdez**. When you are finished creating new category names, close the dialog box.

❸ **Assign a Clip to a Category**

After you have established a category, you can assign any clip to it. Start by selecting the clip in the **Scrapbook**. For example, one clip might be an excerpt from a legal brief on privacy matters, specifically the issue of TV monitoring.

Click the **Categories** button under the list of clips in the **Scrapbook**. The **Assign Categories** dialog box opens and again displays a list of available categories, including any you might have created in step 2. Enable the check box for the category you want to assign to this clip—you can select more than one category

if you want. Then click **OK**. The selected clip is assigned to the chosen categories.

4 Assign Keywords

Keywords allow even more specific classification of clips than categories alone. You can enter keywords to help you search for certain clips within the broader project and category divisions. For example, the privacy excerpt mentions monitoring, electronic data, and the name of a product. You can enter these terms as keywords to assist you in later searches for this particular clip.

Select the clip you want to annotate with keywords in the **Scrapbook**. In the **Keywords** text box, type the words and phrases that can help you identify the clip. Use commas to separate the entries. When you're finished, click **Apply**.

5 Display the Results

Open Entourage, display the **Project Center**, and select the project to which you have assigned the clip. Click the **Clippings** tab to view all the clips you've assigned to this project. The clip appears along with its keywords and category assignments.

KEY TERM

Keywords—Words and phrases for which you can search when trying to locate an item. They're used in the **Scrapbook** and other search routines.

NOTE

Regardless of the order in which you entered the keywords, the program alphabetizes them when they appear in the **Project Center**.

---

8 Search for Clips

The object of organizing **Scrapbook** clips is to be able to find them later. If you have assigned your clips to projects, placed them in categories, and written *keywords* for them, you can use all three factors to search for clips and add them to a document.

1 Select the Project

At the top of the **Scrapbook** window, open the drop-down list that initially is labeled **All**. This menu provides several search options; to search for clips in a particular project, select **Project is**.

A second list opens to the right of the first. From it, select the project to which you've assigned the clip you are looking for—in this case, **Prince William Sound**. The **Scrapbook** display is filtered to display only clips in that project.

Before You Begin

✔ **7** Organize the Scrapbook

TIP

The menu at the top of the **Scrapbook** window also gives you the options of searching by the clip's creation date, its category, the program in which it was created, words in the title, or assigned keywords. If you lose track of a project's project or category assignments, searching by other criteria in this list often can help you find it.

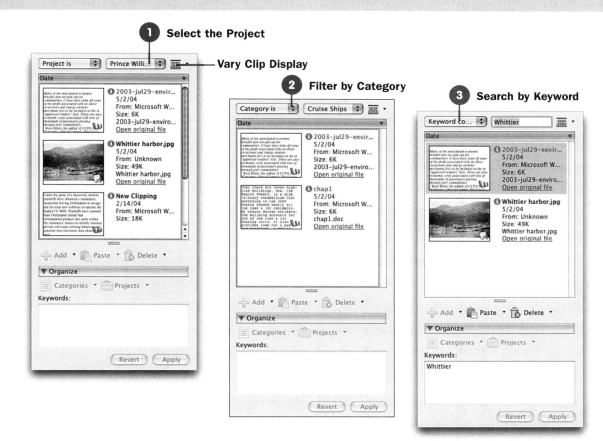

Select the Project

Project is | Prince Willi...

Vary Clip Display

2 **Filter by Category**

Category is | Cruise Ships

3 **Search by Keyword**

Keyword co... | Whittier

<image src="NOTE icon" />**NOTE**

To vary the display of clips in the **Scrapbook** window, click the third button (the **View** button) at the top of the **Scrapbook** window. This button lets you display the clips as a list, with more detail, or in a large preview.

2 **Filter by Category**

If you have assigned the clips to categories, you can use the categories to further filter the display of clips in the **Scrapbook**. From the first drop-down list at the top of the **Scrapbook** window (it now should read **Project is**), select **Category is**.

From the second drop-down list, select the category to which you assigned the clip you're looking for. To search for clips that concern cruise ships, for example, open the second list and select the **Cruise ships** category.

③ Search by Keyword

You might want to make the search more specific by performing a keyword search. From the first drop-down list at the top of the **Scrapbook** window, select **Keyword contains**. A text box opens to the right of this menu. Type the keywords for which you want to search.

Clips to which that keyword was assigned are displayed in the **Scrapbook** list. You then can drag the clips into the document you want to use them in or select the clips and click the **Paste** button to place them in a document.

NOTE

When you search for clips in a certain category, the program scans the entire **Scrapbook**. For instance, you cannot display clips in the **Prince William Sound** project and then further filter those selections for those in the **Cruise ships** category.

TIP

As you type a keyword, the program begins its search and matches the partial or full keyword as it appears in the text box; you don't need to press **Return** to start the search. You need not match the capitalization of the original keyword.

3

Arts and Letters

IN THIS CHAPTER:

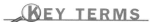

Because they are packaged as a team, the applications of Office 2004 have many things in common. Among these is the capability to manage and use a common source of artwork.

Three of the four major Office programs—Entourage is the exception—have some form of artistic talent. Word can import pictures, Excel can generate graphs, and PowerPoint can use photos and drawings in presentations. All three applications also provide the means to draw basic shapes such as circles and rectangles.

The real graphic power, though, is in the shared graphic utilities available to all three major programs. These include Microsoft Graph, the Clip Gallery, AutoShapes, WordArt, and other tools.

The gateway to these artistic tools is the **Insert**, **Picture** menu command. From its submenu, you can make one of these choices:

- **Clip Art**—This command opens access to the *Clip Gallery*, a built-in source of *clip art*.

- **From File**—This command lets you select any graphics file available on your system or network.

- **AutoShapes**—This command provides access to primitive drawing objects such as squares, circles, and arrows. After you have inserted them, you can color, stretch, join, and otherwise enhance them.

- **WordArt**—This command allows you to stretch, curve, and otherwise distort a block of text.

- **From Scanner or Camera**—This command lets you directly import a picture from a scanner or digital camera. The camera or scanner must have been installed before you can use this command.

In addition, each application has a few options of its own:

- **Horizontal Line**—This command draws just that in a Word document.

- **Organization Chart**—This command lets you insert a hierarchical diagram into Excel or PowerPoint.

- **Chart**—This command imports an Excel chart into Word.

- **Microsoft Word Table**—This command lets you draw a blank table in PowerPoint.

9 Retrieve Clip Art

The **Clip Gallery** is a collection of cartoon-style illustrations called *clip art* you can insert into any Office document. Initially, Office comes with several hundred pieces of this type of art.

1 Open the Clip Gallery

In any Word, Excel, or PowerPoint document, click in the document at the place you want the drawing to appear. Then select **Insert**, **Picture**, **Clip Art**. The **Clip Gallery** opens.

2 Select a Category

Scroll down the **Category** list on the left side of the window. Select a category, and a selection of drawings in that category is displayed in the large pane on the right.

Scroll down the right window if necessary to see the entire selection of clip art in the chosen category. Select a picture.

3 Insert the Picture

Click **Insert**. The picture is inserted into the document at the place you selected in step 1. You can drag the drawing to a new position or use its adjustment handles to change its size.

Because most of the artwork in the **Clip Gallery** uses *vector graphics*, you can enlarge or reduce the drawings without affecting their quality. You can't do much resizing with *raster* graphics.

4 Search the Gallery

As an alternative to selecting art by category, you can search the entire gallery. Each drawing in the gallery has been identified by a set of descriptive *keywords*, so you can search for all the drawings that have a particular keyword.

If necessary, open the **Clip Gallery** by selecting **Insert**, **Picture**, **Clip Art**. In the **Search** text box at the top of the screen, type a word or phrase that describes the kind of art you are looking for. Then click the **Search** button.

The gallery displays any drawings whose keywords match the search terms you entered.

See Also

→ **10** Add Your Art to the Gallery

NOTE

If you want an even broader selection of clip art, install the **Value Pack** addendum to the basic Office package or check out the clip art on the Microsoft Web site at **http://office.microsoft.com/clipart/default.aspx.**

TIP

Enable the **Preview** check box in the lower-right corner of the **Clip Gallery** window to see a larger sample of the selected drawing.

KEY TERMS

Vector—A graphics file that describes its contents by their shapes and colors.

Raster—A graphics file that defines its contents as patterns of colored dots or *pixels*.

1 Open the Clip Gallery

3 Insert the Picture

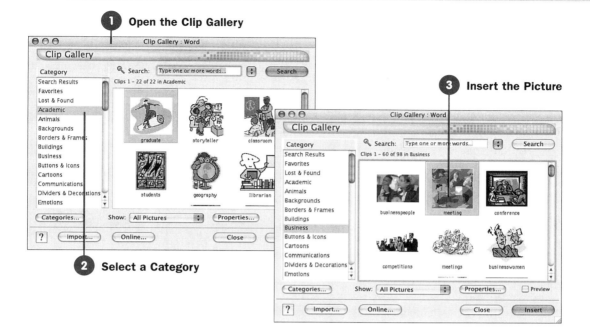

2 Select a Category

4 Search the Gallery

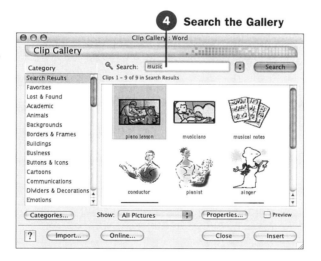

The **Clip Gallery** is not limited to the artwork Microsoft supplies. The gallery is also a resource to which you can add your own work, assigning keywords and categories so that you can search and retrieve your artwork again.

Neither are you limited to the cartoonish drawings that populate most of the gallery. You can add pictures (photos), movies, and various multimedia files as well. Within these boundaries, you can add to the **Clip Gallery** any file you can find on your hard disk or in available network resources.

① Open the Clip Gallery

In an open Word, Excel, or PowerPoint document, select **Insert**, **Picture**, **Clip Art**. The **Clip Gallery** opens.

② Select a File

In the lower-left corner of the **Clip Gallery** window, click the **Import** button. The **Import** dialog box opens.

Navigate to the folder that contains the file you want to use. Select that file, and click **Import** again. The **Properties** dialog box opens.

③ Describe the File

In the **Properties** dialog box, you can add information that will identify the file you are adding to the **Clip Gallery**.

Click the **Description** tab to open that page of the dialog box (if it is not already displayed). In the **Description of this clip** text box, type a brief title. This title will appear under the file's thumbnail in the **Clip Gallery**.

④ Pick a Category

Click the **Categories** tab to open that page of the dialog box. Here, you can place the imported graphic in one or more of the categories that appear in the **Clip Gallery**. Scroll down the list and select as many categories as you want.

Before You Begin

✔ **9** Retrieve Clip Art

See Also

→ **11** Add Your Artistic Touches

TIP

You can use the **Clip Gallery** to add pictures and drawings to Word, Excel, and PowerPoint documents. Only PowerPoint, however, can use multimedia files.

NOTE

The **Import** dialog box has three options: **Copy into Clip Gallery**, **Move into Clip Gallery**, and **Add Alias to Clip Gallery**. The first two options place the graphic directly in the gallery; the third places only a pointer to the file's current location in the gallery. The alias option leaves the original file undisturbed, but you would lose the connection should you someday relocate the file.

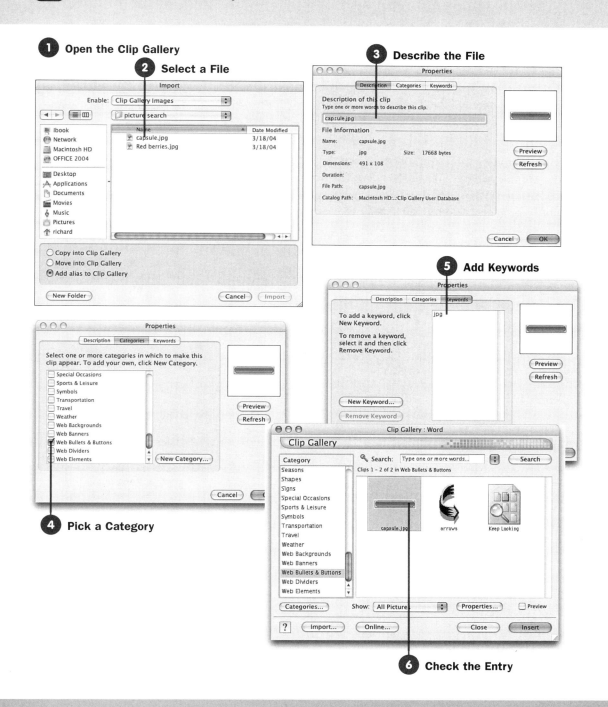

1 Open the Clip Gallery

2 Select a File

3 Describe the File

4 Pick a Category

5 Add Keywords

6 Check the Entry

⑤ Add Keywords

Adding keywords to an image to aid in later searches is an art in itself. Think of all the terms you or someone else might use when searching for a picture like the one you are adding to the gallery. Then think of some of the less likely terms someone might use.

Don't go overboard with terms people are unlikely to use. For example, if you apply the keyword *button* to a picture of an arrow (as the authors of the **Clip Gallery** actually did), you run the risk that a keyword search will produce too many useless results to be of value.

Click the **Keywords** tab to open that page of the **Properties** dialog box. Click the **New Keyword** button. In the small dialog box that opens, type the keyword you want to assign to this image and click **OK**. Repeat this for each keyword you want to assign to the image.

When you're finished adding keywords, click **OK** to close the **Properties** dialog box. You return to the **Clip Gallery**.

⑥ Check the Entry

Check the new entry by selecting its categories and searching by its keywords.

TIP

Remember, it might be you who has to search for this picture someday. Think ahead six months. If you are looking for this picture, under which categories would you look? Be sure to select as many meaningful categories as possible. You can use the **New Category** button to create categories of your own.

---

11 Add Your Artistic Touches

Office's art tools hardly rank with the image-editing products creative professionals usually have at their disposal. Nevertheless, after you insert a picture into a document, the **Formatting Palette** is transformed into a tool that offers what might be a surprising variety of picture-editing features. Sometimes it can be easier to tweak the picture with these tools than to go back to the original image-editing application and start again.

For instance, you can use the **Formatting Palette** to adjust the brightness, contrast, and color of an image; the color adjustment tool is similar to the **Variations** feature in the killer Adobe Photoshop application. You can use the **Formatting Palette** to apply picture effects such as the filters found in other image editors. The **Formatting Palette** also provides ways to make selections and remove red-eye and scratches from photographs.

Before You Begin

✔ **9** Retrieve Clip Art

See Also

→ **12** Create a Transparent Area

→ **13** Add Text to Artwork

→ **43** Turn a Photo into a Painting

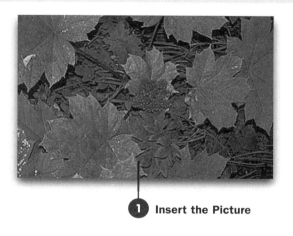

1 Insert the Picture

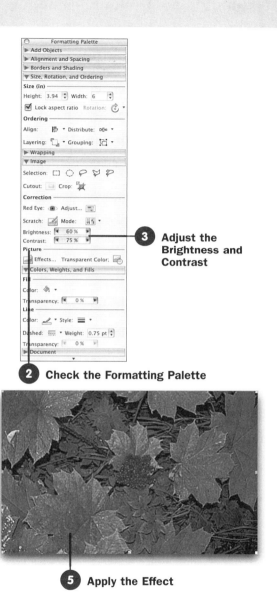

3 Adjust the
Brightness and
Contrast

2 Check the Formatting Palette

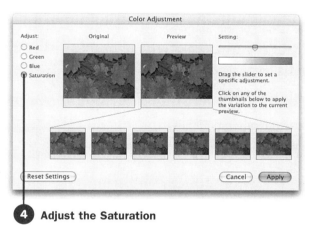

4 Adjust the Saturation

5 Apply the Effect

① Insert the Picture

If the picture is available in the **Clip Gallery**, select **Insert**, **Picture**, **Clip Art** to use the gallery to insert the picture into the

document. To use a picture from your hard disk or network, select **Insert**, **Picture**, **From File**.

Navigate to the folder where the picture is stored, select the picture file, and click **Insert**. The picture is added to the document. Drag it to a new position, if necessary, and use the adjustment handles to set it to the proper size.

2 Check the Formatting Palette

When you select a picture in the document, the **Formatting Palette** undergoes a transformation. Normally oriented to formatting text and documents, the palette instead displays options for formatting graphics.

Click the arrows next to each heading in the **Formatting Palette** to expand or collapse each section. Picture editing functions are found, naturally enough, under the **Image** heading.

3 Adjust the Brightness and Contrast

You might have a picture taken on a rainy day. If so, it probably could use a boost in brightness and contrast. In the **Brightness** and **Contrast** sliders, use the arrow buttons to increase or decrease the percentages of these effects.

4 Adjust the Saturation

In the **Image Correction** section of the **Formatting Palette**, click the **Adjust** icon to open the **Color Adjustment** dialog box. You can use the **Color Adjustment** dialog box to adjust the hues of individual colors or to adjust color saturation.

To overcome the rainy-day effect, for example, select the **Saturation** radio button in the upper-left corner of the dialog box. Then adjust the **Setting** slider in the upper-right corner of the dialog box to get the effect you want.

5 Apply the Effect

Click the **Apply** button in the **Color Adjustment** dialog box. The picture displays the effects you have chosen from the **Formatting Palette** and the **Color Adjustment** dialog box. If you want, you can continue making adjustments to the image from the **Formatting Palette**.

 TIP

If you import a photo into a document, you can make it look like a painting. Select the picture and then select **Effects** from the **Formatting Palette**. Select an effect such as **Palette Knife**, **Angled Strokes**, or **Colored Pencil**. Use the sliders provided to adjust the intensity of the effect. See **43** **Turn a Photo into a Painting**.

 TIP

For more precise resizing, select the picture and then expand the **Size** section of the **Formatting Palette**. There, you can enter specific height and width dimensions.

 TIP

As an alternative to adjusting the saturation of the image, click the image in the row at the bottom of the dialog box that best displays the effect you want.

12 Create a Transparent Area

See Also

→ **11** Add Your Artistic Touches

→ **13** Add Text to Artwork

Photoshop and other professional-level image-editing applications include a transparency option that allows you to create see-through sections of an image that reveal whatever is behind it.

Office 2004 takes advantage of the Mac operating system to let you do the same. You can select a color within a picture and designate it as transparent. Instead of the color, you see whatever is behind it. In a printed document, you see the paper; in a Web page or PowerPoint presentation, you see the background color.

The transparency feature has some limitations. It works only on *raster* graphics, and you can select only one color in an image to be transparent. Nevertheless, this feature gives you a way to clean up a picture by eliminating a distracting background.

✦ NOTE

This technique does not work well with photographs, which seldom have large areas of a single color. What you see as one color (a blue sky for example, or a sunlit wall), might actually be made up of many subtle shades. If you try to select a single color for the transparency, you might actually select only one of those many shades. Dedicated graphics-editing programs let you adjust the "tolerance" (the variations of the color) when selecting a transparency color. The Office graphics editor is not that dedicated.

1 Insert the Picture

Use one of the **Insert**, **Picture** submenu options to place an image in a document. To work best, the image should have a large area of a single color that can be made transparent.

2 Select the Transparency Option

Select the picture if it is not already selected. In the **Picture** section of the **Formatting Palette**, select the **Transparent Color** option.

3 Select the Color to Be Transparent

In the picture, click the color you want to become transparent. In the example shown here, the white background around the pill-shaped button was selected.

4 Check the Results

In the picture, the selected color (the white background) is no longer visible; you see the background color from the document (in this case, a dark color) instead.

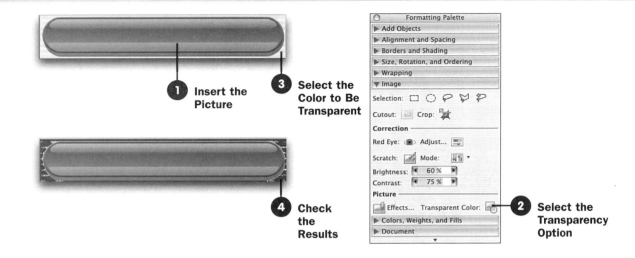

1 Insert the Picture

3 Select the Color to Be Transparent

4 Check the Results

2 Select the Transparency Option

---

13 Add Text to Artwork

Words and pictures go together, particularly in a program such as Microsoft Word. Often, you will be called on to enhance a graphic with text, a caption, or a callout.

There are several ways to combine text and graphics. One is to attach a caption to a picture as described in this task. Others are to insert a callout or add text to an AutoShape. You also can use a text box to apply a label to a graphic. You might use this option if you are preparing a button for a Web page.

1 Create a Text Box

Display the page of the document that contains the graphic you want to label. This can be a page in a Word document, an Excel graph or chart, or an image in a PowerPoint slide. Select **Insert**, **Text Box** from the menu of the application you are using.

Click the graphic. A text box is created. Use the adjustment handles to place the text box in an appropriate position over the graphic. Adjust the size of the text box by dragging the adjustment handles.

Before You Begin

✔ **11** Add Your Artistic Touches

See Also

→ **12** Create a Transparent Area

NOTE

To attach a caption to a picture, select **Insert**, **Caption** from the menu of the program you are using. Options for the caption include setting up a numbering scheme for each illustration. Caption options are available on the **Drawing** toolbar. To insert text in an AutoShape, **Ctrl**-click the shape and then enter the text.

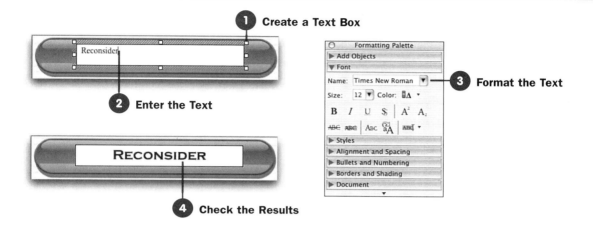

① **Create a Text Box**

② **Enter the Text**

③ **Format the Text**

RECONSIDER

④ **Check the Results**

② **Enter the Text**

Click inside the text box and type the text you want to use for the label or callout.

③ **Format the Text**

Use the **Formatting Palette** to format the text you've just entered. You might want to change the typeface, size, and color of the text so that it can easily be seen against the graphic. If you are adding a button label, for example, you probably will want to center the text as well.

Select the text and apply the formatting by selecting options from the **Formatting Palette**.

④ **Check the Results**

Click outside the text box to remove the selection and see the completed label.

14 Apply Artwork to Text

WordArt is a long-standing Office feature that turns text into artistic shapes. When you're done with WordArt, the text is a piece of art you can insert in a document and manage accordingly.

WordArt lets you place text in a variety of alignments, including an assortment of curves, shadows, and perspective shapes. You then can stretch the dimensions to achieve effects that range from artistic to goofy.

1 Start WordArt

Select **Insert**, **Picture**, **WordArt**. The **WordArt Gallery** opens to present the available WordArt designs. You don't necessarily have to position the insertion point in the text where you want the WordArt to appear; you can drag the art wherever you want it after it is created.

2 Select a Design

Select one of the designs and click **OK**. The **Edit WordArt Text** dialog box opens.

3 Enter the Text

The **Edit WordArt Text** dialog box asks you to enter the text you want to use to create your text art. Type the text.

4 Adjust Text Size and Font

From the **Font** and **Size** drop-down lists, select a font and a font size for your text art. Click the **Bold** or **Italic** button to change the weight of the text. When you're done typing text and formatting it, click **OK** to close the **Edit WordArt Text** dialog box.

5 Check the Results

The competed WordArt is displayed in the center of the current page. If you want, you can use the adjustment handles to change the size and proportions of the art.

See Also

→ **11** Add Your Artistic Touches

→ **13** Add Text to Artwork

 TIP

WordArt is one of the selections on the **Insert**, **Picture** submenu. It is also available from the **Drawing** toolbar.

 TIP

When the program displays the completed WordArt, it also displays a WordArt toolbar. You can use its tools to revise the graphic including, if you must, rewriting the text or picking an entirely new design.

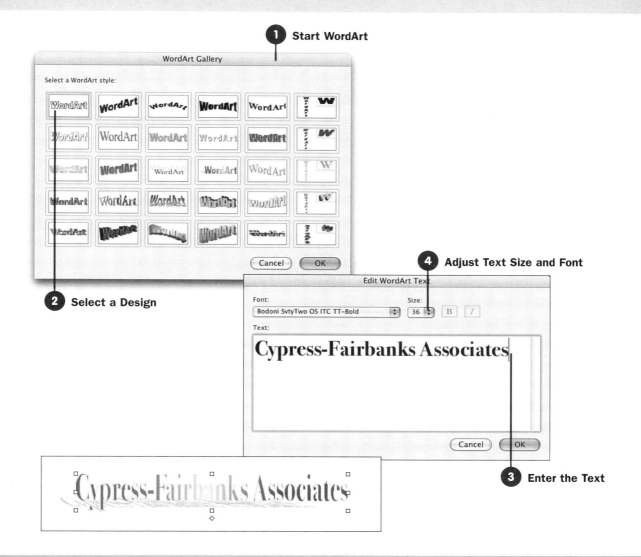

1 Start WordArt

2 Select a Design

4 Adjust Text Size and Font

3 Enter the Text

4

Shaping Your Work with Templates

IN THIS CHAPTER:

KEY TERM

Template—An Office document that can be used as a pattern for creating other documents. When you open a new document based on the template, the contents and appearance of the template appear automatically in the document.

NOTE

Most of the templates initially supplied with Office 2004 are for either Word documents or PowerPoint presentations. You can add templates for other programs by designing your own or by searching the Web for **Microsoft Office Templates**.

A well-designed document can be hard to create. After you've finished putting it together, you might find yourself saying, "I sure hope I don't have to go through that again."

You don't have to do it all over again. You can save the design as a *template* and then apply that design to other documents you create. Say that you've created a workable invoice form built with Word tables or on an Excel worksheet where the program automatically adds up the totals. Or, you might want to duplicate the look of a letterhead or the text of an effective solicitation letter. If you create a template of that design, you can apply it to other documents as well.

You don't even have to create your own templates. All Office 2004 applications come with several templates. A template for a Word document might include layouts; typefaces and sizes; margins; and room for standard text such as your company name, address, and contact information. An Excel template might set up the formulas for an invoice or a bid sheet, including calculations and appearance items. PowerPoint templates come in two forms. *Design* templates apply uniform coloring and design to a presentation; *content* templates provide suggested content for sales pitches, program proposals, and other common types of presentations.

15   Use a Template to Design a Document

See Also

→ **16** Adapt a Template to Your Needs

→ **17** Set Up a New Template

NOTE

The categories and subcategories in this display reflect the folders and subfolders in which the templates are stored.

The command center for Office templates is the **Project Gallery**, where you can choose from multiple types of *templates* for any Office program. You then can open a document based on the chosen template.

① Display the Project Gallery

The **Project Gallery** normally opens when you start Word, Excel, or PowerPoint. If it does not, select **File**, **Project Gallery** to open the gallery. Select the **New** page tab at the top of the screen if it is not already displayed. On the left side of the **Project Gallery** screen is the **Category** list; when you select a category, samples of the templates in that category are displayed in the right pane. Initially, the **Blank Documents** category displays a basic format for each of the four Office programs.

Some of the categories are marked with arrows. Click an arrow to see a list of subcategories.

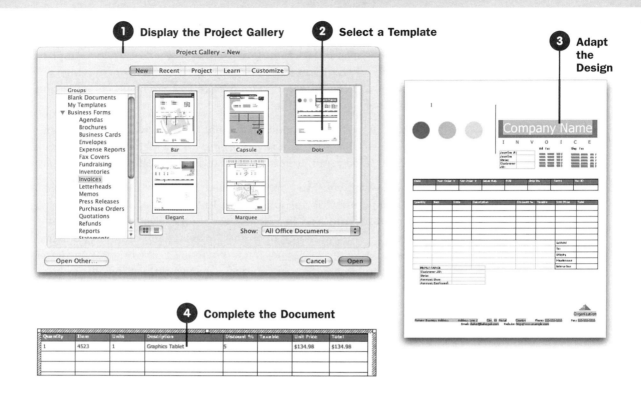

① **Display the Project Gallery**   ② **Select a Template**   ③ **Adapt the Design**

④ **Complete the Document**

② Select a Template

Select a category or subcategory. For example, if you want to create an invoice form, open the **Business Forms** category and select the **Invoices** subcategory. Scroll through the invoice designs in the right pane, select a template, and click **Open**.

A new document in the template design opens. In the case of an invoice design, the new document might include graphic elements, a placeholder for your organization's name, and a table with mathematical formulas to calculate the total bill.

③ Adapt the Design

Replace the placeholders with your company name and other elements unique to your organization.

✎ NOTE

The template dictates the application in which it opens. If you are in Word and select an Excel template, Excel opens a new file based on the template.

The placeholder might be displayed in a direct text form (such as with the text *Company Name* or *Placeholder*), or it might be a small block of programming code, called a *field code*, that creates the placeholder. Either way, you can replace the placeholder entry with your information: Click to select the placeholder contents and type your own information.

④ Complete the Document

You now have a document formatted to a standard style. Complete it as you wish. If you used a letter template, you now can write a formatted letter. If you used an invoice template, you can enter the customer's name and the items purchased.

This is now a conventional document that behaves like any other document file. You must save it under a new filename. You can reopen it, edit and print it, or send it as an email attachment.

If you want, you can apply a different template, although the procedure varies with the application. In Word, select **Tools, Templates and Add-Ins**; click **Attach**; and select the new template to apply. In PowerPoint, open the **Format** menu and select either a design or layout template. If you have an Excel workbook formatted in one template, you can add a new worksheet formatted in a different template. **Ctrl**-click an existing worksheet tab, select **Insert** from the context menu, and then choose a new template. A new sheet formatted with that template is added to the workbook.

Adapt a Template to Your Needs

Before You Begin

✔ **15** Use a Template to Design a Document

See Also

→ **17** Set Up a New Template

 TIP

Some of the supplied templates open with wizards that display forms in which you can enter the local information you want to include. These templates make good candidates for personalization. Some templates have these wizards; some don't. It seems to have been at the discretion of the template writer.

Chances are, you'll find that some of the *templates* supplied with Office are *almost* good enough for your purposes. With a few changes, they could be even better. For example, you could take one of the supplied letterhead templates and add your name and organization. You might want to get more ambitious and choose a different typeface or insert a different graphic.

You can modify an Office template by opening a document based on the template you want to modify. Make the changes you want to that new document and then save *that* document as a template.

❶ Select a Template

Select **File, Project Gallery** to open the **Project Gallery** if it is not already open. Choose a category and select the template you want to modify.

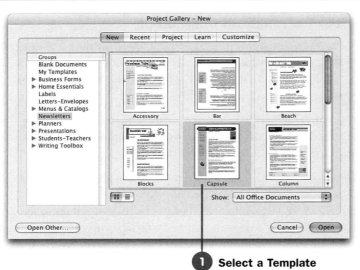

1 Select a Template

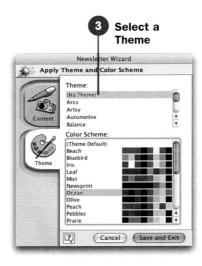

3 Select a Theme

2 Enter the Personalized Information

4 Save the Document

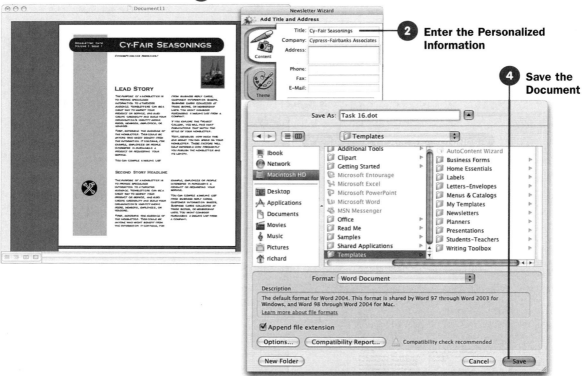

2 Enter the Personalized Information

In this example, the newsletter template comes with a fill-in-the-blanks wizard where you can enter personalized information. You also can make some choices such as the number of pages to print and whether to leave space for a mailing label.

Make sure that the wizard's **Content** tab is selected. Enter your information in the appropriate text boxes and make the choices you want.

If there is no wizard, the template probably does have placeholders. Click them to select the boilerplate text and then enter your own information. Depending on its design, the template might also have text blocks where you can enter longer text such as newsletter articles or the body of a letter. You also can add, delete, and rearrange the placeholders and text blocks.

3 Select a Theme

This step is optional. If the template you selected has a wizard, the **Theme** tab for the wizard displays several options for applying a different theme or color scheme to the document.

Experiment. Select different themes and color schemes. If nothing strikes your fancy, select **No Theme** from the **Theme** list and **Theme Default** from the **Color Scheme** list to return to the template's original layout.

4 Save the Document

When you're done with the template wizard, click the **Save and Exit** button. The newsletter displays the chosen selections.

From the main menu, select **File**, **Save**. In the **Save As** dialog box, save a Word template with a **.dot** extension in a folder named **My Templates**. If this were an Excel template, the extension would be **.xlt**; a PowerPoint template has the extension **.pot**. Together, the extension and the folder assignment ensure that the template will be available in the **Project Gallery** and you will be able to create new documents based on that template.

NOTE

Just because you are presented with a form, there's no need to fill in every blank. Just enter the information you want to place in the document. For example, if you are planning an employee newsletter, you probably need not include an address and telephone number.

TIP

The Mac is comfortable without filename extensions, but the PC is not. If you expect that a Windows user will ever want to use this template, enable the **Append file extension** check box.

You don't have to start with someone else's prebuilt *template*. You can create your own from scratch. Let's say that you've created an Excel workbook that neatly outlines a bid proposal that you would like to keep around for future use. You could save this workbook as a custom template.

In similar fashion, you might create an effective proposal or collection letter in Word and want to reuse this priceless prose in other letters. You can save the letter as a Word template with room for new names and addresses. The presentation that wowed everyone can be saved as a content template for PowerPoint.

① Create the Document

Build a new document that contains the material you want to use in the template. The document can include text such as page headers, headlines, graphics, or table column and row labels. It also can include formulas, styles, macros, and any formatting you want to include.

For example, if you are building a bid form in Excel, you could include headings that identify your company, labels for service and expense categories, and formulas to calculate and total the items.

When you are creating the document you want to use as a template, include only those elements you want to appear in every document based on this template. For example, if you are creating an invoice template, include your company name and address and appropriate headings for line items you include in most invoices. Do not include the specifics for any particular job.

② Save As a Template

When you have finished creating the document you want to use as a template, select **File**, **Save As**. The **Save As** dialog box opens.

Before You Begin

✔ **15** Use a Template to Design a Document

See Also

→ **16** Adapt a Template to Your Needs

→ **63** Enter a Formula

NOTE

Excel gives you two template options. You can save a document as either a *default workbook template* or a *custom template*. The default workbook template is initially applied to every new Excel workbook you open. A custom template is one you can selectively apply as you would other templates in the **Project Gallery**. To serve as a default workbook template, the template must be saved with the filename **Workbook.xlt** in the Excel startup folder **Microsoft Office 2004/Office/Startup/Excel**. Save a custom template using any useful filename within the Office **Templates** folder.

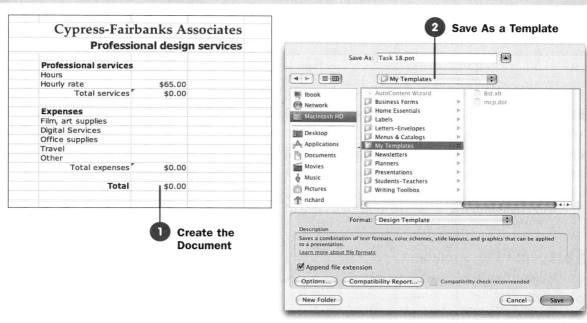

1 Create the Document

2 Save As a Template

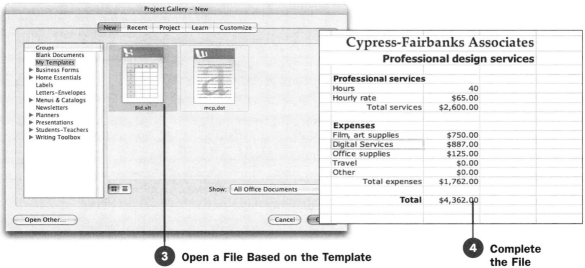

3 Open a File Based on the Template

4 Complete the File

In the **Save As** text box, give the template a name. From the **Format** drop-down list in the lower part of the dialog box, select **Template**. This option appends a designated template filename extension to the filename you provided in the **Save As** box. That extension is **.dot** for a Word template, **.xlt** for Excel, and **.pot** for PowerPoint.

In the folder window in the center of the dialog box, navigate to the **Applications, Office 2004, Templates** folder. Templates saved within that folder are available through the **Project Gallery**. That includes subfolders such as **My Templates**. In the **Project Gallery**, these subfolders appear as expandable category headings.

Click **Save** to close the **Save As** dialog box. The template is saved with the specified filename in the chosen folder.

3 Open a File Based on the Template

Select **File, Project Gallery** to open the **Project Gallery**, and select the category that represents the folder where you stored the template. Scroll through the list of templates in the right pane and click to select the template you just created. Click **OK** to close the **Project Gallery** and create a new document based on the selected template.

4 Complete the File

A new file opens, displaying the elements you have included in the template. In the case of the bid form template created in this example, you can fill in amounts and let the formulas from the template calculate the totals. Then you can save the completed worksheet as an Excel file.

TIP

The Mac is comfortable without filename extensions, but the PC is not. If you expect that a Windows user will ever want to use this template, enable the **Append file extension** check box.

TIP

You can display a thumbnail of the template in the **Project Gallery**. Before you select **File, Save As** to save the template, select **File, Properties** to open the **Properties** dialog box. Enable the **Save preview picture** check box. Then save the template as described in step 2. Unless you enable the **Save preview picture** option, the **Project Gallery** will use a generic thumbnail to represent the template.

---

18 Use an Old Document to Create a New One

Any Office document you've recently used is, in effect, a kind of *template*. Perhaps you recently wrote a sales letter to a client; now, you'd like to send the same message to another prospect. You can resurrect the old letter; change the name, address, and other key wording; and send it to the new destination.

See Also

→ **103** Develop a Presentation from Scratch

→ **107** Insert New Text in a Slide

Suppose that you recently delivered a well-received presentation and now, want to adapt it to a new audience. You can open a new PowerPoint presentation based on the previous one, make the changes you need, and save it as a new presentation template.

❶ Open the Project Gallery

Select **File**, **Project Gallery** to open the **Project Gallery**. Office stores a list of your 50 most recent documents on a **Recent** tabbed page. The recent documents—they could go back for more than a month—are displayed by modification date. If you know you last opened the presentation two weeks ago, you can select that time interval.

❷ Open the New Document

Select the document you want to emulate from the list and click **Open as Copy**. The document you selected opens with a generic filename; otherwise, it is a duplicate of the original.

NOTE

This process is essentially the same for Word, Excel, and PowerPoint documents. If the model document you want is not in the **Recent** list, open the file from its original location and save it under a new name.

❸ Edit and Save the Document

Make the changes you want to the document and then select **File**, **Save**. In the **Save As** text box, enter a filename. In the **Microsoft Office 2004** folder, navigate to the **Templates**, **PowerPoint**, **Design** folder. From the **Format** drop-down list under the folder list, select **Design Template**. Click **Save**; the file is saved as a new template.

❹ Check the Recent Documents

Select **File**, **Project Gallery**. When the **Project Gallery** reopens, select the **New** page. Open the **Presentation** category and select **Design**. The newly saved document is there; you might have to scroll down to find it.

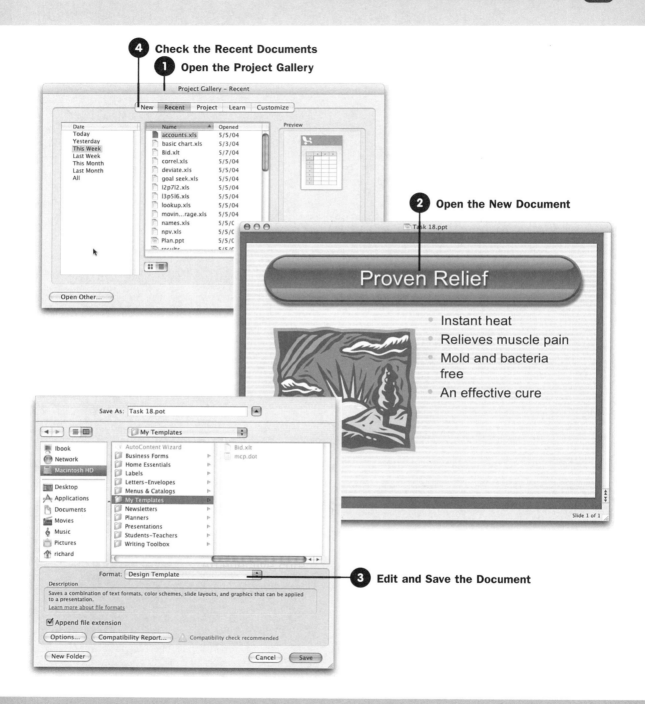

4 Check the Recent Documents

1 Open the Project Gallery

2 Open the New Document

3 Edit and Save the Document

PART II

Word 2004

IN THIS PART:

5

Managing Documents

IN THIS CHAPTER:

A serious Word user creates a lot of documents—*a lot* of documents. You can easily create so many that it becomes hard to keep track of them.

Take this scenario: You wrote a proposal for a client some time back. Now after some delay, the client wants to discuss it. That would be all well and good if you could remember exactly where on your vast hard disk you stashed your copy of the proposal.

Naturally, you have arranged this and all your documents in a logical system of folders and subfolders. Nevertheless, there might be other problems with locating the document. If this was a major proposal, chances are it was reviewed by the boss before it went out. Perhaps a couple of colleagues weighed in with their thoughts, too. Each returned a different file with their revisions added, and each file is now stored in the destination folder. But which of the several versions you now have is the "final" document?

This is not the worst-case scenario. Suppose that you find the proper file, open it, and make some last-minute additions. Just as you are about to change the revised version, the power grid collapses and you are left in the dark with an important unsaved document. It might be good to know that at moments like these, Word offers some help.

19 Open Files from the Project Gallery

See Also

 2 Set Up a Project

 15 Use a Template to
Design a Document

The quick, easy way to open a file in Word is to select **File**, **Open** and select the file. Well, *sometimes* that's the quickest or easiest way. When you use the **Open** command, the first thing you see is a list of the folders, subfolders, and files on your computer. If you have used the folder system to compartmentalize your files, you should be able to find the file you're looking for. If not, you can use the **Project Gallery**.

If you used the **Project Gallery** in previous versions of Office, you might remember it as a source of templates for new documents. Word 2004 features an expanded version that's linked to the new **Project Center**. Even if you don't remember all the details of a previous file, you certainly remember *something* about it. You might recall the last time you worked on it, at least within a week or so. Or, you might have used the **Project Gallery** to associate the file with a particular project. If so, the **Project Gallery** gives you some hope of finding it.

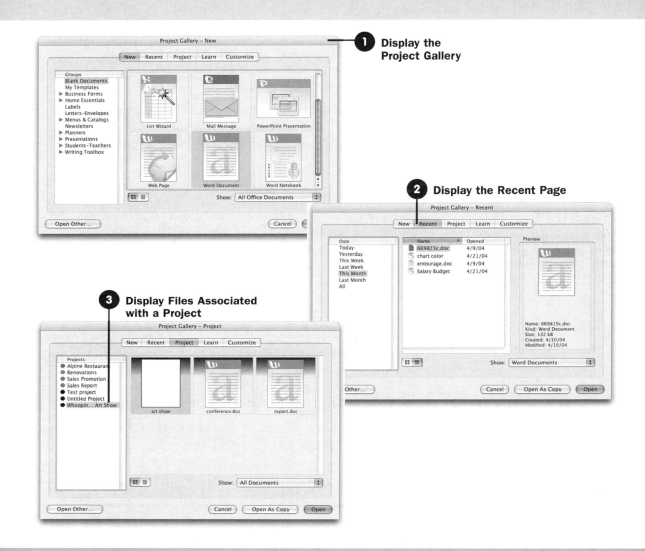

1 Display the Project Gallery

2 Display the Recent Page

3 Display Files Associated with a Project

The 2004 incarnation of the **Project Gallery** is organized into five tabbed pages: The **New** page contains templates, blank documents, and other resources useful when you create a new document. The **Recent** page displays your most recently used documents, organized by the dates they were saved. The **Project** page lists the resources of various projects created in the **Project Center**. The **Customize** page lets you

 TIP

The **Learn** page includes sample documents that demonstrate the new features of Office 2004. It is primarily a resource for new users.

change the settings for the **Project Gallery** display. If you're looking for a file, the **Recent** and **Project** pages will probably be the most useful.

① Display the Project Gallery

If the **Project Gallery** is not open, select **File**, **Project Gallery** to open it. If you have not changed this behavior in the **Customize** page, the gallery opens to the last page that was previously displayed.

② Display the Recent Page

NOTE

The **Recent** page displays files on the basis of when they were last *opened*, not when they were last saved.

Click the **Recent** tab at the top of the **Project Gallery** screen to display the **Recent** page. This page displays files according to the time they were most recently opened. If you know when the file was last used, or can even come within a week or a month of that date, you can find the file listed here.

③ Display Files Associated with a Project

If you have established a project using Entourage and the **Project Center** as described in **②** **Set Up a Project**, you can find its component files in the **Projects** page of the **Project Gallery**. Each active project is displayed in the left pane; each document or other file associated with the project is displayed on the right.

Select a project from the list on the left, and then select the file you want from the list on the right. Click **Open**.

---

20 Live with Older Files

See Also

→ **19** Open Files from the Project Gallery

→ **22** Save Quickly and Automatically

Compatibility isn't just a question for dating services. It's also a major concern for Word users. Word has been around for a long time. There have been at least a dozen different versions, not only on Mac and Windows platforms, but on the old DOS operating system as well. Word has always been Word, but over all the years and variations, there are bound to have been some changes. The people who wrote the older versions couldn't possibly have anticipated all the features that would be added later. Thus, as Microsoft has published new versions of the program, there have been occasional new versions of the Word file format as well.

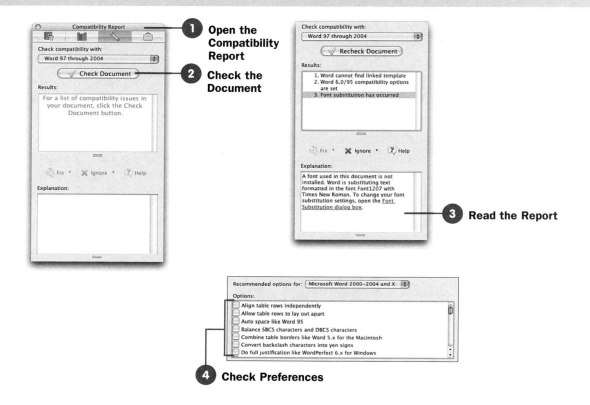

1 Open the Compatibility Report

2 Check the Document

3 Read the Report

4 Check Preferences

You might find yourself using Word 2004 to work with a document created on an older version or on a Windows system. The newer version of Word is designed to open the older document, but it might not do so as smoothly as you would hope. Little glitches in things such as line breaks and graphics handling might need some extra attention.

To deal with problems like these, Office 2004 provides a **Compatibility Check** feature. It reviews an older document and looks for differences that might cause conflicts with the current format. The program notes the differences and suggests ways to resolve them. You can decide whether to make each suggested change.

It also works the other way around. You can check a new document for changes that might be necessary for the file to be compatible with another user's older version of Word.

❶ Open the Compatibility Report

As you work on a document, Word continuously checks it for compatibility with the latest format, **Word 97 through 2004**. If you are working with an older document and the program finds a discrepancy, the **Toolbox** button on the **Standard** toolbar begins flashing. To act on the problem, select **Tools**, **Compatibility Report**. The **Compatibility Report** screen opens.

When you save a new document in an older format, Word offers a **Compatibility Report** button in the **Save As** dialog box. Click the button to open the **Compatibility Report** screen.

❷ Check the Document

In the **Compatibility Report** window, the **Check compatibility with** drop-down list initially displays the version of Word that was used to create the older document.

If the document was created with an older version of Word, select **Word 97 through 2004**. If this is a new document you want to check for compatibility with an older format, select the older format. Then click the **Check Document** button. If you have previously checked the file, the button is labeled **Recheck Document**.

❸ Read the Report

The program checks for potential problems and displays them in the **Results** window. It might show one item, or it might show several. For an explanation of the problems identified, click each item in turn. Details of the problem are reported in the **Explanation** box.

❹ Check Preferences

The explanation often recommends that you make changes in the **Preferences** dialog box. For example, it might suggest that you change the compatibility options to a different file format.

Click the text hyperlink to open the **Preferences** dialog box and make the suggested change. For example, you can open the **Recommended options** list and select a different file format. As an alternative, you can select **Word**, **Preferences** to open the dialog box and then click the **Compatibility** tab.

Click **OK** to close the **Properties** dialog box. The file is modified to reflect your selections and to minimize compatibility problems.

TIP

The **Compatibility Report** feature is also available in the **toolbox**, which has an icon on the **Standard** toolbar. Click the **Toolbox** button; when the **toolbox** opens, click the button that has a wrench icon.

NOTE

A **Recommended options** selection changes the list of items in an **Options** window. You can enable individual options in this window, but you normally want to accept those that the program recommends.

21 Retrieve Recently Used Files

Not all the files you have to find are lost. Your search needs can be as simple as coming back from lunch and reopening the file you were working on this morning. Here's where Word can give you instant recall.

When you open the **File** menu, you can select from a group of recently opened files at the bottom of the menu. As Word comes out of the box, the menu can display the last four documents you opened. You can increase the number to as many as nine, or you can turn off the feature.

1 Display the Recently Used Files

Open the **File** menu. The recently used file list appears at the bottom of the menu. A new file is added to this list whenever you save it for the first time.

2 Open the Preferences Dialog Box

To change the number of files listed at the bottom of the **File** menu or to turn off the recently used files feature altogether, select **Word**, **Preferences**. In the **Preferences** dialog box that opens, select the **General** page from the list of pages on the left. The **Recently used file list** is one of the checklist items on this page.

3 Set the Number of Files to Display

In the box that accompanies the **Recently used file list** option, enter the number of files you want to see on the menu. You can enter any number from 1 through 9. Type the entry or use the spin buttons next to the box. Click **OK** to close the dialog box.

4 Check the Menu

As you open and close files, check the file list at the bottom of the **File** menu. It displays the number of files you specified in step 3.

If you have increased the number of files, the change will not take place immediately. For example, if you changed the maximum number of files from 4 to 9, you will not see nine filenames until you have opened five more files.

See Also

→ **19** Open Files from the Project Gallery

→ **20** Live with Older Files

TIP

If you really don't want to see any recent files on the menu, disable the **Recently used file list** check box.

NOTE

Saving the same file nine times doesn't add the file to the list. To be added to the list, the file must have been saved with a new filename, to a different folder, or both.

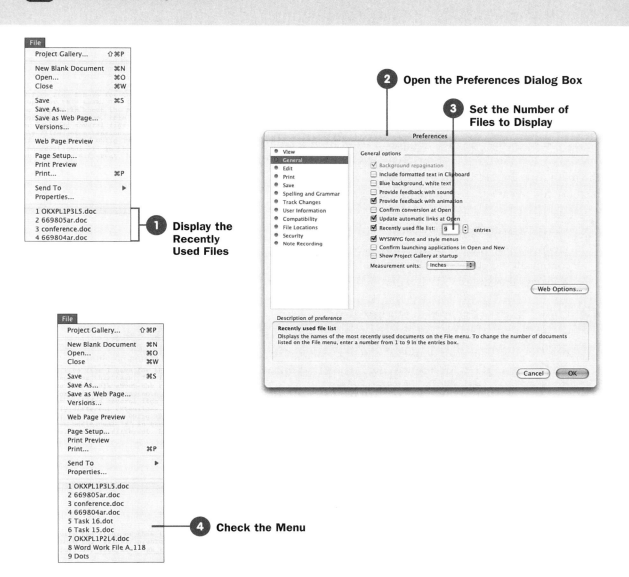

1 Display the Recently Used Files

2 Open the Preferences Dialog Box

3 Set the Number of Files to Display

4 Check the Menu

22   Save Quickly and Automatically

Plenty of advice has been issued over the years about having backup copies of your files available *when*, not *if*, the computer fails. There also seems to be a law of human nature that says, "Ignore that advice."

That's why you can set Word to make periodic backups without your intervention. For example, many people set Word to make backups every 10 minutes. Then, should the worst happen, you lose only 10 minutes' work.

When you set a backup interval, you activate an *AutoRecover* feature that preserves the backed-up material in a *recovery file*. When you restart Word after a program crash or a power failure, the program restores the recovery file and asks whether you want to open it.

That's *almost* a no-brainer. If you open the recovery file and save it under the original filename, the original file is lost. If you pass up the chance to open the recovery file, the recovery file is deleted and gone forever. A third option, which preserves everything, is to save the recovery file under a new name.

1   Open the Preferences Dialog Box

Open a document, any document. Then select **Word**, **Preferences**. When the **Preferences** dialog box opens, go to the **Save** page by clicking **Save** in the list on the left. This page displays several options for saving and preserving your work.

2   Set the AutoRecover Interval

Enable the **Save AutoRecover info every** check box. You then can call for an automatic recovery at any interval between 1 and 120 minutes. For most purposes, 10 minutes is a good interval, but you can make your own choice.

3   Examine Other Options

The **Save** page of the **Preferences** dialog box has other options that also can affect your ability to preserve and recover your work.

See Also

→ 23 Manage Multiple Versions of a File

KEY TERMS

AutoRecover—A Word feature that periodically saves a backup of an open file and recovers it in case of failure.

Recovery file—A backup file that Word can recover in case of a system crash or power failure.

NOTE

In the Windows version of Word, you would open a dialog box comparable to the **Preferences** dialog box by selecting **Tools**, **Options**.

NOTE

Some people swear by AutoRecover; others swear at it. The critics complain that when AutoSave kicks in it cuts off their work in mid-sentence. Not everyone has had this experience, but some do complain about it.

1 Open the Preferences Dialog Box

3 Examine Other Options

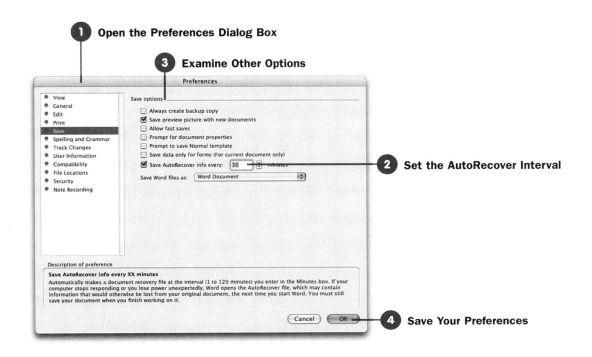

2 Set the AutoRecover Interval

4 Save Your Preferences

TIP

Point to any option in this list, and a description is displayed in the lower part of the dialog box.

The **Always create backup copy** option automatically saves a backup copy any time you save a document. This backup file duplicates the previously saved version, minus any subsequent changes you have made. It could be valuable if you save changes you didn't want to make or if you accidentally delete the original file. This was a feature of older word processors that lacked capabilities such as AutoRecover or the ability to undo errors. It is less necessary now.

If you have to retrieve a backup copy, select **File, Open**. In the **Open** dialog box, open the **Enable** drop-down list and select **All Readable Documents**. Navigate to the folder where you saved the original document. The backup file is in that same folder with the title **Backup of** and the original document's filename.

The **Allow fast saves** option structures a document file so that it can be saved to disk more rapidly. Instead of saving a single continuous document, this feature saves the document in disorganized segments with pointers to indicate which piece fits where.

The price of a fast save is a larger, more complex document file. Modern hard disks operate quickly enough that this feature, too, is often unnecessary.

④ Save Your Preferences

When you're finished selecting options, click **OK** to close the **Preferences** dialog box. The changes will come into play as you continue to work.

 NOTE

A fast save might also be a security risk. Word does not remove deletions from a fast-saved file; it just ignores them. In one case, what were delicately called "unprofessional" comments were supposedly removed from a letter to a business partner. The comments were forgotten but not gone; although hidden, they remained in the file. Naturally, the recipient found them.

23 Manage Multiple Versions of a File

Writing is supposed to be a lonely, solo activity, but it doesn't usually work that way. There are editors to contend with (apologies to those who edit this book), and multiple contributors might work on a joint project.

A common scenario is to complete a document and then send it to several reviewers. Each returns a revised copy of the file. Now, you have several copies of the same file and a problem keeping track of them.

Microsoft likes to promote its projects as collaborative tools, and Word includes several features to help move that process along. As each reviewer's revisions arrive, you can *merge* them into your original document. Then, instead of saving a separate file or overwriting the original, you can save the revised document as a *version* of the original. Instead of being scattered around as separate files, a single file incorporates all the versions.

In addition to accepting multiple revisions into a single file, versions can be useful to lone authors who repeatedly revise their work. Each new revision can be saved as a version, but the earlier work is there if it's needed.

Before You Begin

✔ **22** Save Quickly and Automatically

See Also

→ **19** Open Files from the Project Gallery

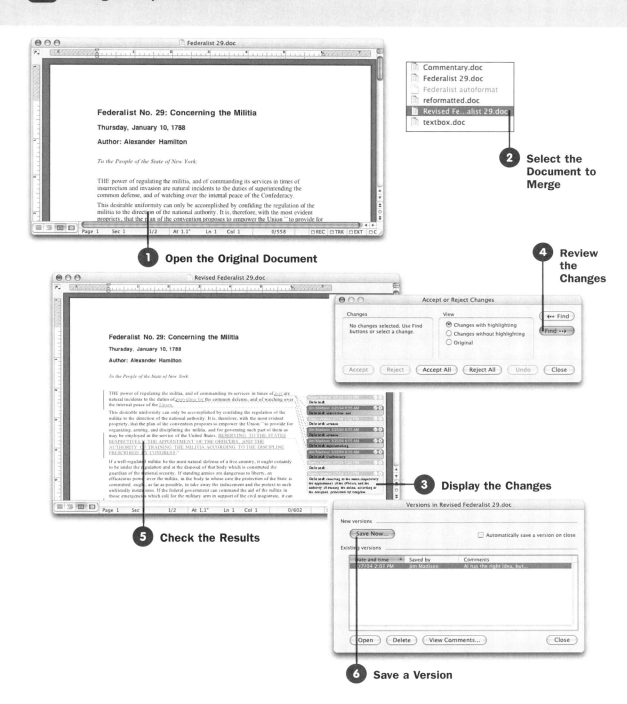

2 Select the Document to Merge

1 Open the Original Document

4 Review the Changes

3 Display the Changes

5 Check the Results

6 Save a Version

1 Open the Original Document

If you have received a revised file from a reviewer, you can examine these changes and decide whether you want to incorporate them into the document's final version. Start by opening the original document.

2 Select the Document to Merge

Select **Tools, Merge Documents**. The **Choose a File** dialog box displays the familiar folder structure. Select the copy of the document the reviewer has submitted and click **Open**.

3 Display the Changes

If the reviewer has used the *Track Changes* feature, the revisions appear in your copy of the document. If the changes are not visible, select **View, Toolbars, Reviewing**. Open the list on the left side of the toolbar and select one of the **Showing markup** options.

If the reviewer did not use the **Track Changes** feature, you can obtain the same results by approaching from the opposite direction. Open the *edited* document and select **Tools, Track Changes, Compare Documents**. Then merge in the original document.

🔍KEY TERM

Track Changes—A Word feature in which changes made by an editor or reviewer are displayed as strikeouts and additions. Other readers then can see what changes have been made.

4 Review the Changes

Select **Tools, Track Changes, Accept or Reject Changes**. The **Accept or Reject Changes** dialog box opens. Click the **Find** button that displays a forward arrow. The first change is highlighted in the document, and the dialog box asks for your decision.

You can accept or reject the suggested change, or you can accept or reject all changes in the document. If you select one of the all-document options, a dialog box asks you to confirm the action. When you're finished, click **Close**.

5 Check the Results

Your accepted changes are merged into the original document. You can repeat steps 1–4 for any other reviewer's documents that arrive. The document can accept multiple viewers' revisions, displaying each person's work in a different color.

6 **Save a Version**

The reviews might not all come in at once. Instead of saving a new file for each revision, you can save a single file that contains successive versions of the same file. This approach simplifies file management and makes it easier for you to track who has submitted their comments so far.

NOTE

After the merge, the document received from the reviewer is still a separate document. Because it also has been incorporated into the version document, you might want to stash the reviewer's document in a backup file somewhere.

With the merged document open, select **File**, **Versions**. In the dialog box that opens, click **Save Now**. The **Save Version** dialog box asks for your comments on the version. These brief comments can help you identify the version: "**With Addie's comments**," or something similar. Type a comment if you want and click **OK**.

You return to the document. Select **File**, **Versions** again. The saved version appears on the list of versions.

6

Writing and Editing

IN THIS CHAPTER:

The first movie makers staged their productions in theaters. The actors performed on stage, and a single camera was set up between rows of audience seats. They did it that way because it was what they knew. Only later did they figure out that they could move the production to different locations, and the *movie set* was invented.

The first word processors were much the same. They emulated typewriters because that's what their inventors knew. About that time, a technologically advanced newspaper printing plant conducted a tour that featured the latest experimental technology. By that time, reporters were writing on computer terminals, but the rest of the process was mainly photographic. Automatic typesetters took pictures of each letter and generated columns of type in long paper strips. These strips then were pasted onto page layout forms that were photographed again to produce printing plates. The highlight of the tour was a device that took the output of the reporters terminals and assembled it electronically into entire pages. It was still experimental at the time, but as an invention it was the typographical equivalent of a movie set.

Now, of course, you can do the same thing on your own, using Word or any number of other word processing products. You can do many other things, too, such as selecting a typeface or finding misspelled words. Nevertheless, if you set out to fill an entire book with really bad writing, Word does absolutely nothing to stop you. In fact, it does all that it can to help.

NOTE

The tasks in this chapter don't try to teach you the fundamentals. Instead, they demonstrate some of the extra tricks you can employ to build a better document.

Word is still basically a word processor. It processes words. This computerized process can aid, but not replace, human judgment. Take the spelling checker, for example. It does not actually identify misspelled words. It flags words that are not in a list of properly spelled words. It's still up to you to decide whether the words are actually misspelled.

Just remember: Word is a tool and so is a hammer. You can use a hammer to build things or to destroy things. The choice is yours. The tool doesn't care.

24 Write an Outline

Beginning management students sometimes have to go through this exercise: The class is split into groups, and each is given an assortment of Lego blocks. The task is to duplicate the figure that has been assembled in the front of the room. The group with the shortest time wins. Your team's clock starts when you move the first block.

That last sentence is the key to the exercise. Victory invariably goes to the team that devotes the most time to planning. Members take the time to study the model figure and plan each move before they touch that first block.

Outlining a written document is much the same. You might have hated it in school—you might even hate it now. Nevertheless, outlining is the key to a well-organized document. Without careful planning, you can wander off on a tangent, forget important points, or overemphasize unimportant ones. And you'll probably take more time than you would if you had done some better planning in advance.

Word can help by displaying a document in an *Outline view*. In this view, each heading is assigned a level in the outline. The main heading is assigned Level 1; major subheadings are Level 2; and so on. You can promote or demote headings to different levels. You also can reorganize the document by moving headings up and down. When you do so, any subordinate headings (or text you might have written) are moved along with the headings. After you fill out the document by writing text to accompany each heading, you can see the heading structure without the subordinate body text if you want.

❶ Display Outline View

As it often does, Word gives you several ways to display a document in Outline view. You can select **View**, **Outline**; you can press ⌘-**Alt-O** (that's the letter *O*); or you can click the **Outline View** icon in the lower-left corner of the screen.

See Also

→ **27** Apply Automatic Numbers

→ **36** Apply a Style to a New Paragraph

→ **104** Outline a Presentation

KEY TERM

Outline view—A view that displays a document in the form of an adjustable outline. You can move headings to different levels, change the order of major topics, and hide or display body text.

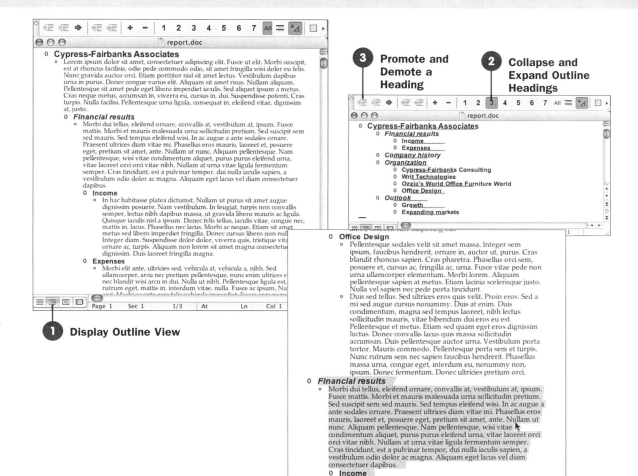

1 Display Outline View

3 Promote and Demote a Heading

2 Collapse and Expand Outline Headings

In Outline view, headings and body text are indented according to their outline levels. An **Outlining** toolbar also opens with tools for managing and rearranging the outline. If you are working with an existing document, you can use Outline view to display and, if necessary, change the document outline. If you are starting a new document, use the outline to sketch in the main and subordinate headings and then add the body text. You can always rearrange things later.

② Collapse and Expand Outline Headings

One way to check the organization of your document is to hide lower levels of the document so that you can see the higher-level headings with less distraction.

The **Outlining** toolbar has a row of numbers, from 1 to 7. Click any of these numbers to see only the headings at that level and above. For example, if you want to see only the top three outline levels, click the **3** in the toolbar. Click **All** to display all levels of the outline.

③ Promote and Demote a Heading

Perhaps you see that a subheading should instead be a main heading or that a main heading should become a subheading. In Outline view, you can promote or demote headings or paragraphs to new levels.

Again, there's more than one way to do this. You can select the heading and click either the **Promote** or **Demote** button at the left end of the **Outlining** toolbar. Alternatively, you can press **Tab** to demote a heading by moving it to the right or **Shift-Tab** to promote the heading by moving it to the left.

④ Reorganize Sections of the Document

All paragraphs in Outline view have small symbols to the left: plus marks next to headings that have subordinate levels and small squares next to those that do not.

 NOTE

Initially, Word ties its outline levels to built-in *styles*. The style **Heading1** is assigned to outline Level 1, **Heading2** is assigned to Level 2, and so on. Every nonheading is designated as **Body Text**. You can change these assignments, but you must leave Outline view to do so. Switch to **Normal** or **Print Layout** view and select an example of the style you want to change. Then select **Format**, **Paragraph**. A button in the **Paragraph** dialog box lets you assign a different outline level to all examples of the selected style.

 TIP

You also can expand or collapse any section of the outline by selecting a heading and clicking the **+** (plus) or **–** (minus) button on the **Outlining** toolbar.

TIP

If you actually want to insert a tab while in Outline view, press ⌘-**Tab**. If you press the **Tab** key by itself, you demote the current heading one level. If you are building a PowerPoint presentation, you can use the same outlining techniques you use in Word. In fact, if you develop an outline in Word, you can import it into PowerPoint. See **104** **Outline a Presentation** and **105** **Import an Outline from Word**.

NOTE

The Latin text in the sample document is traditionally used by page designers who need blocks of "dummy text" to test their designs. It has been traced to an essay on ethics written by Cicero in 45 BC.

If you click the plus symbol next to a heading, you select all subordinate headings and body text beneath that heading. Then, you can drag the selected text to move the entire section up or down within the document. Alternatively, you can select the text and use the up or down arrow in the **Outlining** toolbar or drag the heading to a new position.

25 Expand Abbreviations

See Also

➡ **26** Insert a Symbol

KEY TERM

AutoCorrect—A Word feature in which you can enter a short text passage such as an abbreviation or a commonly misspelled word and then specify substitute text to be inserted into the text instead.

Suppose that you are trying to type a sentence such as *Don't drink the water.* You forget to capitalize the first letter, and you leave out the apostrophe. But when you go back to correct your mistakes, you find there's no problem. The sentence is written just as you intended.

This is an example of *AutoCorrect* at work. AutoCorrect is a multifaceted device that can automatically capitalize the first word in a sentence and correct common typographical errors. If you have a long entry that you often must type (such as a scientific term or the long title of a company), you can enter a short form of the term that AutoCorrect can then expand.

① Add an AutoCorrect Entry

AutoCorrect has two important uses. The first is to help correct misspellings and improper capitalization. The feature comes heavily stocked with commonly misspelled words and other common typing errors. It automatically replaces these errors with the correct versions.

To see the AutoCorrect options, select **Tools**, **AutoCorrect**. The **AutoCorrect** dialog box includes a large window split into two columns. On the left is the text you might type; on the right is the correct version. Scroll down to find the incorrect version of *don't*. Unless the list has been changed, you should find it in the left column, paired with the correct version in the right column. Thus, when you type it wrong, Word still gets it right.

The second use of the AutoCorrect tool is to expand abbreviations. At the top of the list you might notice, for example, that if you type (c), AutoCorrect replaces it with a copyright symbol ©.

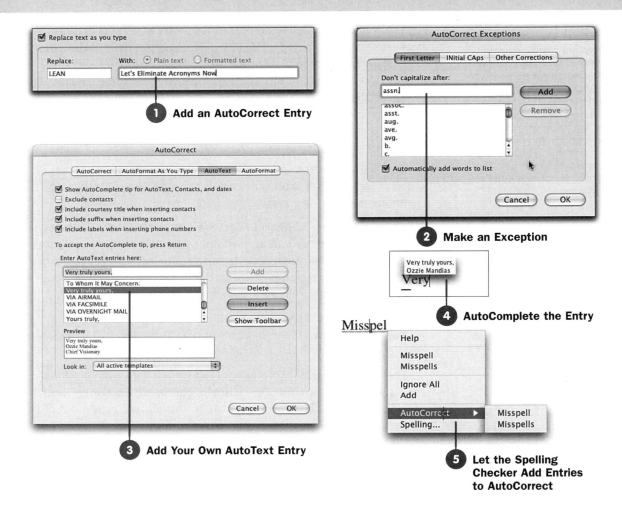

1 Add an AutoCorrect Entry

2 Make an Exception

3 Add Your Own AutoText Entry

4 AutoComplete the Entry

5 Let the Spelling Checker Add Entries to AutoCorrect

You can add your own common misspellings or abbreviations. Suppose that you frequently have to spell out the full name of an organization. You could enter a short form (such as **LEAN**) in the **Replace** window and the long form (such as **Let's Eliminate Acronyms Now**) in the **With** window.

Make sure that the **Replace text as you type** check box is enabled. Click **OK**. Then, whenever you type **LEAN**, Word expands this abbreviation into the full name.

NOTE

The AutoCorrect list is case-sensitive. In the example here, because the abbreviation is fully capitalized, there should be no fear of typing sentences such as *Lean on me*.

TIP

Another check box you might find valuable is the **Replace text as you type** check box. Disabling it turns off AutoCorrect. Some people prefer it that way, including Unix programmers to whom capitalization is important. It also includes people who find AutoCorrect to be just plain irritating.

The AutoCorrect dialog box has several other checklist options. These normally are selected, but you can cancel them if you want. Enable the **Correct Two Initial Capitals** check box for occasions when you leave the **Caps Lock** key pressed by mistake. Enable other check boxes to automatically capitalize the first letters of sentences and of days of the week.

2 Make an Exception

When Word encounters a period, it normally assumes that is the end of a sentence. With impeccable computer logic, it capitalizes the next word.

That isn't always as logical as it seems. Sometimes, the period is at the end of an abbreviation and capitalizing the next word would be wrong. For that reason, AutoCorrect provides for exceptions. It already has listed many common abbreviations as exceptions to the capitalization rule, and you can add your own.

From the **AutoCorrect** dialog box (select **Tools**, **AutoCorrect**), select **Exceptions**. Enter an abbreviation, including the period, and click **Add**.

This dialog box has two other pages to which you can add different kinds of exceptions. For example, you might encounter a corporate name with nonstandard capitalization that runs afoul of the **Initial Caps** rule. You could add that term as an exception on that page. The **Other Corrections** page is for exceptions that don't fit in the other categories.

3 Add Your Own AutoText Entry

AutoText is a close companion to **AutoCorrect**. Instead of substituting one phrase for another, AutoText is a collection of stock phrases such as the closing to a letter. When you begin typing the phrase, the *AutoComplete* function recognizes it and asks whether you want to enter the entire phrase. If so, press **Enter**. If not, just keep on typing. Because most AutoText entries are complete paragraphs, pressing **Enter** inserts the phrase *and* positions the insertion point at the start of a new paragraph. Alternatively, you can press **Tab** to complete the entry without starting the new paragraph.

KEY TERMS

AutoText—A selection of stored text entries available as AutoComplete entries.

AutoComplete—A feature that recognizes the first few keystrokes of a stored text entry and, on command, completes the entry.

AutoText also has its own sources of irritation. When the developers stocked the function with an initial set of AutoText entries, they apparently couldn't resist showing off. AutoText can insert large, fully formatted tables. When you type *comp*, for example, a yellow flag suggests that when you press **Enter** you can complete the word *comparison*. What you get instead is a table designed for a pro/con list. There are several other examples like this, and they tend to show up when you least expect them.

There's no quick way to get rid of these built-in phrases. To do so individually, select **Tools**, **Autocorrect** and select the **AutoText** page in the dialog box. Select each entry in turn, starting with **Asset Inventory** and check its appearance in the **Preview** window. Click **Delete** for each entry you want to remove.

The easiest way to make an AutoText entry, particularly if it's long, is to start by typing it in a document. Select the text you have entered. Then select **Tools**, **AutoCorrect**; in the **AutoCorrect** dialog box, click the **AutoText** page. The first line of the selected phrase appears in the **Enter AutoText entries here** text box. If there are additional lines, the full text appears in the **Preview** box.

Click **Add**, and then click **OK**. The phrase is added to the AutoText list.

④ AutoComplete the Entry

If you have stored an AutoText entry, AutoComplete can insert it into a document.

Type the first few letters of an AutoText entry (for this example, begin to type the closing for a letter, **Very truly yours, Ozzie Mandias**). An AutoComplete tip notes that you have begun to type an AutoText entry. If you want to insert the entry, press **Return**. Otherwise, just keep typing.

⑤ Let the Spelling Checker Add Entries to AutoCorrect

If you're human, you misspell more words than you could possibly think of adding to the AutoCorrect list. And it can be inconvenient to open the AutoCorrect list every time you think of an addition you'd like to make. There's a simpler way: Let the spelling checker add your common mistakes—and the correct words—to the AutoCorrect list for you.

TIP

In addition to any AutoText entries you might have added to Word's repertoire, default AutoText entries you might find useful are dates (begin typing today's date in a common format—such as **April 21, 2004** or **4/21/04**—and the tip pops up with the completed date; press **Return** to enter the complete date in the document) and months of the year.

When the spelling checker flags a word as possibly misspelled, **Ctrl**-click the word. In the context menu, point to the **AutoCorrect** option; the spelling checker displays suggested corrections. Click the one you want to use.

The misspelled word is corrected in the document. In addition, the misspelling and its correct version are added to the AutoCorrect list.

26 Insert a Symbol

See Also

→ **27** Apply Automatic Numbers

→ **108** Format Bullet Points

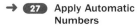 **KEY TERM**

Symbol—A special character or graphic outside the normal assortment of characters and punctuation marks.

 TIP

You can apply custom bullets to text you've already written or to text you are about to type.

 TIP

Selecting a custom bullet displaces one of the standard bullets already displayed. Don't worry. You can use the **Reset** button to restore the original selection.

You can't always complete a document with just the 26 letters of the alphabet plus a handful of punctuation marks. Most fonts have additional characters or *symbols* you can use to enhance a document.

One frequent use of symbols is in the bullets of bullet points. Many documents use bulleted lists, and although Word provides several useful bullet characters, you might want to look further. The **Bullets and Numbering** feature provides a route you can explore.

① Open the Bullets and Numbering Dialog Box

Select the text to which you want to add bullets, or place the insertion point at the spot in the document where you want to add a bulleted list. Then select **Format**, **Bullets and Numbering** to open the **Bullets and Numbering** dialog box. Select the **Bulleted** tab if that page is not already open.

② Customize the Display

Select any of the bullet designs displayed and click the **Customize** button. The **Customize bulleted list** dialog box opens. Click the **Bullet** button to open the **Symbol** dialog box.

③ Select a New Bullet Character

The **Symbol** dialog box displays the contents of one of several fonts that contain symbols instead of the usual alphabetical characters.

Try to stick to universally available fonts such as **Symbol**, **Dingbats**, and **Wingdings**. If a recipient's typefaces differ from yours, the bullets might appear as symbols far removed from what you had intended.

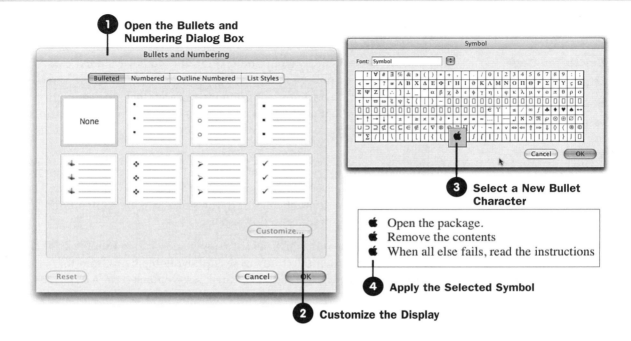

① Open the Bullets and Numbering Dialog Box

③ Select a New Bullet Character

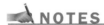 Open the package.
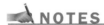 Remove the contents
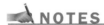 When all else fails, read the instructions

④ Apply the Selected Symbol

② Customize the Display

Check the available symbols. Click any of the symbols to see an enlarged picture. If you want to look into another symbol font, select a different font from the **Font** drop-down list at the top of the dialog box.

④ Apply the Selected Symbol

Select a symbol and click **OK**. Click **OK** again to close the **Customize bulleted list** dialog box and the **Bullets and Numbering** dialog box. When you return to the document, the new symbol is applied to the bulleted list.

⚡NOTES

You might want to insert a symbol other than a bullet point, such as to insert a copyright or trademark symbol. Click where you want the symbol and select **Insert**, **Symbol** to open the **Symbol** dialog box. Select the symbol you want to use and click **OK**.

The Mac operating system has its own symbol feature, generally more sophisticated than the Microsoft system shown here. In many applications, excluding Word but including the Finder, you can select **Edit**, **Special Characters** to open a **Character Palette**. Leave the palette open when you return to Word to use the Mac symbol feature in Word.

27 Apply Automatic Numbers

Before You Begin

✔ **24** Write an Outline

See Also

→ **26** Insert a Symbol

TIP

There's not much difference between a bulleted list and a numbered list as far as the formatting goes, but some folks recognize at least one stylistic difference. A convention among some types of publishers is that if the list represents steps to be taken in order, it should be numbered. If the order of the items in the list doesn't matter, use bullets.

KEY TERMS

Field—A function inserted into a Word document that displays variable information. Fields can display dates, consecutive numbers, or other variable information that can be updated as their values change.

Switch—An entry within a function that modifies the formatting or the value of the displayed result. For example, in a numeric field, a switch could reset the value to **1**.

In most respects, Word's layout and text formatting powers don't compare with professional-level page layout programs such as QuarkXpress and InDesign. But Word has one thing the big boys lack: the capability to apply automatic numbering systems. If the first item in a list is number 1, Word can figure out—all on its own—that the next item in the list is number 2.

There are several ways to apply numbering. The easiest might be simply to select the **Numbered Lists** option on the **Formatting Palette**. This option can produce a numbered list in the same way the companion **Bullet Lists** option produces a bulleted list.

Not nearly as simple is to use *fields* to apply consecutive numbers. Select **Insert**, **Field** and then select any of several available fields from the **Numbering** category. For example, anywhere you insert an **AUTONUM** field, a consecutive number appears. Other numbering fields include **SEQ** (with which you can create several separate named sequences) and **LISTNUM** (with which you can insert outline-style numbers). An **Options** button in the **Insert Field** dialog box lets you name the sequence or add a *switch* that can reset a numbering sequence to **1**.

Midway on the difficulty scale is applying outline numbers to the headings within a document. When you apply an outlining scheme, each heading should be assigned an appropriate outline level. When you apply numbering to the outline, top-level headings are numbered 1, 2, and 3, while lower-level headings might be designated a, b, and c.

You can select variations on this numbering scheme, such as roman numerals or a legal numbering scheme (in which the main heading is 1, the next subordinate is 1.1, and so on). This task explains how to apply numbers to existing outline headings.

❶ Apply a Numbering Scheme

Open the document in Outline view and select a top-level heading. Then select **Format**, **Bullets and Numbering**. The **Bullets and Numbering** dialog box opens. Select the **Outline Numbered** page.

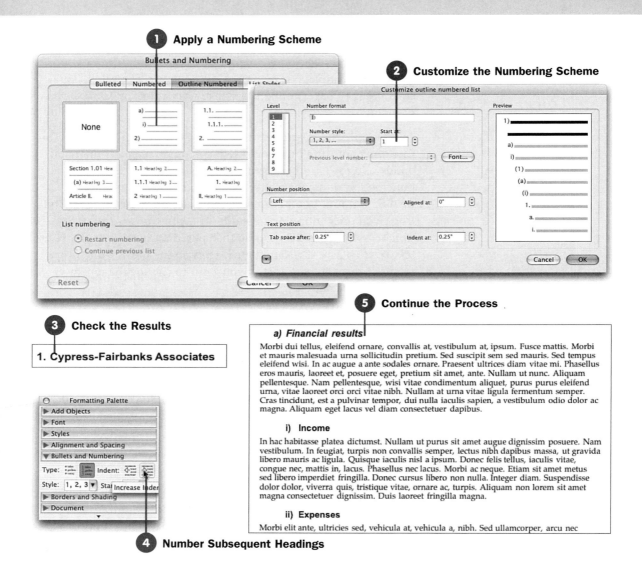

1 **Apply a Numbering Scheme**

2 **Customize the Numbering Scheme**

3 **Check the Results**

5 **Continue the Process**

4 **Number Subsequent Headings**

Select one of the displayed numbering schemes. If it is not exactly what you want to use, you can modify it.

NOTE

In the **Bullets and Numbering** dialog box, the **Bulleted** page provides alternative formats for bullet points; the **Numbered** page does the same for numbered lists.

② **Customize the Numbering Scheme**

The chosen numbering scheme might not be exactly what you want. For example, one available option uses a parenthesis after each number, but you might prefer to use periods or Roman numerals.

To customize the selected scheme, click the **Customize** button. The **Customize outline numbered list** dialog box offers a variety of options. In the **Number format** text box, you can change the punctuation that comes after the number. You can also select **Arabic**, **Roman**, or other numbering styles from the **Number style** list. If you are continuing an earlier list, you can set a starting number other than **1** by typing the desired number in the **Start at** text box. There are also options for setting the indents and alignments of the numbered list. If you want to change the typeface, click the **Font** button.

In the **Level** list, select level **1**. Then set the specifications you want for first-level numbering.

TIP

Select a lower-level heading from the **Level** list and specify the formatting of lower-level numbers without leaving the dialog box.

③ **Check the Results**

When you're finished customizing the formatting, click **OK**. When you return to the **Bullets and Numbering** dialog box, click **OK** again. The numbering scheme is applied to the selected heading in the current document.

④ **Number Subsequent Headings**

You still must number other headings in the document, but you need not reopen the **Bullets and Numbering** dialog box to do so. You can work through the **Formatting Palette**.

Select the next lower-level heading (for example, if you formatted level 1 headings with the **Bullets and Numbering** dialog box, now select a level 2 heading). In the **Bullets and Numbering** area of the **Formatting Palette**, click the **Numbering** button. To the right of that button, click the **Increase Indent** button.

When the **Numbering** button is selected, the **Increase Indent** and **Decrease Indent** buttons select lower or higher outline levels and apply the numbers accordingly.

5 **Continue the Process**

Repeat step 4 to apply numbers to subsequent headings, increasing or decreasing their indents so their numbering reflects their positions in the outline. Unfortunately, numbering does not automatically follow the assigned heading levels; it must be adjusted manually for each heading.

28 Insert an Excel Worksheet

The applications in Office 2004 are designed to work together. If you have some figures from Excel you want to insert into a Word document, you can do that.

Suppose that you are writing a proposal for a potential client. You've written a sales pitch in Word, but the bid figures you want to use are in an Excel worksheet. You can merge these two documents by inserting the Excel figures into the Word letter.

See Also

→ **40** Place Graphics

→ **50** Generate a Form Letter

→ **109** Insert an Excel Table

1 **Write the Document**

Start with the Word document that will accept the Excel figures. If you are preparing a bid proposal, write the text you want to include with the figures.

2 **Select the Excel Data**

Open the Excel workbook that contains the information you want to include in the Word document and select the cells you want to use. Then select **Edit**, **Copy** or press ⌘-**C**. The Excel data is copied to the clipboard.

3 **Link the Two Documents**

In the Word document, click at the spot where you want to insert the Excel material. Select **Edit**, **Paste Special**. The **Paste Special** dialog box opens. Make sure that the **Paste** button (not the **Paste link** button) is selected. From the **As** list box, select **Microsoft Excel Worksheet Object**. Click **OK**.

NOTE

The **Paste Special** dialog box also contains options to paste the clipboard contents as formatted or unformatted text, as a noneditable picture, or in HTML format. The HTML format uses the **Data Merge Manager**, whose main job is to accommodate mass mailings. When pasted in this format, the Excel contents are treated like the name and address variables in a mail merge.

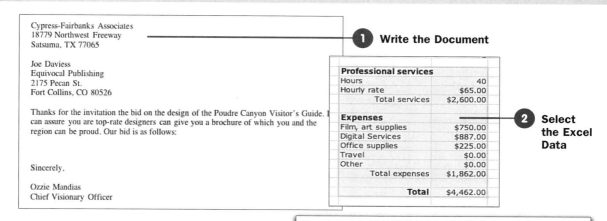

1 Write the Document

2 Select the Excel Data

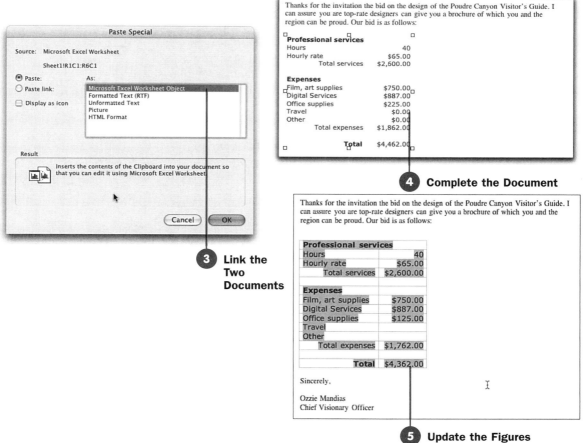

3 Link the Two Documents

4 Complete the Document

5 Update the Figures

4 **Complete the Document**

The worksheet information is pasted into the Word document. It is imported as a graphic, so you can use the adjustment handles to resize it as necessary. You can also move it to a different position.

5 **Update the Figures**

When you receive word of reduced paper cost or any other factor that affects the Excel data included in the Word document, you can go into Excel and adjust the bid accordingly. The Word document automatically updates itself to reflect the changes.

To do this, double-click the Excel data in the Word document. The worksheet opens in Excel. Make the changes there and then return to the Word document where the changes also appear.

29 Select Multiple Items

Perhaps you've seen a financial newsletter that emphasizes important points by underlining them. Or how about a gossip column that bold-faces the names of celebrities? These are among many ways you might want to select isolated pieces of a document to apply special formatting. The obvious solution is to select one block of text at a time and then apply the formatting to each selection. The not-so-obvious solution is to select all these blocks at once, even though they are not adjacent. Then you can apply the formatting to all of them at the same time.

See Also

→ **30** Select an Area

→ **31** Clear Unwanted Formatting

→ **32** Find Formatting Codes

1 **Select the First Item**

Select the first item you want. It can be a word, a sentence, a paragraph, or the contents of a table cell.

2 **Select the Other Items**

Press the ⌘ key and drag the mouse over the next block of text you want to select. Keep the ⌘ key pressed as you drag over all the selections you want to make.

3 **Apply the Formatting**

Use the **Formatting Palette** to select the formatting you want to apply to the selected text.

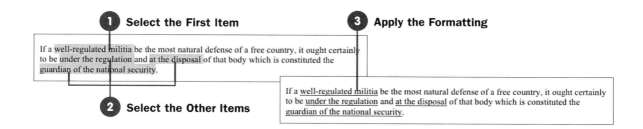

1 Select the First Item   **3** Apply the Formatting

If a well-regulated militia be the most natural defense of a free country, it ought certainly to be under the regulation and at the disposal of that body which is constituted the guardian of the national security.

2 Select the Other Items

If a well-regulated militia be the most natural defense of a free country, it ought certainly to be under the regulation and at the disposal of that body which is constituted the guardian of the national security.

30 Select an Area

See Also

→ **29** Select Multiple Items

→ **31** Clear Unwanted Formatting

→ **32** Find Formatting Codes

 TIP

There is another very practical possibility for selecting an unusually shaped area: Perhaps you have entered a tabular list using the **Tab** key to separate the columns. You could select the first column and boldface the text.

Most of the time, when you make a selection, you select a particular string of text: a word, a section, or a paragraph. If the text breaks onto a new line, the selection breaks right along with it.

Sometimes, you might want to select an area of the screen, regardless of the text structure. For example, you might want to select a rectangular area in the center of a block of text and apply a light-blue highlight to this selected area to create graphic interest on the page. The light-blue rectangle is not related to a particular section of text—it's just an oddly shaped selection. If that's what you want to do, you can readily do it.

1 Make the Selection

The secret to selecting an area is to press the **Option** key while you drag to make the selection.

2 Apply Special Effects

This type of selection falls outside normal text-handling functions. That means you are limited in what you can do with it. For example, most of the alignment and spacing options apply to all the paragraphs included in the selection, not just the selection itself. Nevertheless, you can do a few things such as reformat the text or apply a new typeface. You also can open the **Font** section of the **Formatting Palette** and select a highlight color to be applied to the selection.

THE power of regulating the militia, and of c
insurrection and invasion are natural incidents
common defense, and of watching over the in

This desirable uniformity can only be accomp
militia to the direction of the national authorit
propriety, that the plan of the convention prop
organizing, arming, and disciplining the milit
may be employed in the service of the United
RESPECTIVELY THE APPOINTMENT OF
AUTHORITY OF TRAINING THE MILITI
PRESCRIBED BY CONGRESS."

If a well-regulated militia be the most natural
to be under the regulation and at the disposal

 Make the Selection

THE power of regulating the militia, and of c
insurrection and invasion are natural incidents
common defense, and of watching over the in

This desirable uniformity can only be accomp
militia to the direction of the national authorit
propriety, that the plan of the convention prop
organizing, arming, and disciplining the milit
may be employed in the service of the United
RESPECTIVELY THE APPOINTMENT OF
AUTHORITY OF TRAINING THE MILITI
PRESCRIBED BY CONGRESS."

If a well-regulated militia be the most natural
to be under the regulation and at the disposal

 Apply Special Effects

31 Clear Unwanted Formatting

Just as you can apply formatting to large areas or multiple selections,
you can remove the formatting from text in much the same way. The
Clear Formatting command does just what its name suggests: It clears
away all the formatting from selected text. Select the text—up to the full
document—and then apply the **Clear Formatting** command. The command removes any local formatting, such as boldfaced type, and any
character or paragraph styles that might have been applied.

You might have a heavily formatted document that you want to reformat. Instead of removing each formatting element individually, you can
clear all the formatting at once and start with the proverbial clean slate.

1 Select the Text You Want to Reformat

To reformat a single paragraph, click inside that paragraph (do
not select any text in the paragraph, just position the mouse pointer in the paragraph). To reformat a smaller or larger block of text,
select the text.

Before You Begin

✔ **24** Write an Outline

See Also

→ **29** Select Multiple Items

→ **30** Select an Area

→ **32** Find Formatting Codes

 TIP

Use the **Clear Formatting**
command in conjunction
with the multiselection feature described in **29**
Select Multiple Items.
Select all the instances of
the formatting you want to
change; then use the **Clear
Formatting** command to
make all the changes at
once.

Federalist No. 29: Concerning the Militia

Thursday, January 10, 1788

Author: Alexander Hamilton
To the People of the State of New York:

THE power of regulating the militia, and of commanding its services in times of insurrection and invasion are natural incidents to the duties of superintending the common defense, and of watching over the internal peace of the Confederacy.

This desirable uniformity can only be accomplished by confiding the regulation of the militia to the direction of the national authority. It is, therefore, with the most evident propriety, that the plan of the convention proposes to empower the Union `` to provide for organizing, arming, and disciplining the militia, and for governing such part of them as may be employed in the service of the United States, *reserving to the states respectively the appointment of the officers, and the authority of training the militia according to the discipline prescribed by congress."*

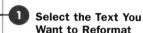 **Select the Text You Want to Reformat**

Federalist No. 29: Concerning the Militia

Thursday, January 10, 1788

Author: Alexander Hamilton

To the People of the State of New York:

THE power of regulating the militia, and of commanding its services in times of insurrection and invasion are natural incidents to the duties of superintending the common defense, and of watching over the internal peace of the Confederacy.

This desirable uniformity can only be accomplished by confiding the regulation of the militia to the direction of the national authority. It is, therefore, with the most evident propriety, that the plan of the convention proposes to empower the Union `` to provide for organizing, arming, and disciplining the militia, and for governing such part of them as may be employed in the service of the United States, reserving to the states respectively the appointment of the officers, and the authority of training the militia according to the discipline prescribed by congress."

2 **Clear the Formatting**

 TIP

You can also clear formatting from the selected text using the **Formatting Palette**. Select the text and open the **Styles** list. Go to the top of the list and click the **Clear Formatting** button.

2 Clear the Formatting

Select **Edit**, **Clear**, **Formats**. All styles and manual formatting are removed. The **Clear Formatting** command behaves differently, depending on the text you select:

- When you place the cursor inside a paragraph, the command removes any character formatting applied within the paragraph. The paragraph is reset to the **Normal** *style*.

- When you select text within a paragraph, the command removes any character formatting applied to the selection and applies the underlying paragraph style.

- When you select one or more paragraphs, the command removes all character formatting within the paragraph and resets the paragraph formats to the **Normal** style.

32 Find Formatting Codes

You might be used to using Word's **Find and Replace** function to search for text you want to edit. But you also can used it to find particular formats such as italic type or instances of a given *style*.

Suppose that you want to replace all the **Heading 3** styles in a document with some different formatting. You could find each example of the style in turn and then replace it with something else. Alternatively, you could find and highlight every instance of the style and then replace it with the new formatting all at the same time.

1 **Expand the Find and Replace Dialog Box**

Select **Edit**, **Find**. The **Find and Replace** dialog box opens. Click the expansion arrow in the lower-left corner of the dialog box to see all the options. The expanded dialog box displays options for refining the selection.

2 **Select a Format to Search For**

At the bottom of the dialog box, open the **Format** list. This list contains a variety of formatting options for which you can search. For example, you can use the **Font** option to search for a particular typeface or the **Paragraph** option to search for paragraphs with various characteristics, such as indentations. You might want to search for a particular style. In that case, select the **Style** option from the list. A dialog box opens to let you select the style you want to find.

You can select options from the **Special** list at the bottom of the dialog box to search for formatting instructions such as tabs and end-of-paragraph markers.

See Also

→ **29** Select Multiple Items

→ **30** Select an Area

→ **31** Clear Unwanted Formatting

 TIP

To remove the formatting from multiple selections, you can highlight every instance of a particular kind of formatting. Then use the **Clear Formatting** command as described in **31** **Clear Unwanted Formatting**.

NOTE

Selections from the **Special** list place codes in the **Find what** text box, such as **^t** for a tab or **^p** for an end-of-paragraph marker. If you are familiar with these codes, you can bypass the menu and type them in the **Find what** text box.

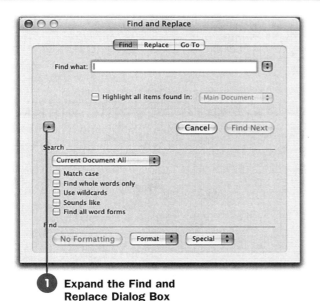

1 Expand the Find and Replace Dialog Box

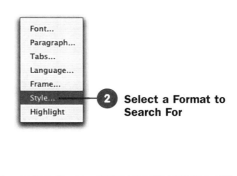

2 Select a Format to Search For

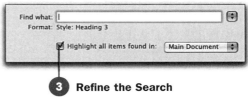

3 Refine the Search

Organization

Nunc gravida, dolor in ultricies tincidunt, tellus velit lobortis turpis, in laoreet mi urna vel velit. Morbi gravida. Nulla facilisi. Integer a nunc. Vestibulum sem lectus, venenatis nec, vestibulum quis, pellentesque at, risus. Suspendisse molestie. Pellentesque quis mi. Nulla blandit enim a nulla. Aenean tincidunt, turpis quis sollicitudin tincidunt, libero erat eleifend diam, a congue felis dui sed augue. In hac habitasse platea dictumst. Vestibulum sem neque, faucibus non, placerat vitae, fringilla vel, risus. Vivamus dictum vehicula est. Vivamus sed ante sed turpis vestibulum vulputate. Sed sed dui. Etiam at n

Cypress-Fairbanks Consulting

Maecenas id turpis id justo aliquet cursus. Proin non ligula eu tortor pellen Vestibulum urna est, dignissim sit amet, imperdiet vitae, fringilla quis, aug augue. Pellentesque posuere, nunc in blandit tempus, nunc nibh fermentur mattis enim tellus non leo. Proin porta, lacus eget interdum porta, quam ar nibh, sit amet sodales lorem lectus nec ligula. Suspendisse potenti. Vivamu dui et mattis condimentum, ante leo congue ipsum, quis lobortis libero leo Mauris tincidunt accumsan lorem. Fusce quis sapien.

Writ Technologies

Aliquam ipsum quam, commodo vel, commodo sit amet, luctus at, ligula. I libero, ullamcorper vel, pharetra quis, ultrices id, felis. In vel nibh. Donec d

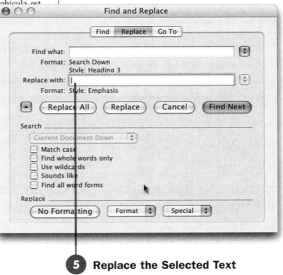

4 Execute the Search

5 Replace the Selected Text

❸ Refine the Search

Make a selection from the **Format** or **Special** menu. If you make a formatting selection, that formatting appears under the **Find what** box. Here you see that the **Style** option was selected from the **Format** list and that the **Heading 3** style was selected.

If no text is in the **Find what** text box, the program finds all the examples of the chosen formatting. If you type text in the **Find what** box, the program finds only items that have *both* the indicated text and formatting.

If you want to highlight all examples of the selection at the same time, enable the **Highlight all items found in** check box and select **Main Document** from the pop-up list.

❹ Execute the Search

Click the **Find All** or **Find Next** button. (The wording of the button varies with the nature of your selection.) The search finds the first example of the indicated formatting. If you opted to highlight all items, all examples in the document are selected. Here you see that only the text formatted with the **Heading 3** style has been selected.

❺ Replace the Selected Text

You can do several things with the selected text. For example, if you want to apply a new typeface to the selections, you can select a new font from the **Formatting Palette** and apply it to all the selections simultaneously. Alternatively, as shown here, you can replace the selected style with a different one: Click the **Replace** tab at the top of the **Find and Replace** dialog box, fill in the text or select the special formatting you want to replace the found text with, and click **Replace**.

 TIP

If a format has a keyboard shortcut, such as ⌘-**B** for bold type, click in the **Find what** text box and press the keyboard shortcut. Pressing the shortcut again cycles through other options such as finding text that is not bold or turning off the selection altogether. If you find things getting away from you, click the **No Formatting** button in the expanded dialog box to erase all formatting selections and start over.

7

Formatting Your Work

IN THIS CHAPTER:

Typewriters and early word processors were limited in their flexibility. They could hammer out business letters, manuscripts, and other documents that required only straight lines and single typefaces. They were—and still are—perfectly adequate machines for those purposes. They couldn't do much else, though, and in truth not much more was expected.

Word has none of these limitations. It can produce typeset documents in multiple type sizes and faces. It can insert titles and subheadings in a well-regimented hierarchy. But because Word can do so much more, more is often expected.

NOTE

The formatting tools available in Word are best suited for office documents, small newsletters, and similar publications. Commercial publishers would probably prefer the extra strength of high-end page layout programs such as InDesign and QuarkXpress.

Instead of the traditional business letter or double-spaced manuscript, your audience might have become accustomed to seeing well-formatted documents with a typeset look, neatly ordered headings and subheadings, and plenty of illustrations.

Word has the tools to do these things and many more. To tell the truth, some of these tools work better than others. But they're all available, and they can help produce a well-designed result.

33 Apply Automatic Formats

See Also

→ **34** Select a Gallery Style

→ **35** Space and Indent a Paragraph

→ **36** Apply a Style to a New Paragraph

Often, the difference between Word and traditional typewriting is in the small things. For example, you can place a true dash (—) into a document, whereas old-school typists had to settle for a pair of hyphens (--) instead. Typewriters had only one kind of quotation marks (""), but typesetters can use so-called *smart quotes* (" and ") that differ at the beginning and end of the quotation.

Other relics of the typewriter age are still around and often condemned by serious typographers. For instance, it is considered bad typesetting form to use multiple carriage returns to create space between lines—use line and paragraph spacing instead.

KEY TERM

Hyperlink—A text string that contains a Web page or an email address. Clicking the link takes you to the Web page or initiates an email message to the address.

These are the sorts of things *AutoFormat* can cure. This feature can automatically apply formats such as headings, bulleted and numbered lists, borders, numbers, and symbols to your text. It also formats Internet and email address as *hyperlinks* that can lead directly to a Web site or initiate an email message. Then, it corrects old typewriting conventions such as removing multiple carriage returns and inserting dashes and smart quotes.

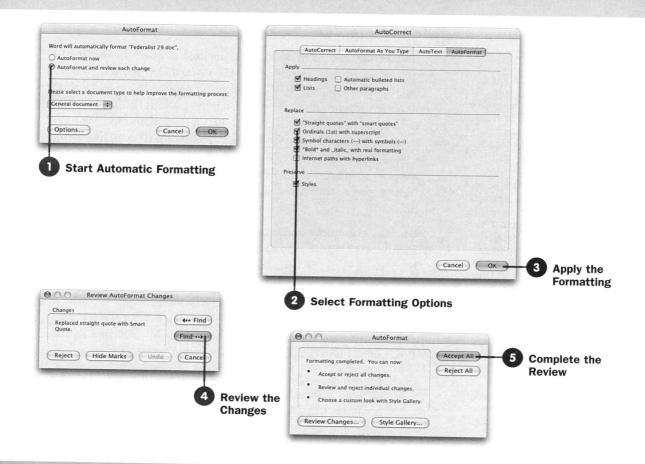

1 Start Automatic Formatting

2 Select Formatting Options

3 Apply the Formatting

4 Review the Changes

5 Complete the Review

There are two ways to use the AutoFormat feature:

- **Format text automatically as you write**—As you work, Word tries to detect and automatically format things such as bulleted or numbered lists. For example, if you begin a line with a number, a period, and a tab, Word assumes that this is part of a numbered list and formats it accordingly.

- **Format an existing document**—When you execute the **Format, AutoFormat** command, Word scans the document and suggests changes. You have a chance to accept or reject the suggested changes.

NOTES

Some fonts available to Word have limited character sets that lack dashes, smart quotes, and other characters of this type. This is particularly true of typefaces such as Courier that originally were developed for typewriters.

When Word inserts a dash, it is an *em dash*, a dash that is about as long as the type is high. The measurement *em* gets its name because in most typefaces it is about the width of the letter *M*. There is a shorter dash called an *en dash* that, yes, is about the width of the letter *N*.

 TIP

Like most features that begin with *Auto*, AutoFormat is a loose cannon that can—and often does—rip through a document and make unwelcome changes. In a large document, just reviewing all the changes can be daunting. To save some work, copy a representative section of the document into a new document and run AutoFormat on the copy. This can alert you to problems before they infest the entire main document.

① Start Automatic Formatting

If you want to format an existing document, open the document and select **Format**, **AutoFormat**. The **AutoFormat** dialog box opens. Select the option of reformatting now or of having a chance to review the proposed changes first; the latter is usually the wiser choice. From the drop-down list, select a document type. Word applies different formats to general documents, letters, and email messages, so select the type of document that most closely matches the document you want Word to format. Then click the **Options** button to open the **AutoCorrect** dialog box to the **AutoFormat** page.

You also can apply automatic formatting as you write a new document. Select **Tools**, **AutoCorrect**. When the **AutoCorrect** dialog box opens, click the **AutoFormat As You Type** tab. You can use this page to select the types of formatting you want to apply.

② Select Formatting Options

On the **AutoFormat As You Type** tab of the **AutoCorrect** dialog box, check these options for the formatting process:

- **Headings**—If this option is checked, the program applies automatic heading styles, **Heading 1–Heading 9**, to the headings in outlines or legal documents.

- **Lists**—When the program encounters items with list formatting such as bullet points, it automatically applies a *list style* to them.

- **Automatic bulleted lists**—If the program finds a paragraph that begins with an asterisk, a hyphen, or similar character (other than a space or tab), it formats the item as part of a bulleted list.

- **"Straight quotes" with "smart quotes"**—The program replaces any straight quotes (") it finds with smart or curly quotes (" ").

- **Ordinals (1st) with superscript**—In a formation such as *2nd*, the program applies superscripts like this: *2nd*.

- **Symbol characters (--) with symbols (—)**—This option replaces one hyphen with an en dash (–) and two hyphens with an em dash (—).

- ***Bold* and _italic_ with real formatting**—The program applies bold formatting to words bracketed by asterisks and italic to words enclosed by underscores.

- **Internet paths with hyperlinks**—This option formats Internet paths (constructions that begin with **http://** or **www.**) as clickable links.

The final items on the two pages differ. The **AutoFormat** page allows you to keep existing paragraph styles; the **AutoFormat As You Type** page gives you the option of creating new styles. For more on styles, see **36** **Apply a Style to a New Paragraph**.

3 Apply the Formatting

After selecting your options, click **OK**. When you return to the **AutoFormat** dialog box, click **OK** again.

The **AutoFormat** dialog box gives you the options of accepting or rejecting the changes or of reviewing each individually.

4 Review the Changes

If you clicked the **Review Changes** button, you will notice that the passages to be removed are marked with strikeout, and new additions are underlined.

In the **Review AutoFormat Changes** dialog box that opens when you click **Review Changes**, use the forward or backward **Find** button to locate a suggested change. Click **Reject** if you do not want to make the change. If you want to accept the change, click the **Find** button again; the change will be made after you complete the review.

5 Complete the Review

When the review is complete, select **Cancel**. You return to the **AutoFormat** dialog box. Now, you can click the **Accept All** button to implement all the changes you did not reject.

NOTE

A list style is a standard set of formatting instructions applied to selected paragraphs. In this case, the style governs the formatting of items in a list. For more on styles, see **36** **Apply a Style to a New Paragraph.**

NOTE

The **Review Changes** option formats the changes in your document using the same markings used by the **Track Changes** feature described in **23** **Manage Multiple Versions of a File.**

34 Select a Gallery Style

34 Select a Gallery Style

Before You Begin

✔ **33** Apply Automatic
Formats

See Also

→ **35** Space and Indent a
Paragraph

→ **36** Apply a Style to a
New Paragraph

In **33** **Apply Automatic Formats**, you might have noticed that the
AutoFormat dialog box includes a **Style Gallery** button. The **Style
Gallery** is an array of formatting options available as alternatives to the
current *template*. You can choose different type, colors, and other effects
to give the document a different look.

The **Style Gallery** is also available directly from the main menu. You
can use it and an accompanying **Theme** collection to completely
change the appearance of a mundane document.

1 **Open the Style Gallery**

You can open the **Style Gallery** from the **AutoFormat** dialog box
(select **Format**, **AutoFormat**) by clicking the **Style Gallery** button.
Alternatively, you can open the **Style Gallery** from the main
menu by selecting **Format**, **Theme**. When the **Theme** dialog box
opens, click the **Style Gallery** button.

On the left of the **Style Gallery** window is a column of templates
you can apply. The large **Preview** window displays a preview of
how the selected template looks when applied to the currently
open Word document.

NOTE

The **Theme** dialog box also
offers alternatives to a document's initial appearance.
You can select variations of
typefaces and colors. The
Style Gallery has a similar
purpose, but it works by
applying a new template to
the document.

2 **Select a Template**

Scroll down the list of templates. When you select one, the **Preview**
window shows how that template looks when applied to the current document. Experiment by selecting various templates from
the list until you find one that is appropriate for the current document.

3 **Apply the Selection**

Click **OK**. The new template is applied to the document.

1 Open the Style Gallery

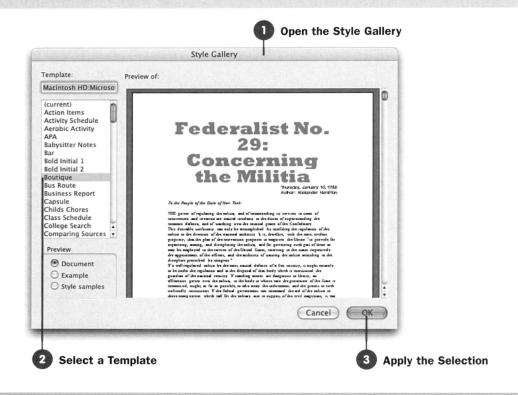

2 Select a Template

3 Apply the Selection

35 Space and Indent a Paragraph

Paragraph formatting is at the heart of document formatting. The document, after all, is only the sum of its paragraphs. When you think of a paragraph, you probably think of a paragraph of body text. That fits with the way your English teachers probably explained it some time back. But in Word, any block of text between two paragraph markers is a paragraph. It can be a long block of type, a headline, or even an empty space. The **Paragraph** dialog box has two pages of specifications you can apply to any paragraph. Your use of these options has a major effect on the overall document design.

See Also

→ **36** Apply a Style to a New Paragraph

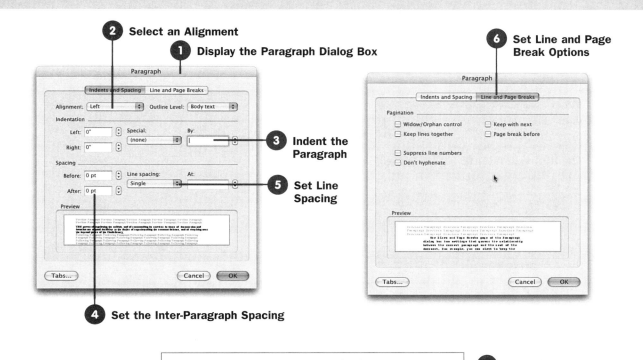

2 Select an Alignment

1 Display the Paragraph Dialog Box

6 Set Line and Page Break Options

3 Indent the Paragraph

5 Set Line Spacing

4 Set the Inter-Paragraph Spacing

7 Apply the Formatting

Thanks for the invitation the bid on the design of the Poudre Canyon Visitor's Guide. I can assure you are top-rate designers can give you a brochure of which you and the region can be proud. Our bid is as follows:

1 Display the Paragraph Dialog Box

Place the cursor in the paragraph you want to modify. Then select **Format**, **Paragraph**. The first page of the **Paragraph** dialog box contains options for **Indents and Spacing**.

2 Select an Alignment

There are four possible alignment settings for a paragraph: **Left**, **Right**, **Centered**, and **Justified**. For most body text paragraphs, the only real choices are **Left** and **Justified**. But even with only two alternatives, the choice is something more than a coin toss.

Left, also known as *left-justified*, *flush left*, or *ragged right* aligns the type along the left margin and lets the right edge of the paragraph

run ragged (or unaligned). It's the most readable alignment and usually is the best choice for letters, reports, and similar documents. It's also a good choice for text laid out in narrow columns.

Justified, also known as *full justification,* aligns the type on both the left and right margins. It is a more formal layout and is best used with hyphenation turned on (select **Tools, Hyphenation** and turn on hyphenation).

The **Right** and **Centered** alignments are special-effects settings and are best used sparingly. In particular, few advanced designs employ the forced symmetry of centered type.

③ Indent the Paragraph

You can indent the left or right margin or both. Independent of these settings, you also can set the first line indentation.

For example, if you include an extended quote in a report, you might want to indent it half an inch on both the left and right. To do that, type .5" in both the **Left** and **Right** text boxes.

If you want to indent the first line of the paragraph, the instinctive method often is to press **Tab.** The better method is to set a separate first line indentation. To do that, select **First line** from the **Special** drop-down list and type a measurement such as **.25"** in the **By** text box.

If you want to set a hanging indent (such as with a bulleted list), you can do it here. The full paragraph is indented to the **Left** indentation setting, but the first line is extended to the left by the amount you specify.

④ Set the Inter-Paragraph Spacing

There are two kinds of paragraph spacing: the spacing between each line and the spacing between each paragraph. Do not, even by accident, use the **Enter** key to add space between paragraphs. Use the paragraph spacing fields in the **Paragraph** dialog box instead.

The **Before** and **After** settings set the space between paragraphs. You can enter the settings manually, or you can use the spin buttons next to each text box to adjust the spacing 6 points at a time.

TIP

In the **Hyphenation** dialog box, you can elect to automatically hyphenate the document, in which case Word hyphenates words at their syllable breaks when they fall within the **Hyphenation zone** at the right end of each line. You can adjust the width of the zone. A narrower zone produces a neater edge by hyphenating more words; a wider zone hyphenates fewer words but produces a more ragged appearance. You also can limit the number of consecutive lines that end in hyphenated words. As an alternative to automatic hyphenation, you can select manual hyphenation, which steps you through the document and asks you to accept or reject each proposed hyphenation individually.

NOTE

The Outline Level setting is discussed in **24** Write an Outline.

NOTE

When you apply bullets or numbering to a paragraph, the indentations set in that process also appear in the **Paragraph** dialog box. For example, if you position the cursor in a paragraph and click the **Bullets** button in the **Formatting** toolbar, the paragraph dialog box reports a **Before Text** indent of **.25"**, the **Hanging** option selected in the **Special** drop-down list, and a **By** value of **.25"**. You can modify the settings in the **Paragraph** dialog box to affect the way the bulleted list appears.

A *point* is a typographical measurement that amounts to 1/72 of an inch. Thus, 12-point type is 12/72 or 1/6 inch high. In addition, to improve readability, *leading* (which originally was indeed made of lead) is inserted between lines, and additional space is often added between paragraphs. A common spacing for text paragraphs is 6 points; 12–15 points is common after larger headings.

⑤ Set Line Spacing

The options in the **Line spacing** drop-down list affect the spacing between lines within the paragraph. Several of the settings, such as **Single** and **Double**, are intended primarily for typewriter-style applications. In typeset documents, the most useful setting is **Exactly**. Then in the **At** box, type the value you want for the spacing between lines in points.

For example, if you are using 12-point type, it is common to use 14-point line spacing to improve readability by injecting a little air between the lines.

⑥ Set Line and Page Break Options

The **Lines and Page Breaks** page of the **Paragraph** dialog box has settings that govern the relationship between the current paragraph and the rest of the document. For example, you can elect to keep the paragraph's lines together when they would otherwise fall across a page break.

You also can specify that the current paragraph be kept with the one that comes after it. This is a valuable setting in instructional literature, where you want an instruction to stay on the same page as the explanations and comments in the next paragraph.

⑦ Apply the Formatting

Make the adjustments you want in the **Paragraph** dialog box and click **OK**. The new settings are applied to the paragraph.

TIP

To quickly set the spacing of a single paragraph, click to position the insertion point in the paragraph and then press ⌘-**0** (zero). The program adds 6 points of space above the paragraph *except* when it appears at the top of a page.

36 Apply a Style to a New Paragraph

You can format a single paragraph the way you want it; you might want to apply this format to other paragraphs of the same type. The best way to do this is to save the paragraph formatting as a *style*. Then you can apply that style to any other paragraphs in the document.

Styles come in two forms: paragraph and character. Most often, you'll use paragraph styles that are applied to entire paragraphs at one time. Character styles are applied only to selected characters within the paragraph. There also are specialized paragraph styles you can apply to tables and numbered or bulleted lists.

When you create a new style, you can set and save any formatting you want, including indentions, spacing, typefaces, and other appearance items. If you already have applied the formatting to a paragraph, you can save that formatting as the style.

1 Establish the Format

Select a paragraph whose formatting you want to use as the style. If you want to make any changes in formatting or typefaces, you can do so now.

When the paragraph has been formatted the way you want, select **Format**, **Style**. The **Style** dialog box opens. The **Description** field shows the specifications of the selected paragraph.

2 Start a New Style

Click the **New** button. The **New Style** dialog box opens. In the **Name** text box, enter a name for the style you are creating.

3 Select the "Based On" Style

Open the **Based on** drop-down list to see a list of all existing styles. If you want to start with one of these styles and adapt it for your new style, select the style and make the adaptations you want. If you want to turn the current paragraph format into a style, scroll to the top of the list and select **No Style**.

See Also

→ **33** Apply Automatic Formats

→ **35** Space and Indent a Paragraph

KEY TERM

Style—A set of formatting directions saved so that they can be applied to other text.

NOTE

Be sure that the style name is original. Word has many built-in styles that take most of the logical names, such as **Body** and **List Bullet**. You will not be allowed to overwrite these with your new style.

TIP

If you want to modify the style as it currently stands, click the **Format** button near the bottom of the dialog box. You then can select the type of formatting you want to change. When you do so, you open the same dialog box you would see if you were applying the formatting from the main menu.

1 Establish the Format **2** Start a New Style

3 Select the "Based On" Style

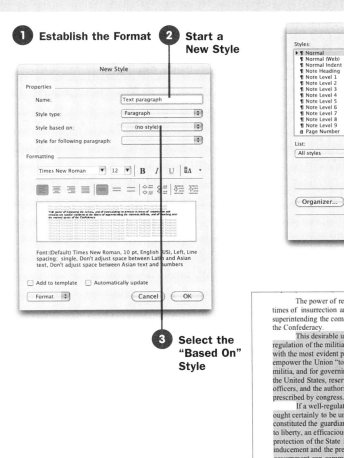

4 Apply the Style

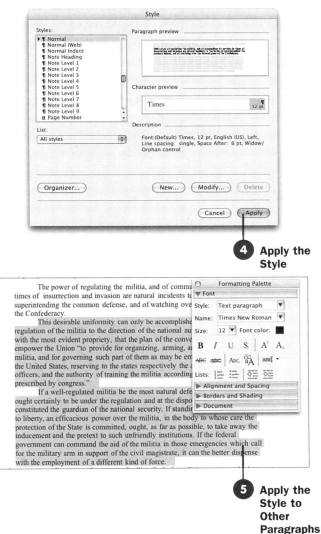

5 Apply the Style to Other Paragraphs

4 Apply the Style

Click **OK** to close the **New Style** dialog box. When you return to the **Style** dialog box, click **Apply**. The paragraph formatting is now a style, and the style name appears in the **Formatting Palette**.

5 Apply the Style to Other Paragraphs

Select the paragraphs to which you want to apply the new style. In the **Formatting Palette**, open the **Style** list. Find and select the name of the newly created style. It is immediately applied to all the selected paragraphs.

NOTE

You also can apply an existing style to selected paragraphs by selecting **Format**, **Style**. In the **Styles** list, select the style you want to use and click the **Apply** button.

37 Get Your Margins Out of the Gutter

Setting page margins might normally be simple enough. But as you might have inferred from that last sentence, that isn't always the case.

There's a difference in the margins used in documents such as letters and reports and margins used in documents such as brochures and position papers. The margins you'd use for a memo are vastly different from the margins required in a multipage booklet made up of folded pages. You might want to use a complex set of margins to accommodate the *gutter* within the fold.

For any document, you can set the left, right, top, and bottom margins. For a multipage document, you must set all these margins plus a margin for either side of the middle.

1 Start the Page Setup

Select **Format**, **Document**. The **Document** dialog box displays margin and layout settings. Click the **Margins** tab to display that page of the dialog box.

You can enter values for the **Top**, **Bottom**, **Left**, and **Right** margins for pages in the document. If you use these text boxes to set margins, all the pages in your document will be identical, with the same margins on each page. This approach works well for single-sided documents such as reports. However, if you want to print your document on two sides of the paper and bind it (for example, staple the pages in the middle), you'll want the margins to be mirrored, so that the center margins are wider—on a left-hand page the right margin is wider, and on a right-hand page the left margin is wider.

Before You Begin

✔ **35** Space and Indent a Paragraph

See Also

→ **36** Apply a Style to a New Paragraph

→ **38** Set a Section in Multiple Columns

KEY TERM

Gutter—An area between columns of type or between printed pages.

NOTE

Windows users might be accustomed to finding margin settings by way of **File**, **Page Setup**. You still can do that on a Mac, but it's a long, difficult trip through multiple dialog boxes on a route that is not well marked.

① **Start the Page Setup**

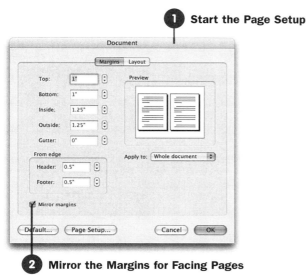

② **Mirror the Margins for Facing Pages**

③ **Enter the New Margin Settings**

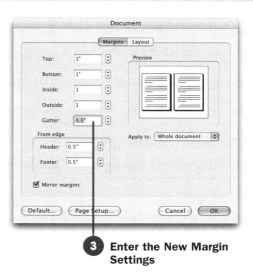

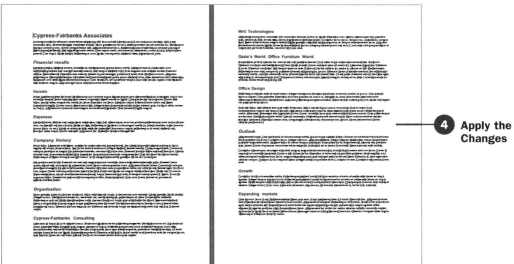

④ **Apply the Changes**

② **Mirror the Margins for Facing Pages**

If you're working with a document that will be printed on two sides of the page (as this book is printed), enable the **Mirror margins** check box in the lower-left corner of the dialog box. This

option sets up the facing pages for a booklet. The **Preview** window shows the two pages, and instead of **Left** and **Right** margin text boxes, the dialog box now calls for **Inside** and **Outside** margins. The **Inside** margin is at the center of the document near the fold or binding; the **Outside** margin falls at the outside edges of the two-page layout.

You also can use the **Gutter** setting to provide wider margins on the inside edges of bound pages.

3 Enter the New Margin Settings

Enter any changes you might want to make in the margin settings. For example, you might want to set narrower outside margins than those you would use for a single sheet. You also can use the **Gutter** setting to widen the gap between the two pages.

4 Apply the Changes

Click **OK** to close the **Document** dialog box. The changes are applied to the document. Select **View, Zoom, Many Pages** to see how two pages of your document look with the new margin settings.

TIP

The various margin settings can be confusing, and one setting often interacts with another. The safe course is to check the **Preview** window and change the settings if necessary before you click **OK**.

---

38 Set a Section in Multiple Columns

Publications such as newsletters look best with multiple columns. Not only that, but long lines impair readability; it is better to use columns to shorten them up.

You can set an entire document in multiple columns, but you probably don't want to. For example, you'd probably want a title to span the entire page even if the smaller text were arranged in columns. For situations like this, you can divide the document into *sections*.

You might start a new section for many reasons. One is to apply different formatting to the section. While headlines above are set in one column across the page, the second section can be divided into two columns.

Strictly speaking, you don't have to start a new section to start a new column arrangement. But confining the column structure to a designated section makes the text easier to manage.

Before You Begin

→ **37** Get Your Margins Out of the Gutter

See Also

→ **39** Flow Text Through Multiple Boxes

KEY TERM

Section—A division within a document. A new section is often used when you want to vary the margins, the number of columns, or other characteristics of the page.

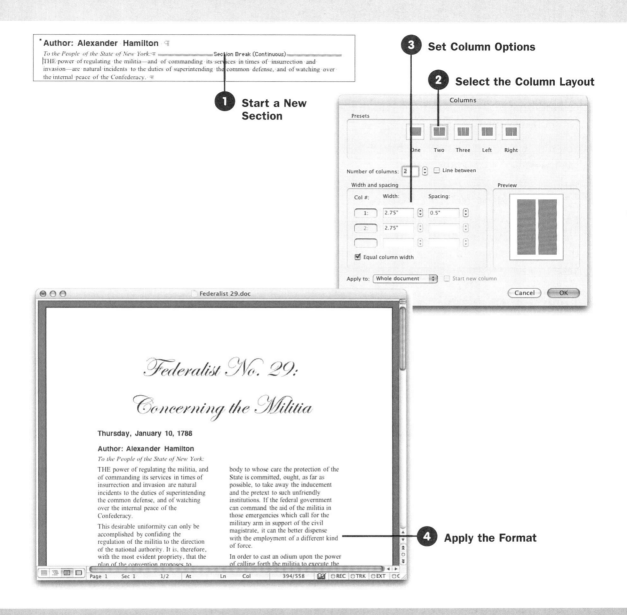

Start a New Section

Select the Column Layout

Set Column Options

Apply the Format

1 Start a New Section

Click at the start of the text you want to set into columns. Then select **Insert**, **Break**. A submenu offers a choice of page, column,

and section breaks. The **Section Break (Continuous)** option starts a new section but, unlike the other section breaks, does not start the section on a new page.

Select the type of break you want; the break is inserted in the document.

If you want, you can place another section break later in the document. In that case, the column formatting will end at the second section break. If you create only one section, the new section extends from the section break to the end of the document.

② Select the Column Layout

Click to position the insertion point just after the section break. Then select **Format, Columns**. The **Columns** dialog box opens. In the row of diagrams at the top of the box, select the number of columns you want to use. You need do nothing more to set your text into columns unless you want to.

③ Set Column Options

If you want a rule to appear between the columns, enable the **Line between** check box. If you want, you also can vary the column widths and the spacing between the columns. Disable the **Equal column width** check box and type the desired widths and spacing for the individual columns in the **Width and spacing** section of the dialog box.

From the **Apply to** drop-down list, choose whether to apply the columnar format to the entire document, to the current section, or to the document from this point forward.

④ Apply the Format

When you're finished adjusting the column options, click **OK**. The column structure is applied to the document.

NOTE

You can set any of several types of breaks. The **Page Break** starts a new page without starting a new section, and the **Column Break** moves to the top of a new column. You can set a section break with or without starting the section on a new page. For example, the **Odd Page** and **Even Page** options are for use when you always want to start a new chapter on a left or right page. This setting remains in effect despite changes earlier in the document that affect the page layout.

TIP

You can see the break by selecting **Word, Preferences**. On the **View** page under **Nonprinting characters**, enable the **All** check box. More quickly, you can open the **Document** section of the **Formatting Palette** and click the **Show/Hide** button in the **Layout** row.

Flow Text Through Multiple Boxes

See Also

→ Set a Section in Multiple Columns

NOTE

The text boxes as drawn might conceal text beneath them. If so, **Ctrl**-click the border of each box. From the menu that opens, select **Format Text Box**. When the **Format Text Box** dialog box opens, click the **Layout** tab to go to that page. From the **Wrapping style** options, select **Square** and click **OK**. The "hidden" text now wraps around the text box.

TIP

You also can copy the text to be inserted and then paste it into the first of the linked text boxes. The pasted text flows through the linked boxes.

NOTE

After the text is in the boxes, you can format it as you like. For example, you might want to set the sidebar in a different typeface from the rest of the document. If the boxes still do not accommodate all the text, you can add more linked boxes or resize the existing ones.

Sidebars are short articles that accompany and expand longer pieces of text. You'll often find a sidebar in a box on a page with the main article. You might also find a sidebar that flows through two boxes, often on different pages.

You can use Word text boxes to set up just such a flow of one block of text within another on a page. If the contents of one text box exceed the box's capacity, you can link two text boxes. The article that begins in one box flows directly into the other. *Seamlessly* is an overused marketing term, but you truly cannot find many seams in Word's text box features.

① Create the Text Boxes

With the document open, select **Insert**, **Text Box**. The cursor changes to a crosshair symbol.

Drag to draw the first box where you want it to be. Then repeat the **Insert**, **Text Box** command and draw one or more additional boxes.

② Link the Boxes

If you want to link two text boxes so the text you add to the first one flows into the second one, **Ctrl**-click the border of the first text box. From the menu that opens, select **Create Text Box Link**. The mouse pointer changes to a pitcher icon with an arrow. Click the second box in the chain of text boxes you want to link.

If you want to link more than two text boxes, repeat this step, linking each box in the order in which you want the text to flow through the boxes.

③ Add the Text File

Click to position the insertion point in the first of the series of linked text boxes. Select **Insert**, **File** and select the document you want to insert in the text boxes. When you've selected the file, click **Insert**. The text flows through the boxes in order.

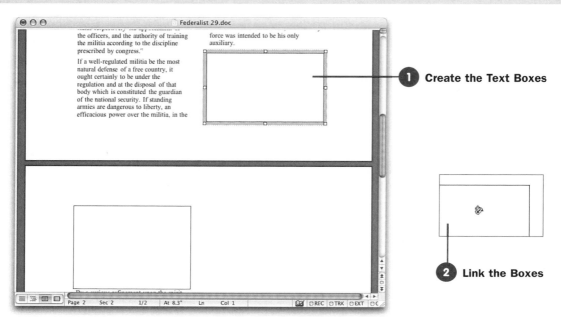

1 Create the Text Boxes

2 Link the Boxes

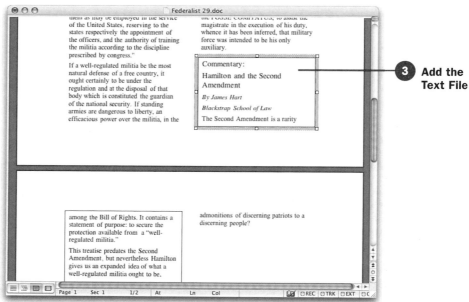

3 Add the Text File

40 **Place Graphics**

Before You Begin

✔ **9** Retrieve Clip Art

See Also

→ **41** Reposition a Picture

→ **42** Wrap Text Around a Graphic

NOTE

Vector art, which is made up of lines and shapes, accepts resizing much better than *raster* art, which is made up of patterns of dots.

TIP

It helps to enlarge the page display so that you can work with the graphics and page elements more readily. Select **View**, **Zoom**, **Page Width**. Also make sure that the **View**, **Page Layout** option is selected. Note that graphics do not appear in **Normal** and **Outline** views and that **Online Layout** view does not display printed page breaks.

KEY TERM

Bounding box—The box that surrounds an illustration when it is selected. You can adjust the size and location of the picture by resizing or moving the bounding box.

The world is full of *clip art*, royalty-free pictures, and other forms of artwork, most of it inexpensive. Most of it is also the wrong size. It's rare to import a piece of art into a Word document and find it exactly the size you want. In some way, the art you import into a Word document will have to be resized, cropped, or both.

It's not unusual, for example, to import a drawing that takes up excessive room and creates awkward page breaks or, at the other extreme, is too tiny to see. In those cases, you can crop the picture to concentrate on its good points and resize it to fit the design of the page.

1 **Insert the Clip Art**

Open the document. To insert a graphic, select **Insert**, **Picture**. Then choose whether you want to import the graphic from the **Clip Art Gallery** or from a file on your hard disk (see **9** **Retrieve Clip Art**).

2 **Select the Illustration**

Click to select the illustration you want to resize. In this example, the document has two pictures, both imported in their original sizes. The tree on the first page seems about the right size, but the tulip drawing is so large that Word has created a second page to hold it.

3 **Select the Crop Tool**

Sometimes you need to zero in on part of a picture, eliminating some elements, rather than trying to fit the whole thing into the page design. In the case of the tulip drawing, you might want to crop the image so that only the two tulips on the left remain, eliminating the distracting stem on the right.

When you click to select an illustration, adjustment handles appear around its edges. These delineate the image's *bounding box*. When you move the handles, you resize the box and the picture inside.

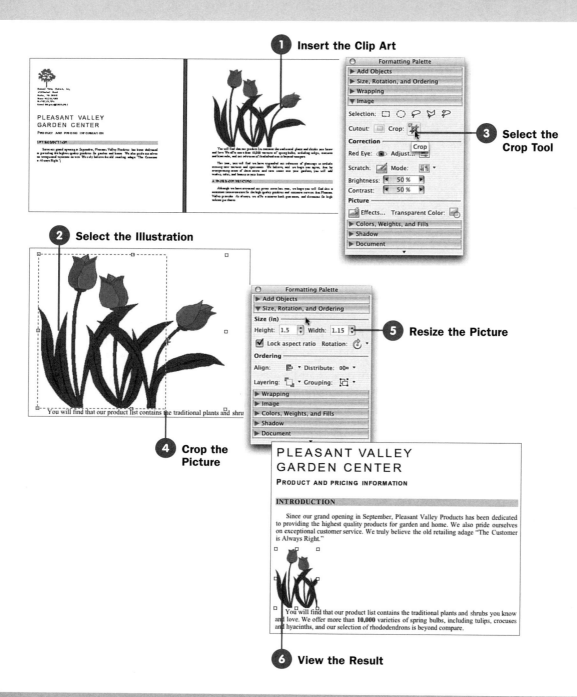

1 Insert the Clip Art

2 Select the Illustration

3 Select the Crop Tool

4 Crop the Picture

5 Resize the Picture

6 View the Result

When a picture is selected, the **Formatting Palette** changes to display picture-editing features. If you open the **Image** section of the **Formatting Palette**, the tools group includes a **Crop** tool. Select it.

④ Crop the Picture

When you select the **Crop** tool, the mouse pointer changes into a crop symbol. Click the adjustment handle on one side of the image's bounding box and drag it to crop the picture. A dotted line guides you. In the case of the tulip drawing, you might drag the upper-right handle to the left until only two tulips are visible. When you're satisfied with the portion of the image indicated by the cropping lines, release the mouse button. The portion of the image outside the dotted lines is deleted.

⑤ Resize the Picture

You can resize a picture by dragging the adjustment handles. To ensure that you maintain the same height-to-width proportion, press **Shift** while you drag one of the corner handles.

For more precise resizing, use the **Size** section of the **Formatting Palette**. There you can enter the desired height and width of the image. If the **Lock aspect ratio** check box is enabled, a change in height or width changes the other dimension proportionately.

In the tulip example, you might decide that a height of 1 1/2" is about right. Enter that height and enable the **Lock aspect ratio** check box. The illustration is scaled accordingly. It also is moved to the first page.

⑥ View the Result

The resized picture appears in the document. If you want, you now can reposition the image (see **41** **Reposition a Picture**), add a caption (see **13** **Add Text to Artwork**), or wrap the text around it (see **42** **Wrap Text Around a Graphic**).

☝ TIPS

If you crop too far, you can drag the adjustment handle back to a new position. If all else fails, select **Edit**, **Undo** and try again.

Because cropping changes the size of a picture, Word might reposition it on the page when you are finished cropping. If so, scroll until you find the picture again. You can correct the placement later.

✎ NOTE

A more comprehensive picture editing option is available in the **Picture** section of the **Formatting Palette**. Select **Format Picture**, and a dialog box offers options for sizing, text wrapping, borders, and cropping.

---

41 Reposition a Picture

Usually, when a picture first is inserted into a document, it appears as a *floating object*. CSI connotations aside, this means the object can be placed anywhere on the page, including the margins, headers, or footers. You probably don't want your illustrations to move around this freely. In that case, you have several options:

- Set the picture to occupy a precise location on the page.

- Make the picture an *inline object* with the text. When you do this, the image functions like a letter of text. A large picture can be a paragraph in its own right.

- Anchor the picture to a text paragraph. This ensures that, if the anchor paragraph is moved, the picture moves with it.

1 Select the Picture

Select the picture you want to move. Make sure that the picture is floating and is not inline with the text.

2 Display Formatting Symbols

In the **Standard** toolbar, select the **Show/Hide** button. Displaying the paragraph symbols makes it easier to relocate the picture. In particular, it displays an anchor symbol that indicates the paragraph to which the illustration is anchored.

3 Move the Picture

Click the picture and drag it to a new location in the document. In the brochure shown here, you might want to drag the tulip picture until it aligns along the left side of the first paragraph. Drag until the anchor symbol appears next to the first paragraph.

4 Set a Precise Position

Although you can drag a picture into position, you might want to set its position on the page more precisely. You can specify that the picture be a certain distance from the anchor paragraph, for example, or at a certain position on the page.

Before You Begin

✔ **40** Place Graphics

See Also

→ **42** Wrap Text Around a Graphic

KEY TERMS

Floating object—A picture or other graphic object that can be moved freely on the page, regardless of text or other contents.

Inline object—A picture or other graphic object inserted into the text like a letter or paragraph.

TIP

Floating graphics display adjustment handles in the form of hollow boxes. Inline graphics display solid black handles. To change the status, go to the **Wrapping** section of the **Formatting Palette** and select a different wrapping style.

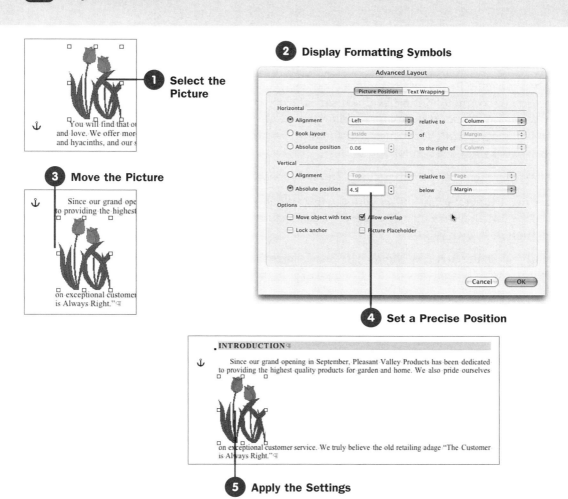

1 Select the Picture

2 Display Formatting Symbols

3 Move the Picture

4 Set a Precise Position

5 Apply the Settings

For example, if you set the illustration to appear 4 1/2" below the top margin, the picture remains in that position regardless of changes in its immediate surroundings. If the anchor paragraph is moved to another page, the picture then appears 4 1/2" below the top margin of *that* page.

Select **Format**, **Picture**. In the **Format Picture** dialog box, select the **Layout** page and then click the **Advanced** button to display the **Advanced Layout** dialog box.

Select the **Picture Position** page, which gives you several options for both horizontal and vertical alignment. You can set both the distance and the distance from what. For example, you could set the picture to be on the left relative to the current column and 4 1/2" below the top margin.

5 Apply the Settings

Click **OK** to close the **Advanced Layout** dialog box. Click **OK** to close the remaining dialog boxes and return to the document. If you want, you also can adjust text wrapping, as explained in 42 **Wrap Text Around a Graphic**.

TIP

There are several ways to display the **Format Picture** dialog box. You can click the **Format picture** button in the **Formatting Palette**, or you can ⌘-click the picture and select **Format Picture** from the context menu that opens.

42 Wrap Text Around a Graphic

Unless a picture takes up the full width of a column—or comes close—you probably will want some text to appear on one or both sides of the image. In typical Microsoft Office fashion, the text wrapping function gives you a host of ways to do so.

You can set the direction in which the text wraps around the graphic, in what direction, and how closely it wraps.

1 Select a Wrapping Style

You can select wrapping methods, including several advanced options, from the **Format Picture** dialog box. If your needs are basic, however, it might be easier to use the **Wrapping** section of the **Formatting Palette**.

In the **Wrapping** section of the **Formatting Palette**, open the **Style** list, which includes several wrapping styles you can apply. The **Square** option wraps the text around the bounding box; the **Tight** option adheres more closely to the contours of the actual image (and not the square outlines of the *bounding box*). The **Top and Bottom** option essentially provides for no wrapping at all.

Click to select the wrapping style you want from the **Style** list.

Before You Begin

✔ 40 Place Graphics
✔ 41 Reposition a Picture

NOTE

There are other wrapping options, but those described here are the ones you will use most often.

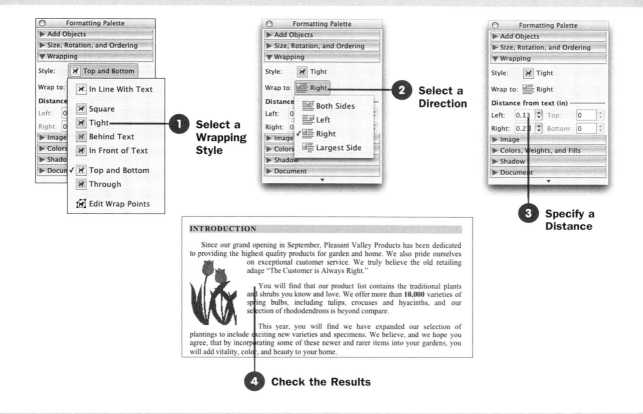

Select a Wrapping Style

Select a Direction

Specify a Distance

Check the Results

Select a Direction

The text can wrap on either side of the picture, or sometimes on both. You can select the way you want the text to wrap from the **Wrap to** drop-down list. The safe but generic selection here is **Largest Side**. If the picture is on the left side of the page or column, the text wraps to the right. If the picture is on the right side, the text wraps to the left. You can also force the text to wrap to one side or the other by selecting **Left** or **Right** from the **Wrap to** list.

Specify a Distance

You might want more room between the picture and the text than Word's default spacing provides. In the **Distance from text** group,

you can use the spin buttons to inject a little more air on any of the four sides of the picture.

④ Check the Results

As you make selections from the **Formatting Palette**, the image and text in the document adjust based on your specifications. You can use the **Formatting Palette** to fine-tune the wrapping until the page looks just the way you want.

43 Turn a Photo into a Painting

Word's picture-editing capabilities are hardly on par with high-end professional tools such as Adobe Photoshop. Nevertheless, over the years Word has gained enough picture-editing features to rival some of the less-expensive image editors.

In particular, after you have imported a picture into a Word document, you can apply a variety of special effects. These effects are counterparts to the *filters* available in image-editing software packages.

① Import the Image

Select **Insert, Picture**. Select the source file (the photograph) from either the **Clip Gallery** or an image file stored on disk.

② Select an Effect

Click to select the picture if it is not already selected (look for the *bounding box* and the *adjustment handles*). In the **Picture** section of the **Formatting Palette**, click **Effects**. The **Effects Gallery** opens.

The **Effects Gallery** displays an assortment of effects you can apply to the selected picture. Scroll through the gallery to see samples of how the effects would look when applied. Click to select the effect you want to work with.

Before You Begin

✔ **9** Retrieve Clip Art

✔ **11** Add Your Artistic Touches

✔ **40** Place Graphics

KEY TERM

Filters—Image-editing features that apply painting, drawing, and other effects to a picture.

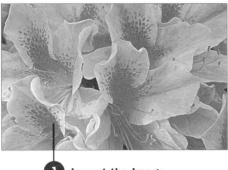

1 Import the Image

2 Select an Effect

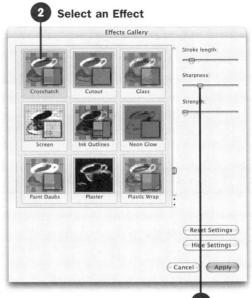

3 Adjust Effect Options

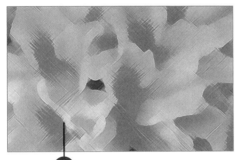

4 Apply the Effect

3 Adjust Effect Options

Each effect has a set of controls you can use to adjust its impact. For example, if you select the **Crosshatch** filter, you can adjust the length, sharpness, and strength of the strokes the effect applies to the image. Drag these sliders to change the impact of the filter on the image.

 TIP

You can apply more than one effect, overlaying **Paint Daubs**, for example, on top of the **Crosshatch** filter. The effects are unpredictable, so be prepared to use **Undo** often.

4 Apply the Effect

Click **Apply** to close the **Effects Gallery** and apply the filter to the picture. If you want to apply a different effect or settings—and you probably will—select **Edit**, **Undo** and try again.

8

Arranging Tables

IN THIS CHAPTER:

The IBM Selectric typewriter was a classic of industrial design. In the days just before the first personal computers, the Selectric was on the desk of nearly every serious typist in the nation.

One measure of skill with the Selectric was its capability to make creative use of tab stops. If you were a basic Selectric user, you could use tab stops to indent the first line of a paragraph. If you were good at it, you could use tabs to format tabular text such as price lists. You could put the items in one column and the prices in another. If you were *really* good it at, you could use tab stops to center lines of type.

The one unfortunate result was that so many typewriting habits carried over to the computer. Word can indent paragraphs, center lines, and set up tables much more easily than a typewriter could ever do. Yet there are people who still treat the Mac as a kind of typewriter. In particular, they punch the **Tab** key to set up tables when a Word table could do the job so much better and more easily.

44 Insert a Table into a Document

See Also

→ **45** Apply an Automatic Format to a Table

→ **47** Add and Delete Rows and Columns

At its simplest, a *table* is simply an assembly of rows and columns with a cell at each intersection. On a higher level, the table becomes a way to organize and format the material that occupies those rows and columns. For example, you could arrange a training class schedule with neatly arranged columns for class titles and dates. If you wanted, you could include a title row across the top.

In another document, you could insert an itemized bid quotation with items and amounts, including a total of the numeric figures.

1 Insert the Table

Open the document and select the place where you want to insert the table. In the **Standard** toolbar at the top of the screen, click the **Insert Table** button.

A table outline grid opens. Click the upper-left cell and drag down and to the right until you have selected the number of rows and columns you want to include. For instance, you might want to include a table of seven rows and two columns. Drag until the legend at the bottom of the grid reads **7 x 2 Table**. The grid starts small, but it expands as you approach its limits. When you release the mouse, the table is inserted into the document.

TIP

Consider the expected contents of the table before you pick the table dimensions. If you expect to put column headers in the first row, be sure to allow for that. You can add and remove rows and columns, but it's easier if you get it right in the first place.

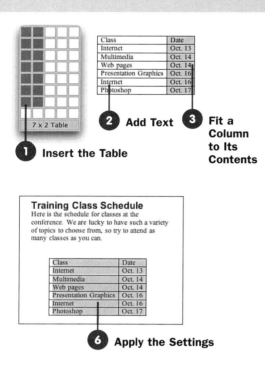

7 x 2 Table

1 Insert the Table

2 Add Text

3 Fit a Column to Its Contents

Training Class Schedule
Here is the schedule for classes at the conference. We are lucky to have such a variety of topics to choose from, so try to attend as many classes as you can.

Class	Date
Internet	Oct. 13
Multimedia	Oct. 14
Web pages	Oct. 14
Presentation Graphics	Oct. 16
Internet	Oct. 16
Photoshop	Oct. 17

6 Apply the Settings

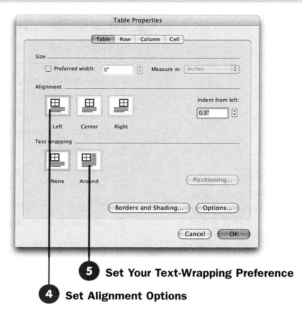

5 Set Your Text-Wrapping Preference

4 Set Alignment Options

Initially, the table fits between the margins of the page or the column (if you formatted the document with multiple columns, as described in **38** **Set a Section in Multiple Columns**) where it is inserted and all columns are the same width.

2 **Add Text**

Click in the upper-left cell of the table. Type the text you want to place in that cell. For example, it might be the column heading **Class**. Press **Tab**. The insertion point moves to the next cell to the right. Type the text you want in that cell, perhaps **Date**. Press **Tab** again.

If you have reached the right side of the table, the insertion point moves to the first cell in the next row. As you continue, pressing **Tab** moves the insertion point from left to right, and then to the next row of cells.

Continue until you have completed entering data into the table.

 TIP

If you reach the end of the table, pressing **Tab** adds a new row to the table.

CHAPTER 8: Arranging Tables

③ Fit a Column to Its Contents

Initially, the table appears in a pretty basic form. It occupies the width of the page or the text column where it has been inserted, and each table column is the same width. In the example shown here, the right column was originally much wider than its rather brief contents. You can set the column width to match its contents; this technique works whether the column is too narrow or too wide for its contents.

With the mouse, point to the column you want to reset. Click when the cursor becomes a down-facing arrow. The column is selected. From the main menu, select **Table, AutoFit**. From the submenu that opens, select **AutoFit to Contents**.

④ Set Alignment Options

A table fits into a Word document much like a graphic does. It has an adjustment handle in the lower-right corner; you can use the handle to adjust the table's size. When you point to the table, you also display a larger handle on the upper-left corner of the table. You can use that handle to move the table to a new location. In some instances, you might want to wrap text around a table, and of course, Word lets you do that.

The **Table Properties** dialog box is where you can make many adjustments to the table. In this example, with one of the table columns reduced in width, the table no longer extends across the full width of the page or text column. Among other things, you can set the **Table Properties** dialog box to adjust the position of the table between the margins.

Point to the table and pause for a moment until the handles appear. Click the larger handle at the upper-left. The entire table is selected. Then select **Table, Table Properties**. The **Table Properties** dialog box opens. Click the **Table** tab. This page lets you set the width, the alignment, and other properties of the full table.

To set the width of the table to a specific measurement, enable the **Preferred width** check box and type the width you'd like the table to be. From the **Measure in** drop-down list box, select the unit of measurement (inches, centimeters, points, or picas). If you want

NOTE

In the **AutoFit** menu, the **AutoFit to Window** option is for documents that will be converted to Web pages. This setting spreads the table across the browser window. The other options can be set more precisely by selecting **Table, Properties**.

NOTE

Other buttons on this page let you set borders and shading and set margin and spacing options for individual cells. Other tabs let you set the properties of individual rows, columns, and cells.

the table to autofit in the current page or text column, disable the **Preferred width** check box. If the text is wider than the width of its column, the text wraps to new lines as necessary.

In the **Alignment** section, you can align the table to the left, center, or right of the page or the text column. You can also indent the table a specific distance from the left margin.

⑤ Set Your Text-Wrapping Preference

In the **Text wrapping** section of the dialog box, click the button that descibes your preference for how text around the table should behave. For example, if you don't want the text to wrap around the table, no matter how much room is to the side of the table, click **None**. If you want the text in the paragraph below the table to wrap on the side of the table, click **Around**.

⑥ Apply the Settings

Make the settings you want to apply and then click **OK**. The settings are applied to the table.

NOTE

If the total column widths within a table are wider than the page, the table extends past the right side of the page. You cannot readily adjust the sizes of these unseen columns. To get the table back within the page boundaries, you must adjust the sizes of the visible columns.

㊺ Apply an Automatic Format to a Table

Most tables are made up mainly of text. Like the other text in a Word document, you can format the text in a table by changing the typeface and altering its size and alignment. You also can change the borders and shading of a table. You often will want to remove at least some borders to relieve the strict row-and-column look of a basic table. You also might want to emphasize rows and columns that contain labels or totals.

If you are familiar with formatting data in an Excel worksheet, formatting a Word table works much the same way. Nevertheless, changing all these formats can consume more time than you want to devote to the process. The alternative is to shortcut the process and apply a predetermined format. A collection of *table AutoFormats* can do the formatting for you.

Before You Begin

✔ ㊹ Insert a Table into a Document

See Also

→ ㉝ Apply Automatic Formats

→ ㊿ Automatically Format a Worksheet

KEY TERM

Table AutoFormat—A Word feature that applies standard combinations of colors, type specifications, and other formatting features to a table. This is distinct from a text AutoFormat, which applies formatting rules to an entire document.

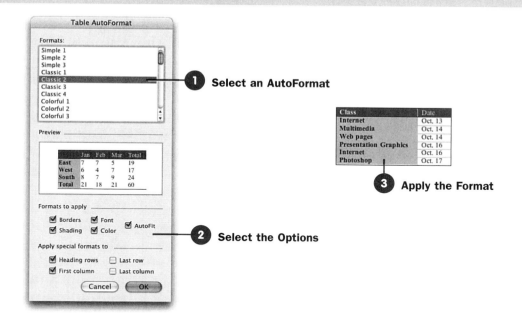

1 Select an AutoFormat

3 Apply the Format

2 Select the Options

Although these formats are standardized, you can be selective in how you apply them. You can decide, for example, whether to apply an AutoFormat's borders, typeface choices, and other properties to the table at hand. You can omit any formatting options you don't want to use.

1 Select an AutoFormat

Click anywhere in the table. Then from the main menu, select **Table, AutoFormat**. The **Table AutoFormat** dialog box displays a list of available AutoFormats. Each format is a combination of type styles, borders, and colors. Scroll down the **Formats** list. When you select a format, its design appears in the **Preview** window.

2 Select the Options

The lower part of the dialog box displays options for applying the selected format. In the **Formats to apply** section, enable the check boxes for the options you want to apply and disable the check boxes for the options you don't want to apply. Watch the **Preview** pane to see how your selections affect the formatting of the sample

table. In the **Apply special formats to** section, you can select distinctive formatting for top and bottom rows and outside-edge columns that might contain labels or totals. Again, watch the **Preview** pane to see how these selections affect the sample table.

❸ Apply the Format

After making your selections from the **Table AutoFormat** dialog box, click **OK**. The chosen format is applied to the table you selected in step 1.

46 Apply a Style to a Table

Word *styles* are a way to ensure that a document maintains a uniform format. For example, styles make it easier to ensure that all body text is the same type face and size, as are all first-level headings, figure captions, and other standard elements. Table styles do the same thing within the boundaries of the table. You can apply styles to ensure that each table in your document uses the same type face and size and that all table headings are uniformly formatted.

❶ Select a Table Element

You might want to set a uniform style for table headings—for example, setting them in bold type, a larger size, or a different typeface.

Select the text in the table you want to format. If you want to format the table headings, select the heading row of a table.

❷ Establish a New Style

In the **Style** section of the **Formatting Palette**, click the **New Style** button. You also can select **Format**, **Style** from the main menu and then click the **New** button.

The **New Style** dialog box opens. In the **Name** text box, type a name for the style you are creating. From the **Style type** drop-down list, choose between a **Paragraph** style that applies the formatting to an entire paragraph and a **Character** style that applies the formatting only to selected text. Normally, you will use a **Paragraph** style because it applies the formatting to the contents of any selected table cell.

Before You Begin

✔ **45** Apply an Automatic Format to a Table

See Also

➔ **36** Apply a Style to a New Paragraph

🖌 NOTE

You also can establish a style for the table grid, ensuring that each table in the document has a uniform set of borders. The option is available in the **Styles** section of the **Formatting Template**.

💡 TIP

You can select one row of a table by pointing to the left end of the row. Click when the mouse pointer becomes an angled arrow.

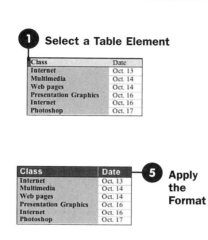

① **Select a Table Element**

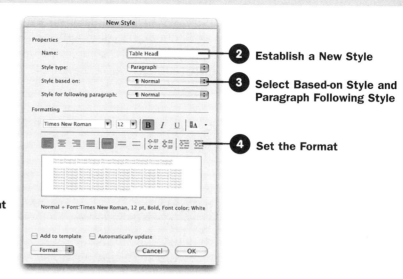

② **Establish a New Style**

③ **Select Based-on Style and Paragraph Following Style**

④ **Set the Format**

⑤ **Apply the Format**

③ **Select Based-on Style and Paragraph Following Style**

From the **Style based on** drop-down list, select the existing style on which you want to base the style you are creating. Select the **Normal** style unless another style is available that more closely resembles the formatting you want. Word defines your new style as a set of variations from the style you select here (in this example, the **Normal** style).

The **Normal** *template* initially assigned to a document comes with a host of built-in styles, including one that is itself called **Normal**. There also are styles for several levels of headings plus body text, bulleted lists, and many others. Other templates usually have a multitude of available styles. You can use any of these as the basis of a new style.

From the **Style for following paragraph** drop-down list, select the style you want to assign to the paragraph that succeeds the one formatted with the current style. If you are creating a new **Table Head** style, for example, you might want the paragraph that comes after the **Table Head** style to be formatted in a **Body Text** style. If so, select that style from the drop-down list. You can

always override this behavior by assigning a different style to the paragraph.

4 Set the Format

In the **Formatting** area of the dialog box, set the formatting you want to use. For example, you can select a new type face, size, weight, and even color. You can also set alignment and spacing options. As you select the formatting options you want to apply to the new style, watch the preview window to see how this new style interacts with other paragraphs in a sample document.

When you make a selection from the **Format** drop-down list, dialog boxes open where you can set additional specifications. These dialog boxes include expanded font specifications and alignment options plus settings for tabs, borders, and numbering. Selecting the **Add to Template** check box automatically adds any changes you make to the document template, from where they will be applied to all examples of the current style.

When you're finished selecting formatting options for the new style, click **OK**. The new style is added to the list of styles displayed in the **Formatting Palette**.

5 Apply the Format

Select the text to which you want to apply the new style formats (in this example, the top label row of a table). In the **Formatting Palette**, click the new style. Repeat this step for other similar blocks of text (other table headings) in the document.

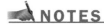

NOTES

The **Automatically Update** option automatically applies any formatting changes you make to a paragraph of table style to every example of that style. It can cause unwanted changes, so it is best used with great caution.

The **Table Properties** dialog box has additional provisions for aligning and spacing the contents of each row, column, or cell. From the main menu, select **Table, Properties**.

Tables are often imperfect when you first create them. You might have to add rows or columns to include new information. Conversely, you might have to remove some rows or columns to reduce clutter, make the table more readable, or fit it into a smaller space.

Before You Begin

✔ **44** Insert a Table into a Document

See Also

→ **48** Nest a Table Within a Table

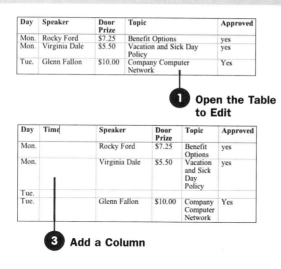

1 Open the Table to Edit

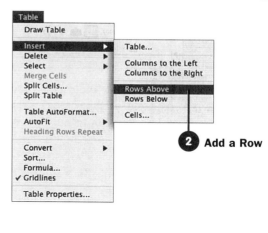

2 Add a Row

3 Add a Column

4 Delete a Column

A work done by committee is a typical example. The seminar agenda shown here is a case in point. You draw up an agenda based on the information you have at a given time. But then the planners add another speaker to the schedule, and a critic points out that the dates are listed but not the times. Another critic notes that the **Approved** column is unnecessary—if the presentation was not approved, it would not be on the agenda in the first place.

That means you have to make some changes to the table. You have to add a row for the new speaker, add a column for the time entries, and remove the unnecessary column.

1 Open the Table to Edit

Open the document containing the table you want to edit.

TIP

You initially selected one row, so only one row is added to the table. The number of rows added matches the number of rows selected. Thus, if you had selected three rows, three rows would have been added. Column insertions work the same way.

2 Add a Row

The new speaker is scheduled to be next-to-last on the agenda. That means the new row must be added above the last row.

Select the last row in the table (click just to the left edge to select the entire row); then select **Table, Insert, Rows Above**. The new row is added above the selected row. If you prefer, the menu also gives you the option of adding rows *below* the selected row.

3 Add a Column

The new **Time** column should be the second from the left (to the right of the current **Date** column). Select the left column (click just above the top edge of the column to select the entire column); then select **Table, Insert, Columns to the Right**.

The new column is inserted. Later, you might want to use the **Table, AutoFit** command to adjust the column width to its contents.

4 Delete a Column

Select the column to be deleted (in this case, click just above the last **Approved** column to select the entire column). Then select **Table, Delete, Columns**. The column is removed from the table. Had you selected more than one column, all the selected columns would be deleted.

48 Nest a Table Within a Table

Is one table not enough to contain the data you want to present? How about nesting a table inside another table?

You might want to prepare a sales report in a Word document for eventual publication as a Web page. For many reasons—lack of other Web formatting tools being the main one—Web page designers have learned to make elaborate use of table structures. They routinely nest one table within another.

You can do the same thing to prepare a Word document that also can be exported to the Web.

1 Set Up the Basic Table

Suppose that you are preparing a sales report for both printed and Web publication. Start by preparing a basic table. Within that table, you can nest a second table that reports monthly sales by division or sales representative.

The first step is to set up the outer table that will contain the second table. The first table can be fairly simple, such as a sales report that contains room for one or two additional tables.

Before You Begin

✔ **44** Insert a Table into a Document

See Also

→ **49** Add Numbers in a Column

NOTE

Commercial Web designers want the flexibility and added features of a professional-level Web-authoring application such as Dreamweaver or GoLive. Web pages exported from Word are not up to that level, but they often are adequate for internal corporate publications, as is the project in this exercise.

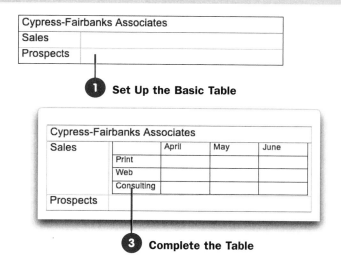

1 Set Up the Basic Table

3 Complete the Table

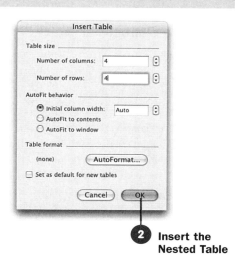

2 Insert the Nested Table

2 Insert the Nested Table

Click the cell where you want to insert the new table. Select **Table**, **Table Options** to set the column width large enough to hold the information the new table will contain. When inserted, the nested table automatically fills the width of its host cell; the host cell does not automatically widen itself to accommodate the inserted table.

The height of the cell, on the other hand, is no problem. The host cell expands vertically to accommodate the number of rows in the inserted table.

From the main menu, select **Table**, **Insert**, **Table**. The **Insert Table** dialog box opens. Select the number of rows and columns you want the new table to contain and click **OK**.

3 Complete the Table

The nested table is inserted into the outer table. You now can complete it by typing headings and other information.

NOTE

The remaining sections of the **Insert Table** dialog box let you apply *AutoFit* and *AutoFormat* settings to the new table. You can do so now, or you can wait until later. See **44** Insert a Table into a Document and **45** Apply an Automatic Format to a Table.

49 Add Numbers in a Column

A Word table is not an Excel worksheet. Excel can calculate sophisticated formulas and apply automatic formats. Word, on the other hand, can calculate some simple formulas and align numbers on a tab stop. Sometimes, however, even Word's limited calculation capability is valuable.

For example, if you are submitting a bid proposal, you can use the basic addition and multiplication functions in Word to figure the total. You also can use decimal tab stops to align the numbers on their decimal points for better presentation.

1 Enter a Formula

In this example of a bid proposal, the quotation includes an estimated number of working hours multiplied by an hourly rate. You can calculate the total labor bill by multiplying the contents of those two cells.

Click the cell where you want the results of the formula to appear. If you are multiplying a number of hours by an hourly rate, this might be a cell next to the label **Total**.

In the main menu, select **Table, Formula**. A **Formula** dialog box opens.

In the dialog box, enter the formula you want Word to calculate. If you want to multiply the hours in cell **B2** by the hourly rate in cell **B3**, enter: **=B2*B3**. The equal sign is a signal to Word that this is a formula.

2 Select a Number Format

From the **Number format** drop-down list, select a numerical format. For example, you might want to format the number as **Currency**, so that a dollar sign ($) and a decimal point are applied to the number (negative numbers appear in parentheses). The **Number format** you select is applied only to the calculated number. The formats of other numbers are not changed.

Before You Begin

✔ **44** Insert a Table into a Document

See Also

→ **48** Nest a Table Within a Table

→ **63** Enter a Formula

 TIP

Although the cells are not labeled, the rows and columns in a Word table are identified just like those in Excel: Rows are numbered, and columns are identified by letters. Thus, the cell in the second column of the third row is identified as cell **B3**. You can use these cell references to make entries in a formula.

TIP

The program makes assumptions about what you want to do. For example, if you are placing the formula under a column of several numbers, the **Formula** dialog box might contain the formula **SUM(ABOVE)**. The program assumes that you want to add the preceding numbers. If that's not what you want to do, erase the formula and enter your own.

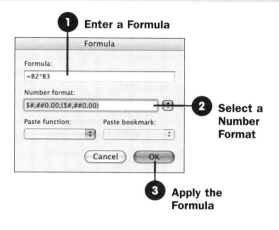

1 **Enter a Formula**

2 **Select a Number Format**

3 **Apply the Formula**

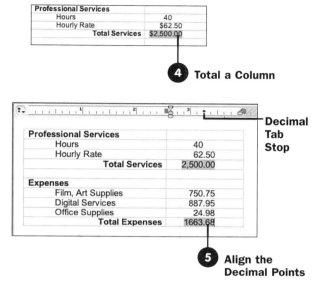

4 **Total a Column**

Decimal Tab Stop

5 **Align the Decimal Points**

3 Apply the Formula

Click **OK**. The results of the calculation appear in the table cell you selected in step 1.

4 Total a Column

The **SUM** function automatically totals any numbers it finds in the column above the cell in which the function is located. It searches upward until it finds an empty space and then assumes that these are the numbers you want to add.

For example, if you used this function under a column of three expense items, the **SUM** function would automatically add the expenses. Click the cell below the figures you want to add. Open the **Table** section of the **Formatting Palette** and click the **AutoSum** button.

The formula =**SUM(ABOVE)** is executed, and the total appears in the selected cell.

⑤ Align the Decimal Points

A Word table doesn't have all the number formatting powers of Excel, but there is one thing you can do: Align all the numbers in a column on their decimal points. You do this with tab settings.

From the main menu, select **View, Ruler**. Rulers appear along the top and side of the document window; the top ruler contains symbols that indicate locations of the tab stops.

Tabs are normally set flush left, so that text you type after the tab appears to the right. You can also select a flush-right tab, in which the text appears to the left of the tab, or a centered tab that centers the text on either side of the tab position. For number formatting, use the decimal point tab that aligns numbers on their decimal points.

In any number format that uses decimal points, the decimal point is placed on the tab and the cents appear to the right of the tab position. All figures are aligned on the decimal tab, no matter how many dollars or cents each entry has.

You can select a tab type by clicking the small tab symbol in the upper-left corner of the document windows, at the junction of the two rulers. From the menu that drops down, select **Decimal**.

Now, when you click in the upper ruler, you insert a decimal tab at that position. Go to a point on the ruler above the column in the table where you want to set the tab. In the table in this exercise, a decimal tab for the second column would be at about the 3.2" mark. If you are not satisfied with the position of the tab, you can drag the tab back and forth on the ruler.

As soon as you set the tab stop, figures in the selected column are aligned on their decimal points. This example includes the value **40** without a decimal point, but this number is aligned as though it had one (**40.00**).

NOTE

In the **Formula** dialog box, the **Paste Function** drop-down list allows you to paste a prewritten formula into the **Formula** text box at the top of the dialog box. If you want to use numbers in the formula that appear outside the table, you can apply bookmarks to those numbers (select the value; select **Insert, Bookmark**; name the bookmark; and press **Return**). To use the bookmark in the formula, select the bookmark from the **Paste bookmark** drop-down list.

TIP

When the rulers are ostensibly hidden, you still can display them temporarily by bringing the mouse pointer near their positions at the edges of the document window.

9

Delivering the Mail

IN THIS CHAPTER:

The first popular word processing program for personal computers was actually two programs. The combination had the formal name WordStar and Mail Merge. The fact that form letter generation held nearly equal billing with the word processing component says something about the importance of mail merge in business offices across the land.

Never mind that Mail Merge and other programs of its ilk made it easy for nearly anyone to join the junk mail industry. The ability to individualize copies of standard form letters has many valuable and more acceptable uses. That's why mail merging still has a central place in today's implementations of Word and its Office companions. For example, you can use personalized form letters to send out confirmations to people who have registered for a conference. Or you can send email meeting notices to a selected group of co-workers.

In Word 2004, the mail merge function is called **Data Merge**. The process joins two documents, which can come from any of several Office components. A *main document* contains the fixed text that is common to all the form letters—that might be the location and schedule of the conference. A *data source* contains the recipients' names, addresses, and other variable information.

The main document must be a Word document, but the data source need not be. It can be an Entourage address list or an Excel database list. The main document includes *fields* that accept the contents of the data source. These fields read records in the data source and generate a new letter for each record. One field could retrieve a recipient's last name, another the first name, and another the street address. This is how a letter addressed to John Cass can include not only his name and address but the salutation *Dear Jack*.

50 Generate a Form Letter

See Also

→ **51** Designate a Data Source

→ **53** Complete a Merge

One cynical way to describe a mail merge is that it has the capability to irritate thousands of people, individually and by name. Mail merges can also be good for many legitimate purposes, particularly when addressed to willing recipients. In this example, you are preparing a *main document* to be sent to the people who have registered for a conference. In **51** **Designate a Data Source**, you'll match the letter you write here with the list of names and addresses, also called the *data source*.

The letter, or main document, consists of general text such as the conference schedule and driving directions. It will be merged with names and addresses from a data source. The result is a personalized letter addressed to each conference participant.

① Write the Main Document in Word

Start by writing the letter. Welcome the recipient to the conference and include information people need to know. In the area where you normally would insert a name and address, leave room for the merge *fields* you will add later (see **51** **Designate a Data Source**).

② Open the Data Merge Manager

When you finish typing the main document, save it with a descriptive name. From the main menu, select **Tools, Data Merge Manager**. The **Data Merge Manager** is a toolkit you can use to assemble the merge letter. It looks and works much like the **Formatting Palette**. It is divided into several sections; you can expand or collapse each section by clicking the arrow next to the section title.

③ Designate the Main Document Type

In the **Main Document** section of the **Data Merge Manager**, click the C:eate button. The menu that opens offers several options for the type of file you can create. Select **Form Letters**.

Other types of main documents you can create include labels and envelopes. You could set up a standard envelope with your return address and merge fields for the recipients' names and addresses. You could do the same with standard mailing labels. You can use the **Catalog** to create a catalog from the pictures and descriptions in a data source.

④ Select a Document

If more than one document is open, you are asked to choose which is to become the main document. If only one document is open, it is automatically chosen. The selected document is designated as the main document.

KEY TERMS

Main document—The body of a merged form letter, containing the common information sent to every recipient.

Data source—A document that contains variable information to be used in a merge letter.

Fields—In a Word document, codes that instruct the program to insert variable information. In a merge document, fields are used in the main document to insert information from the data source.

TIP

Veteran Word users might expect to find the mail merge features with the menu command **Tools, Merge Documents**. This command now is limited to merging main documents and data sources that already have been prepared. The **Data Merge Manager** provides tools to both prepare and merge the documents.

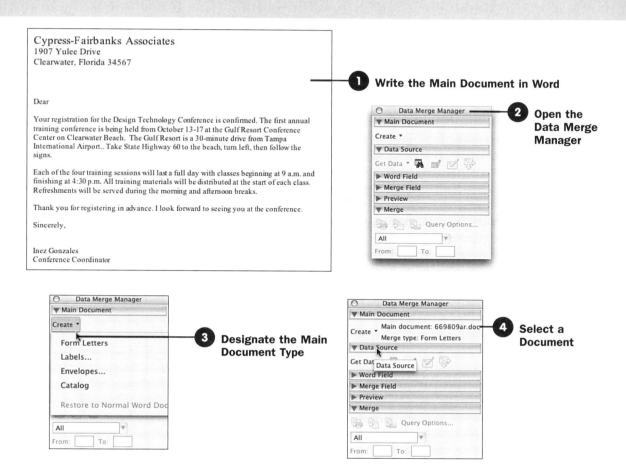

Cypress-Fairbanks Associates
1907 Yulee Drive
Clearwater, Florida 34567

Dear

Your registration for the Design Technology Conference is confirmed. The first annual training conference is being held from October 13-17 at the Gulf Resort Conference Center on Clearwater Beach. The Gulf Resort is a 30-minute drive from Tampa International Airport.. Take State Highway 60 to the beach, turn left, then follow the signs.

Each of the four training sessions will last a full day with classes beginning at 9 a.m. and finishing at 4:30 p.m. All training materials will be distributed at the start of each class. Refreshments will be served during the morning and afternoon breaks.

Thank you for registering in advance. I look forward to seeing you at the conference.

Sincerely,

Inez Gonzales
Conference Coordinator

1 Write the Main Document in Word

2 Open the Data Merge Manager

3 Designate the Main Document Type

4 Select a Document

---

51 Designate a Data Source

Before You Begin

✔ **50** Generate a Form Letter

See Also

→ **52** Use an Address Book List As the Data Source

→ **84** Set Up a Database List

The *data source* is the second half of the data merge partnership. This file can be (and often is) another Word document that lists the recipients' names, addresses, and other individual data. But it also can be many other things, including an Excel worksheet, the Office Address Book, and data from outside sources such as the FileMaker Pro database program. The data source information usually is in table form, with a row for each recipient and a column for each type of information such as the name, street address, city, state, and postal code.

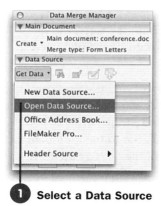

1 **Select a Data Source**

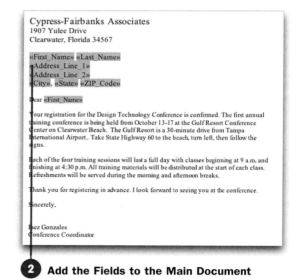

2 **Add the Fields to the Main Document**

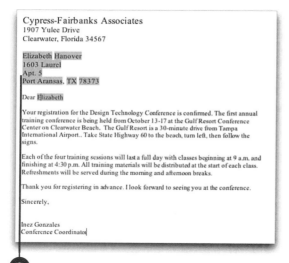

3 **Preview the Document**

1 Select a Data Source

In the **Data Source** section of the **Data Merge Manager**, click the **Get Data** button. A menu opens, offering you several options for the source file of the data you want to use.

Select **New Data Source** if you want to create a new data source in a Word document. If you have a large mailing, though, you

NOTE

Selecting the **Office Address Book** option from the **Get Data** menu uses as a data source the Address Book you maintain in Entourage. Selecting **Header Source** selects a file that contains only a list of column headings. You might use such a file if you want to use a uniform set of column headings as field names for a variety of data sources.

should create the data source in advance. When your data source already exists, select **Open Data Source** from the **Get Data** menu. A **Finder** window opens. Navigate to the data source file, select it, and click **Open**.

If you select an Excel file as your data source and the workbook has named ranges, an **Open Workbook** dialog box asks you to select a range that contains the merge data. If the Excel file you designated contains only data you want to use in the mail merge, select **Entire Workbook** in the top pane of the dialog box and **Entire Worksheet** in the bottom pane. Click **OK**.

❷ Add the Fields to the Main Document

Word uses *fields* for many things. They can contain variable information such as dates and page numbers. In a data merge, fields can contain the names and addresses of the recipients.

Column headings from the data source file appear in the **Merge Field** section of the **Data Merge Manager**. From there, you can drag the column headings as data fields into the main document. Drag the fields into the main document and drop them in the places where they would appear (for example, drag the **Address_Line_1** field from the **Data Merge Manager** in to the place in the main document it would normally occupy in a business address).

Insert new line breaks as needed. Be sure you add spacing and punctuation as necessary—for example, insert a space between the first and last names and a comma after the city.

TIP

You can personalize the salutation by adding a second instance of the first name field after *Dear*.

❸ Preview the Document

Open the **Preview** section of the **Data Merge Manager**. On the left end of the window, click the **View Merged Data** button. A sample of the main document using the first name and address from the data source appears. You can use the control buttons in the **Preview** section to check other records.

 NOTE

The {a} button at the far right of the **Preview** section of the **Data Merge Manager** is the **View Field Codes** button. It displays in full the codes used to insert the merge data.

52 Use an Address Book List As the Data Source

Entourage includes an Address Book that is available to all other Office applications, including Word. Because the Address Book is an existing *data source*, you can use it as a data source for a data merge. And because contacts in the Address Book can be grouped into categories, you can use those categories to select only the recipients you want.

1 Identify the Data Source

After establishing a *main document*, you can specify the Address Book as a data source. In the **Data Merge Manager**, open the **Data Source** section and click the **Get Data** button. From the menu that opens, select **Office Address Book**. The current Address Book is designated as the data source.

2 Set Up the Fields

The **Merge Field** section of the **Data Merge Manager** displays the fields available in the Address Book. Drag the fields into position in the main document. Available fields when using the Address Book include **First_Name**, **Last_Name**, and a combined **Full_Name** field.

3 Filter the Data

It's unlikely that you would want to send the same letter to everyone in your Address Book. The book probably contains a combination of personal and business addresses. You might want to limit the mailing to business contacts—or to a certain class of business contacts such as customers or suppliers.

In the **Merge** section of the **Data Merge Manager**, click the **Query Options** button. The **Query Options** dialog box asks you to select the recipients to be included in the mailing.

The **Query Options** dialog box displays the categories into which Address Book listings are sorted. The program provides an initial list of categories such as **Friends**, **Work**, and **Travel**. You can add categories of your own including, perhaps, a category for junk mail or a category of people involved in a renovation project.

Before You Begin

✔ **50** Generate a Form Letter

✔ **51** Designate a Data Source

See Also

→ **1** Display the Project Center

→ **53** Complete a Merge

→ **125** Keep Track of Contacts

TIPS

If you are creating a mail merge for an internal company message, you might want to use the **Department** field instead of physical mailing addresses.

See **137** **Personalize Your Address Book** for information on how to assign contacts to categories and projects and add other identifying information such as postal codes, professions, and employment. You can use these identifying assignments to tailor a mailing list.

NOTE

The **Query Options** dialog box appears only when the Office Address Book is used as a data source. If a different data file is used as the data source, a query-building dialog box lets you select the conditions under which names are added or omitted. It is described in **53** **Complete a Merge**.

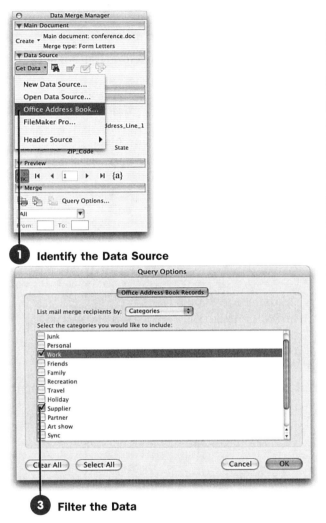

1 Identify the Data Source

3 Filter the Data

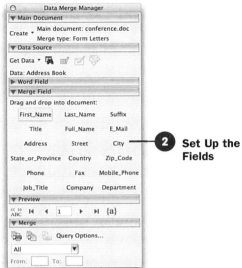

2 Set Up the Fields

TIP

From the **List mail merge recipients by** drop-down list, select the **Complete Record** option to see a list of all your contacts by name so that you can select or omit them individually.

Enable the check boxes for the categories of recipients you want to include in this mailing. All categories are initially selected, so you might want to click the **Clear All** button and then enable the check boxes for the categories you want to include.

Select the categories or individuals you want to include in the mail merge and then click **OK**. The mailing is restricted to the people and categories you have selected.

53 Complete a Merge

When you are ready to merge the *main document* with the *data source*, you have two options. The choice depends on how confident you are about your previous work.

If you feel that you have properly set up the main document, including the merge *fields*, and if what you see in the **Preview** section of the **Data Merge Manager** looks satisfactory, you may feel safe in sending the merge directly to the printer. This approach prints multiple copies of the letter, each addressed to a different recipient.

If you have any doubts about how well you've organized the mail merge, you can save the merged document as a new file. The multiple copies of the letter are all in this file, again individually addressed. You can check this file and make any needed corrections (just as you would with any normal Word document) before you send it to the printer.

1 Select Query Options

If you have a large data source, you might not want to send a letter to everyone whose name appears in it. You might want to send the mailing only to people in a certain state or postal code. In the case of the conference example used in this chapter, your data source might include a column to indicate whether the individual has registered in advance. You could send a verification letter only to those people who have already registered.

In the **Merge** section of the **Data Merge Manager**, click **Query Options**. The **Query Options** dialog box gives you the opportunity to filter and sort the records as they will appear in the final merge.

Before You Begin

✔ **50** Generate a Form Letter

✔ **51** Designate a Data Source

ⓘ TIP

As you proceed with this task, you have several opportunities to verify your work. Remember this basic principle: When in doubt, check it out.

NOTE

This version of the **Query Options** dialog box is entirely different from the one that appears when you use the Address Book as a data source. That alternative is described in **52** **Use an Address Book List As the Data Source**.

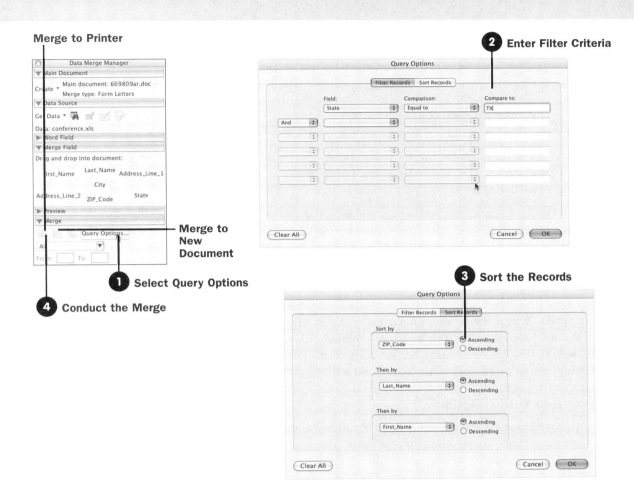

Merge to Printer

2 Enter Filter Criteria

Merge to New Document

1 Select Query Options

4 Conduct the Merge

3 Sort the Records

2 Enter Filter Criteria

On the **Filter Records** page of the **Query Options** dialog box, you can enter criteria for selecting the records to be merged. For example, if you want to include only residents of a certain state, from the **Field** drop-down list select **State**; from the **Comparison** drop-down list, select the operator **Equal to**. In the **Compare to** text box, type the state.

You can enter additional filter criteria by filling out additional lines in this dialog box. For example, if you want to include only those records from a specific state *and* who have previously registered for the conference, in the second line leave the **And** operator selected, select **Registered** from the **Field** drop-down list, and select **is not blank** from the **Comparison** drop-down list.

The dialog box provides several other opportunities to specify which records from the data source you will use. Instead of **Equal to**, you can select the comparison options **Less than** or **Greater than**.

On the additional criteria lines, an **And** operator says the record must meet *all* conditions; the **Or** alternative says the record can meet *any* of the stated conditions.

③ Sort the Records

Use the **Sort Records** page of the **Query Options** dialog box to set the order in which the merged records are printed. For example, if you have a large mailing, sorting by postal code might qualify you for reduced postage costs.

Open the **Sort by** list, and select the field on which you want to sort. If you select **ZIP_Code**, for example, the records are sorted based on that field. You also can select **Ascending** or **Descending** order.

You can specify additional sorting options as well. For example, you can specify that the merged records be sorted by postal code, then within each code by the recipient's last name. If more than one recipient has the same last name, you can sort again by first name.

When you have completed your sorting and filtering choices, click **OK**. The dialog box closes, and your selections are applied to the data source.

④ Conduct the Merge

In the **Merge** section of the **Data Merge Manager**, click either the **Merge to Printer** or **Merge to New Document** button. (Point to the buttons in the top row of the **Merge** section to display their labels.) The documents are merged to the selected destination.

 TIP

Ever notice that when you're entering your address on a Web site, you're asked to select your state from a drop-down list? That's to ensure that the entries are consistent—all the state names are either abbreviated or spelled out. Otherwise, if they tried to filter out all the customers from *Texas*, they would get an entirely different list than if they filtered all the customers from *TX*. This kind of consistency is vital to properly using any database, including the Address Book.

 TIP

An **And** operator reduces the number of records selected; the **Or** operator increases the number.

 TIP

You can check the effects of your filtering and sorting choices by opening the **Preview** section of the **Data Merge Manager**. Click the **View Merged Data** button and scroll through the records. In the **Merge** section, you can open the **Data Range List**, which initially is labeled **All**. Change it to **Current Record** or **Custom**. If you select **Custom**, specify a range of pages. You then can perform a test merge of the selected pages.

54 Send Letters by Email

Before You Begin

✔ **50** Generate a Form
Letter

✔ **51** Designate a Data
Source

✔ **53** Complete a Merge

🖎 NOTE

The email merge feature in Word is available only if you have designated Entourage as your default email program. If some other mail program now holds that status, you must change the default. Under OS X 3 (Panther), make the change using the **Finder** menu: Select **Go**, **Applications**; double-click **Mail**; select **Preferences**; and click the **General** icon. Open the **Default Email Reader** menu and select **Entourage**. Under OS X 2 (Jaguar), open the **Apple** menu and select **System Preferences**, **Internet**. Click the **Email** tab to open the **Default Email Reader** menu. In either case, if Entourage is not one of the menu choices, click **Select**, navigate to the **Office 2004** menu, and select **Entourage**.

Postal delivery is often derided as *snail mail*. Electronic mail is faster and often less expensive than the traditional alternative.

If you use Entourage as your default email program, and if your **data source** includes a **field** for email addresses, you can deliver a mass mailing using email.

1 Set Up the Email Merge

Set up the form letter data merge using the **Data Merge Manager** to identify a **main document** and data source and to insert merge fields into the main document.

In this case, insert the recipients' email addresses instead of their postal addresses.

2 Set the Terms of the Merge

In the **Data Merge Manager**, open the **Merge** section and click the **Merge to E-Mail** button. This is the third button from the left; you can identify it by pointing to the button with the mouse and reading the ToolTip that pops up.

The **Mail Recipient** dialog box opens. Make sure that the **To** drop-down list is set to **E_Mail**. In the **Subject** text box, type a subject as you would for any email message.

From the **Send As** drop-down list, select one of these options:

- **Text**—Sends the form letters as plain-text email messages. This is the quickest, simplest way to get the word out.

- **Attachment**—Sends the letters as attachments to email messages. This is a good choice for long messages.

- **HTML Message**—Sends the letters in an HTML format that preserves headings, tables, and other special formatting. A drawback is that not everyone is equipped to receive it.

When you've specified the terms of the email merge, click the **Data Merge To Outbox** button. The merged letters are placed in your Entourage Outbox.

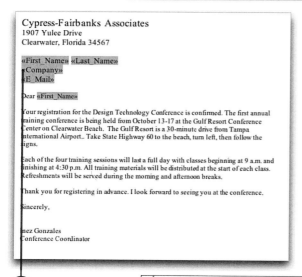

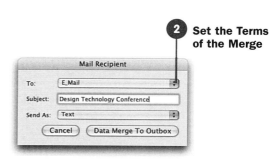

2 Set the Terms of the Merge

3 Complete the Transmission

1 Set Up the Email Merge

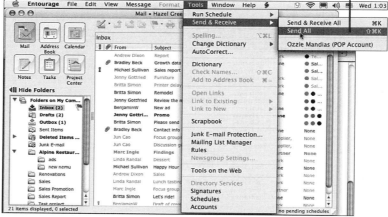

3 Complete the Transmission

Open Entourage. From the main menu, select **Tools, Send & Receive, Send All**. All the mail messages that Word's **Data Merge** feature placed in the Outbox are sent.

NOTE

Before you send the message, check the **Preview** section of the **Data Merge Manager**. Also be sure to set any query options, as explained in **52** Use an Address Book List As the Data Source and **53** Complete a Merge, before you proceed.

10

Using the Notebook

IN THIS CHAPTER:

You can display a Word document in any of several views: a **Normal** view for quick text entry, a **Page Layout** or **Online Layout** view to see how a finished document will look, and an **Outline** view to help organize your work.

Word 2004 has another view: the **Notebook Layout** view. This view looks like a ruled notebook page and is intended to be used like one. It is a place where you can jot down ideas, record your thoughts, gather research material, or take notes at a lecture or presentation.

Notebook Layout view is like the highly organized expert who walks into someone's messy office and compartmentalizes everything into files, drawers, and designated places for everything. It can make an orderly structure of seemingly random entries. Nevertheless, if you prefer a piling system to a filing system, you can use the **Notebook Layout** view that way, too.

In **Notebook Layout** view, you work in a **notebook**, which is more or less a regular Word document. You can write text, insert text, check spelling, and find and replace text just as you would in any Word document. But this view has a distinct display and several unique features designed to make taking and organizing notes easier.

The **Notebook Layout** view emulates a physical notebook with ruled pages and tabbed sections. You can name the sections, create new sections, and drag them into a new order. Within each page, you can establish an outline structure in which your notes are organized under headings and subheadings.

If something needs checking or a follow-up action, you can flag the item to remind you it requires attention.

NOTE

The **Notebook Layout** view is unique to the Mac version of Word. Windows users can purchase a separate product called One Note that has many of the same features as **Notebook Layout**.

KEY TERM

Notebook—A Word view that formats a document as a notebook with tabbed places.

TIP

The **Notebook Layout** view has its own version of Word's **Standard** toolbar. If this toolbar is not open, you can display it by selecting **View**, **Toolbars**, **Notebook Layout View Standard**.

55 Set Up a Notebook

See Also

→ **19** Open Files from the Project Gallery

→ **58** Build an Outline

You can create a new notebook document from the **Project Gallery** or by converting an existing file to **Notebook Layout** view.

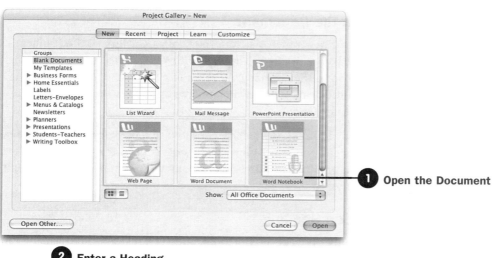

1 Open the Document

2 Enter a Heading

3 Label the Section Tabs

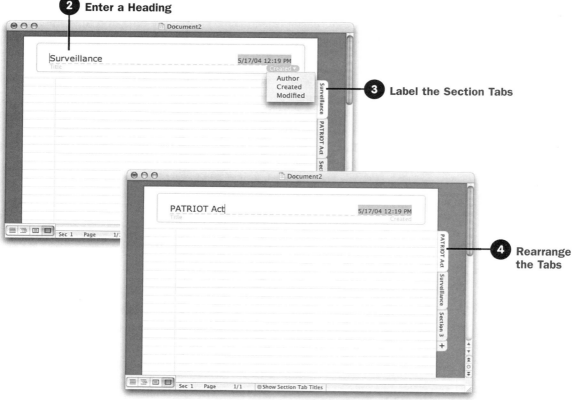

4 Rearrange the Tabs

❶ Open the Document

Create a new notebook from the **Project Gallery**. If the **Project Gallery** does not open when you start Word, select **File**, **Project Gallery**. In the **Groups** column, select **Blank Documents**. Scroll down the display of new documents and select **Word Notebook**. Then click **Open**.

To convert an existing document to a notebook, open the existing document and select **View**, **Notebook Layout** from the main Word menu, or click the **Notebook Layout View** button in the lower-left corner of the window.

❷ Enter a Heading

The upper part of the notebook page is a heading area, where you can enter a title for the current section. You also can select from codes that display the author's name, the date and time the notebook was created, or when it was last modified.

Click in the left part of the title area and type a title. Then point to the dimmed legend just under the name or date on the right side of the heading area. The legend becomes a button; click it. A menu offers the choices **Author**, **Created**, and **Modified**. Depending on which option you select, your name, the date the document was created, or the date it was last edited appears in the document heading.

❸ Label the Section Tabs

A notebook document initially has three section tabs with the prosaic names **Section 1**, **Section 2**, and **Section 3**. You can change these labels to section titles that identify the contents of those pages. The tab titles can be the same as the section titles in the page headings, but that's not required.

Double-click the tab you want to rename. The name is selected, and you can type a new name. To add a new tab, click the + button at the bottom of the row of tabs.

❹ Rearrange the Tabs

You can rearrange the section tabs to suit your needs. For example, you might want to move one tab to a position ahead of another. Click the tab and drag it into the new position in the row of tabs.

Because the notebook is a Word document, you can save and reopen it just like any other Word document (it bears the familiar **.doc** file extension). When you reopen it, it appears in the **Notebook Layout** view.

If a document initially was in **Normal**, **Page Layout**, or some other view, you can change it to **Notebook Layout** view, but a **Notebook Layout** document cannot be changed to another view.

 TIP

If you don't want to display section names on the tabs, you can display numbers instead. In the **Status Bar** at the bottom of the window, click the section labeled **Show Section Tab Titles**. That feature is disabled, and the tabs are numbered simply **1**, **2**, and **3**. Click the same place again to restore the tab labels. If you move a numbered section tab, the tabs are renumbered to reflect the new order. Their titles, however, are unchanged.

56 Take Written Notes

Entering notes can be a freeform kind of process. Say, for example, you are doing a research project and want to take notes as you read an article on the subject. You could type your notes in any form you want. You could start on the top line and type everything in one big paragraph. Or, as is done in this example, you can enter the notes in outline form with headings and supporting points.

❶ Type a Heading

Click the first line of the notebook page. Type a top-level outline heading. It can be anything descriptive, such as **Grocery list** or **Einstein's theory**.

❷ Enter a Note

Click to move to the next line and press **Tab**. Pressing **Tab** indicates that your next entry is a subsidiary to the heading in the previous line.

Type whatever you'd like to record about the subject. You can use paragraph-style text or a bullet-point format to jot down shorter thoughts.

Before You Begin

✔ **55** Set Up a Notebook

See Also

→ **58** Build an Outline

NOTE

Notebook Layout view works much like Word's **Outline** view. Entries appear in outline format. Tab labels and page heading are the top-level outline entries, and headings and subheadings on the notebook page are positioned at lower levels of the outline. You can ignore the outline and enter freeform text, but the notebook tends to impose an outline structure. See **58** **Build an Outline**.

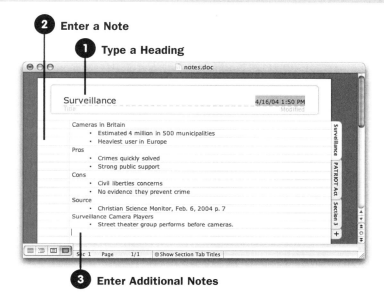

2 Enter a Note

1 Type a Heading

3 Enter Additional Notes

3 Enter Additional Notes

Continue to enter notes as you encounter the information. You can cut and paste notes from other sources, too, as long as you're careful to avoid plagiarism and copyright violations. Don't worry too much about organizing the chunks of text; you can take care of that as described in **58** **Build an Outline**.

57 Record Audio Notes

Before You Begin

✔ **56** Take Written Notes

See Also

→ **59** Note a Task to Be Done

→ **61** Flag Important Information

Your notes don't have to be in writing. If your computer has a microphone (as most Macs do), either built-in or attached, you can dictate audio notes.

You can add audio notes in many situations. If you're on the move, you can record a quick audio note. If disk space and battery power permit, you can record an entire meeting or lecture. You can also make quick reminders to yourself about some task you have to complete. This

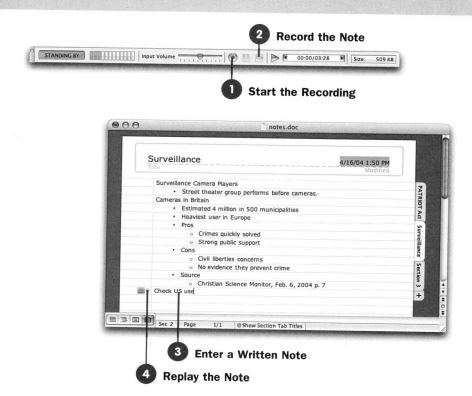

2 Record the Note

STANDING BY | Input Volume | 00:00/03:28 | Size: 509 KB

1 Start the Recording

3 Enter a Written Note

4 Replay the Note

exercise features notes about the use of surveillance cameras in Great Britain. If you learn of a source of comparable information in the United States, you could record an audio note to remind yourself to check with that source.

When you record a note, an audio icon is inserted into the notebook. To identify the audio note, type a companion text note about what you are recording. This text is linked to the recording. You can find the recorded note later by searching for the text. Then you can click the audio icon to replay the audio note. Without the text note, you still can look for the audio icon, but the text makes the note easier to find and identify.

NOTE

It is discourteous and unwise to record people without asking their permission.

TIP

Audio recording can use a lot of disk space. For example, a 4-minute recording can consume more than 600KB on your disk.

 NOTE

You can delete an audio note in two ways; neither is entirely satisfactory. On the main menu, select **Tools, Audio Notes, Delete Audio Marker**. This command unlinks the recording from the note but does not delete the recording itself; it still is there, leaving your flubs and unguarded comments for others to find and hear. The alternative is to select **Tools, Audio Notes, Delete Audio from Document**. This option deletes the recording— *along with all the other audio notes* recorded for that document.

❶ Start the Recording

Place the cursor at the point in the notebook where you want to insert the recorded note. Select **View, Toolbars, Audio Notes**. The **Audio Notes** toolbar is displayed at the top of the notebook page.

On that toolbar, click the **Start Recording** button. A **Recording** signal at the left end of the toolbar is lit.

❷ Record the Note

Record your note. When finished, click the **Stop** button in the toolbar.

❸ Enter a Written Note

Enter a written note that describes the nature of the recording. Enter it as you would any other note. You don't need the written note, but you'll appreciate it later if you have to search for the audio note.

❹ Replay the Note

To replay the audio note, find it in the notebook. If you have included a text note, you can search for the text. Click the line where the audio note appears; then click the audio icon (the speaker) that appears in the left margin of the note.

---

58 Build an Outline

Before You Begin

✔ **56** Take Written Notes

See Also

→ **24** Write an Outline

→ **104** Outline a Presentation

Although **Notebook Layout** view doesn't require that you arrange your notes in an outline format, the program definitely encourages it. The program applies a structure of headings and subheadings to the text you type in the notebook and encourages you to use them.

In a notebook, the headings and subheadings correspond to outline levels determined by the relative level at which text is indented. Starting from the left, you can indent note levels, placing them at successively lower levels. You can use as many as nine of these note levels.

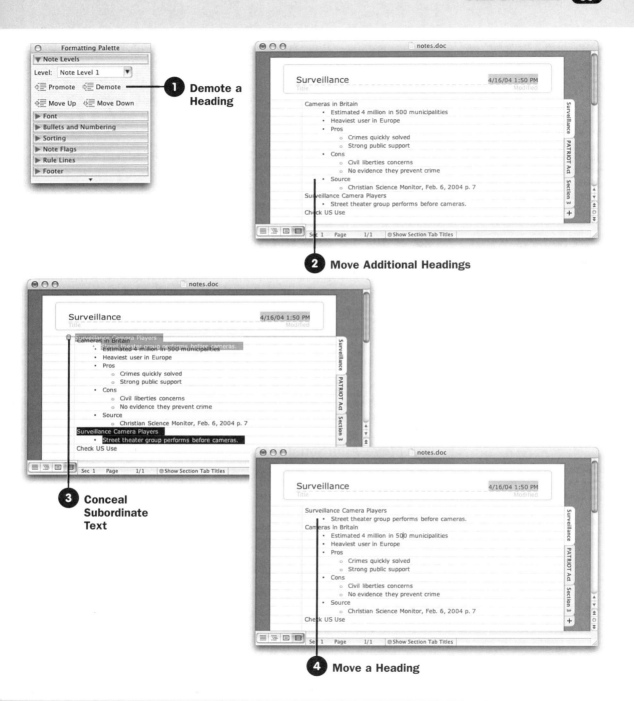

1 Demote a Heading

2 Move Additional Headings

3 Conceal Subordinate Text

4 Move a Heading

TIP

If you are preparing a long document such as a major report or a book, the notebook can store notes for the project and help you organize it. You can assign material to various note levels, move notes to different headings, and reorganize the structure. The result can be a well-structured outline for the project.

 NOTE

The **Formatting Palette** reconstitutes itself in **Notebook Layout** view to display tools for managing notes. For example, a **Note Levels** section displays tools for promoting and demoting headings.

 TIP

The **Formatting Palette** also has a **Level** drop-down list that contains all nine heading levels. You can select a heading in the notebook and then use that list to assign it to a new heading level. This approach is useful if you want to promote or demote the heading by several levels.

You can use this outline structure to organize your information. Indent subheadings to make them subordinate to headings; then place text under these headings and subheadings to organize it within the structure. You can promote or demote headings to different note levels, and you can move headings along with their contents to different parts of the structure.

You also can collapse or expand the heading display. Point to any heading that has subordinate material, and a blue arrow appears in the left margin. Click the arrow to display only the heading. Click the arrow again to redisplay the full content.

1 Demote a Heading

You might have a collection of notes that you jotted down as they occurred to you. Now you want to better organize them. For example, the headings **Pros** and **Cons** are part of the discussion about British surveillance cameras. They should be demoted to lower levels—levels under the heading **Cameras in Britain**. The **Source** heading also refers to British cameras and should also be on a subordinate level to the **Cameras in Britain** heading.

Click one of the headings that you want to demote. In the **Formatting Palette**, click the **Demote** button. The heading is moved to a lower level—that is, it is indented once more.

2 Move Additional Headings

Repeat step 1 to assign new levels to the headings in your notebook. If it fits your design, you can also promote some headings to higher levels: Click the heading you want to promote and then click the **Promote** button in the **Formatting Palette** to outdent the selected heading.

3 Conceal Subordinate Text

When an outline grows to become larger and more complex, it is sometimes useful to collapse lower-level entries so that you can concentrate on higher-level headings. Any heading that has subordinate text can be collapsed to display only that heading.

The subordinate text is still there and moves with the heading if you promote, demote, or move it. The subordinate text is just not displayed for the moment.

In this example, the heading **Cameras in Britain** has several subordinate headings and notes that can be collapsed. Point to that heading and click the blue triangle that appears to the left of the heading. The heading is collapsed. Click the triangle to the left of the heading to reopen, or expand, the heading to show all the subordinate text.

4 Move a Heading

In addition to promoting or demoting a heading, you can move it to a position higher or lower in the notebook outline. For example, you might decide that the note about the **Surveillance Camera Players** would make a good lead-in to the entire discussion.

Collapse both the **Cameras in Britain** and the **Surveillance Camera Players** headings following the instructions in step 3. Doing so ensures that their contents stay with them during the move.

Select the **Surveillance Camera Players** heading. In the **Formatting Palette**, click the **Move Up** button. The heading is moved up one position in the outline.

Open both collapsed headings by clicking the triangle to the left of each heading to see the results.

TIP

In this example, you want to move the **Surveillance Camera Players** heading up only one position. If several more headings are in the notebook outline, you can click **Move Up** more than once.

---

59 Note a Task to Be Done

The Entourage tasks list is a versatile tool that, among other things, can remind you when a task is due. You can link the reminder to a notebook entry to help you keep track of notebook items.

For example, you might have made a note to check with a source of information. In addition to the notebook entry, you can enter the note as an Entourage task and ask to be reminded at the proper time. Entourage displays an **Office Notification** at the appointed hour.

Before You Begin

✔ **56** Take Written Notes

See Also

→ **61** Flag Important Information

→ **126** Maintain Your Meeting Schedule

1 Select the Note and Create the Task

Open the notebook and click the note you want to record as a task. In the ongoing survellience camera example, you might select the **Check US Use** notebook entry.

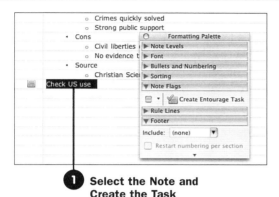

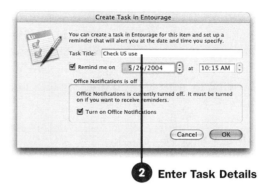

1 Select the Note and Create the Task

2 Enter Task Details

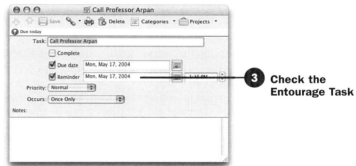

3 Check the Entourage Task

 TIP

When you open the task in Entourage, you can add or edit details that were not available when you created the task in the notebook. For example, you can set a due date and priority and, in the **Occurs** list, indicate whether this is a one-time or recurring task. When the task has been completed, you can reopen the task in Entourage and check it off as complete.

In the **Formatting Palette**, open the **Note Flags** section and select **Create Entourage Task**. The **Create Task in Entourage** dialog box opens.

2 **Enter Task Details**

The **Task Title** text box repeats the notebook entry you selected in step 1; you can change that title if you want.

Enable the **Remind me on** check box if it is not already selected. Then enter a date and time you want to receive the reminder. When finished, click **OK**.

3 Check the Entourage Task

Open Entourage. In the group of buttons on the left side of the window, click **Task**. The task list opens and includes the newly created task. Select the task listing and, in the Entourage toolbar, click **Edit**. Details of the task are displayed.

60 Scribble a Note

Want to scribble in your notebook? This might be your first opportunity since kindergarten. The *Scribble tool* is a notebook equivalent to the pen or pencil tool in other applications. With it, you can use the mouse or touchpad to draw directly on a notebook page. If you have a more sophisticated tool such as a drawing tablet, that's even better.

If you want to jot down a quick note, you might sometimes find it quicker to do it by hand instead of using the keyboard. Granted, most people's attempts to write by mouse leave something to be desired. That something is legibility. A more productive use of the **Scribble** tool might be to make a quick drawing. You could diagram a workflow or sketch a map to a destination.

1 Select the Scribble Tool

The **Scribble** tool comes in an assortment of pen sizes and colors. A black medium point often does the job, but if you prefer, you can use a finer point and a different color.

On the **Standard** toolbar, click the arrow next to the **Scribble** tool button. A menu of pen sizes is displayed. Point to the size you want to use, and a color palette opens. Select a color.

2 Draw the First Line

Click the **Scribble** tool button (not the arrow next to the button) to select the tool. The tool opens, using the pen size and color you selected in step 1. Drag a line on the page with the **Scribble** tool.

The line is a graphic object. It displays adjustment handles you can use to move or resize it. The **Formatting Palette** changes to display an assortment of graphic editing tools.

Before You Begin

✔ **55** Set Up a Notebook

See Also

→ **56** Take Written Notes

🔍 KEY TERM

Scribble tool—A drawing tool available in **Notebook Layout** view to take notes or make drawings by hand.

📝 NOTE

In **Notebook Layout** view, Word's **Standard** toolbar is modified to display buttons for notebook functions such as the **Scribble** tool.

💡 TIP

Unless your hand is extremely steady, don't expect a perfect line on the first try. A little practice will help. Don't be afraid to delete the line (select it and press the **Delete** key) and start over.

1 Select the Scribble Tool

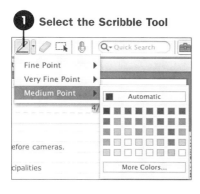

2 Draw the First Line

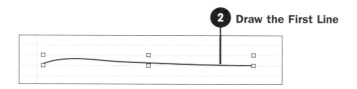

3 Draw Additional Lines

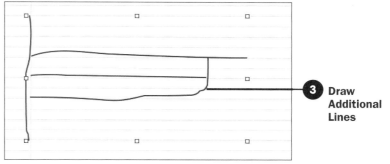

4 Add Text Labels

---

3 **Draw Additional Lines**

Draw any additional lines you want to add to the graphic you are creating. When you add lines that touch or are close together, the program automatically groups them as a single object. Should the need arise, you can select and move the entire group simultaneously.

4 **Add Text Labels**

It would be hard to tell that the assemblage of lines in this example is intended as a map. If you have a steady hand or a graphics tablet, you can use the **Scribble** tool to add text labels such as the names of streets. The most legible alternative—adding typed labels to your scribbled lines—unfortunately is not available.

61 Flag Important Information

Some notes are more important than others. The notebook includes the means to *flag* notes so that you can readily come back to them. You might want to act on the note, give it further research or study, or send it to someone else. You might also want to be able to leave a check mark next to the note when you have completed the follow-up.

1 Select a Flag Type

Open the notebook that contains the notes you want to flag. Click anywhere in the paragraph you want to flag. In the **Note Flags** section of the **Formatting Palette**, the current note flag symbol appears on the left side of the window. Click the arrow next to the symbol to display all the available flag types.

Select a flag type. If you select either of the three check box types, you can use that flag icon later to identify a completed task. Otherwise, there are no set rules for the type of flag you select. Pick a type that is meaningful to you. After you click the flag you want, the flag icon appears to the left of the selected paragraph in the notebook.

2 Check Off a Completed Task

If you have used one of the check box flag types, you can use it to flag a completed project. Click in the check box; the task is checked off.

3 Flag for Follow-up

A separate flag type allows you to set a reminder to follow up on a particular note. Select the note you want to flag for follow-up and then click the **Flag for Follow Up** button in the **Standard** toolbar. The icon on this button is a red flag.

A dialog box asks you to set a date and time to receive the reminder. Type the date and time or use the spin arrows to change the settings. When you're finished, click **OK**. You can expect an **Office Notification** at the date and time you selected.

Before You Begin

✔ **56** Take Written Notes

See Also

→ **59** Note a Task to Be Done

KEY TERM

Flag—To identify a notebook entry for further attention.

NOTE

The ability to flag notes is a companion to identifying them as Entourage tasks as described in **59** **Note a Task to Be Done**. You can do either or both; the choice is yours. Staying within the notebook is the simpler choice. Making the note an Entourage task might be preferable if the notes you are taking are part of a larger project.

TIP

You must apply flags individually to every line you want to flag. If you select multiple lines, the flag is applied only to the first line in the selection.

NOTE

The notebook flag features are similar to designating a note as an Entourage task and can be used as an simpler alternative when the full Entourage features are not needed.

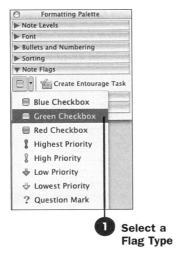

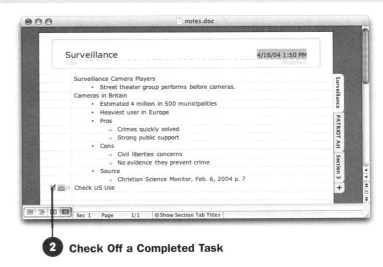

① Select a Flag Type

② Check Off a Completed Task

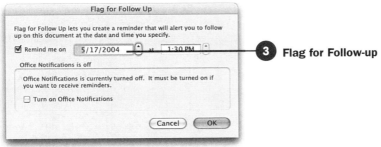

③ Flag for Follow-up

---

62 Quickly Find Resources

Before You Begin

✔ **56** Take Written Notes

See Also

→ **59** Note a Task to Be Done

→ **61** Flag Important Information

A notebook can quickly fill a sheaf of pages of randomly collected information. Even if you have painstakingly arranged the material on tabbed pages and in outline form, you might want to retrieve a note from a place you can't quite remember.

You can use *Quick Search* to find key words and phrases within the notebook. The feature highlights these phrases and the tabbed pages on which they occur.

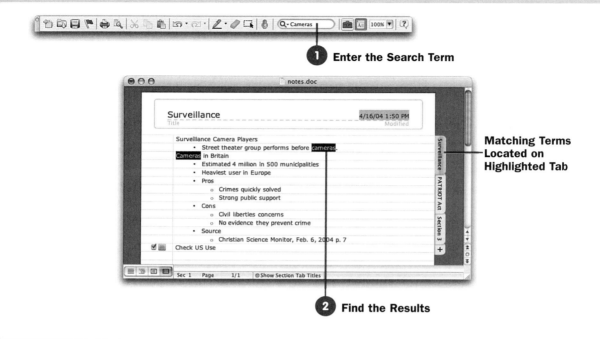

1 **Enter the Search Term**

**Matching Terms
Located on
Highlighted Tab**

2 **Find the Results**

1 **Enter the Search Term**

In the notebook's **Standard** toolbar, click in the **Quick Search** window. Enter the word or phrase you want to find. Note that you can start the search from any page in the notebook; the search is conducted throughout the entire notebook.

2 **Find the Results**

The program highlights every instance of the search term in the notebook. If the term appears on a different page, the program also highlights the tab for that page. You can scroll to the pages and items that contain the highlighted terms.

KEY TERM

Quick Search—A Word notebook feature that finds and highlights key words and phrases.

PART III

Excel 2004

IN THIS PART:

11

Building Worksheets and Workbooks

IN THIS CHAPTER:

Excel is an example of a venerable class of programs known as *spreadsheets*. Like other applications of its kind, Excel shows you a screen that is laid out in rows and columns like an accountant's worksheet. You can put numbers on the sheet along with text labels to help you understand what the numbers represent. Then, you can add those numbers, compare results, figure percentages, and conduct a seemingly infinite array of calculations.

In their basic form, spreadsheets can smear these numbers and calculated results over vast acres of row-and-column real estate. A single Excel *worksheet*, as it's now called, gives you room to spread your work over 256 columns and 65,536 rows. Each intersection of a row and column is a *cell* where you can make entries or display the results of calculations. Nearly 17 million cells are available for your use and possible amusement in a single worksheet.

A cell is usually identified by its coordinates. For example, the cell in row 2 of column B is cell **B2**. You also can identify *ranges* of cells. The cells in rows 1–3 of columns B–D can be identified as **B1:D3**.

Fortunately for both yourself and your audience, you usually won't have to extend yourself nearly so far. Just as fortunately, the modern versions of programs like Excel provide the means to break up large blocks of figures into more workable subdivisions. Instead of spreading numbers all over a single sheet, you can organize even the most expansive exercises into multiple worksheets assembled into multipage *workbooks*.

If all you want to do is add up the cost of a shopping list, you probably don't have to worry too much about spreading numbers over vast territory or multiple worksheets. On the other hand, consider the workbook designed by an oil company engineer to assess the possible costs and returns of prospective drilling projects. This workbook covered nearly every possible contingency, starting with geology, the cost of drilling, and the likelihood of success. The analysis then went further to apply economic factors such as oil price trends and anticipated revenue. Each of these factors was evaluated with a host of mathematical formulas.

TIP

Your needs might be much less complex than the engineer's. Nevertheless, you easily could find yourself in a position where the ability to do things like that can pay long-term benefits to you and to the people who read your work.

The engineer built a workbook of multiple worksheets. One analyzed the drilling cost, another the likely output, another the anticipated revenue, and so on—more than a dozen worksheets in all. They were topped by a wrap-up worksheet that summarized the results.

63 Enter a Formula

Excel is a device you can use to figure things out. It is the leading tool of that class of computer operators called *number crunchers*. And Excel truly excels at crunching numbers. It does math—higher math, lower math, postgraduate math, Excel doesn't really care what kind of math you ask it to do.

As you work with Excel, you will make entries in **cells**, which are the rectangles at the junctions of rows and columns. The most important entries will be the numbers you want Excel to calculate, but you probably will use more than numbers. We humans need text labels to help us identify what's on the screen. We often find it greatly helpful to have a graph or some other kind of illustration to help us understand the numeric data. But things like that are just for our benefit. Excel itself needs only the numbers.

After the numbers are in place, you probably want to do something with them—add or subtract them, or calculate their standard deviation, or some such.

One way to do that is to enter a **formula**. This can be as simple as basic arithmetic, subtracting the contents of cell A2 from the contents of cell A1. Or it can be exceedingly complex like the oil engineer's equations.

1 Start the Formula

Click the cell where you want the results of the formula to appear. Type an equal sign (=). This symbol signals Excel that you want to enter a formula, not just a text or numerical entry.

2 Make an Entry

Enter a value to be used in the formula. You can type a number, or you can refer to the contents of another cell. A cell is identified by the row and cell headers, such as cell **B2**. With the equal sign in place, you can then type the cell reference. Often, though, it is easier just to click the cell. If you do this while writing a formula, the cell reference is added to the formula.

See Also

→ **64** Make an Automatic Calculation

→ **65** Make an Advanced Calculation

NOTE

Excel has an optional toolbar called the **Formula** bar, where the contents of the currently selected cell also appear; you can write or edit the cell contents there. The **Formula** bar is not automatically displayed, but you can open it by selecting **View**, **Toolbars** and selecting, or placing a check mark next to, the **Formula Bar** option.

KEY TERM

Formula—A mathematical expression that performs a calculation.

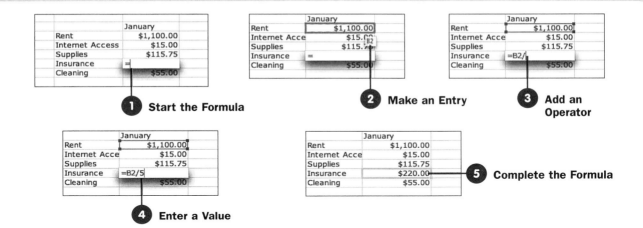

1 Start the Formula

2 Make an Entry

3 Add an Operator

4 Enter a Value

5 Complete the Formula

3 Add an Operator

Excel formulas can use these operators:

+ for addition

– for subtraction

* for multiplication

/ for division

^ for an exponent

Every formula needs an operator; it is the action of the numerical sentence, the action you want Excel to perform on the values you provide.

4 Enter a Value

Enter a second value. As before, this value can be a number or the cell reference of another cell.

5 Complete the Formula

Press **Return** to complete the formula. The result of the formula appears in the cell you selected in step 1. In this example, you might want to calculate the cost of insurance for a small business. The agent quotes an insurance premium of half of the monthly rent. Because the rent can vary, you can enter the current rent

payment in cell **B2** (where it is clearly labeled and you can easily adjust it). In the insurance value cell (cell **B5**), enter the formula =**B2/2** (monthly rent divided by 2). Now if the rent changes, the insurance value also changes. (And if you find another insurance agent, you may be able to enter a more favorable formula in cell **B5**).

64 Make an Automatic Calculation

A formula can be as complex as the engineering calculations required for an oil field project. But unless you have the kind of expertise to write that type of equation, you'll probably instead turn to Excel's *functions*.

Functions are built-in formulas that make many commonly used calculations. Some are fairly simple, such as the **SUM** function that totals a group of numbers. In fact, there is an **AutoSum** feature that not only totals a column of numbers, but also scans the worksheet and finds numbers to be totaled. Other functions perform statistical, engineering, or financial tasks. Chapter 14, "Forecasting Results," contains examples of how some of the more advanced functions work.

① Start the Formula

Click the cell where you want the results of the formula to appear. This can be any place that makes sense. For example, the logical place for the sum of a column numbers is at the bottom of the column.

② Select an Automatic Function

Because you want to total the values in the cells above the current cell, you can click the **AutoSum** button in the **Standard** toolbar. The **AutoSum** function automatically assumes that you want to total those figures. The function looks for numerical entries above it in the column and assumes, usually correctly, that these are the numbers you want to add. It ignores any text or blank cells. You can second-guess the function's decision by selecting a different range of cells.

You don't need to enter an equal sign before you apply a function; the function includes that symbol for you.

Before You Begin

✔ **63** Enter a Formula

See Also

→ **65** Make an Advanced Calculation

KEY TERM

Function—A prewritten formula, often used as a shortcut to enter a complex formula.

TIP

The drop-down arrow to the right of the **AutoSum** button opens a list of other common functions that work automatically in the same fashion.

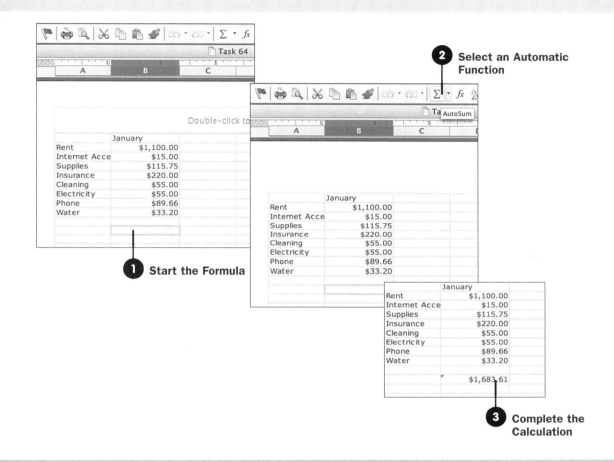

2 Select an Automatic Function

1 Start the Formula

3 Complete the Calculation

3 **Complete the Calculation**

Make sure that the function plans to total the cells you want it to work with. The cells the function plans to total appear outlined by a dashed line; the cell range is shown between the function's opening and closing parentheses—**(B2:B10)** in this example. If necessary, you can drag over a different range of cells or edit the cell names in the formula displayed.

When you are satisfied with the cells the function will use, press **Return**. The sum of the selected entries is displayed in the cell you selected in step 1.

65 Make an Advanced Calculation

The basic Excel *functions* readily handle simple calculations. More advanced functions incorporate much more complex mathematics and can save you a great deal more work.

Excel functions observe a standard format, or *syntax*. As with any other type of formula, a function begins with an equal sign. Next is the function's name followed by a list of *arguments* to be used in its calculations. These arguments can be values, cell references, or ranges of cells. Separate the arguments with commas and enclose them in parentheses. For example

    =SUM(34,45,56)

    =AVERAGE(B6:B88)

    =PMT(1%,60,15000)

If a function is fairly simple or if you're familiar with it, you can enter it and its arguments directly into a cell. Many functions are more complex, though, and you might not always be familiar with how to properly assemble them. (For some functions, the order of the arguments is crucial; switch the order of a couple arguments, and your function's results are skewed.) In that case, Excel can build the calculation for you using its **Paste Function** feature. The **Paste Function** feature not only assembles the arguments, but also inserts the proper punctuation for you.

Start this process, logically enough, by selecting **Insert**, **Function** from the menu system. The **Paste Function** dialog box opens to let you select from a list of available functions. If you display the **Standard** toolbar, it includes a **Paste Function** button you can click instead of choosing from the menu.

After you select the function, a **Function Arguments** dialog box displays a group of text boxes in which you can enter each of the required arguments in addition to any optional ones. As you click in each box, an explanation of the argument appears in the lower part of the dialog box. You can type values here, or you can click a text box, return to the worksheet, and select a cell or range of cells that hold the values you want to enter as the argument.

Before You Begin

✔ **63** Enter a Formula

✔ **64** Make an Automatic Calculation

See Also

→ **66** Format Numbers Automatically

KEY TERMS

Syntax—The language in which a formula or function is expressed, including values, their order, and punctuation. If these elements are not in the proper order, the formula produces an incorrect result (if it works at all).

Arguments—The values a function uses in its calculations.

 TIP

Find the function you're looking for in the **Paste Function** dialog box by scrolling down the **Function name** list. Narrow the choices by using the list in the **Select a category** window.

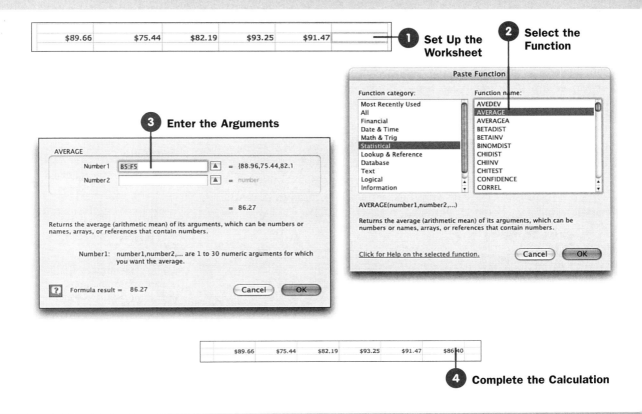

$89.66	$75.44	$82.19	$93.25	$91.47	

1 Set Up the Worksheet

2 Select the Function

3 Enter the Arguments

4 Complete the Calculation

$89.66	$75.44	$82.19	$93.25	$91.47	$86.40

1 Set Up the Worksheet

Open or create a worksheet that has the data you want to use in the function. Click the cell where you want the function to display its results.

2 Select the Function

In the main menu, select **Insert, Function**. The **Paste Function** dialog box displays an ape's arm-length list of Excel's available functions. Because it's a long list, Microsoft has seen fit to group

the functions into categories. These appear in the **Function cate-gory** list on the left side of the dialog box. Select a category, and you see a more selective list of functions in the right window.

Select the function from the **Function name** list; then click **OK**. A new dialog box opens to let you enter the values the function will use.

③ Enter the Arguments

The function requires arguments to make its calculations. You could type specific values into the various argument text boxes in the **Function Arguments** dialog box, but more likely you will want to use the contents of one or more cells. Click the text box where you want to make the entry; then go to the worksheet and select the cells to be included. (Don't forget to look at the bottom of the dialog box when you click each argument text box for an explanation of the argument.) When you click in the worksheet, the selected cell or range of cells is automatically entered in the argument text box; you don't actually have to copy any informa-tion to the dialog box.

When copying cell contents from the worksheet to the dialog box, the **Function Arguments** dialog box *will* get in the way of your worksheet, but the problem usually is self-correcting. When you make a selection in the worksheet, the dialog box automatically collapses to give you some extra room. If you want, you can man-ually collapse the dialog box by clicking the small graphic at the right end of each text box. A similar graphic lets you reinflate the dialog box.

④ Complete the Calculation

Click **OK** to close the **Function Arguments** dialog box. The func-tion makes its calculations and displays the result in the cell you selected in step 1.

 TIP

Many **Function Arguments** dialog boxes present a series of text boxes labeled **Number 1**, **Number 2**, and so on. You need not fill out all of them—in fact, you'll find it hard to do. As you complete one text box, Excel adds another, up to a limit of 30. Fill in only the number of arguments you need. Often, it is enough just to enter a range of cells in the **Number 1** box.

66 Format Numbers Automatically

Before You Begin

✔ **63** Enter a Formula

See Also

→ **67** Automatically Format a Worksheet

→ **68** Format Results Depending on Circumstances

 TIP

If you expect to format a range of cells in the same way, select the empty cells in advance and apply the format. Then, the entries you make are properly formatted as you enter them.

 TIP

A quick way to select a range of cells is to hold down the **Shift** key, click the upper-left and lower-right cells of the range.

 TIP

An alternative to using the **Formatting Palette** is to select **Format, Cells**. When the **Format Cells** dialog box opens, select the **Number** tab.

When you make an entry in a cell, the results might not look exactly the way you would like. For example, you might want to enter an amount of $5. You could type the **5**, which is all Excel would need to do its work. Or, you could type **$5.00** including the dollar sign and decimal point. This requires some extra work and, if you have many entries to make, entering numbers in this way requires a *lot* of extra work.

There is a third choice: Let Excel do the formatting for you. Excel can format numbers in many ways, such as currency, percentages, dates, and times of day. You can use any reasonable number of decimal places. If you change the information, the formatting remains in place.

No matter how you format a cell, you do not change the data itself—only its appearance. In any calculation, Excel treats a $5 entry as a value of **5**, no matter how you display it. The same is true of decimal places. If you choose to display **3.1416** as **3.14**, Excel still uses the full number in calculations.

1 Select the Cells to Be Formatted

You can select a single cell or an extended range. It's okay to include cells that contain text labels; Excel simply ignores them when it formats the numerical cells.

2 Pick a Format

In the **Formatting Palette**, open the **Number** section if it is not already open. Open the **Format** list and select the format you want to use. For example, if you want a dollars-and-cents format, select **Currency**.

The **Formatting Palette** also lets you change the number of decimal places if you want. If you made the choice in the **Format Cells** dialog box, you might have several other options, such whether to precede the figure with a currency symbol such as a dollar sign and the way you want to display negative numbers. To set these options, select your preferred display setting from the lists provided.

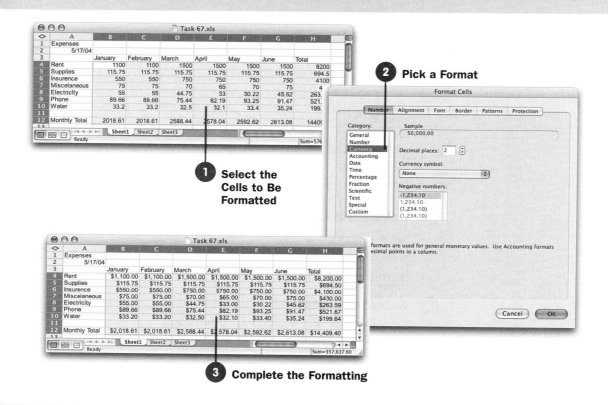

1 Select the Cells to Be Formatted

2 Pick a Format

3 Complete the Formatting

3 Complete the Formatting

If you make your formatting selections from the **Formatting Palette**, they take effect immediately. If you use the **Format Cells** dialog box, make your selections and click the **OK** button at the bottom of the dialog box.

The entries are displayed in the selected format. For example, if you chose the **Currency** format (as in the example) and made no other choices, the numbers are displayed with dollar signs, commas for thousands, and two decimal places.

67 Automatically Format a Worksheet

See Also

✔ **66** Format Numbers
Automatically

Chances are, you won't be fully satisfied with a plain-Jane words-and-numbers worksheet. Particularly if you're a Mac user, you probably want to jazz up your work a bit. But detailed formatting can be time-consuming, and you might not always have the time to consume.

There's an alternative. Excel's **AutoFormat** feature provides an assortment of predesigned formats you can quickly apply to give your worksheet some visual appeal.

1 Select the Cells to Be Formatted

Select the range you want to format. It can be the entire worksheet, but often you will want to limit the formatting to a particular table of data.

2 Select a Format

Select **Format**, **AutoFormat** from the menu. The **AutoFormat** dialog box opens with a list of available automatic formats. Click any item in the **Table format** list, and the **Sample** window displays an example of how the format will look.

Click the **Options** button to see additional choices. You can use this checklist to make selective use of particular elements of the packaged formats, such as selecting the fonts used by the format but omitting the horizontal or vertical rules.

3 Apply the Format

Make your selections from the **AutoFormat** dialog box and click **OK**. The chosen format is applied to the selected cells. Click outside the formatted area to remove the selection and see the formatted cells more clearly.

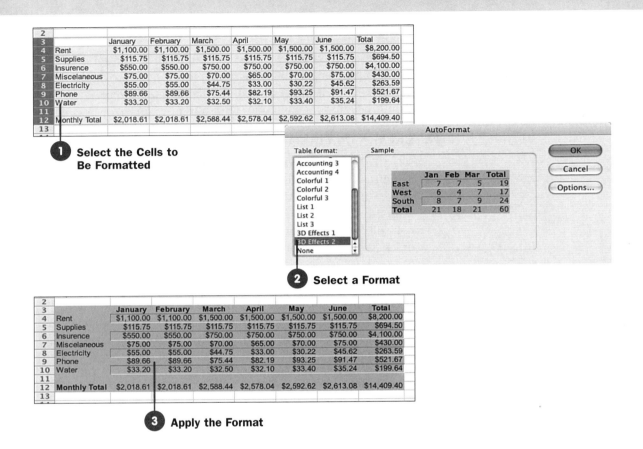

1 Select the Cells to Be Formatted

2 Select a Format

3 Apply the Format

68 Format Results Depending on Circumstances

Good information can sometimes hide in a busy worksheet. You might want to call attention to a good sales month, for example. Or, you might want to flag expenses that exceed normal limits.

You can use *conditional formatting* to emphasize results when—but only when—they fall outside the limits you set. You can use bold-faced type, different colors, borders, or backgrounds to ensure that exceptional or unexpected results get your attention.

Before You Begin

✔ **64** Make an Automatic Calculation

✔ **65** Make an Advanced Calculation

✔ **66** Format Numbers Automatically

See Also

→ **69** Build a Decision-Making Formula

KEY TERM

Conditional formatting—
Formatting applied to
emphasize specific data
only when it falls outside
certain limits.

 TIP

If the dialog box gets in the
way, click the arrow symbol
at the end of any condition
statement to collapse the
dialog box so that only the
condition is displayed. A
similar arrow restores the
dialog box.

① Select the Cells for Conditional Formatting

Suppose you have set up a worksheet that totals your monthly
household expenses. You want to flag those months where the
expenses exceeded your budget. In this example, I've selected the
monthly totals for conditional formatting.

② Set the Conditions

Select **Format, Conditional Formatting** from the menu. The
Conditional Formatting dialog box asks you to set the conditions
under which specific formatting will be applied. Make selections
from the drop-down lists or enter them in the text boxes. Usually,
you will enter an expression that says a particular value is greater
or less than a stated limit.

You can enter more than one condition. For example, you might
want to flag amounts that fall between $1,500 and $2,000. You could
start by entering the condition that the cell value is greater than
1500. Then click the **Add** button and state as a second condition that
the cell value is less than 2000. If you change your mind about entering a condition, the **Delete** button will accommodate you.

③ Set the Text Format

Click the **Format** button. The **Format Cells** dialog box opens.
Normally, it is set to display text-formatting options; if it is not
already displayed, click the **Font** tab to display the text-formatting
options.

Set the format to be applied when the condition is met. You can
boldface the entry, change its color, underline it, or apply a
strikethrough.

In the example of the household expenses, you might want to format the value in the monthly results cells in boldface when the
value exceeds your budget of $1,500.

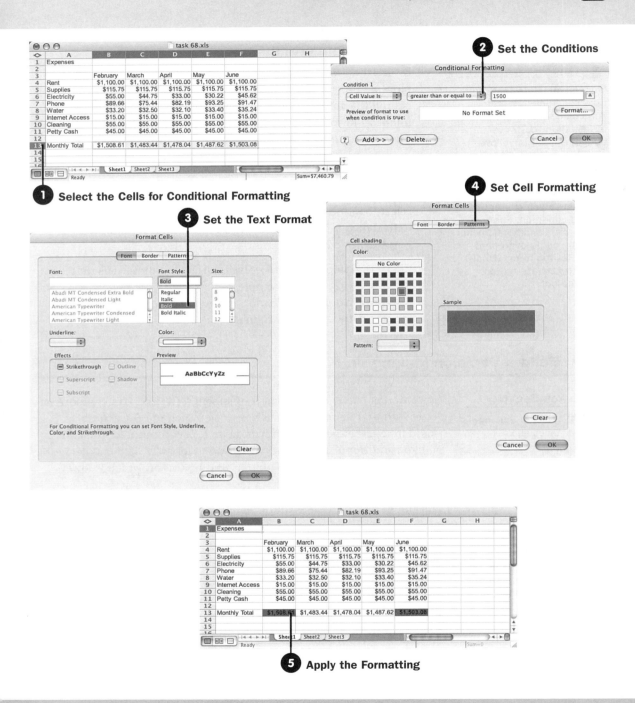

2 Set the Conditions

1 Select the Cells for Conditional Formatting

4 Set Cell Formatting

3 Set the Text Format

5 Apply the Formatting

You can stipulate that multiple conditions be met. You could state that items of less than $150 over budget appear in yellow and that greater differences appear in red. Click the **Add** button, and the **Format Cells** dialog box expands so you can enter a second condition. Enter even more conditions if you want. If you go overboard and enter too many conditions, the **Delete** button bails you out.

④ Set Cell Formatting

By selecting the tabs at the top of the dialog box, you also can place a border around the results cells or add a pattern or color behind the value that appears in those cells. In the example, you might want to highlight the results cell with a thin border and fill the cell with a blue background when the value in any of the results cells exceeds the budget of $1,500.

⑤ Apply the Formatting

Select the formats you want from the various tabs of the **Format Cells** dialog box; then click **OK**. You return to the **Conditional Formatting** dialog box.

Click **OK** again. The formatting is applied to those cells that meet the conditions. In the example, you exceeded the budget of $1,500 in February and June. The formatting calls attention to these months without any additional effort.

⑥⑨ Build a Decision-Making Formula

Before You Begin

✔ **64** Make an Automatic Calculation

See Also

→ **68** Format Results Depending on Circumstances

EY TERM

Conditional statement—A function that compares two values and returns one of two results depending on the comparison.

No computer can exercise human judgment, but Excel can compare one value with another and tell you how they match up. For example, would it be less expensive to buy or lease a new computer? You can build a *conditional statement* to suggest an answer. Such a statement compares the costs of the two options and reports on which is lower.

The data that goes into a conditional statement can be simple enough that the statement merely confirms the obvious. Alternatively, as a working professional, you might want to assess whether the income from a prospective assignment exceeds the costs and whether it does so by a large enough margin to make the project worthwhile.

① Prepare the Worksheet

Set up a worksheet that contains the terms you want to compare. Click the cell where you want to report the results of the comparison. That will be a yes-or-no response; either the project is feasible or it is not.

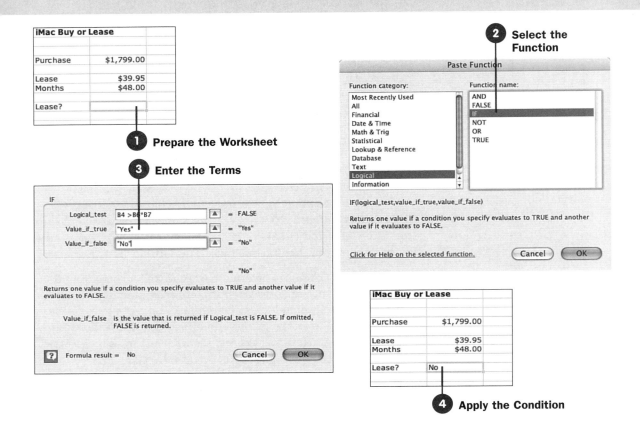

2 Select the
Function

1 Prepare the Worksheet

3 Enter the Terms

4 Apply the Condition

---

2 ## Select the Function

Select **Insert**, **Function** from the menu. In the **Paste Function** dialog box that opens, select the **Logical** category from the **Function category** list on the left. From the **Function name** list on the right, select a function from that group.

Click **OK**. A dialog box specific to the function you selected opens. These steps detail the **IF** function, but the dialog boxes for the other five function options work in a similar way.

NOTE

IF is the most commonly selected function for a conditional statement. Its logic is to evaluate a particular statement and then return one answer if the result is true and another if the result is false.

3 Enter the Terms

In the **Logical_test** box of the **IF** dialog box, enter the condition to be tested. This must be a statement that produces a true or false answer. Simple examples are **1 < 2** (true) and **2+2=5** (false). Of course, rather than simple values such as **1**, **2**, and **5**, you would reference cells in your worksheet.

Other functions also return true-or-false responses. The **NOT** function is the opposite of **IF**. Its oxymoronic response is to report true if the statement you entered is false, and vice versa. The **AND** and **OR** functions accept multiple arguments. **AND** reports true if *all* the arguments are true; **OR** reports true if *any* of the arguments are true. The **TRUE** and **FALSE** functions simply enter those words into the worksheet. You might as well just type **TRUE** or **FALSE** yourself.

Suppose that you want to determine whether the income from a job will exceed the expenses—and will do so by at least 15%. Your logical test, then, would look something like this: The total revenue is greater than the total expenses multiplied by 1.15. If the total revenue is calculated in cell **D4** and the total expenses is calculated in cell **G5**, your logical test would read **D4 > G5*1.15**.

NOTE

If you make no entries in the two **Value_if** boxes, the function reports either **TRUE** or **FALSE**.

In the **Value_if_true** box, enter the result you want to report if the condition statement is true. You might select to return a simple **Yes**, or you might want to report the phrase **Go for it**. In the **Value_if_false** box, enter the result you want to report if the condition statement is false: **No** or **No way**. If you want to return a textual answer, you must surround the word or phrase with double quotation marks, like this: **"No way"**.

4 Apply the Condition

Click **OK**. The function evaluates the statement and reports its answer. In this example, the object is to determine whether it made sense to purchase a computer outright or to lease it for a certain period of time. The logical test is simple: If the purchase price (contained in cell **C5**) is more than the monthly lease (in cell **C7**) multiplied by the number of months of the lease (in cell **C8**), it makes sense to lease; otherwise, purchasing the machine is more cost effective. The results displayed in the worksheet do not tell how much the lease would cost—the conditional statement just reports that leasing is not a good idea.

70 Convert Kilometers to Miles

The metric system might make great mathematical and technical sense, but to many Americans it remains an alien language. So, when you see a sign that reports it is 120 kilometers to a destination, you still might want to know how far that is in miles.

Excel has a **CONVERT** function that can give you answers like that. It can also make many other conversions such as Celsius to Fahrenheit, teaspoons to fluid ounces, and days to years. All you have to do is enter a value and identify the units you want to compare.

1 Select the Function

Select the worksheet cell where you want the results of the conversion to appear. Then select **Insert, Function** from the menu. Select the **Engineering** option from the **Function category** list box and select **CONVERT** from the **Function name** list box. Click **OK**. The CONVERT dialog box opens.

2 Enter the Criteria

In the **Number** box, enter the number you want to convert. You also can enter a cell reference.

In the **From_unit** box, enter the units from which you want to convert. You can use familiar abbreviations such as *km* for kilometers or *mi* for miles.

In the **To_unit** box, enter the units to which you want to convert the value.

3 Complete the Conversion

Click the **OK** button in the lower-right corner of the dialog box. The result appears in the selected cell of the worksheet. The state of Ohio was a pioneer in posting metric distances on its highway signs, so if you are leaving Columbus you might see a sign that says it is 120 kilometers to Dayton. Even if you know the conversion factor, it's hard to do in your head, so you can ask Excel to make the conversion for you.

Before You Begin

✔ **63** Enter a Formula
✔ **64** Make an Automatic Calculation

TIP

If the **Paste Function** dialog box does not display an **Engineering** category, you must install the optional **Analysis ToolPak**. Close the **Paste Function** dialog box by clicking **Cancel**. Then select **Tools, Add-Ins, Analysis ToolPak** and click **OK**. The extra functions are installed.

NOTE

There's no handy list of the units or their abbreviations, so you're reduced to trial and error. If you make a text entry, Excel automatically places quotation marks around it.

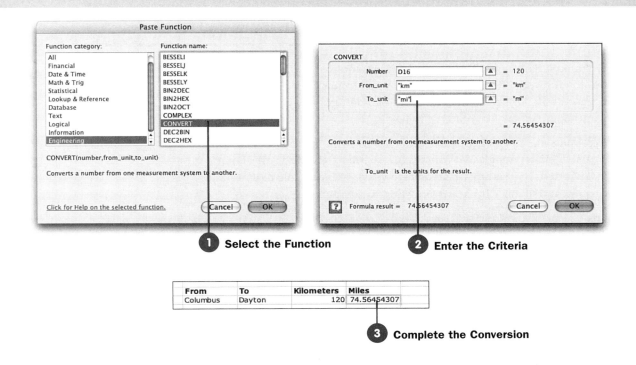

1 Select the Function

2 Enter the Criteria

From	To	Kilometers	Miles
Columbus	Dayton	120	74.56454307

3 Complete the Conversion

71 **Display the Page Layout**

See Also

→ **72** Set Up a Printed Page

→ **73** Print Only What You Need

→ **74** Print Multiple Pages on One Sheet

NOTE

Page Layout view is new to Office 2004 and is exclusive to the Mac, at least so far.

Excel has always had an uneasy relationship with standard office printers. Take a typical profit-and-loss worksheet that neatly totals and subtotals various categories of income and expenses. It might do a good job of projecting financial results into future years, but it does not always do a good job of fitting itself onto a sheet of paper 8 1/2 inches wide.

The new **Page Layout** view does not really solve that problem, but it makes printing easier to manage. Conventional Excel displays have used dotted lines to show where printed pages would divide, but **Page Layout** view shows the pages in better detail. This view also makes adding things such as headers and footers for multiple pages easier.

1 Display a Blank Document in Page Layout View

Open a blank document. By *default*, the worksheet opens in Excel 2004 in **Page Layout** view. To the right, you might see a grayed-out area labeled **Click to add data**. If you scroll down, you'll see similar areas below and to the right of the main page.

Page Layout view emphasizes only the area of a worksheet that appears on a printed page. If you go beyond this single page, you must click one of the additional pages.

2 Display an Active Worksheet in Normal View

Open or create a worksheet; then select **View**, **Normal**. This is the traditional Excel display. If the worksheet is larger than the printed page, dotted lines show where the page boundaries are.

In this example, the projections for Year 4 are beyond the page boundary and would be printed on a separate page. Rows that extend below the bottom of the current page are moved to separate pages as well.

3 Display a Worksheet in Page Layout View

Select **View**, **Page Layout**. The display shows page boundaries, indicating more clearly how the printed pages will look.

4 Edit the Header and Footer

This worksheet is already formatted with the sheet title at the top of the page and a page number at the bottom. You might want to edit this text or add new elements to the header or footer.

For example, you could add the date in the upper-left corner of each page (in the header area). The header and footer areas are each divided into three segments: left, center, and right. Double-click any of these segments to add to or edit its contents.

To add the date at the upper left, double-click that segment. The segment opens for editing, and the **Header and Footer** toolbar opens. Click the **Insert Date** button. A code to display the current date is inserted into the segment.

KEY TERM

Default—A setting that remains in place unless you do something to change it. This term sometimes intimidates newcomers because it suggests some kind of negligence. That's not the case here.

TIP

You might want to readjust this particular worksheet so everything falls on a single page. In this instance, selecting the data and specifying a slightly smaller type size probably would do it. **Page Layout** view just shows you the pages; it's up to you to make any necessary corrections.

NOTE

The same header and footer options are also available through the **Page Setup** dialog box. The **Page Layout** view simplifies the process of editing the headers and footers by making them more directly accessible.

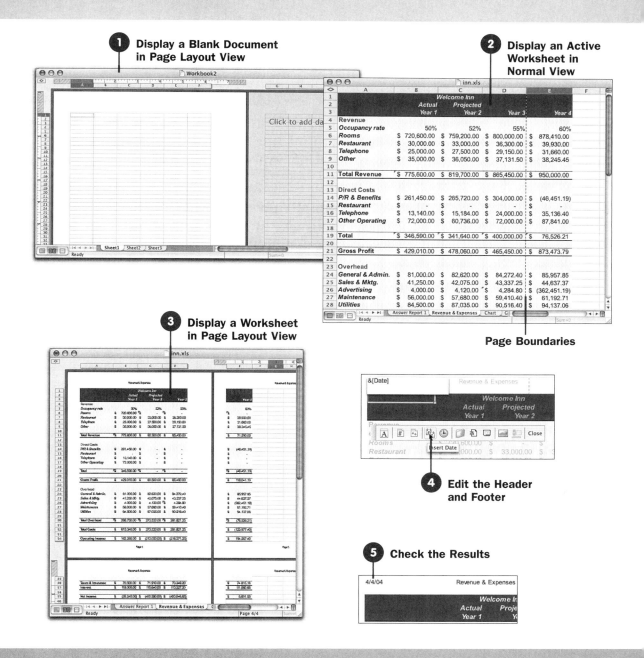

1 Display a Blank Document in Page Layout View

2 Display an Active Worksheet in Normal View

Page Boundaries

3 Display a Worksheet in Page Layout View

4 Edit the Header and Footer

5 Check the Results

5 **Check the Results**

Click the **Close** button on the **Header and Footer** toolbar. The toolbar closes, and the date is displayed in the worksheet.

72 Set Up a Printed Page

In one sense, it's easy to print from Excel. Just select **File**, **Print** from the menu and let 'er rip. But the results of such an action are only semipredictable. It's not uncommon to print a sheet in which a few columns don't fit on the first page and are shunted off to a page of their own.

Scotch tape is one answer, but there is a better one. You can improve the organization of your printed work if you take some care to set up the printed page. One option is to adjust the page boundaries so everything that should be together on one page actually is.

See Also

→ **73** Print Only What You Need

→ **74** Print Multiple Pages on One Sheet

1 **Display the Page Breaks**

To display the existing page breaks (that is, where Excel plans to break the worksheet when it prints to the currently selected paper size in the currently selected printer), select **View**, **Page Break Preview** from the menu. The worksheet shows dotted lines where the page breaks will be.

2 **Adjust the Page Breaks**

Drag these dotted lines to make the page breaks fall where you prefer. In this example, the page break originally fell between the **Year 3** and **Year 4** results columns. If you want all four years to appear on the same page, drag the dotted line to the right of the **Year 4** column (you can't see the dotted line in this position because it coincides with the end-of-worksheet border).

3 **Check the Results**

Select **File**, **Print Preview**. The layout of the printed page is displayed. Check to ensure that all the information you were expecting to see on the page is indeed included. If it is not, click the **Close** button on the **Print Preview** window to return to the pagebreak view of your worksheet and drag the dotted lines again.

TIP

If you see a dialog box titled **Welcome to Page Break Preview**, it just means the program has identified you as a firsttime user of this feature. Click **OK**.

NOTE

There's one possible drawback to the process of forcing additional information on the page. If you ask Excel to fit added material on the page, it accommodates you by reducing the type size. The tradeoff for a well-organized page might be type that is hard to read.

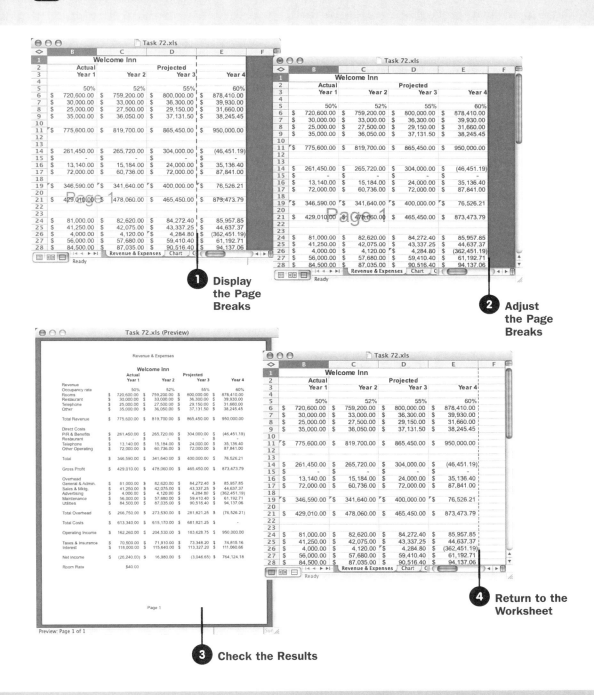

1 Display
the Page
Breaks

2 Adjust
the Page
Breaks

4 Return to the
Worksheet

3 Check the Results

Don't worry if the preview shows rows of # symbols in place of more meaningful contents. These symbols are used as placeholders for the actual cell contents. When you print, the printed page includes all the correct numbers.

4 Return to the Worksheet

Click the **Close** button in the upper-right corner of the window to close the **Print Preview** window and return to the page-break view of your worksheet. To return to the normal worksheet view, select **View**, **Normal** from the menu.

73 Print Only What You Need

When planning an Excel print job, you might want to ask, "Do I really need to print the whole thing?"

Often, you don't. Depending on the intended audience, printing a key section of a workbook without printing long sheets full of supporting data might be sufficient.

You can select a range of cells and define them as a *print area*. Then you can print just the print area so that only the information you want to include is sent to the printer.

1 Define the Range

Select the cells you want to print. The cells don't necessarily have to be adjacent.

2 Set the Print Area

Select **File**, **Print Area**, **Set Print Area** from the menu. Page boundaries are formed so that the area you select becomes a page in its own right.

3 Check the Results

Select **File**, **Print Preview** from the menu. The preview shows that only the area you selected will be printed on the page. If there is more than one page, press **Page Down** to see subsequent pages. If you are satisfied, close the preview and select **File**, **Print**.

Before You Begin

✔ **72** Set Up a Printed Page

See Also

→ **71** Display the Page Layout

→ **74** Print Multiple Pages on One Sheet

KEY TERM

Print area—A range of spreadsheet cells selected to appear alone on a printed page.

NOTE

To select nonadjacent ranges, press and hold the **Ctrl** key while making the selections. When you designate them as print areas, each selection becomes a separate page.

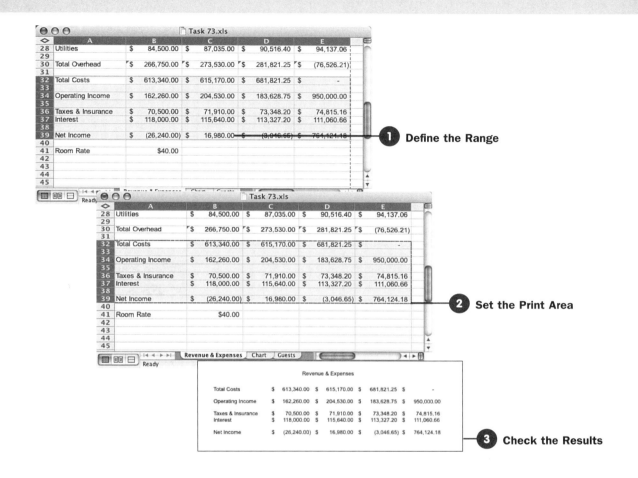

1 Define the Range

2 Set the Print Area

3 Check the Results

74 Print Multiple Pages on One Sheet

74 **Print Multiple Pages on One Sheet**

See Also

→ **71** Display the Page Layout

→ **72** Set Up a Printed Page

→ **73** Print Only What You Need

Sometimes the page layout that makes sense onscreen does not work out as well on paper. The best onscreen design often is one that compartmentalizes material into compact groups. These might be on different worksheets, or you might have decided to print only selected parts of a worksheet. In either case, Excel normally prints these selections on separate pages. In that case, though, you might find yourself printing several sheets with small amounts of information and large blank areas.

In such a case, you can print several "pages" on a single sheet, dividing them with borders if you like.

① Display the Layout Options

Select **File**, **Print** from the menu. When the **Print** dialog box opens, open the drop-down list that initially reads **Copies and Pages** and instead select **Layout**.

The dialog box changes to display multipage layout options.

② Select the Number of Pages

From the **Pages per Sheet** list, select the number of pages you want to print on one sheet. You can choose as many as 16. Your choice can be governed by the number of small ranges you want to print on one sheet. Remember, though, that readability will suffer if you select more than 4 pages.

The chosen number of pages is reflected in the preview box on the left side of the dialog box. The layout preview shows the order in which the pages will be printed on the sheet.

③ Select a Layout Direction

From the group of **Layout Direction** thumbnails in the middle of the dialog box, click the thumbnail that represents the direction in which you want the pages to go on the sheet.

④ Select a Border

If you want to display a border around each page, select a border style from the **Border** drop-down list.

⑤ Print the Document

Click the **Print** button at the bottom of the dialog box to send your work to the currently selected printer.

NOTE

This dialog box is generated by the printer driver, so what you see might vary from what's shown here, depending on the printer you use. For most printers, though, the **Print** dialog box works about the same as described here.

TIP

You can choose to have consecutive pages go down in columns or across in rows. You also can choose to have them go backward in either direction.

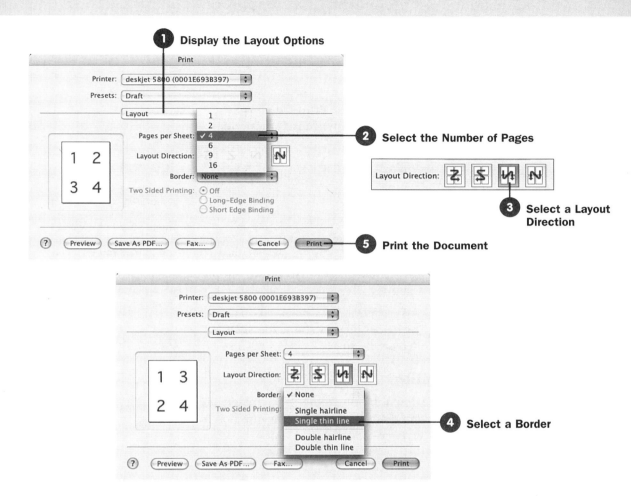

1 Display the Layout Options

2 Select the Number of Pages

3 Select a Layout Direction

4 Select a Border

5 Print the Document

12

Charting Data

IN THIS CHAPTER:

Legend to the contrary, it takes a really good picture to be worth a thousand words. Few, if any, Excel graphics ever rise to that level.

Nevertheless, it would be hard to overestimate the value of visual communication, particularly when the subject matter is as dense as some Excel projects tend to be. A well-executed *chart*—Excel's name for a graph—can summarize long columns of numbers into an easy-to-grasp illustration.

Mac users are known for their artistic temperaments. If you share that quality, you might find this number-crunching application surprisingly accommodating. You can choose from a variety of charts—from the common bar, line, and pie charts to custom designs that include one called **Outdoor Bars**. Each basic chart offers several variations such as 3D effects. Then you can embellish the chart with a choice of colors, typographic effects, and other artistic variations.

And if all of the above fails to satisfy, you can go even further and design a chart type uniquely your own. Those advanced excursions, though, are not usually the sort of thing you can do *In a Snap*.

75 Plot a Chart

See Also

→ **76** Format the Text in a Chart
→ **78** Add Color and Texture

The key to an effective chart is to pick the type of chart that best illustrates your data. For example, bar and column charts are good for comparing two sets of data. A line chart shows progress over time, and a pie chart is the traditional way to illustrate portions of a whole.

Excel has a **Chart Wizard** that can guide you through the process of selecting a chart type and applying other effects.

1 Start the Chart Wizard

Start by selecting the range of worksheet cells that contain the data you want to chart. Select **Insert**, **Chart** from the menu. The **Chart Wizard** opens to **Step 1 of 4**.

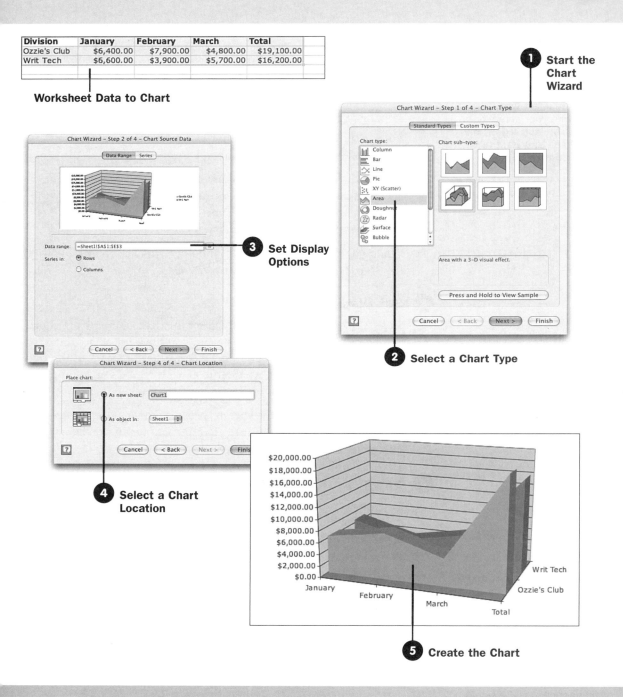

Division	January	February	March	Total
Ozzie's Club	$6,400.00	$7,900.00	$4,800.00	$19,100.00
Writ Tech	$6,600.00	$3,900.00	$5,700.00	$16,200.00

Worksheet Data to Chart

1 Start the Chart Wizard

3 Set Display Options

2 Select a Chart Type

4 Select a Chart Location

5 Create the Chart

TIP

If you want to see how the selected chart type will look with your actual data, follow the instructions on the **Press and Hold to View Sample** button.

2 Select a Chart Type

The wizard presents a list of available chart types. From the **Chart type** list in the left column, select the type that seems most appropriate to your data. A variety of subtypes appears on the right side of the dialog box. The **Chart sub-type** list usually includes variations such as stacked and 3D charts. Initially, a basic chart is selected. If you prefer, click a subtype to select it.

If none of the standard chart types does exactly what you want, click the **Custom Types** tab to see an expanded variety with variations such as glass or metallic surfaces. If you have seriously modified an existing chart, you can add it to the custom types list.

When you've selected the basic kind of chart, click **Next** to go to the **Step 2 of 4** page of the **Chart Wizard**.

3 Set Display Options

Steps 2 and 3 of the wizard let you set the details of how the chart will be displayed. If, for some reason, you have not selected the correct data range, you can make a correction in Step 2 of the wizard. You can also decide whether to chart the labels of columns (in this case the months) or rows (the business units).

On the **Step 3** page of the wizard, you can add a chart title and axis labels. Unless you want to change these items, you can skip past these two steps by clicking **Next** twice.

4 Select a Chart Location

The options on the **Step 4** page of the **Chart Wizard** let you choose whether to display the new chart on a separate new worksheet or to include it on an existing page in the workbook. In either case, you can select or enter the name of the sheet where you want the chart to appear.

TIP

After you have generated a chart, the **Formatting Palette** transforms itself to display formatting options for the chart. Click any element of the chart—text, the background, or one of the chart elements—and the palette displays formatting options for the selected item.

5 Create the Chart

Click **Finish** to close the wizard and complete the chart. The completed chart is displayed.

76 Format the Text in a Chart

Although a *chart* may be a visual medium, it often is not complete without text. A typical chart uses text in a title, to label the values of each axis, and in a legend that explains what the chart elements are.

The **Chart Wizard** lets you add, omit, or vary some of these labels when you generate the chart. Nevertheless, later, you might want to upgrade the text display to make it more readable and to explain the chart better.

You can change the text in any chart area by selecting the text, then applying a new typeface, type style, or other enhancements.

1 Select the Text to Be Reformatted

Click the text you want to modify. You select all the text of that type. For example, if you want to enlarge the text on one chart axis, click any of that text. The entire axis is selected.

Small boxes identify the edges of the selected area.

2 Open the Formatting Options

There are several ways to open the chart-formatting options. One requires no action of your own: When you select the text, the **Formatting Palette** displays options for reformatting it.

You can double-click or **Ctrl**-click the text, and then select the **Format Axis** option from the context menu that appears. Either action opens the **Format Axis** dialog box. Click the **Font** tab to see the text-formatting options.

3 Select a New Format

In either the **Formatting Palette** or the **Format Axis** dialog box, select a new typeface from the **Font** list, a style from the **Font Style** list, a type size from the **Size** list, or a text color from the **Color** drop-down list. If you have selected numbered labels, you also can format them as you would worksheet entries by adding dollar signs or adjusting decimal places.

You can make other formatting changes as well, such as choosing single or double underlining from the **Underline** drop-down list and specifying either a transparent or opaque background.

Before You Begin

✔ **75** Plot a Chart

See Also

→ **66** Format Numbers Automatically

→ **77** Compress Large Numbers

NOTE

Sometimes the boxes that identify the edges of the selected area are really small boxes, so check carefully. In the illustration for this step, the two names on the right side of the graph are selected.

NOTE

The **Format Axis** selections appear only if you are formatting axis labels. If you are formatting a title or a legend, the menu item and dialog box labels read **Format Title** or **Format Legend**.

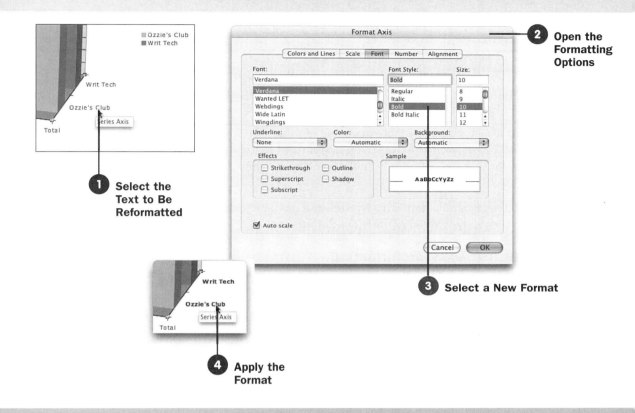

2 Open the Formatting Options

1 Select the Text to Be Reformatted

3 Select a New Format

4 Apply the Format

4 **Apply the Format**

Press **Return** or click **OK** to close the **Format Axis** dialog box. The labels you selected in step 1 appear with the new formatting.

---

77 Compress Large Numbers

Before You Begin

✔ **75** Plot a Chart

See Also

→ **79** Annotate a Chart

→ **78** Add Color and Texture

A well-designed chart often can help readers make sense of numbers and gain insight into data that might otherwise be obscured in a detailed worksheet. Sometimes, though, the charts themselves can be confusing—particularly when the display units along their axes are unclear. This is most likely to happen when the values in an axis extend over a wide range of large numbers, say 1 million–50 million.

In that case, the ability to change the display units can help make things clearer. You could display the numbers 1–50 along with a legend that explains that the values are in millions.

1 Generate or Display the Chart

Create a chart using the values in your worksheet (see **75** Plot a Chart), or display the portion of the worksheet containing the chart if you've already created it.

2 Simplify a Numerical Axis

Double-click the axis you want to change. The **Format Axis** dialog box opens. Click the **Scale** tab to view the formatting options for scaling numeric entries.

For example, you might have a list of salaries that vary from $30,000 to $90,000. Normally, a graph generated from this list might show values from 0 to 100,000, with all the results grouped in the upper two-thirds of that scale. If you set the **Minimum** value at $20,000, the values would be more evenly distributed and probably easier to read.

You also can select the **Major unit** and **Minor unit** values to be displayed—those that are listed next to the longer and shorter tick marks along the axis. For example, in the salary range, each $10,000 would be a major unit and display a longer tick mark. Each $5,000 might be a minor unit with a shorter tick mark.

The **Display units** section offers a particularly good opportunity to simplify a scale. Open the drop-down list and select a unit such as **Hundreds** or **Thousands**. Make sure that the **Show display units** check box is enabled. This way, values of 25,000 or 50,000 will be displayed as **25** and **50** with a legend pointing out that the measurements are in thousands.

3 Simplify a Text Axis

A chart often displays numbers on one axis and text labels on another. When you double-click a text axis, the **Scale** tab of the **Format Axis** dialog box displays a different set of options.

 NOTE

A chart might have problems such as an axis on which the numbers are hard to read or a scale that's large enough that some labels are skipped. This might happen if one axis displays the months of the year. If they are spread over too narrow a space, only every third month might be displayed.

TIP

You can also click the **Number** tab to change the style of the numbers, such as by reducing the number of decimal places or removing dollar signs.

TIP

A key option when adjusting the scale of labels on a text axis is **Number of categories between tick mark labels**. If this item is set at any number greater than **1**, only some of the labels appear in the chart. This would have the same effect as the compressed scale described earlier. This might not be important if you are charting a recognizable series such as months or a 1-2-3 sequence. If each tick represents the results for an individual, though, it's important to include all the names.

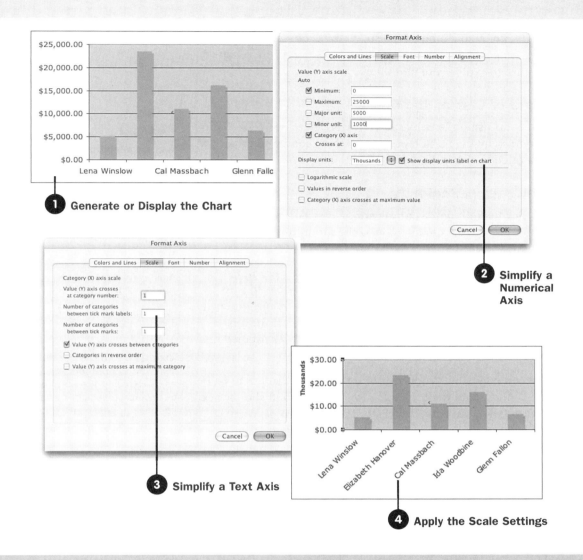

① Generate or Display the Chart

② Simplify a Numerical Axis

③ Simplify a Text Axis

④ Apply the Scale Settings

④ Apply the Scale Settings

Click **OK** to close the **Format Axis** dialog box. The chart displays the changes you made to the scale of the axis labels.

78 Add Color and Texture

In the early days of the World Wide Web—actually, just a few years ago—it was important to use so-called Web-safe colors. These are colors that browsers and graphics cards could reproduce even if their capacity was limited. The result was a collection of 216 colors that could be reproduced easily using a limited range of numeric values.

The problem with Web-safe colors is that the colors were selected for mathematical, not aesthetic, reasons. Serious designers looked at the limited color palette and cringed. Fortunately, higher-capacity computer systems provide more options and mean Web-safe colors are no longer a necessity.

Nevertheless, Excel's stock charting colors have a certain Web-safe aura. They look like they were chosen on a rainy day in Seattle (which may well have been the case). Microsoft says the colors chosen for Excel 2004 are brighter than before, but your design sense still might dictate whether different colors would look better.

You can do something about that. You can select any element of a chart—one set of bars in a bar chart, for example—and not only change its color, but give it some texture and other graphic snap.

1 Select a Data Series

An Excel chart shows one or more *data series*. For example, in a graph that shows different classes of office expenses, each expense category would be a data series. Rent would be one series, office supplies another, and so on. In a column or bar graph, each data series is represented by a different color.

Hover the mouse pointer over a chart element and see a description of the series it represents. For example, if you point to a graph element that represents office supplies, a label displays the description in the form **Series Office Supplies, Value $550**.

The first step in brightening a chart is to select a data series so you can change its color and appearance. Click a chart element that represents the series you want to change, such as one of the bars that represents outlays for rent.

Before You Begin

✔ **75** Plot a Chart

See Also

→ **76** Format the Text in a Chart

→ **77** Compress Large Numbers

KEY TERM

Data series—Chart elements that show related data such as one person's performance or an expense category.

 TIP

If the **Formatting Palette** is displayed, the **Format** section includes a drop-down list of chart elements you can reformat. Open the list and make a selection from there to select a data series.

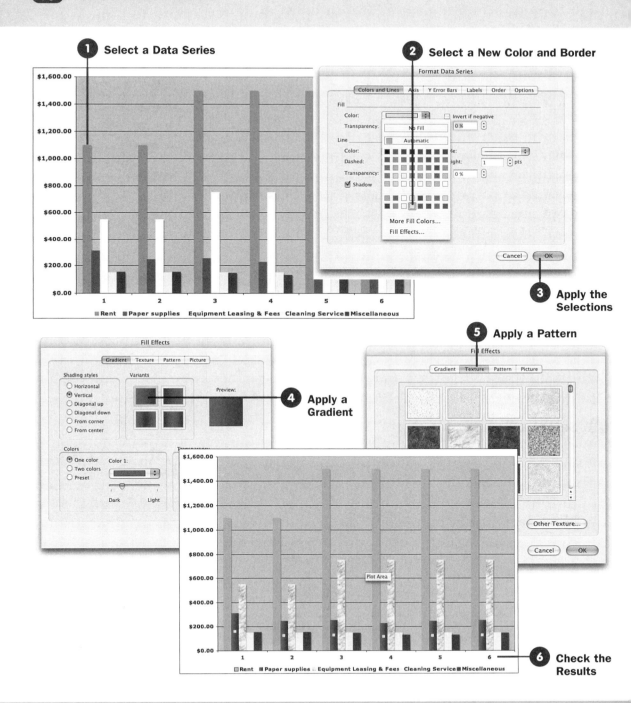

① Select a Data Series

② Select a New Color and Border

Format Data Series

Colors and Lines | Axis | Y Error Bars | Labels | Order | Options

Fill

Color:

Transparency: No Fill

Invert if negative

Line Automatic

Color:

Dashed:

Transparency:

☑ Shadow

More Fill Colors...

Fill Effects...

Cancel | OK

③ Apply the Selections

Rent | Paper supplies | Equipment Leasing & Fees | Cleaning Service | Miscellaneous

⑤ Apply a Pattern

Fill Effects

Gradient | Texture | Pattern | Picture

Fill Effects

Gradient | Texture | Pattern | Picture

Shading styles

○ Horizontal
◉ Vertical
○ Diagonal up
○ Diagonal down
○ From corner
○ From center

Variants

Preview:

④ Apply a Gradient

Colors

◉ One color
○ Two colors
○ Preset

Color 1:

Dark   Light

Other Texture...

Cancel | OK

Plot Area

Rent | Paper supplies | Equipment Leasing & Fees | Cleaning Service | Miscellaneous

⑥ Check the Results

2 Select a New Color and Border

Select **Format, Selected Data Series** from the menu. The **Format Data Series** dialog box opens. Click the **Colors and Lines** tab if it is not already selected. The **Colors and Lines** page presents options for applying new colors, borders, and fill effects to a data series. Although you clicked only one bar in the bar chart, for example, *all* the bars in that series are affected with the modifications you make here. (In the example shown, all six of the tallest Rent bars are affected.)

In the **Line** section, select any effects you want to apply to the borders of the selected data series. For example, if you want to apply a drop shadow to the bars for the selected data series in your bar chart, enable the **Shadow** check box. You also can set the weight and style of the border lines by choosing from the drop-down lists.

Open the **Color** drop-down list and select a more pleasing color for the data series. For example, you might want to use a lighter shade of blue for the **Rent** data series in the sample chart.

3 Apply the Selections

Click **OK** to close the **Format Data Series** dialog box. The changes are applied to the data series you selected in step 1. Click outside the selection to cancel the selection and see the full effect.

4 Apply a Gradient

Select another data series (such as the **Equipment & leasing fees** bar in the sample chart) and select **Format, Selected Data Series** to open the **Format Data Series** dialog box again.

Select a new color and border effect, as explained in step 2, if you want. Then open the **Color** drop-down list and select **Fill Effects** to open the **Fill Effects** dialog box. Tabs across the top of the **Fill Effects** dialog box let you apply *gradients*, patterns, and other effects to the selected data series.

Click the **Gradient** tab if it is not already selected. The **Gradient** page offers a host of ways to apply gradient effects. You can vary the direction of the gradient by selecting one of the **Shading styles** options, selecting a **Variant** of that style, selecting one or more colors from the **Colors** area, using the slider to specify whether that

KEY TERM

Gradient—A block of color that varies from one shade or color to another.

TIP

A gradient works best when you have selected a bright color before you apply the gradient options.

TIP

In a bar graph, the most effective gradient goes opposite the bar's length. For a vertical bar, select a **Horizontal** gradient and vice versa.

color is dark or light, and using the **Transparency** sliders to combine the shades and colors.

The **Gradient** page of the **Fill Effects** dialog box is ripe with experimental possibilities. Try different settings and check the **Preview** window to see what you've done.

When you are satisfied with your choices, click **OK** to apply the gradient you've created to the selected data series.

⑤ Apply a Pattern

Select another data series (such as the **Paper supplies** bar in the sample chart) and select **Format, Selected Data Series**. When the **Format Data Series** dialog box opens, you can again select a border effect. Don't worry about choosing a new color. When you select a pattern, it overrides any color selection you might have made. Then click the **Fill Effects** button. When the **Fill Effects** dialog box opens, click the **Texture** tab.

The **Texture** page displays a group of texture effects from which you can select. Select one; then click **OK** to close the **Fill Effects** dialog box.

⑥ Check the Results

In the **Format Data Series** dialog box, click **OK** again to apply the texture to the selected data series. The chart displays the effects of your changes. In the sample shown, you can see that the color of the Rent bars was changed, a gradient was applied to the **Equipment & leasing fees** bars, and a texture was applied to the **Paper supplies** bars. For all three of these bars, I also enabled the **Shadow** check box on the **Patterns** tab of the **Format Data Series** dialog box to provide a drop shadow for each bar.

79 Annotate a Chart

A chart can have a great visual impact, but there is one important condition: People must understand what they're seeing. Without explanation, a viewer might not know whether a chart plots monthly sales performance or caribou migrations in the Arctic. That's why a chart usually requires *annotations*.

Excel offers several ways to annotate charts, all of which are available in the **Chart Options** dialog box:

- **Titles**—These are for the chart and for each axis.

- **Legend**—This is a free-standing text box that explains what the colors in the chart are supposed to mean.

- **Data labels**—These show the specific value for each chart element.

- **Data chart**—This is a text box included in the chart to show the data on which the chart is based.

1 Select the Chart

Open the chart and click its background area. Black adjustment handles around the border indicate that the entire chart is selected.

Be sure to select the entire chart, not one of its components. If the chart is selected, the adjustment handles appear around the entire chart. If you click a component by mistake, the handles appear around only the selected component.

2 Add Titles

In the main menu, select **Chart**, **Chart Options**. The **Chart Options** dialog box displays a selection of options, including the annotation features.

Click the **Titles** tab if that page is not already selected. Text boxes on this page let you give titles to the chart and each axis.

Type the titles you want to use in the appropriate text boxes. A sample of the results appears in the preview window.

Before You Begin

✔ **75** Plot a Chart

See Also

→ **76** Format the Text in a Chart

→ **78** Add Color and Texture

KEY TERM

Annotation—In an Excel chart, titles, legends, and other additional information that helps explain the chart.

NOTE

If you are generating a new chart, these options are also available as you progress through the **Chart Wizard**. Many are also available in the **Formatting Palette**.

NOTE

The x-axis is the horizontal axis. It typically contains category information such as expense items, months, or individual names. The y-axis is the vertical axis and typically contains amounts or other numerical values.

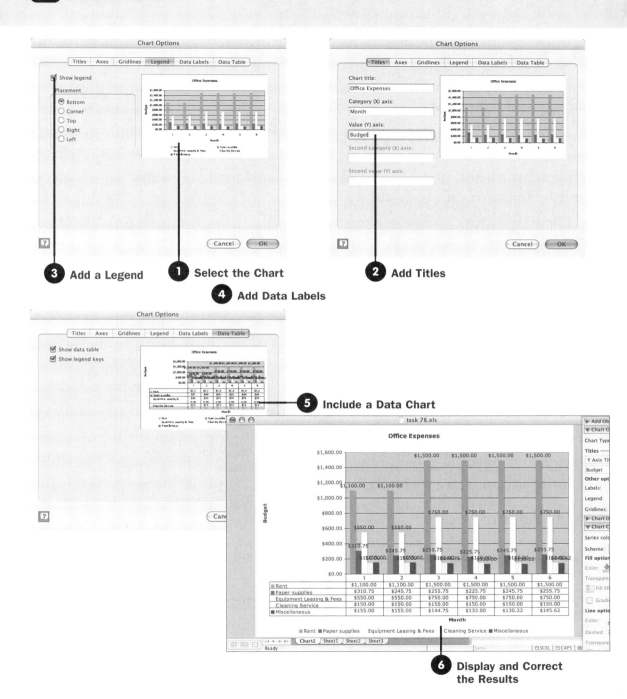

3 Add a Legend

1 Select the Chart

2 Add Titles

4 Add Data Labels

5 Include a Data Chart

6 Display and Correct the Results

3 Add a Legend

Click the **Legend** tab. On this page, you can opt to display a legend in the chart and, if so, select its placement.

A legend explains the bars, lines, and other colored elements of the chart. To include a legend in your chart, enable the **Show legend** check box and then select its placement from the five **Placement** options.

4 Add Data Labels

Click the **Data Labels** tab. This page lets you apply labels to each element of the chart.

A chart might show a wide range of values—perhaps from 0 to 50,000. Bars, lines, or pie slices in such a chart show approximate values at best. Data labels display the specific values of each item. Depending on the type of chart you're working with, you might be able to display other values instead. In a bar chart, you have the alternative of applying the same labels that appear on the y-axis. If you enable the **Legend key next to label** check box, the labels include color codes similar to those in the legend.

To add data labels, select the **Show value** option or the any alternative option you want to use.

5 Include a Data Chart

Click the **Data Chart** tab. A *data chart* is a copy of the data on which the chart is based. Because the chart is based on data in the worksheet, there might seem to be little reason to include a data chart in the chart as well.

But consider this: You might not want to distribute the rest of the worksheet along with the chart. The worksheet might be too complex for a brief presentation, or it might contain confidential information. If you include only the data used to create the chart, readers can see the underlying figures without perusing the entire worksheet.

Enable the **Show data table** check box to do just that. If you also enable the **Show legend keys** check box, the labels in the data table are color-coded in the same style as they are in the legend.

 NOTE

You can't select types of values that don't fit the type of data you are charting. For example, if you are working with text labels, Excel does not let you attempt to compute percentages, so those options are grayed out and you can't select them.

⑥ Display and Correct the Results

Click **OK** to close the **Chart Options** dialog box. The upgraded chart is displayed.

There's an excellent chance you won't like it. Additions such as the titles, legend, and data table leave less room for the chart itself. You might find that the graphics have been scrunched beyond legibility. Also, the data labels might be the wrong size or overlap each other.

The quickest solution is to click the background of the chart to select the entire chart and use the adjustment handles to increase its height, width, or both. Everything within the chart, both text and graphics, adjusts to a new scale.

You can adjust the data labels or any other text by selecting the text and then selecting **Format**, **Selected Data Labels**. In the dialog box that opens, click the **Font** tab and change the typeface and size of the selected text (see ⑦⑥ **Format the Text in a Chart**).

⑧⓪ Track Multiple Tasks

Before You Begin

✔ ⑦⑤ Plot a Chart

See Also

→ ⑦⑥ Format the Text in a Chart

→ ⑦⑧ Add Color and Texture

Life is not a single project; it is a succession of smaller projects that start and stop on an irregular schedule. You often must complete one before you can begin another.

Even on a smaller scale, an individual project can consist of multiple interlinked activities. Suppose that you have volunteered to produce a neighborhood newsletter. You find it is not just one job but several. You must cajole association officers and other contributors to get their submissions in on time. You must edit the text, lay out pages, and then see to printing and distribution.

Were this a commercial publishing venture, the publisher might use a specialized project management program. Such programs can track the progress of a multitask project, showing the starting and completion dates of each task and tracking the progress of each step. The program displays this information in a type of bar chart called a *Gantt chart*.

If yours is a typical newsletter, your budget will probably just about cover a trip to a quick-print shop. Project management software is well outside the realm of financial possibility. But you can customize a

stacked bar graph in Excel to emulate a Gantt chart. As tasks within the project are partly or fully completed, you can note the progress in a worksheet. As you do so, the chart is updated to display your current progress.

❶ Start with a Worksheet

Start by outlining the project schedule on a worksheet. Enter each task—for the newsletter example, the tasks include writing, layout, printing, and so on—in its own row. Enter the task name in column **A**. Enter the starting date in column **B**. Use the **Format**, **Cells** command to format the cells in column **B** as dates.

Column **C** holds the number of days of work completed so far. Leave it blank for now; as the work is completed, you can update this entry. Column **D** holds a formula that keeps track of the number of days of work remaining before the deadline for each task (the deadline date minus the starting date minus the number of days of work already completed). Enter the deadline dates in column **E**. Again, format the cells in column **E** as dates.

If you subtract the starting date from the completion date, you get the total number of days' work in the task. If you then subtract the number of days completed, you get the number of days remaining. In cell **D2**, the formula to do this is **=E2-B2-C2**. You then can copy this formula to the remaining cells in column **D** to make the same calculations for the other tasks.

❷ Set Up the Chart

Select the entries to be charted. In this case, that would be cells **A2:D6**. If you have entered completion dates in column **E**, do not select them. They are not needed for the chart and, if included, would just mess things up. Also do not select any column headings you might have provided.

Select **Insert**, **Chart** from the menu. The **Chart Wizard** asks you to select a chart type. From the **Chart type** list, select **Bar**. In the **Chart sub-type** collection, select **Stacked Bar**. The name of the selected subtype is displayed near the bottom of the dialog box.

Click **Next** twice until you reach the **Step 3** page of the wizard. Open the **Legend** tab and make sure that the **Show Legend** option is selected. Then select a **Bottom** position.

NOTE

Selecting the right starting and completion dates is critical to the project management process. Some dates depend on others. For example, you can start editing material before all of it is submitted. But you can't send the newsletter to the printer before all the preceding tasks are completed, and you obviously cannot distribute the newsletter until it has been printed.

TIP

To copy a formula, select the cell that contains it. Then drag over this cell and the destination cells to select them as a group. When you release the mouse button, the formulas are copied and their results displayed.

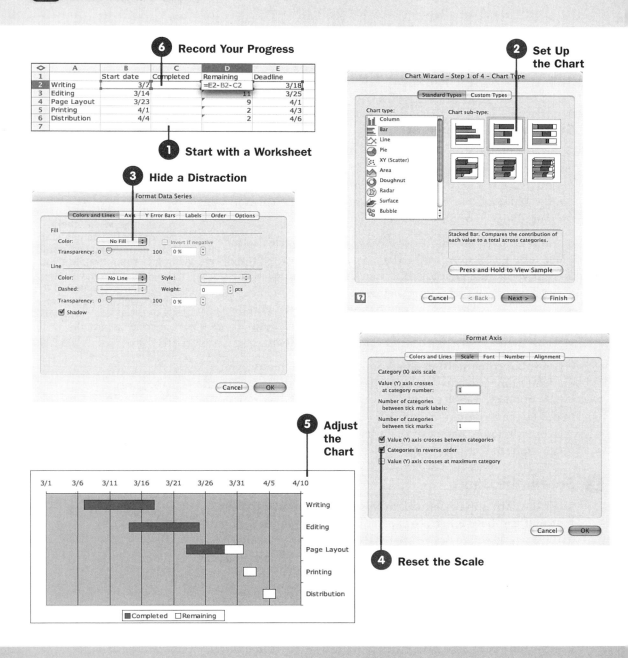

6 **Record Your Progress**

2 Set Up the Chart

1 Start with a Worksheet

3 Hide a Distraction

5 Adjust the Chart

4 Reset the Scale

Click the **Finish** button, skipping the final step. A primitive version of the chart appears on the worksheet, but it probably still needs some work.

3 Hide a Distraction

Locate the **Start Date** data series in the chart. This is the first series in each bar; unless you have changed the color, it is the set of blue bars. These bars chart the starting date entries. A true Gantt chart does not trace these entries, so you can make them disappear.

Double-click the **Start Date** data series in the chart. The **Format Data Series** dialog box opens. Click the **Colors and Lines** tab if it is not already selected. In both the **Fill** and **Line** sections, select **No Fill** or **No Line** and click **OK**. The start data bars are now invisible, just as they would be in a real Gantt chart.

4 Reset the Scale

If you want this chart to look realistic, you must reset the position and direction of the x- and y-axes.

Double-click the vertical axis in the chart, the one with the task names. When the **Format Axis** dialog box opens, click the **Scale** tab. Enable the **Categories in reverse order** check box and click **OK**. The tasks now appear from top to bottom in order of their starting dates. The horizontal axis is now located above the chart.

Back in the chart, double-click the horizontal axis (the dates across the top of the chart) to reopen the **Format Axis** dialog box for the horizontal axis. Enable the **Value (X) axis crosses between categories** check box and click **OK** to place the category labels on the right side of the chart.

The **Minimum** and **Maximum** numbers in the **Format Axis** dialog box represent the beginning and ending dates of the chart; they are a little earlier and a little later than the project dates in the worksheet. The dates are expressed as *serial numbers*. Add 1 to the serial number, and you add one day to the date.

In this case, when you hid the starting dates, you concealed the results for 11 days. You can improve the display of the finished chart by starting the sequence 10 days later than the program originally suggests. To do this, increase the number in the **Minimum** box by **10**.

 NOTE

A Gantt chart has a very specific format that differs from the charts Excel normally produces. You can customize the Excel chart, though, to produce a good simulation of a Gantt chart.

NOTE

Although Excel normally displays dates in a fashion familiar to us, it records them as serial numbers. This is the number of days since, for some reason, January 1, 1904. These serial numbers appear in the dialog box. If you want to see the serial number of a date or time in a worksheet, select the cell and change the number format to **General**. Dates appear as whole numbers, times as decimal portions of a day.

Because there is no visible **Start date** bar, **Ctrl**-click that item in the legend and press **Delete** to delete it.

5 Adjust the Chart

Microsoft seems to have decreed that when you generate an Excel chart, it appears in distorted proportions that make it hard to read. You usually can make a great improvement by selecting the entire chart (click its background) and dragging the adjustment handles to give the chart better and more readable proportions.

> **NOTE**
>
> To change a number format, go to the **Number** section of the **Formatting Palette** and make a selection from the **Format** list. Alternatively, select **Format**, **Cells** to open the **Format Cells** dialog box where you can make a number of formatting choices.

6 Record Your Progress

Initially, the chart shows only uncompleted tasks (the bars are empty, or white). As tasks are partly or wholly completed, enter the number of days in the **Completed** column of the worksheet from which you generated the chart. The chart is immediately updated to show the completed activity.

81 Generate a See-Through Chart

Before You Begin

✔ 75 Plot a Chart

See Also

→ 82 Rotate a 3D Chart

Sometimes, you can get too fancy with a chart. When a chart has multiple layers, as it does in many 3D designs, a front layer can obscure important information on a layer behind. In that case, you can reveal the hidden content by making the front layer semitransparent.

This effect works by applying a ***gradient*** to the front layer. When applied to a chart element, the gradient adds some partial shading to the element, making it appear semitransparent.

1 Select a Data Series

Double-click the chart element you want to make transparent. In the case of an area graph, it almost certainly would be the frontmost data series. The **Format Data Series** dialog box opens.

2 Select a Gradient

Make sure that the **Patterns** tab is selected. Click the **Fill Effects** button. When the **Fill Effects** dialog box opens, be sure it displays the **Gradient** tab.

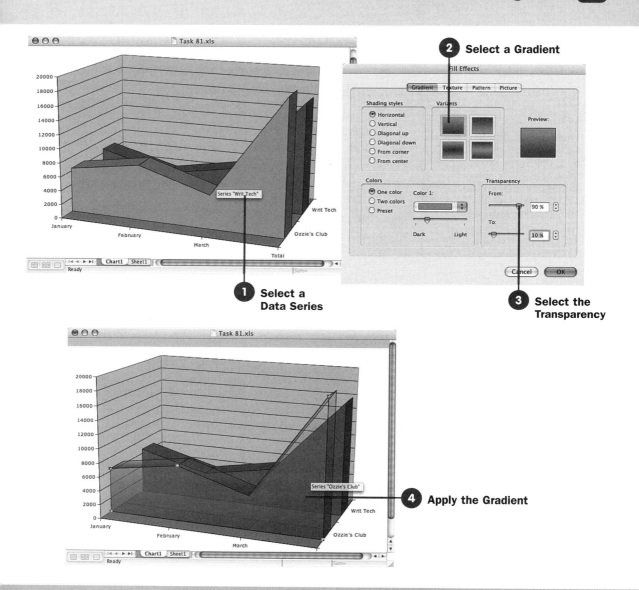

2 Select a Gradient

1 Select a Data Series

3 Select the Transparency

4 Apply the Gradient

Select a shading style and the degree of transparency you want to apply. For this example, a horizontal gradient works well. Select the **Variant** option that applies a darker shade at the bottom and a lighter shade at the top.

Set the **Dark/Light** slider toward the dark end of the scale. Use the **Preview** window as a guide.

NOTE

The upper slider controls the darkest shade in the gradient; the lower slider controls the lightest. When the darker shade is on the bottom, as it is here, it's easy to get them reversed.

3 Select the Transparency

Use the **Transparency** sliders to select the degree of shading. Set the **From** slider to a fairly dark shade; set the **To** slider to a fairly light shade. You can experiment with these until you get the right effect.

4 Apply the Gradient

Click **OK** twice to close both dialog boxes. The gradient is applied to the selected data series. You now can see the element behind it.

82 Rotate a 3D Chart

Before You Begin

✔ 75 Plot a Chart

See Also

→ 81 Generate a See-Through Chart

Nearly all the standard chart types have 3D variants. The added dimension provides room for added information. Whereas a conventional chart might show sales by division or sales by the month, a 3D chart lets you show sales for each month in each division.

There's one drawback. Trying to chart too much data in one place can lead to a kind of visual information overload. Because a 3D chart has a front-to-back dimension, there's also a risk of hiding information in the back rows.

One solution is to make the front ranks transparent, as explained in **81 Generate a See-Through Chart**. Another is to elevate and rotate the chart so that every data series is visible. You can elevate the chart so that you appear to be looking at it from a higher or lower position, or you can rotate it from left to right and back again. Another option is to drag the chart's adjustment handles to change its perspective.

1 Create or Display the Chart

Use the **Chart Wizard** to create a chart. The best candidate for the rotated 3D treatment is a 3D chart that has several front-to-back rows. In its standard alignment, such a chart might conceal some of its elements, as is the case with the sample chart shown.

Increase/Decrease Elevation

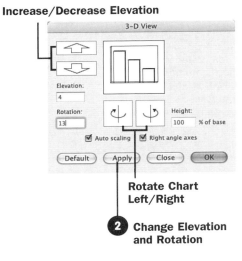

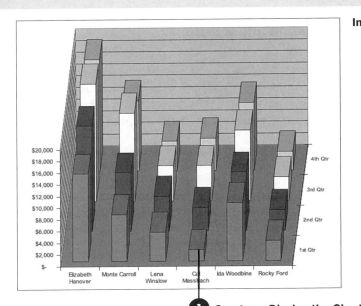

1 Create or Display the Chart

Rotate Chart Left/Right

2 Change Elevation and Rotation

3 Fine-tune the Results

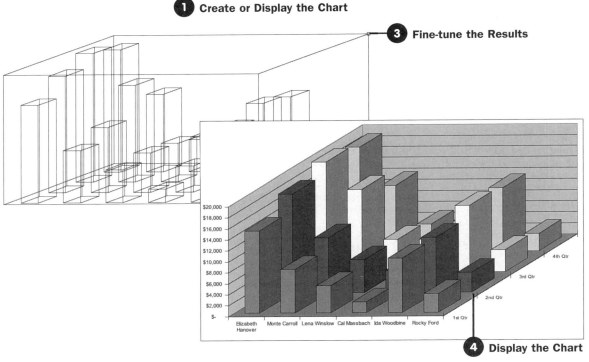

4 Display the Chart

② Change Elevation and Rotation

Select **Chart**, **3-D View** from the menu. The **3-D View** dialog box provides the means to rotate a chart and change its perspective. You can use the arrow buttons to the left of the chart diagram to increase or decrease the elevation from which you view the chart. You can use the rotation arrows below the diagram to swing the chart to the left or right.

The **3-D View** dialog box also has check boxes for **Auto scaling** and **Right angle axes**. When these options are enabled, Excel applies standard settings for scale and perspective. If you disable these check boxes, the dialog box shows additional options. Now you can use the **Height** window to scale the chart's height as a percentage of its base. A separate set of windows lets you alter the perspective.

Use the arrows or the text boxes to reset the elevation and rotation. For the chart in this case, an elevation of **4** moves you to a lower apparent viewpoint and a rotation of **13** turns the chart so that all the bars on it are more readily visible.

Click **OK** to close the dialog box. The chart is reoriented to the new settings.

③ Fine-tune the Results

Click the gray chart background. Adjustment handles appear on all corners of the chart. Click the handle in the upper-right corner. A wire-frame outline of the chart is displayed. Even with the change in perspective, some of Cal Massbach's data still might be hidden behind Ida Woodbine's taller bars. To fix that, you can drag the corner a short distance up and to the right.

④ Display the Chart

Release the mouse button. The chart is displayed in its new perspective.

83 Track Long-term Trends

The numbers you chart are often part of a pattern. It helps to not only chart the raw statistics, but also to see where the numbers are taking you. For example, if you have generated a bar chart, Excel can add a *trendline* to average out the values and let you see what might happen in the future.

As you do so, you will encounter features that involve higher mathematics. Don't be intimidated. Those whose talents are not mathematical still can get good results from the basic settings.

1 Display a Chart

A bar graph is an ideal candidate for a trendline. It often displays a series of periodic readings. Adding a trendline helps you see any pattern that might be developing. For example, if you are charting caribou migrations, a trendline might help you determine whether the migration level is going up or down and, if so, how quickly.

2 Select a Line Style

Click the background of the chart to select the entire chart; then select **Chart**, **Add Trendline** from the menu. The **Add Trendline** dialog box displays an assortment of options.

The **Trend/Regression type** section offers several options that involve higher mathematics. Most users will want to stick with the most basic **Linear** type. A rule of thumb for the other choices is if you understand them, feel free to use them. Otherwise, you probably don't need them.

3 Select the Data Series to Use

In the lower part of the dialog box, select a **Based on series** option. For example, if you want to chart trends in caribou migrations for a chart that also tracks migration trends for polar bears, grizzly bears, and arctic foxes, select the **Caribou** option.

Before You Begin

✔ **75** Plot a Chart

See Also

→ **101** Track a Long-term Average

🔍 **KEY TERM**

Trendline—A line added to a chart that averages a series of values and projects the trend into the future.

📝 NOTE

The **Chart** menu option is available only when a chart is selected. If you can't access this menu option, you've probably selected an element in the chart and not the entire chart. Click the background of the chart to display the selection handles around the chart, which indicate that the chart is selected.

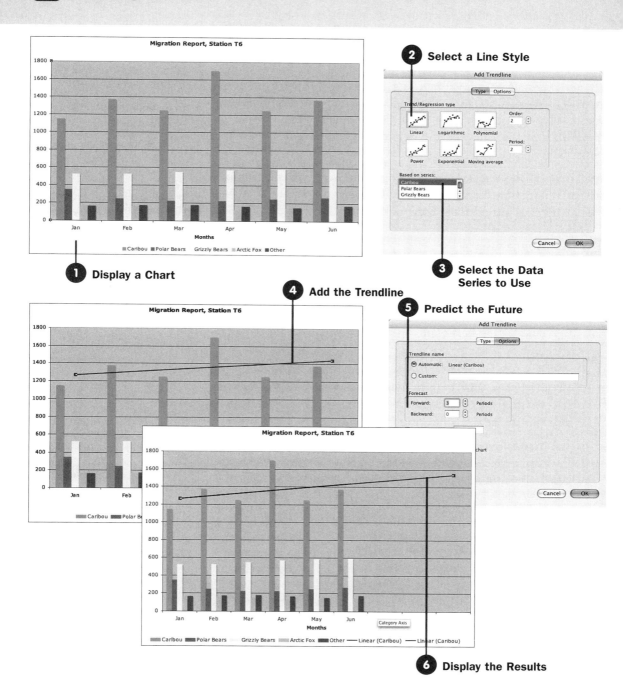

1 Display a Chart

2 Select a Line Style

3 Select the Data Series to Use

4 Add the Trendline

5 Predict the Future

6 Display the Results

4 Add the Trendline

Click **OK** to close the **Add Trendline** dialog box. The trendline is added to the graph. In the case of the migrating caribou, although the monthly figures vary up and down, they have a slight upward trend.

5 Predict the Future

As an option, you can extend the trendline to the future to see what it might hold. Reopen the **Add Trendline** dialog box and click the **Options** tab.

In the **Forecast** section, select the number of periods you want to predict, keeping in mind that the longer the term, the less reliable the prediction. You can also opt to extend the trendline backward.

6 Display the Results

Click **OK** to close the **Add Trendline** dialog box. The chart displays the extended trendline, predicting the future for the specified number of periods.

 NOTE

The linear trendline created in this exercise is intended for simple data sets. Other options on the **Options** tab are mainly for the benefit of those who understand the mathematics involved. In very general terms, a logarithmic trendline is most useful when the data changes greatly at first and then levels out. A polynomial trendline levels out large fluctuations, and a power trendline is best used with measurements that increase at a specific rate. Apply an exponential trendline when the values rise or fall at increasingly higher rates. A moving average smoothes out fluctuations to show a pattern or trend more clearly.

13

Managing Database Lists

IN THIS CHAPTER:

The world of major computer applications is built on **databases**. The scanner at the checkout counter checks a bar code and retrieves information from a database. When you go to an online auction, you check items retrieved from a database, and when you make a bid, that information also is entered in a database.

Databases are all around us—including in Excel. Almost all databases are set up as tables of rows and columns. Excel also uses a structure of rows and columns. It doesn't take a computer scientist to figure out that Excel and databases have something in common.

The databases used in activities such as e-commerce are large, complex networks of interrelated tables. Excel can give you no more than a single table that must fit within the limits of a standard worksheet. Nevertheless, Excel can do what any good database can do: look into its database and selectively retrieve information.

A database in Excel is called a **list**. A list is a block of data set up to be used as a database. You can type columns of data into a worksheet and call it a list. Or, you can use the **List Manager** tool that designates a list by outlining it in a **list frame** and by providing extra buttons and toolbars to help manage your data. The List Manager is unique to the Mac edition of Excel; the PC editions don't have it.

The List Manager provides added tools and visual cues that simplify common database operations, such as sorting a list or filtering selected records. Using the List Manager rules out some of the more advanced database maneuvers of which Excel is capable. This book sticks with List Manager activities; most of the advanced actions are beyond the scope of things you can do *In a Snap*.

KEY TERMS

Database—A collection of data organized in table form from which an application can retrieve selected information.

List—In Excel, a tabular set of data organized for use as a database.

List Manager—A tool used to manage lists, making conducting basic tasks easier.

List frame—Within an Excel worksheet, a boundary that defines the contents of a list.

84 Set Up a Database List

An Excel database list fits into the rows and columns of a worksheet. In database parlance, the rows represent *records*. Each record contains information about a single subject such as an employee, an item in an inventory, or a sales transaction. The columns represent *fields*. Each field contains a particular kind of information, such as the employee's name, the item's price, or the number of items sold.

Each field has a name represented by a column heading. One advantage of using the List Manager is that Excel recognizes the headings as such; it will not accidentally sort them into the middle of a table or retrieve them in a database search.

After you have established a list, you can do such things as sorting it into a new order as explained in **85** Sort Records into a New Order or retrieving particular items of information as explained in **86** Find Selected Records.

1 Collect the Data

Open a worksheet. You can enter data now, or you can collect it from another worksheet.

You also can retrieve data from an external source such as an Access database, but this requires that you install the auxiliary program Microsoft Query. It's available on the Office application CD, but you have to install it separately.

The data should be arranged in row and column format, with a record in each row and a field in each column. Avoid empty rows and columns; they'll just cause trouble when you later try to retrieve information from the list.

If you create a list using existing data, you can use the existing column headings or create new ones. You can also format column headings and other entries, as you often might for other kinds of worksheet entries.

Before You Begin

✔ **63** Enter a Formula

✔ **64** Make an Automatic Calculation

✔ **65** Make an Advanced Calculation

See Also

→ **66** Format Numbers Automatically

→ **67** Automatically Format a Worksheet

KEY TERMS

Record—A row in a database table, containing information about a single subject.

Field—A column in a database table, containing a certain type of information.

NOTE

Be careful not to include leading or trailing spaces in your data entries. These spaces can affect the order in which the data is sorted.

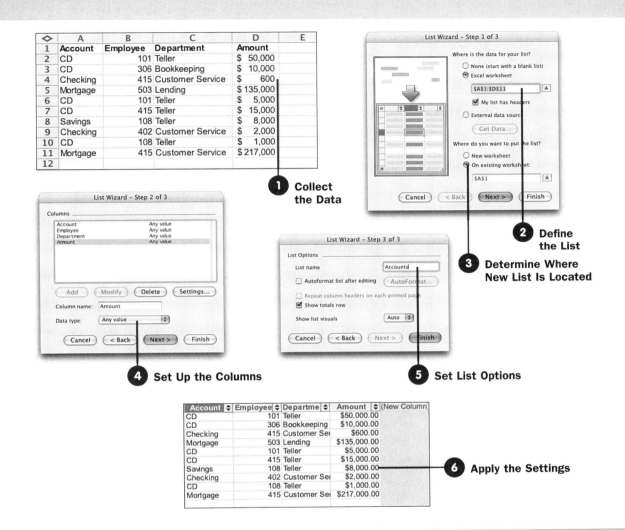

1 Collect the Data

2 Define the List

3 Determine Where New List Is Located

4 Set Up the Columns

5 Set List Options

6 Apply the Settings

2 Define the List

When you have collected the data you want to turn into a database list in a worksheet, select **Insert**, **List** from the menu. The **List Wizard** opens the first of three steps in creating a list. The wizard also invokes the List Manager.

The first step gives you the choice of starting with a blank list or using existing worksheet data. If you select an Excel worksheet as

the source, go to that sheet and select the range of data you want to include in the list. If you include the column headers in the range you select, enable the **My list has headers** check box in the List Wizard.

③ Determine Where New List Is Located

You can choose whether to place the list you are going to create on a new or existing worksheet. In the text box, enter the cell where you want the upper-left corner of the list to fall.

④ Set Up the Columns

Click the **Next** button to go to the **Step 2 of 3** page of the wizard, which asks you to set up the columns. If you are using an existing data source that includes column headings, these column headings appear in the **Columns** list at the top of the window. You can use the existing names as they appear here, or you can select a name from the **Columns** list and type a new name in the **Column name** text box.

From the **Data type** drop-down list, select an option that defines the nature of the data in the selected column. Excel is more flexible in this regard than most database management programs that require that each field be designated as text, numbers, dates, or some other data type. Excel gives you the option of just saying **Any value**. It's a good idea, though, to open this list and set a data type for each field.

Click the **Settings** button to access a more varied range of formatting options such as formatting numbers as currency or decimals.

⑤ Set List Options

Click the **Next** button to advance to the **Step 3 of 3** page of the wizard. The third step provides some list options, the most important of which is to give the list a name. The name you type is applied to the range of cells that make up the list.

If you enable the **AutoFormat list after editing** check box, you then can apply an AutoFormat to the list. You also have the option of showing a row of totals; if the list will cover more than one printed page, you can enable the **Repeat column headers on each printed page** check box to show the column headers on each

NOTE

In its finite wisdom, the **List Wizard** gives you the option of starting with a blank list. But then it just asks you to create columns and fill them with data, so you might as well do that before you turn it into a list.

TIP

Always start a List Manager list in cell **A1** of a fresh worksheet. If the worksheet contains additional data above or to the left of the list, it could be hidden by later database operations. You also should limit yourself to one list per worksheet. These restrictions don't apply to lists that do not use the List Manager.

TIP

Some numerical fields are better treated as text. This includes any numbers that will not be used in calculations, such as employee numbers, telephone numbers, or postal codes.

AutoFormats are pre-designed formats you can apply to Excel data, including the contents of a list. See 66 Format Numbers Automatically.

page. If you elect to turn on the **Show list visuals** option, each column head appears with a set of arrows you can use to sort or filter the information. Alternatives are to turn off the visuals or to select **Auto**, in which case Excel decides whether to display them.

6 Apply the Settings

When you've selected the appropriate options for your database list, click the **Finish** button. The List Manager sets up and displays the list.

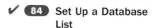
85 Sort Records into a New Order

Before You Begin

✔ **84** Set Up a Database List

See Also

→ **86** Find Selected Records

→ **87** Filter by Multiple Criteria

When a list is created, it usually is a random collection of records, probably assembled in the order in which they were entered. Often, you will want to sort the data so it appears in order of dates, names, or amounts.

There are several ways to do this. The List Manager places arrow-shaped visuals in the column headings; you can use them to sort or filter the list. If you display the **Formatting** toolbar, you can select a column and then click the **Sort Ascending** or **Sort Descending** toolbar button. You can find additional sort options in the **Data** menu.

1 Do a Quick Sort

Click the arrows at the heading of the column you want to sort. A drop-down menu displays sorting and filtering options.

Select **Sort Ascending** to sort the records in alphabetical order (if the data is textual) or least to greatest order (if the data is numerical). Select **Sort Descending** to sort the records in reverse alphabetical order (if the data is textual) or greatest to least order (if the data is numerical). See **86 Find Selected Records** for more information about the other sorting options.

2 Sort More Than One Column

You can sort the database on multiple factors. Perhaps you'd like to sort the list in **Department** order and then by **Employee** number within each department.

Select **Data, Sort** from the menu. The **Sort** dialog box lets you sort as many as three columns in this fashion.

1 **Do a Quick Sort**

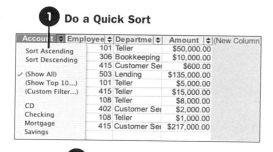

Result of Sorting the List in Ascending Order on the Accounts Column

2 **Sort More Than One Column**

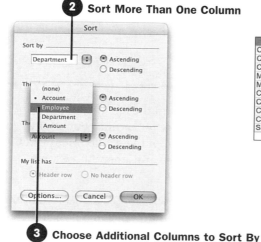

4 **Check the Results**

3 **Choose Additional Columns to Sort By**

From the **Sort by** list, select or enter the field on which you first want to sort the data. You can type the field name or click the arrow button and select the field. In the example, we first want to sort on the **Department** field. Next, select how you want to sort this field: in **Ascending** or **Descending** order. You normally use **Ascending**, but occasionally you might want to select the **Descending** option.

3 **Choose Additional Columns to Sort By**

In the **Then by** window, enter or select the secondary sort field. In the example, I want to sort first by **Department** and then by **Employee**, so I select the **Employee** field name. Then select

> ## TIP
>
> Unless you have absolute trust in your memory, it probably is better to select field names for sorting from the drop-down list of valid field names. However, if you do decide to type your own field names, you need not worry about capitalization—only spelling.

whether you want to sort the second criteria in **Ascending** order or **Descending** order.

If you want to sort on a third field, you can enter it in the remaining **Then by** box.

4 Check the Results

Click **OK** to close the **Sort** dialog box. The records are sorted first by department—note that the records are in alphabetical order based on the department. Within each department, the employee numbers are sorted in ascending order.

86 Find Selected Records

Before You Begin

✔ **84** Set Up a Database List

See Also

→ **87** Filter by Multiple Criteria

KEY TERM

Filter—To search a list and display only those records that meet the stated criteria.

TIP

In a longer list, the number of employees in the drop-down menu can be overwhelming. If you select the **Show Top 10** option, you select only the 10 employees who appear most frequently. The **Custom Filter** option lets you construct a query such as **Employee does not equal 101.**

Most Excel database lists are much larger than the one used in these illustrations. You easily can have several hundred records, but at any time you need to find only a selected fraction of them. You might want to find the sales records of a certain employee or list only those mortgages of more than $200,000.

To do this, you can *filter* the list, displaying only those records that meet your criteria. Excel condenses the display so that it includes only the records you want to see.

1 Display the List

Open a database list that has been set up using the **List Wizard** and List Manager. Make sure that the arrow graphics are displayed next to each column heading.

If the arrows are not displayed, select **View**, **Toolbars**, **List**. In the **List** toolbar, make sure that both the **Autofilters** and **Visuals** buttons are selected.

2 Select the Filter Condition

Using the Employee Bank Account database developed in the preceding tasks, suppose you want to check the account for a particular employee. Click the arrows next to the **Employee** column head. From the drop-down menu that opens, select the employee's name or number (in these illustrations, the employees are identified only by number).

1 Display the List

Account	Employee	Departme	Amount	(New Column)
CD			$50,000.00	
CD	Sort Ascending		$10,000.00	
Checking	Sort Descending	eeping	$600.00	
Mortgage	✓ (Show All)	mer Sei	$135,000.00	
CD	(Show Top 10...)	ng	$5,000.00	
CD	(Custom Filter...)		$15,000.00	
Savings			$8,000.00	
Checking	101	mer Sei	$2,000.00	
CD	108		$1,000.00	
Mortgage	306	mer Sei	$217,000.00	
	402			
	415			
	503			

Account	Employee	Departme	Amount	(New Column)
CD	101	Teller	$50,000.00	
CD	101	Teller	$5,000.00	

3 Check the Results

2 Select the Filter Condition

3 Check the Results

The list displays only the records of the selected employee.

To restore the full list, reopen the drop-down menu for the **Employee** column and select **Show All**.

87 Filter by Multiple Criteria

Sometimes you might want to filter a list on more than one factor. Using the Employee Bank Account database developed in the preceding tasks, for example, you might wonder how many mortgages were originated by the Customer Services department or how many of the new CDs were for $5,000 or more.

To answer questions like these, you can filter the list twice and, when necessary, apply a *custom filter*.

1 Select the First Filter Condition

Click the drop-down arrow next to the first field you want to filter. Select the value by which you want to filter the list. For example, if you want to filter the **Accounts** column to display only CDs, select **CD** from the list.

Only the records where **CD** is the value in the **Accounts** column are displayed.

Before You Begin

✔ **86** Find Selected Records

See Also

→ **85** Sort Records into a New Order

KEY TERM

Custom filter—A database filter built by entering your own conditions.

2 Apply a Custom Filter

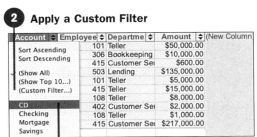

1 Select the First Filter Condition

Custom AutoFilter

| equals |
| does not equal |
| is greater than |
| is greater than or equal to | 5000 |
| is less than |
| is less than or equal to |
| begins with |
| does not begin with |
| ends with |
| does not end with |
| contains |
| does not contain |

Cancel   OK

3 Enter the Conditions

Account	Employee	Departme	Amount	(New Column
CD	101	Teller	$50,000.00	
CD	306	Bookkeeping	$10,000.00	
CD	101	Teller	$5,000.00	
CD	415	Teller	$15,000.00	

4 Apply the Filter

2 Apply a Custom Filter

Open the drop-down list for the next column you want to filter. If none of the listed terms exactly fits the filter you want to perform, select the **Custom Filter** option.

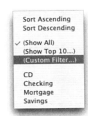

In this example, if you wanted to apply a filter to the **Amount** column, the drop-down list would give you a choice of specific amounts. You could display all amounts of $1,000, for example, or of $5,000. But if you wanted to display all records where the amount was $5,000 or more, you would have to apply the custom filter.

When you select the custom filter, the **Custom AutoFilter** dialog box opens.

3 Enter the Conditions

Open the first drop-down list and select the relationship you want to apply. If you want to display all amounts of $5,000 or more, select **is greater than or equal to**.

In the text box to the right, enter the value. In this example, you would type **5,000**.

A second pair of boxes lets you apply additional conditions if you want.

④ Apply the Filter

When you're finished defining the custom filter, click **OK**. The database list displays only the records that meet both filter conditions.

NOTE

You can apply a custom filter only to the contents of a single column. You cannot use the same dialog box, for example, to filter the **Account** column on **CD** and the **Amount** column on a certain range of values. However, there's nothing to keep you from applying separate custom filters to each of these columns.

88 Join Names for a Mailing List

Names can be a list management problem. On one hand, you might want to sort a list with the last names in alphabetical order. To do that, you need a column in which the last names appear in a format such as **Smith, Joe**.

On the other hand, you might want to produce a mailing list in which the first names appear first. In this case, you would want the names to appear in **Joe Smith** order.

The solution: Maintain separate columns for the first and last names. Put **Smith** in one column and **Joe** in another. Then, use formulas in a third column to produce the sequence **Joe Smith**.

Before You Begin

✔ **63** Enter a Formula

See Also

→ **85** Sort Records into a New Order

→ **86** Find Selected Records

① Separate First and Last Names

Start with a list that includes separate columns for first and last names. The list probably will have other information, too, such as addresses or positions. In this example, though, the names are the important elements.

You will also need a blank column to hold the joined names.

② Enter the Formula to Combine Fields

Select the cell where you want the first joined name to appear. In the example shown here, cell **C1** will hold the combined names in cells **A1** and **B1**. Enter this formula in cell **C2**:

=B1&" "&A1

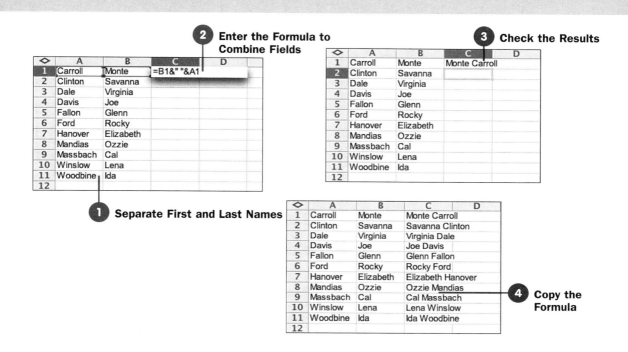

2 Enter the Formula to Combine Fields

3 Check the Results

1 Separate First and Last Names

4 Copy the Formula

Make sure that there's a space between the quotation marks. This formula writes the first name (the name in cell **B1**), a space, and then the last name (the name in cell **A1**)—just what you want for the mailing list.

3 Check the Results

Press **Return**. The first and last names are joined in cell **C2**. If you see an error message, check the formula and try again.

4 Copy the Formula

Click to select the formula cell (cell **C2**); then drag over the remaining cells where you want the joined names to appear (cells **C3–C11**). When you release the mouse button, the remaining joined names are displayed.

89 Find Relationships Between Data

The row-and-column format of an Excel worksheet is good for many things, but it is not the best way to find relationships between data. This is particularly true of a large list with a lot of complex data.

You might want to find the average salary levels for people in various job specialties. Or you might be preparing for a budget meeting in which department heads want to know how much they are spending on salaries this year. A raw list of employees' names, departments, and salaries contains this information—somewhere. But a large roster sorted only on the employees' names is unlikely to reveal the information you need very readily.

But a *PivotTable* can do the job. PivotTable is Microsoft's name for a *cross-tabulation* in which one type of information is related to another. For example, you could list each department and sum up its total payroll. Or, you could go even further and break down the payroll by shift.

1 Set Up the Data

The worksheet shown here is a list of nearly 100 employees, their positions, salaries, job assignments, and other information. You can use this list to generate a PivotTable that breaks down the payroll expenses by both department and shift.

2 Start the Process

Click anywhere in the data area. Then select **Data, PivotTable Report** from the menu. The **Step 1** page of the **PivotTable Wizard** opens.

You can select any of several sources from which to import the information. Because you are using the data in an Excel list, the **Microsoft Excel list or database** option should already be selected. Select it if it is not. Click the **Next** button.

3 Select a Range

The **Step 2** page of the wizard asks you to identify the range of data you plan to use. Again, Excel makes a selection for you. Make sure the selection covers the full data area but avoids extraneous cells. Click **Next**.

Before You Begin

✔ **84** Set Up a Database List

See Also

→ **90** Rearrange PivotTable Data

→ **91** Add Data to a PivotTable

→ **92** Generate Different Summaries

→ **93** Format a PivotTable

→ **99** Identify Causes and Effects

KEY TERMS

PivotTable—A cross-tabulation as implemented in Excel.

Cross-tabulation—A table in which one type of information is related to another.

TIP

You might look at the range name in the **Step 2** page of the wizard and be glad Excel has made the selection. This name refers to the **Employees** worksheet as identified by the exclamation mark and the range of cells on that sheet. The dollar signs identify *absolute references* that always refer to the specific rows and columns, as opposed to *relative references* that can vary if rows or columns are added and subtracted.

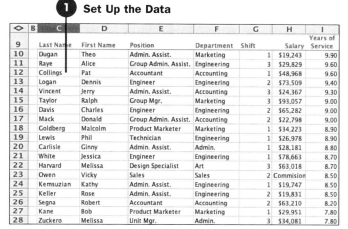

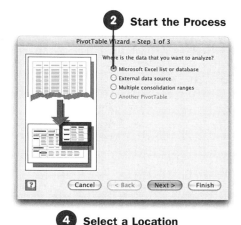

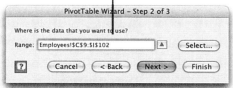

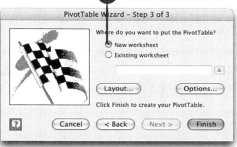

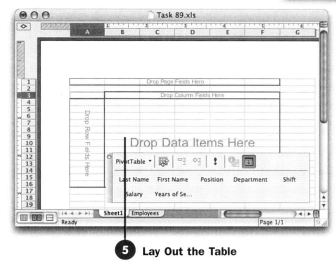

1 Set Up the Data

	Last Name	First Name	Position	Department	Shift	Salary	Years of Service
9	Last Name	First Name	Position	Department	Shift	Salary	Years of Service
10	Dugan	Theo	Admin. Assist.	Marketing	1	$19,243	9.90
11	Raye	Alice	Group Admin. Assist.	Engineering	3	$29,829	9.60
12	Collings	Pat	Accountant	Accounting	1	$48,968	9.60
13	Logan	Dennis	Engineer	Engineering	2	$73,509	9.40
14	Vincent	Jerry	Admin. Assist.	Accounting	3	$24,367	9.30
15	Taylor	Ralph	Group Mgr.	Marketing	3	$93,057	9.00
16	Davis	Charles	Engineer	Engineering	2	$65,282	9.00
17	Mack	Donald	Group Admin. Assist.	Accounting	2	$22,798	9.00
18	Goldberg	Malcolm	Product Marketer	Marketing	1	$34,223	8.90
19	Lewis	Phil	Technician	Engineering	1	$26,978	8.90
20	Carlisle	Ginny	Admin. Assist.	Admin.	1	$28,181	8.80
21	White	Jessica	Engineer	Engineering	1	$78,663	8.70
22	Harvard	Melissa	Design Specialist	Art	3	$63,018	8.70
23	Owen	Vicky	Sales	Sales	2	Commision	8.50
24	Kemsuzian	Kathy	Admin. Assist.	Engineering	1	$19,747	8.50
25	Keller	Rose	Admin. Assist.	Engineering	2	$19,831	8.50
26	Segna	Robert	Accountant	Accounting	2	$63,210	8.20
27	Kane	Bob	Product Marketer	Marketing	1	$29,951	7.80
28	Zuckero	Melissa	Unit Mgr.	Admin.	3	$34,081	7.80

2 Start the Process

3 Select a Range

4 Select a Location

5 Lay Out the Table

6 Add the Data

Count of Salary	Department							
Position	Accounting	Admin.	Art	Engineering	Marketing	R and D	Sales	Grand Total
Accountant	4							4
Admin. Assist.	4	7		3	4			18
Chief Scientist						3		3
Design Specialist			5					5
Engineer				14		2		16
Group Admin. Assist.	3			1	3	3		10
Group Mgr.					1			1
Product Marketer					9			9
Sales							15	15
Technician				9		1		10
Unit Mgr.		2						2
Grand Total	11	9	5	27	17	9	15	93

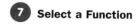

7 Select a Function

Sum of Salary	Department							
Position	Accounting	Admin.	Art	Engineering	Marketing	R and D	Sales	Grand Total
Accountant	196900							196900
Admin. Assist.	89989	183940		65572	91734			431235
Chief Scientist						254282		254282
Design Specialist			263649					263649
Engineer				871714		97963		969677
Group Admin. Assist.	75516			29829	82437	86317		274099
Group Mgr.					93057			93057
Product Marketer					312723			312723
Sales							0	0
Technician				26872		34693		303420
Unit Mgr.		75843						75843
Grand Total	362405	259783	263649	123584	579951	473255	0	3174885

8 Check the Results

4 Select a Location

The **Step 3** page of the wizard asks whether you want to place the table on a new or an existing worksheet. If you choose an existing worksheet, you are also asked for the name of that worksheet. Make a choice, and click **Finish**.

5 Lay Out the Table

A worksheet is opened with a diagram of the table. There also is a **PivotTable** toolbar that contains the column titles in the source list. You can design the table by dragging the column titles to the row, column, and data areas of the diagram.

If you want to organize the table by department, for example, drag the **Department** button from the toolbar to the chart area labeled **Drop Column Fields Here**. To cross-tabulate with job

⚓ NOTE

On the **Step 3** page of the wizard, click the **Layout** button for an alternative way to lay out the table; it emulates older versions of Excel. The **Options** button lets you specify such details as whether columns in the table are totaled and subtotaled.

TIP

It usually works best to put the longer of the two lists in the row position. For example, if you have hundreds of employee records but only half a dozen column headings, put the employees in the row position.

assignments, drag the **Position** button to the **Drop Row Fields Here** block.

6 Add the Data

Drag the **Salary** button into the central data area. The chart is generated, but initially it might not make much sense. The generated chart now merely counts the number of salary items in each classification. You probably already knew or did not care that the Accounting department has four accountants. Your goal is to show total salaries instead. You can take care of that. **Ctrl**-click the data area. From the menu that opens, select **Field Settings**.

7 Select a Function

The **PivotTable Field** dialog box indicates that the table is currently set to display **Count of Salary**. In the **Summarize by** list, select **Sum**. This option totals the salary figures instead of counting the number of salaries.

8 Check the Results

Click **OK** to close the dialog box. The table now totals the salaries for each department and job classification. You can format any of the table's contents to make it look more appealing.

90 Rearrange PivotTable Data

Before You Begin

✔ 84 Set Up a Database List

See Also

→ 91 Add Data to a PivotTable

→ 92 Generate Different Summaries

→ 93 Format a PivotTable

→ 99 Identify Causes and Effects

If a PivotTable uses a large data source, the PivotTable might contain more information than you really want to see. It will be better organized than the source data, but the quantity of data can still be overwhelming.

Suppose that you are a department head who is presented with a PivotTable that breaks down salary information by department and employee. That's all well and good, but all you really want to know is the overall payroll expense for your department.

① Open the PivotTable

	A	B	C	D	E	F
1			Drop Page Fields Here			
2						
3	Sum of Salary		Shift			
4	Department	Position	1	2	3	Grand Total
5	Accounting	Accountant	48968	147932		196900
6		Admin. Assist.	21020		68969	89989
7		Group Admin. Assist.	29569	45947		75516
8	Accounting Total		99557	193879	68969	362405
9	Admin.	Admin. Assist.	58173	71512	54255	183940
10		Unit Mgr.	41762		34081	75843
11	Admin. Total		99935	71512	88336	259783
12	Art	Design Specialist	62681	93956	107012	263649
13	Art Total		62681	93956	107012	263649
14	Engineering	Admin. Assist.	19747	19831	25994	65572
15		Engineer	414686	207631	249397	871714
16		Group Admin. Assist.			29829	29829
17		Technician	26978	156011	85738	268727
18	Engineering Total		461411	383473	390958	1235842
19	Marketing	Admin. Assist.	41507	23816	26411	91734
20		Group Admin. Assist.	28042	54395		82437
21		Group Mgr.			93057	93057
22		Product Marketer	88099	98606	126018	312723
23	Marketing Total		157648	176817	245486	579951
24	R and D	Chief Scientist	170506		83776	254282
25		Engineer		41435	56528	97963
26		Group Admin. Assist.	33320	27344	25653	86317
27		Technician	34693			34693
28	R and D Total		238519	68779	165957	473255
29	Sales	Sales	0	0	0	0
30	Sales Total		0	0	0	0
31	Grand Total		1119751	988416	1066718	3174885
32						

② Open the Field Settings

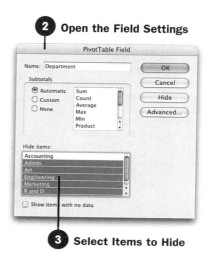

③ Select Items to Hide

④ Check the Results

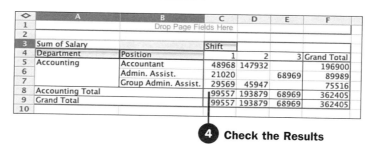

	A		B	C	D	E	F
1			Drop Page Fields Here				
2							
3	Sum of Salary			Shift			
4	Department		Position	1	2		3 Grand Total
5	Accounting		Accountant	48968	147932		196900
6			Admin. Assist.	21020		68969	89989
7			Group Admin. Assist.	29569	45947		75516
8	Accounting Total			99557	193879	68969	362405
9	Grand Total			99557	193879	68969	362405
10							

You can tailor the table to those specific needs. A PivotTable is set up so that you can change field settings in the row and column headings and choose only the information that interests you. The rest of the data is still contained in the PivotTable, but you can concentrate on the most important data. For example, in the **Department** column, you can hide the information for all departments but your own.

NOTE

In constructing the PivotTable as described in **89** Find Relationships Between Data, when you drag a field into position next to another column or row field, you create a table that subtotals the second field within the first. In this example, positions are subtotaled by department.

TIP

You can press ⌘ or **Shift** to select multiple items at one time.

❶ Open the PivotTable

A large database table can lead to what is also a large PivotTable. The shaded headings represent column headings in the original database. You can alter the field settings of any of these shaded headings.

❷ Open the Field Settings

Ctrl-click the heading you want to alter. If you want to suppress the display of other departments' information, for example, **Ctrl**-click the **Department** heading. From the context menu that opens, select **Field Settings**. The **PivotTable Field** dialog box opens.

❸ Select Items to Hide

The upper part of the dialog box controls the display of row and column subtotals for the selected field. The lower part contains a list of items you can hide. In the case of the **Position** field, these would be the job titles found in that field.

Select the items you want to hide; in this case, these would be the names of other departments. Click the **Hide** button. After you have made the selections, click **OK**.

❹ Check the Results

The display of the PivotTable is compressed to show only the single department (the department whose data you did *not* hide in step 3).

---

91 **Add Data to a PivotTable**

Before You Begin

✔ **84** Set Up a Database List

See Also

→ **90** Rearrange PivotTable Data

→ **92** Generate Different Summaries

→ **93** Format a PivotTable

→ **99** Identify Causes and Effects

PivotTables are seldom perfect when you first create them. If necessary, you can add or remove entire fields. For example, instead of a salary breakdown by department and position, you can change the table to relate salary information to years of service.

You can alter the table to display the new breakdown. It involves little more than dragging one field off the table and dragging another onto it.

---

1 **Display the Toolbar**

PivotTable ▾						
Last Name	First Name	Position	Department	Shift		
Salary	Years of Se...					

2 **Drag the Old Field from the Table**

	A	B	C	D	E
1	Position	(Show All) ⬍			
2					
3	Sum of Salary	Shift			
4	Department	1	2	3	Grand Total
5	Accounting	99557	193879	68969	362405
6	Admin.	99935	71512	88336	259783
7	Art	62681	93956	107012	263649
8	Engineering	461411	383473	390958	1235842
9	Marketing	157648	176817	245486	579951
10	R and D	238519	68779	165957	473255
11	Sales	0	0	0	0
12	Grand Total	1119751	988416	1066718	3174885
13					

3 **Drag the New Field onto the Table**

	A	B	C	D	E	F
1	Position	(Show All)	⬍			
2						
3	Sum of Salary		Shift			
4	Department	Years of Service	1	2	3	Grand Total
5	Accounting	1.4		43145		43145
6		4.5	21020			21020
7		5.1	29569			29569
8		6.2		41577		41577
9		7			26361	26361
10		7.5		23149	18241	41390
11		8.2		63210		63210
12		9		22798		22798
13		9.3			24367	24367
14		9.6	48968			48968
15	Accounting Total		99557	193879	68969	362405
16	Admin.	1.7	41762			41762
17		3.6	29992			29992
18		5.3			54255	54255
19		6.4		26696		26696
20		6.8		21942		21942
21		7.7		22874		22874
22		7.8			34081	34081
23		8.8	28181			28181
24	Admin. Total		99935	71512	88336	259783

1 **Display the Toolbar**

From the main menu, select **View, Toolbars, PivotTable**. The **PivotTable** toolbar contains field names available for use in the table plus icons that represent some commonly used functions. You can drag field names from the toolbar to the table and back again.

2 **Drag the Old Field from the Table**

In the PivotTable, click the field you don't want to use—in this case, the **Position** field—and drag it onto the toolbar. The position breakdown is removed from the table.

NOTE

The PivotTable shows only the years of service of employees within the department. If the original table had been less detailed—showing only full years of service, for example—the PivotTable would be somewhat simpler.

3 **Drag the New Field onto the Table**

Now, reverse the process. In the toolbar, click the field you want to add (in this case, the **Years of Service** field) and drag it into position in the table. The table now shows salary breakdowns by years of service.

92 Generate Different Summaries

Before You Begin

✔ **84** Set Up a Database List

See Also

→ **89** Find Relationships Between Data

→ **90** Rearrange PivotTable Data

→ **93** Format a PivotTable

→ **99** Identify Causes and Effects

Sometimes you'll only *think* you've done everything. For example, you might create a PivotTable that sums groups of data only to find out that the client also wants the table to show averages.

But changing the information the PivotTable presents isn't difficult. You can add an averaging function to the table, leaving or removing the sum function as you prefer.

1 **Display the PivotTable**

Open the PivotTable to be revised. If the **PivotTable** toolbar is not displayed, select **View**, **Toolbars**, **PivotTable** to make it appear.

2 **Add the Summary Function**

Summary functions appear in the upper-left corner of the PivotTable. In this example, that area already contains a **Sum of Salary** button. It identifies the information that appears in the data area of the table.

In the toolbar, select the field you want to summarize. Drag it into the table into a position just below the existing summary function button.

Both fields now appear in the table, but not quite the way you intended. In the case of the **Salary** field, Excel assumes that you want to add a count of the salary items rather than the average you really want. Never mind that this assumption is usually wrong. You can correct it.

Function of Table

1 Display the PivotTable

2 Add the Summary Function

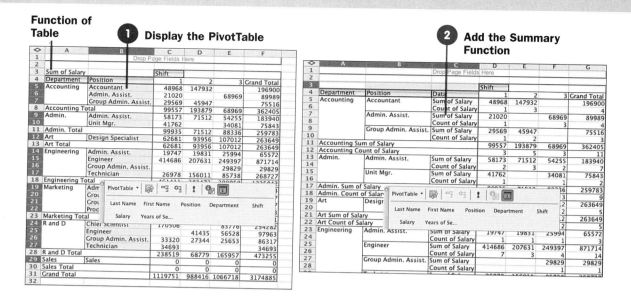

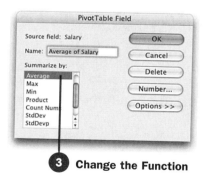

3 Change the Function

4 Apply the Change

③ Change the Function

Ctrl-click any of the cells that contain the count data. From the menu that opens, select **Field Settings**. The **PivotTable Field** dialog box opens. In the **Summarize by** list, select the function you want to use. In this case, it is the **Average** function.

④ Apply the Change

Click **OK** to close the dialog box. The new **Average** function replaces the old **Count** function. You also might want to change other aspects of the table, such as removing the **Position** breakdown. To do that, drag the **Position** button back onto the toolbar.

 TIP

You might want to change the format of the numbers in this table. For example, if an average produces long fractional amounts, select them; select **Format**, **Cells**; and convert to a format with fewer decimal points.

---

93 Format a PivotTable

✔ **84** Set Up a Database List

See Also

→ **89** Find Relationships Between Data

→ **90** Rearrange PivotTable Data

→ **92** Generate Different Summaries

✎ NOTE

This is the same AutoFormat feature you can use on any Excel worksheet.

A completed PivotTable has a slight industrial look. Good formatting can improve readability and make the table look a lot more appealing.

One of the easiest ways to buck up a PivotTable is to use the **AutoFormat** command. You can use it to select one of Excel's prebuilt AutoFormats and apply it to the entire field or to selected fields.

① Select a Format

Click anywhere in the PivotTable you want to format. Then select **Format**, **AutoFormat** from the menu. The **AutoFormat** dialog box offers a selection of prebuilt formats.

Scroll down the **Table format** list and select a format. A preview is displayed in the **Sample** window. Continue selecting formats until you find something you like.

② Apply the Format

Click **OK** to close the dialog box. The format is applied to the selected PivotTable. The results still might not be entirely satisfactory. If so, you can change the format of individual fields.

③ Reformat a Field

Click the heading of the field you want to change. From the main menu, select **Format**, **Cells**. The **Format Cells** dialog box opens.

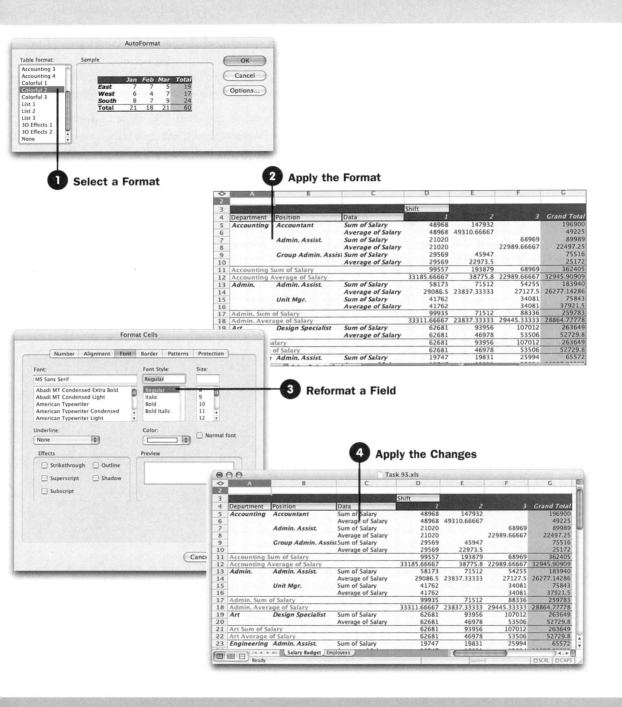

1 Select a Format

2 Apply the Format

3 Reformat a Field

4 Apply the Changes

Tabs across the top of the dialog box present several types of formatting options. You can change the display of a number, display text in a different type, or make other changes. You can apply any one of these formatting options or several of them all at once.

Click the tab that represents the effect you want to apply. For example, you might feel that the typeface in which one field is displayed is too large and loud. Click the **Font** tab to see typeface options. Make the changes you want to the typeface, style, and size of the font.

 NOTE

Click other tabs in the **Format Cells** dialog box and make other formatting selections before you click **OK** to close the dialog box. When you click **OK**, all the formatting changes are applied.

④ Apply the Changes

Click **OK** to close the dialog box. The changes are applied to the PivotTable.

14

Forecasting Results

IN THIS CHAPTER:

There are said to be three kinds of falsehoods: "lies, damned lies, and statistics." Often misattributed to Mark Twain—more likely, the quip came from Benjamin Disraeli, British prime minister of the Victorian era—this remark reflects a cynical but popular view of statistical analysis. It's in the same class with, "Figures lie, and liars figure."

Statistics are easily and often misused, but if properly calculated, the figures themselves don't really lie. Whether you're a corporate financial manager or a homeowner considering a new car loan, statistical analysis can tell you a great deal about how well things are going. Excel has a host of tools to help you conduct multiple kinds of analysis such as looking up key values, calculating the potential return on an investment, or even projecting past experience into the future.

Excel conducts most of its statistical operations by way of **_functions_**. As explained in **64** **Make an Automatic Calculation**, a function is a prewritten formula that can make advanced calculations—you need only fill in the blanks.

Often, you can fill in these blanks using the contents of cells or **_ranges_**, which are simply groups of cells. You can enter a range of cells with a notation such as **A1:A27**, or you can name the range and enter the range name into the function.

It isn't absolutely necessary that you complete a function with items from a worksheet. You could open the function dialog box and type the information directly there. Usually, though, it's easier to enter your information in the worksheet where you can readily see it.

If you enter your terms directly in the worksheet, you have another option. If, for example, you want to test the effect of a different interest rate, you can change that entry in the worksheet. You need not rewrite the entire function; the existing function can simply calculate the new information.

NOTE

To name a range, select the cells, then select **Insert**, **Name**, **Define** from the menu. Type the name you want to give the range—give the range a meaningful name that explains its purpose, such as **Monthly Payments** or **Sales for Region 1**—and press **Enter**.

94 Calculate Payments on a Loan

If you are considering a mortgage, a new car, or some other major purchase, you probably expect to make monthly payments toward the balance. If you know the amount, the term (the length of time the loan will be in effect), and the interest rate, you can use Excel to figure out what the payments will be.

You aren't limited to calculating monthly payments. For example, a business investment might call for annual payments. Shoppers at the low end of the used car market might find themselves making weekly payments. Excel simply asks for a number of regular periodic payments. The length of each period does not matter. However, when using a payment function, make sure the interest period and the payment periods match. For example, you might want to calculate the monthly payments on a 5-year loan at 12% annual interest. To match the payment interval, convert both the loan term and the payment period to months. Enter the transaction as a 60-month loan at 1% monthly interest.

You also aren't limited to computing the terms of installment loans. You can use payment functions to calculate the costs and returns of single-payment instruments such as annuities and investments. You also can calculate loan terms from the standpoint of the lender. In this case, you would ask Excel how much you would earn in payments after you advance the loan. Whatever the nature of the transaction, enter money you pay out as a negative figure and money you receive as a positive amount.

1 Enter the Terms

In a worksheet, enter the amount of the loan, the interest rate, and the number of payments. Where you enter them doesn't particularly matter. Put them in a column, in a row, or spread all over the place. It makes sense, though, to put them together and identify them with text labels. You'll have to find them again later.

In this example, you want to calculate the monthly payments for a $25,000 car loan. The credit union quoted a 5.5% annual interest rate on a 5-year loan.

Before You Begin

✔ **64** Make an Automatic Calculation

See Also

→ **95** Evaluate an Investment

→ **96** Calculate the Return on an Investment

→ **100** Set and Meet a Goal

 TIP

Excel has several loan calculation functions. Each of them uses four factors: the loan amount, its term, the interest rate, and the periodic payments. If you know three of the four, you can select a function that gives you the fourth.

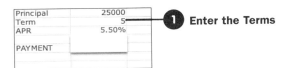

1 Enter the Terms

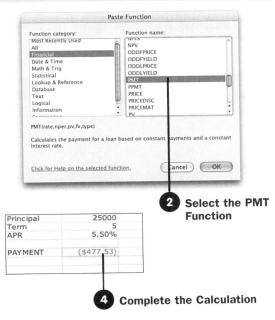

2 Select the PMT Function

3 Enter the Arguments

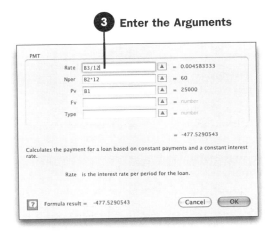

Principal	25000
Term	5
APR	5.50%
PAYMENT	($477.53)

4 Complete the Calculation

---

2 **Select the PMT Function**

Select the cell where you want the results to appear. From the menu, select **Insert**, **Function**. From the **Paste Function** dialog box that opens, select the **PMT** function from the **Function name** list on the right. You can scroll down the list of functions until you find the right one. To narrow the list, select **Financial** from the **Function category** list on the left. When you have selected the function you want to use, click **OK**. A dialog box specific to the function you select opens.

3 **Enter the Arguments**

If you already have entered the terms in a worksheet as described in step 1, you can enter the cell references that contain these terms in text boxes of the function arguments dialog box.

If you have not already converted the terms to a common time period, you can do so when you enter the function arguments. For example, if you have entered an annual percentage rate in cell **C4**, you could enter **C4/12** in the **Rate** text box to convert the annual rate to a monthly rate. If the loan term is 5 years, you could enter **5*12** in the **Nper** (number of periods) box. Both actions convert the terms to months. The amount of the loan goes in the **Pv** (present value) text box.

4 Complete the Calculation

Click **OK** to complete the function and close the dialog box. The payment amount appears in the worksheet in the cell you selected in step 2. Because the calculated value represents money you will pay out, it appears as a negative figure (in parentheses).

With the terms used in this example, the function quotes a monthly payment of $477.53. Now you have to decide whether you can afford a $25,000 car loan.

95 Evaluate an Investment

When you're deciding whether to make an investment, the overriding question is, "What's the payoff?" Will the return be large enough to justify the investment? You can go further and ask whether the return will be better than that of some alternative investment.

Excel has several functions to help you answer this question. One of the most useful is the **NPV** function. It calculates the *net present value* of a future return—what that return would be worth right now. An investment with a positive NPV is profitable. The higher the NPV, the more profitable it is.

Say that you are considering the purchase of a new graphics workstation. You know what it would cost, and you can make a fair estimate of its useful life. Although it might not have much value at the end of that period, you might be able to get a little something for recycling it. Given these values, you can use the **NPV** function to help decide whether this investment would be worthwhile.

Before You Begin

✔ **94** Calculate Payments on a Loan

See Also

→ **96** Calculate the Return on an Investment

KEY TERM

Net present value—The current value of income or payments that will take place in the future.

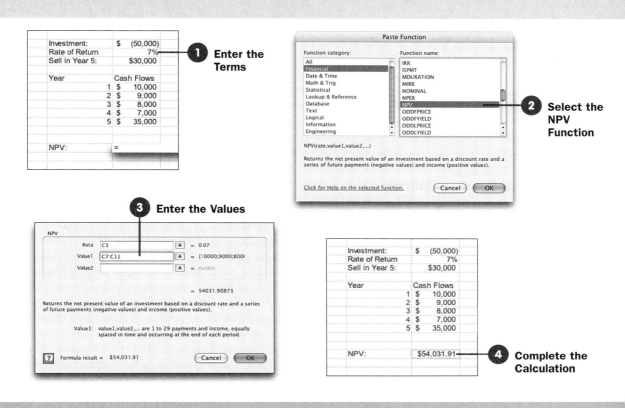

You also can use the **NPV** function to compare alternative investment possibilities. Someone in your organization might be arguing that the money you expect to spend on the workstation would be more profitably spent on staff training. This advocate might even have worked up some numbers to show the potential return on this option.

In that case, you could calculate the **NPV** of your proposal in comparison with the alternative. When calculating your own NPV, enter the expected return from the training option as a **hurdle rate**. You then can determine whether the expected return from your proposal is greater than that of the training alternative.

1 Enter the Terms

It's easiest to enter the terms of the investment in a worksheet column. The **NPV** function takes two kinds of arguments:

- **A rate of return**—This is a percentage that can be the interest rate on a loan to finance the equipment or the hurdle rate for a competing investment. It doesn't have to be a firm figure—it can be an estimate.

- **One or more values that represent periodic income from the investment**—If you are lending money, it might be the repayments with interest. If you are purchasing equipment or training the staff, the periodic income might be reduced cost or the value of higher production.

Enter the amount of the investment (in the example, what you'll pay for the workstation). Because this is an expense, show it as a negative figure. Then enter a rate of return, which is actually a return to someone else, not you. This can be the interest it'll cost to finance the purchase or the hurdle rate of a competing investment.

Add any expected salvage value (what you expect to sell the equipment for at the end of its useful life). Then enter the cash flow expected in each year of the investment's useful life.

For example, you might expect the workstation to save $10,000 in its first year of operation, tapering off as the equipment gets older. By the fifth year, you might figure it will be of limited value to you but someone else would still pay $30,000 for it.

The sponsor of the training alternative projects a 7% return on that investment. If you buy the workstation, you will have to forego the benefits of the training, so the benefits of your investment will be reduced by that rate.

Excel just makes calculations. It does not guarantee that your expectations are realistic.

NOTE

Unlike conventional installment loan payments, the periodic income values represent returns that can vary from period to period. An investment might pay high returns in its earliest years but taper off as equipment gets older. Also, if you sell the used equipment at the end of the term, add your estimated income from the sale of the equipment to the final-year return.

2 Select the NPV Function

Select the cell where you want the results to appear. Select **Insert**, **Function** from the menu. The **Paste Function** dialog box opens.

Select the **NPV** function from the **Financial** category. Click **OK**. A dialog box specific to the function you select opens. In this case, the **NPV** function arguments dialog box opens.

TIP

If you enter these values in a single worksheet column, you can refer to this range of cells when you build the function.

3 Enter the Values

In the **NPV** function arguments dialog box, click to select the **Rate** text box. Enter the expected return rate or click to select its cell from the worksheet.

In the **Value1** text box, enter one or more expected cash flow amounts such as the return expected during each year. If you have entered the expected series of returns in a single worksheet column, you can click the **Value1** text box and then select the range of values. All the cells will be entered in the single text box. Because all the values are included in this box, you need not enter anything for **Value2**.

4 Complete the Calculation

Click **OK** to close the dialog box and complete the function. The result appears in the worksheet cell where you entered the formula (the cell you selected in step 2). In this case, the original $50,000 investment will ultimately be worth a little more than $54,000—thus its net present value.

If you want, you can go to another cell and calculate the difference between the original investment and its net present value. If you entered the investment as a negative figure, add the two values, don't subtract them.

◣NOTE

If you want to enter the returns individually, type the first entry in the **Value1** text box, the second in **Value2**, and so on. As you go, the dialog box expands to display new blank value boxes up to a limit of 30.

---

96 Calculate the Return on an Investment

Before You Begin

✔ **64** Make an Automatic Calculation

See Also

→ **95** Evaluate an Investment

→ **100** Set and Meet a Goal

When you make a major investment, you often have to finance it with borrowed money. At the very least, you'll want to ensure that the return on the investment exceeds the cost of the loan.

There are several ways to do this. **95** **Evaluate an Investment** provides a way to calculate the relative costs. Alternatively, you can calculate an *internal rate of return*. The **IRR** function evaluates a series of cash flows, including the investment, its anticipated returns, and any resale value it might have at the end of the period. It reports its results as a percentage—in effect, an interest rate that represents the potential return on the investment.

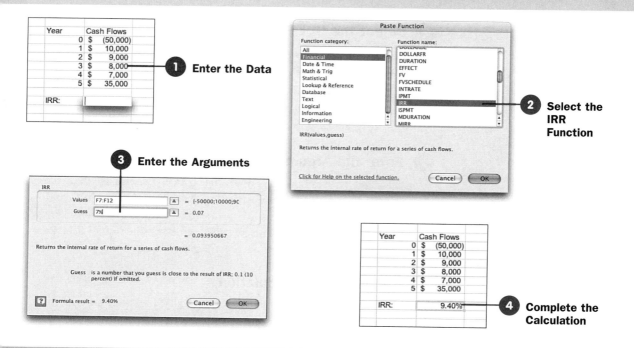

1 Enter the Data

2 Select the IRR Function

3 Enter the Arguments

4 Complete the Calculation

The arguments for the **IRR** function include one called **Guess**. You might ask whether Excel isn't supposed to eliminate guesswork. That's a good point, but in this case there's a reason to take even a wild stab at it. The **IRR** function works by making repeated passes through the data, coming closer to the result with each repetition. If it fails to find a result after 20 passes, it declares failure and issues an error message. Entering your guess gives the function a starting point. The function works more quickly and has a better chance of finding the right result when it starts at a reasonable beginning point.

KEY TERM

Internal rate of return— The percentage return on an investment, comparing the investment's total cost and the income it generates.

1 **Enter the Data**

In a worksheet, enter the initial investment. Because it is an expense, enter this value as a negative amount. Then enter the expected returns over the life of the investment. These values are usually a series of monthly or yearly cash flows. Finally, enter any salvage value the investment might have at the end of the period.

② Select the IRR Function

Select the cell where you want the result to appear. Select **Insert**, **Function**. The **Paste Function** dialog box opens.

In the **Function category** list, select **Financial**. From the **Function name** list, select the **IRR** function. The **IRR** function arguments dialog box opens.

③ Enter the Arguments

Click the **Values** text box, go to the worksheet, and select the range of cells that contains your anticipated income figures. In the **Guess** box, enter your best estimate of a rate of return. Your guess does not have to be accurate or even reasonable. It just gives the **IRR** function a place to begin its calculations.

④ Complete the Calculation

Click **OK** to close the dialog box. The cell where you entered the formula displays the rate of return you can expect from the costs and income data you have entered. You then can compare this return with the cost of financing the investment.

97 Look Up a Price

Before You Begin

✔ **64** Make an Automatic Calculation

See Also

→ **84** Set Up a Database List

→ **86** Find Selected Records

A typical retail business sells multiple products whose prices can change rapidly and often. When you fill out an order form, you can look up the current price the hard way: Pull out a written price list and enter the amount. Or you can ask Excel to look up the price for you.

If you maintain a price list in an Excel worksheet, you can enter any price updates in that worksheet. On another sheet, you can maintain an order form. When you fill out the order, you can ask Excel to go to the price list worksheet, find the item, look up the current price, and enter it in the form.

A lookup function looks for an item in a designated *table array*. The function then scans across the table to the price column, retrieves the price, and places it in the order form.

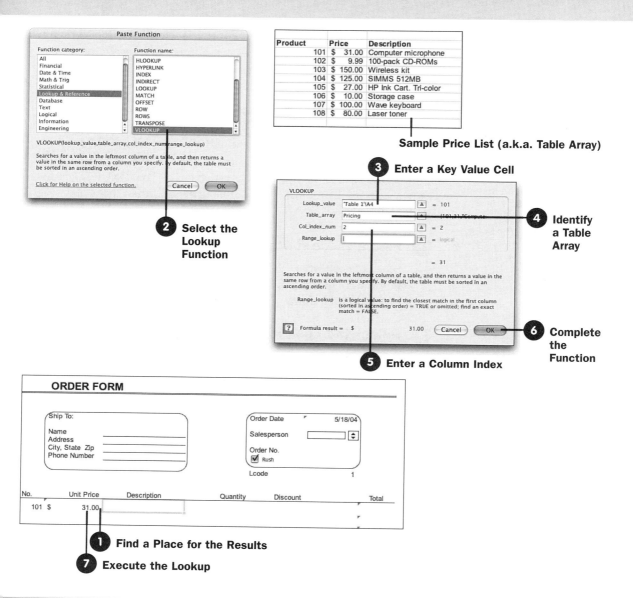

Sample Price List (a.k.a. Table Array)

③ **Enter a Key Value Cell**

② **Select the Lookup Function**

④ **Identify a Table Array**

⑤ **Enter a Column Index**

⑥ **Complete the Function**

① **Find a Place for the Results**

⑦ **Execute the Lookup**

The lookup function requires a **key value** it can look up in the table array. When it finds that value, it also needs instructions about how far and in what direction to find the **lookup value** it must retrieve. For

KEY TERMS

Table array—A range of rows and columns within which a lookup function works. The table array typically is a named range in which key values are arranged down the left column or across the top row.

Key value—The value for which the function searches within the table array.

Lookup value—The value the lookup function returns to the worksheet.

example, you could type a stock number in the order form and then tell the lookup function to locate that stock number (the key value) in the table array (the price list). You then could tell the function to look three cells to the right of the stock number to find the price.

Excel has two lookup functions, identical except for the directions in which they look. The **VLOOKUP** function searches for a key value by looking vertically down the left column in a table array. When it finds that value, the function then looks a specified number of columns to the right to find the results you want to retrieve. The **HLOOKUP** function searches across the top row of the table array and then looks down for the lookup value.

1 Find a Place for the Results

Select the cell where you want the results of the function to appear. If you were looking up a price for an order form, this cell would be in the price column.

2 Select the Lookup Function

Select **Insert**, **Function** from the menu. The **Paste Function** dialog box opens. Select one of the two lookup functions and click **OK**. The **VLOOKUP** and **HLOOKUP** functions are in the **Lookup & Reference** category.

3 Enter a Key Value Cell

The lookup function arguments dialog box displays a text box for each of the function's arguments. In the first box, you can type a key value or enter a cell reference. This might be the cell in an order blank where you will later enter a stock number.

4 Identify a Table Array

The **Table_array** argument refers is a range of cells you want the function to search. In the case of a vertical lookup, this range can have any number of columns. The first column must contain the key values, such as the stock or product numbers, sorted in ascending order. The second column might contain the prices of each item, and the third could hold product descriptions.

Such a table layout lends itself to two lookup functions. Each could search for the same key value, such as the stock number. After

finding the stock number, one function could search one column to the right, retrieve the price, and place it in one cell of the order form. Another could look two columns to the right of the stock number and place the description in another cell of the order form.

5 Enter a Column Index

In the **Col_index_num** box, enter the column or row from which to retrieve the lookup value. In a vertical lookup, if the lookup values are in the second column, enter an offset of **2**. In the table array, count the column in which the key value is located as 1 and then count to the right to the column in which the lookup value is located. In this example, the product number (the key value) is in column 1; the price is in column 2 and therefore has an offset or index of 2. The item description is in column 3 and has an offset or index of 3.

The **Range_lookup** box is optional. If the function cannot find an exact match to the key value, a blank entry or an entry of **TRUE** tells the function to look for the nearest match. An entry of **FALSE** tells the function to look only for an exact match. In this example, if you are looking up an item to place on an invoice, you want to be sure you find the exact item.

6 Complete the Function

Click **OK** to close the function arguments dialog box. A lookup value appears in the cell where you entered the formula. The response Excel returns initially might be an error message. If you have designated an empty cell as the source for the key value (for example, if you entered a cell reference for the order form that has not yet been filled out), the function will have nothing to look up.

7 Execute the Lookup

To test the function, enter a valid key value in the blank cell; the function should return a more satisfactory result. In this price-lookup example, when you enter a product number of 101, the **VLOOKUP** function refers to the price list and returns the correct price for a computer microphone of $31.00.

 TIP

The table array can be a named range. You'll usually find it more convenient to maintain the array in a separate worksheet. For example, you could select the contents of the table array; select **Insert**, **Name**, **Define**; and give the range a name such as **Pricing**.

 TIP

You can copy the function to other cells and then edit it to retrieve additional information. For example, you could copy a function that uses a stock number to retrieve the price and change only the column index to retrieve the item description.

98 Measure Deviations from Average

Before You Begin

✔ **63** Enter a Formula

✔ **64** Make an Automatic Calculation

See Also

→ **84** Set Up a Database List

→ **99** Identify Causes and Effects

→ **101** Track a Long-term Average

KEY TERM

Standard deviation—A measurement of how greatly a range of values deviates from its average.

NOTE

There are various types of averages. In the case of standard deviations, we are discussing the *mean*, the average you calculate by adding the values and dividing the total by the number of items. This is distinct from the *median*, which is the midpoint between the extremes, and the *mode*, which is the value that occurs most often.

In one major city, the total rainfall for a recent year was just about average. That might suggest an easy year for weather forecasters, but that "average year" included an extended drought and a record-breaking flood.

Sometimes, it's important not only to know an average, but also to know what it's an *average of*. In particular, is it an average of a narrow range or a wide one? For example, you might have the results of a customer survey. Do their responses show a wide range of responses to your questions, or were the answers fairly consistent? The **STDEV** (*standard deviation*) function can measure how widely the survey responses vary from the calculated average.

❶ Assemble the Data

If you are working with survey responses, enter them into a worksheet. A useful table format is to list the respondents down the first column. Then create a column for the responses to each question. In this example, the respondents are listed by number in column A; their responses to the first question are listed in column B.

Select the cell in which you want to locate the standard deviation calculation (in this example, that's cell **B36**).

❷ Select the STDEV Function

Select **Insert**, **Function**. The **Paste Function** dialog box opens. From the **Function category** list, select the **Statistical** category. From the **Function name** list for that category, select the **STDEV** function. Click **OK**. The **STDEV** function arguments dialog box opens to ask asks for a series of numbers.

❸ Enter the Conditions

Click to select the **Number 1** text box; then go to the worksheet and select the range of cells that contain the values you want to use to calculate the average. In the case of the survey results, this would be the full range of responses to a particular question (cells **B4–B33**).

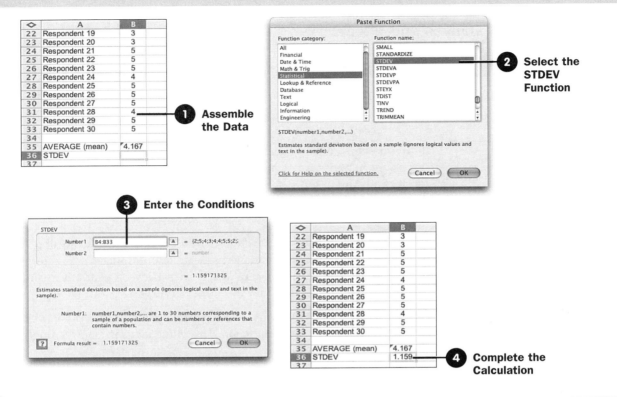

① Assemble the Data

② Select the STDEV Function

③ Enter the Conditions

④ Complete the Calculation

That's all that's necessary. As you make entries in this dialog box, it expands to display another blank text box, but there's no need to fill them all.

④ Complete the Calculation

Click **OK**. The dialog box closes, and the standard deviation is displayed in the worksheet. The lower the deviation, the more tightly grouped the responses.

Suppose that, for example, the survey question asked customers to rate their satisfaction on a scale of 1 (extremely unsatisfied) to 5 (extremely satisfied). If the average response was 4 and the standard deviation was 1 or less, you can conclude that most respondents are reasonably well satisfied. A standard deviation of 3, on the other hand, would be a clue that despite the good average, you have some *very* unsatisfied customers.

 TIP

In the **STDEV** function arguments dialog box, you can enter as many as 30 values in individual text boxes. However, if you have a large number of values, as you would in the responses to a survey, it is much easier to select the spreadsheet range that contains the responses and enter the range in the **Number 1** text box.

Identify Causes and Effects

Before You Begin

✔ **64** Make an Automatic Calculation

See Also

→ **94** Calculate Payments on a Loan

→ **98** Measure Deviations from Average

KEY TERM

Correlation—A measure of how well one set of values relates to another set. A strong correlation suggests a cause-and-effect relationship.

NOTE

Most likely, the **CORREL** function will produce a fractional result between the two extremes. Whether the comparison is positive or negative indicates the nature—plus or minus—of the correlation between the two sets of values. The larger the number, either plus or minus, the stronger the correlation.

A customer survey can have the proverbial good news and bad news.

Suppose that you had taken a survey in which customers expressed their satisfaction on a scale of 1 to 5. The survey also asked for their postal codes and any products they have bought recently.

In this example, most customers are reasonably satisfied, but a significant minority is not. You'd like to identify the source of their dissatisfaction. You might suspect that customers in one area have had unpleasant experiences with a regional service center. Or, perhaps one piece of merchandise is the source of the unhappiness.

In another scenario, you might wonder how effective your advertising has been. Does an increase in advertising produce an increase in sales? You can test to see whether a **correlation** exists between your advertising expenditures and sales levels for the same period.

To test for such causes and effects, you can calculate a *coefficient of correlation* using Excel's **CORREL** function. This value measures how strongly two sets of values are linked.

When you execute the **CORREL** function, it produces a decimal between 1 and –1. A positive value means that advertising does increase sales; a negative number means it has just the opposite effect. Most likely in this case, the result will be positive. The larger the value, the greater the effect.

① Identify the Data to Be Compared

Set up two ranges, each containing one of the sets of data to be compared.

One range should identify the "effect" side of the relationship you want to explore. For example, if you are comparing expenses with revenue, designate one column to include the monthly revenue figures. Then provide a range that contains the possible cause. This might be a column of monthly advertising expenses.

As far as the **CORREL** function is concerned, these values can be arranged in multiple columns or just about anywhere you like. Good worksheet practice, though, suggests that each set of numbers should normally appear in a single column.

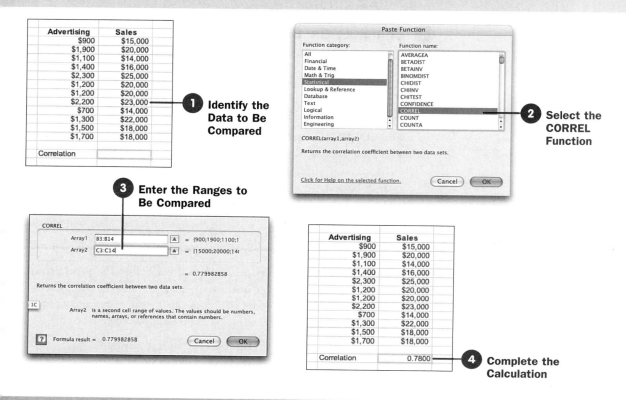

Advertising	Sales
$900	$15,000
$1,900	$20,000
$1,100	$14,000
$1,400	$16,000
$2,300	$25,000
$1,200	$20,000
$1,200	$20,000
$2,200	$23,000
$700	$14,000
$1,300	$22,000
$1,500	$18,000
$1,700	$18,000
Correlation	

1 Identify the Data to Be Compared

2 Select the CORREL Function

3 Enter the Ranges to Be Compared

4 Complete the Calculation

② Select the CORREL Function

Select the cell in which you want the result of the comparison function to be displayed. Select **Insert**, **Function** to open the **Paste Function** dialog box. From the **Function category** list, select the **Statistical** category. From the **Function name** list for that category, select the **CORREL** function.

③ Enter the Ranges to Be Compared

The **CORREL** function arguments dialog box asks you to enter two *arrays*. Each array is one of the ranges you want to compare. Click the **Array1** text box. Then go to the worksheet and select the first of the two ranges. Click the **Array2** text box and select the other range you want to compare.

 TIP

It can be helpful to assign names to ranges, particularly if you are comparing data in a large list. Then, you need enter only the range names in the function's arguments. If you need to find the range later, it will be in the **Name** list at the left end of the **Formula** bar.

CHAPTER 14: Forecasting Results

4 Complete the Calculation

Click **OK** to close the **CORREL** function arguments dialog box. The result appears as a decimal value.

In this case, the result is fairly high and positive. It suggests that your advertising dollars are indeed getting results.

The **CORREL** function sometimes displays the error message **#DIV/0!**. This result means the correlation is zero, which means the function found absolutely no relationship between the two sets of numbers.

100 Set and Meet a Goal

Before You Begin

✔ Make an Automatic Calculation

See Also

→ **94** Calculate Payments on a Loan

→ **99** Identify Causes and Effects

→ **101** Track a Long-term Average

 NOTE

Goal seeking modifies the contents of a worksheet. If you want to preserve the original numbers, work with a copy of the data.

Modern business is goal driven. Sometimes it is not enough just to total existing or prospective incomes and expenses and then see what the difference would be. Often, you want to focus on the outcome and then work backward to see what it takes to meet that objective.

Say, for example, you hope to end the year with a particular profit level. Given the expenses you are likely to have, what level of sales would it take to achieve that profit goal? Excel's **Goal Seek** tool can help you find out.

1 Set Up the Data

Set up or open a worksheet with the values you want to examine. For example, you might want to restrict payments on a loan to a certain amount. Given the desired payment, loan term, and prevailing interest rate, you could set the monthly payment as a goal and then ask Excel to calculate the maximum loan you could afford under those terms. For help, see **94** **Calculate Payments on a Loan**.

Alternatively, suppose that you are operating a bed and breakfast and want to achieve a certain amount of revenue from room rentals. You could use Excel's **Goal Seek** tool to determine the occupancy rate necessary to meet the revenue goal.

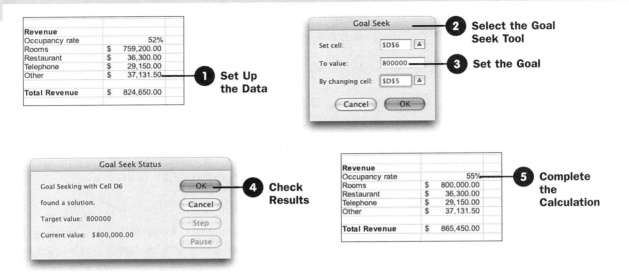

1 Set Up the Data

2 Select the Goal Seek Tool

3 Set the Goal

4 Check Results

5 Complete the Calculation

Whatever the objective, start by selecting the cell where you have entered the formula that states your goal value. In this example, the cell that displays anticipated room revenue, $759,200, contains a formula that multiplies the nightly room rate by the occupancy rate (in the cell just above it). You can ask Excel to calculate what the occupancy rate would have to be to raise the room revenue to $800,000.

2 **Select the Goal Seek Tool**

From the main menu, select **Tools, Goal Seek**. The **Goal Seek** dialog box opens.

3 **Set the Goal**

In the **Set cell** text box, enter the cell that contains the goal you want to achieve. If you have selected a cell in advance (as directed in step 1), that cell is already entered. If the incorrect cell appears in the dialog box, go to the worksheet and click the correct cell to select it.

In the **To value** text box, enter the goal you want to achieve. For example, if you are seeking a certain profit level, enter this profit as the goal.

NOTE

The **Goal Seek** tool works by recalculating a formula. Therefore, the cell that states your goal must contain a formula to be recalculated.

In the **By changing cell** box, enter or select the cell that will contain a variable amount. If you are trying to calculate the sales level that would meet your profit goal, enter the cell that contains the sales revenue. Click **OK** to close the **Goal Seek** dialog box.

> **NOTE**
>
> Normally, this goal-seeking process goes very quickly. At times, though, Excel must make multiple passes through the data; in that case, it displays an ongoing status report. In addition, sometimes Excel reports that it cannot find a solution. In either of these cases, click the **Cancel** button in the **Goal Seek Status** dialog box to halt the process and return to the original values.

④ Check the Results

There are some goals so far out of reach that Excel cannot calculate them within its prescribed 20 passes through the data. Unless you have sent Excel on such an impossible mission, the program reports success in a **Goal Seek Status** dialog box.

⑤ Complete the Calculation

Click **OK** to close the status dialog box. Excel adjusts the amount in the variable cell to meet the goal you have stated. In this case, the worksheet shows that to earn $800,000 from room rentals, you would need an occupancy rate of 55%.

101 Track a Long-term Average

Before You Begin

✔ 65 Make an Automatic Calculation

✔ 75 Plot a Chart

See Also

→ 99 Identify Causes and Effects

→ 100 Set and Meet a Goal

> **KEY TERM**
>
> *Moving average*—A tool that calculates long-term averages, dampening out short-term variations.

A clothing retailer would not normally assume that December sales are typical of the entire year; likewise, a ski shop would not usually make long-term plans based only on its sales in June and July.

Seasonal businesses are typical of situations where you might want to look past wildly fluctuating values and concentrate on the long-term average. The **Moving Average** tool can do this for you. This tool can take a series of values such as monthly sales totals and dampen periodic swings. It then can use its averages to project some short-term future results.

You can use a *moving average* to track sales trends in a seasonal business, to keep track of long-term inventory levels, or to schedule equipment maintenance based on periods of light or heavy use. The **Moving Average** tool looks at sequential values over a number of months or other intervals. You then can ask it to project the results for the next interval or two. For example, if you calculate a moving average of monthly sales for a calendar year, you can ask the function to predict sales for January and February.

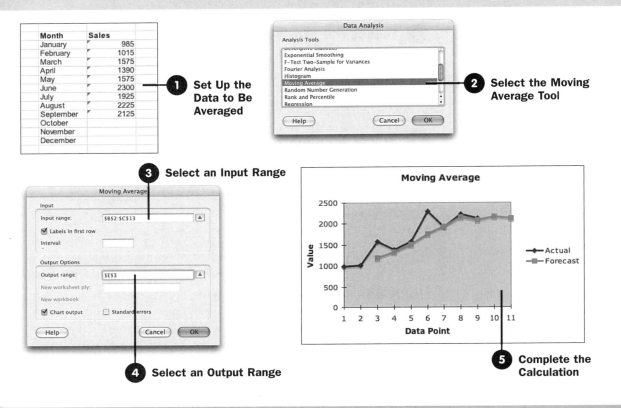

1 Set Up the Data to Be Averaged

2 Select the Moving Average Tool

3 Select an Input Range

4 Select an Output Range

5 Complete the Calculation

---

1 ## Set Up the Data to Be Averaged

For the **Moving Average** calculation, you might use a worksheet that lists monthly sales totals for the year. You then could provide a column in which a moving average is calculated for each month, including projections for the next two months.

The **Moving Average** tool requires at least three intervals to work with before it calculates the first average. If you are tracking monthly sales starting from the beginning of a year, it would calculate no averages for January or February but would pick up the sequence starting in March. At that point, it would report the per-month average for January through March. On the other hand, if the last entry is for September, the function continues to report projected averages for the next three months (through December).

NOTE

The **Moving Average** tool is part of the **Data Analysis ToolPak**, which you must specifically include when you install Excel. If the **Tools**, **Data Analysis** command is not an available menu option, you can install the tool from the **Value Pack** folder on the installation disc, or you can ask your technical support people to install it.

❷ Select the Moving Average Tool

Select **Tools, Data Analysis** from the menu. The **Data Analysis** dialog box opens, offering a choice of analytical tools. Select the **Moving Average** tool and click **OK**. The **Moving Average** dialog box opens.

❸ Select an Input Range

Click the **Input range** text box. Then go to the worksheet and select the range of values you want to average. If you are averaging monthly sales, for example, select the range that includes those figures.

The range must be in a single column or row. If the selection includes column or row titles such as **Sales**, enable the **Labels in first row** check box. If you do that, the function ignores the labels.

Select one to three blank cells beyond the current data, such as the cells that would represent sales for the next three months. The **Moving Average** tool calculates projections for these months as well. Be careful, though. Because this function works with data from the previous three periods, these projected averages are likely to use seasonal data to forecast off-season results.

❹ Select an Output Range

Click the **Output range** text box and select the first cell where you want the moving averages to appear.

If you enable the **Chart output** check box in the **Moving Average** dialog box, Excel generates a graph as well as the numerical report in the specified **Output range**.

❺ Complete the Calculation

Click **OK**. Excel calculates the moving averages for the selected intervals and displays the calculated averages in a new column. Because Excel calculates no averages for the first two months, the code #N/A appears in these cells. You also will see an error code if you try to extend the projection more than two periods from the end of your present data.

🔔 TIP

If you enable the **Chart output** check box in the **Moving Average** dialog box, a line graph of the actual and forecast averages also appears. You might want to use the black-box handles around the edges of the chart box to make the chart larger and more readable. Because this is a standard Excel chart, you can use any of the chart options in the **Formatting** palette to dress it up. See **76 Format the Text in a Chart** and **78 Add Color and Texture** for ways to do this.

PART III: Excel 2004

PART IV

PowerPoint 2004

IN THIS PART:

15

Building a Show

IN THIS CHAPTER:

I once attended a seminar at which a speaker's PowerPoint presentation consisted of multiple slides with 10–15 bullet points each. In rote fashion, the speaker read off every word on the screen—and nothing else.

In a critique of the session, I suggested that instead of just reading the screen, the speaker use his knowledge to expand on the points he presented. Later at another session, the same speaker acknowledged the critique but said, "I'm going to keep on doing it my way."

And he did, demonstrating why so many people equate PowerPoint with really bad presentations. At its best, PowerPoint can guide and enhance a presentation with a series of visual *slides* that outline and illustrate the subject matter. It has the power to help even the most reluctant public speakers make polished, effective presentations.

But the program has also been around long enough to be often and easily misused. With the help of the PowerPoint software, we've all been able to experience countless presenters whose fear of public speaking is entirely well founded.

It doesn't have to be that way. You can develop an effective presentation by implementing a few design principles. You probably are already familiar with one of them: KISS, or keep it simple, stupid.

NOTE

Unlike most Microsoft Office applications, PowerPoint was first developed for the Mac and was later adapted to Windows.

Because PowerPoint has so many creative features, it's easy to overuse them and either bore or overwhelm your audience. The right way is to use these features selectively to build an overall presentation that delivers a focused message.

As you develop your own presentation, keep these points in mind:

- **Simplify**—Limit each slide to a single main concept. Use no more than half a dozen bulleted points, and be sure that all these support the main concept.

- **Stick to the main point**—Make sure that everything on a slide supports the main point. For example, if you use a pie chart, present the main point in an exploding slice with a distinctive color.

- **Use readable text**—You might have 318 fonts on your computer, but stick to 1 or 2 in a presentation. Use short, direct phrases rather than complete sentences.

- **Keep the slides uniform**—Use a template to ensure that backgrounds, typefaces, and other elements are the same from slide to slide.

- **Use color with restraint**—Choose high-contrast hues that promote readability. It's no accident that so many presentations use yellow text on a blue background.

Make sure that the PowerPoint presentation supports your subject matter and does not distract from it. Remember, your goal is to express, not impress.

TIP

Avoid red and green. Color-blind viewers have trouble distinguishing these colors from one another.

102 Select a Presentation Type

A lot of Mac users are well qualified to manage the text, graphics, and color designs of a presentation. For those who are not or do not want to take the time, PowerPoint can do a lot of the design work for you.

As you prepare a presentation, you can select from a number of design *templates*, which are prepared combinations of color, graphics, typefaces, and other design elements. You can choose from an equally broad selection of content templates. These contain model text and graphics for presentations on subjects such as an employee orientation, a financial report, or a project proposal. Or you can choose both.

You can select either a design or content template from the **Project Gallery** that opens when you first start PowerPoint.

1 Open the Project Gallery

Launch PowerPoint. If the **Project Gallery** does not open, you can display it by selecting **File**, **Project Gallery**.

This window offers several options. You can start a new presentation by clicking the **PowerPoint Presentation** graphic on the right side of the window. If you want step-by-step guidance, select the **AutoContent Wizard**.

Alternatively, you can make a selection from the list on the left side of the window. Click the arrow next to **Presentations** and you are given a choice between the **Designs** or **Content** template.

2 Select a Template Type

Click either **Content** or **Designs**. Thumbnail views of master template designs are displayed in the right pane.

See Also

→ **103** Develop a Presentation from Scratch

→ **104** Outline a Presentation

→ **106** Apply a Slide Master

KEY TERM

Template—A predesigned presentation shell that provides design or content elements for a standard presentation.

TIP

If you choose a content template, you are not irrevocably bound to its design; you can apply a different design template later.

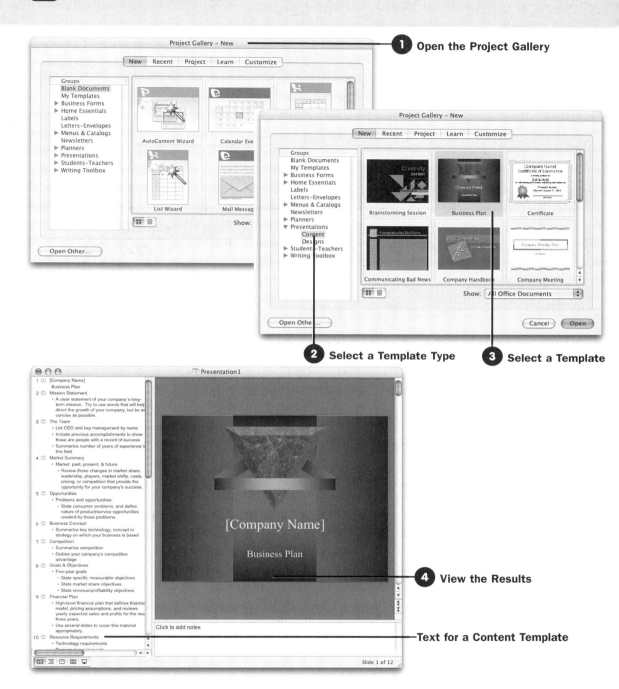

1 Open the Project Gallery

2 Select a Template Type

3 Select a Template

4 View the Results

Text for a Content Template

❸ Select a Template

Scroll through the thumbnails on the right side of the window. Select the design you'd like to base your presentation on and double-click its thumbnail.

❹ View the Results

A presentation opens in that design. If you have chosen a **Content** template, the new presentation includes a series of slides with model text that is shown in an Outline pane on the left side of the window.

 TIP

If you have a choice between a Content template you'd like to use and a design you'd like to display, select the content template first. Then you can select **Format, Slide Design** to apply your preferred design.

103 Develop a Presentation from Scratch

So, you don't want to depend on Microsoft to design a presentation for you. That's understandable. Although PowerPoint provides a lot of handholding for those who want or need it, you can push it out of the way if you want to apply your own colors, graphics, and content.

When you take this route, instead of offering layouts for an entire presentation, PowerPoint lets you select a layout for each slide in the presentation. You can select one layout for a title page and another for a page with graphics and some bullet points.

These are generic pages. You can enhance them by applying an existing design style, or you can use your own design.

Before You Begin

✔ **102** Select a Presentation Type

See Also

→ **106** Apply a Slide Master

→ **107** Insert New Text in a Slide

→ **108** Format Bullet Points

❶ Start a New Presentation

From the **Project Gallery**, double-click the **PowerPoint Presentation** graphic on the right side of the window.

A new presentation opens. In the **Formatting Palette**, open the **Add Objects** group and point to the **Slides** icon. Thumbnails of about two dozen slide types are displayed; you can click the arrow buttons to scroll down and see the entire list. Each provides a basic framework for a new slide in the presentation. When you point to each thumbnail, its label is displayed.

You normally would first select a title slide then proceed by selecting other generic slides that provide spaces for various combinations of text and graphics. There is one blank slide for those who want to start with a clean slate.

 TIP

If the **Project Gallery** is not open, select **File, New Presentation** from the main PowerPoint menu.

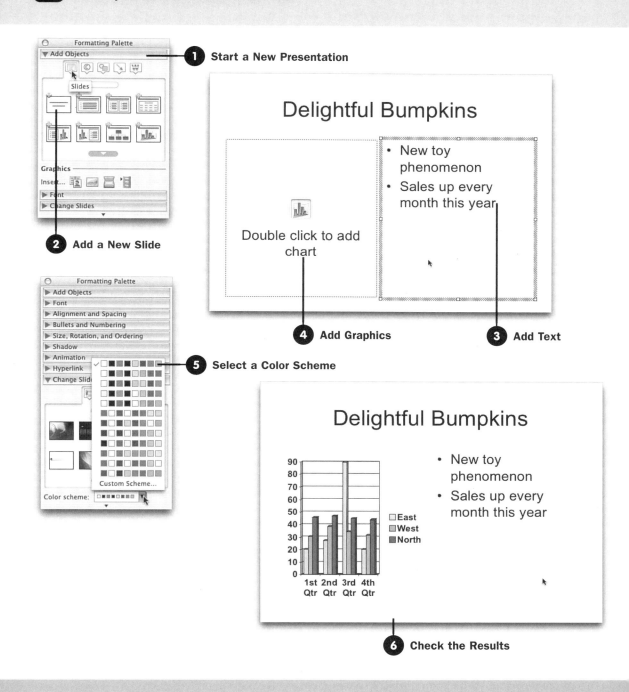

1 Start a New Presentation

2 Add a New Slide

Delightful Bumpkins

Double click to add chart

- New toy phenomenon
- Sales up every month this year

4 Add Graphics

3 Add Text

5 Select a Color Scheme

Delightful Bumpkins

- New toy phenomenon
- Sales up every month this year

6 Check the Results

❷ Add a New Slide

Double-click the layout you want to use for the first slide. Unless you have chosen a totally blank layout, the new slide appears with *placeholders* for text or graphics.

❸ Add Text

In most layouts, you can click the placeholder boxes to add text such as a title for the slide and a bullet-point list. Whatever you type appears in the slide.

❹ Add Graphics

If the placeholder calls for a chart, the auxiliary program **Microsoft Graph** opens so you can construct a graph. Microsoft Graph displays a data sheet you can fill in to generate a graph. When you're finished, click anywhere in the slide window. The graph places itself into the PowerPoint placeholder you originally selected.

❺ Select a Color Scheme

A quick way to spice up an unadorned chart is to apply one of PowerPoint's standard color schemes. At the bottom of the **Formatting Palette**, open the **Change Slides** section; then click the arrow next to the **Color Scheme** drop-down list. A selection of color-coordinated options is displayed. Select one to apply it to all the charts in the presentation.

❻ Check the Results

The slide appears in the new color scheme. If you want, you can select the text, background, or other elements of the slide and use the **Format** menu options to change the appearance of any of these elements.

KEY TERM

Placeholder—A box in a slide layout where you can add text or graphics.

NOTE

If the placeholder calls for clip art, when you click the placeholder, the **Clip Gallery** opens. Select a drawing and click **Insert**. If the placeholder calls for a picture, a Finder window opens; select a picture file and click **Insert**.

TIP

If you want to create your own color scheme, open the **Color Scheme** list and select **Custom Scheme**. A dialog box displays multiple options for applying your own colors.

104 Outline a Presentation

Before You Begin

✔ **102** Select a
Presentation Type

✔ **103** Develop a
Presentation from
Scratch

See Also

→ **105** Import an Outline
from Word

Whether you're preparing a book report, postgraduate thesis, or computer book, the key to success is to get organized. And the key to getting organized is to prepare a good outline.

The same is true of a good presentation. An outline can help you make your points in an organized, orderly way. PowerPoint can help you outline your presentation and keep it on track. In fact, to a great extent, PowerPoint *is* an outlining tool.

As you develop a presentation, it creates its own outline. Slide titles appear at the first outline level, main bullet points at the second level, and subordinate bullet points at successively lower levels. You can display this outline, edit the text, and move elements around to present them in a different order. Any change you make in either the slide text or the outline is immediately reflected in the other.

1 Display the Outline View

You can display a presentation-in-progress in any of several *views*. Normally, you first see a presentation in Normal view, in which each slide appears with the outline in a separate window to its left. Other views include an Outline view in which the outline appears in a larger window and the slide in a smaller one.

To display your presentation in Outline view, click the **Outline View** icon in the lower-left corner of the screen.

2 Reorganize the Outline

In the outline on the left side of the window, click a slide title and drag it to a new position in the outline. The slide in the right side of the window is moved in the presentation series to appear in the new order.

3 Add Some Text

Perhaps you have a blank slide that is waiting for the addition of some new bullet points. You can make that change in the outline; you also can edit existing text on slides by editing the text in the outline on the left side of the window.

KEY TERM

View—A manner of displaying a presentation. You can display a **Normal view** of a slide and the presentation outline, an **Outline view** that emphasizes the outline, and a **Slide view** that displays the slide alone. Other choices are a **Slide Sorter view**, in which you can move the slides into a different order, and a **Slide Show view** that emulates the finished presentation. Choose a view by selecting it from the **View** menu or by selecting one of the view icons in the lower-left corner of the screen.

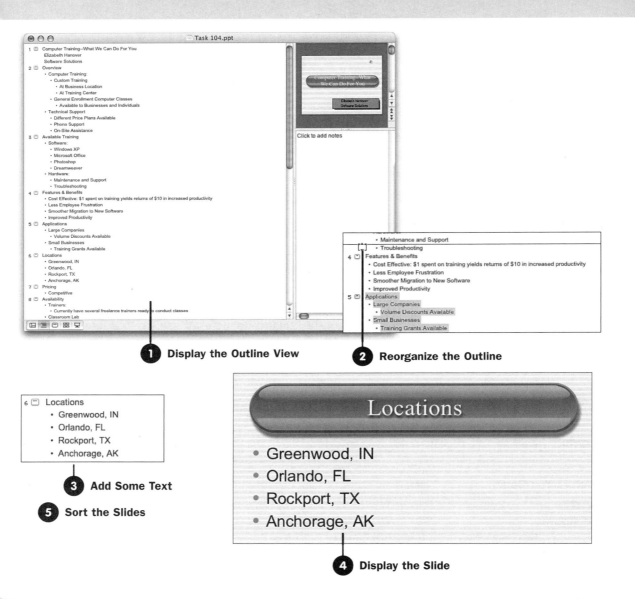

① **Display the Outline View**

② **Reorganize the Outline**

③ **Add Some Text**

⑤ **Sort the Slides**

④ **Display the Slide**

In the outline on the left side of the screen, click at the end of the slide title where you want to add the text. Press **Enter** and then press **Tab**. These keystrokes position the insertion point for you to enter a new bullet point below the slide title.

NOTE

Press **Tab** and **Shift+Tab** to promote or demote entries, whether in the slide or the outline. In step 3, you press **Tab** to demote the text you are adding to a bullet point. If you don't press **Tab**, the text you enter would be at the highest outline level, and thus the title of a new slide.

TIP

In either Normal or Outline view, the boundary between the outline and slide windows is movable. You can slide it in either direction to enlarge one window relative to the other.

Type the new text; as you type, the text also appears in the slide on the right side of the window. You can type multiple bullet points within the outline; press **Enter** after each. You also can use **Tab** and **Shift+Tab** to move the entry to higher or lower outline levels.

④ Display the Slide

Select **View**, **Normal** to switch from Outline view to Normal view. The new entries you made in the outline on the left side of the window appear in the slides on the right side.

⑤ Sort the Slides

You can use the outline to rearrange the order in which the slides appear, but there's another way that probably is more fun.

Select **View**, **Slide Sorter**. This view displays thumbnails of the slides on a single screen. You can move the thumbnails around like a kind of shell game. The new order of the thumbnails is reflected in the finished presentation.

When you're finished, you can use the **View** menu or click a View icon in the lower-left corner of the screen to display a different view.

---

105   Import an Outline from Word

Before You Begin

✔ **24** Write an Outline

✔ **102** Select a Presentation Type

✔ **103** Develop a Presentation from Scratch

✔ **104** Outline a Presentation

See Also

➔ **106** Apply a Slide Master

PowerPoint has a useful outlining feature, but Word can do some really serious outlining. Word has an expanded ability to format text, organize and reorganize, expand or collapse the display of subordinate levels, and many other outlining features. If planning is critical to success— and it is—Word's outliner is a major-league planning tool.

If you are planning an important presentation, it makes sense to get your thoughts together by building an outline in Word. Then you can start a new PowerPoint presentation by importing that outline. PowerPoint uses the Word outline to build the slideshow presentation for you.

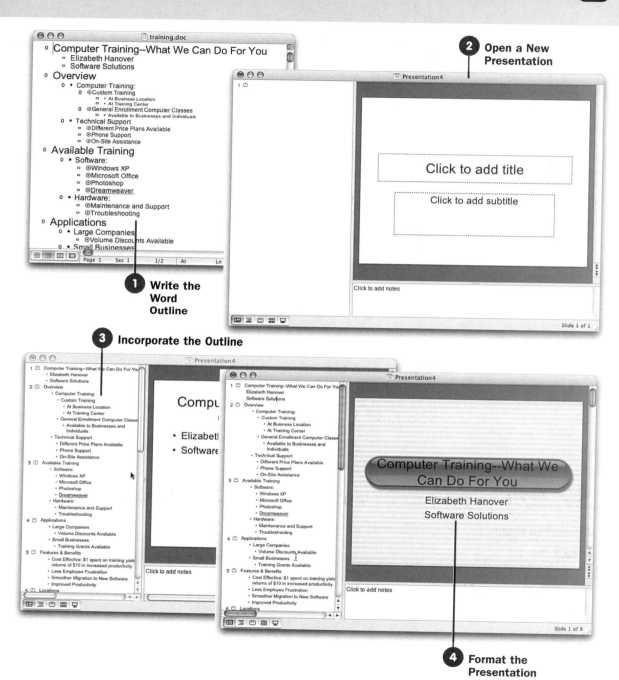

1 Write the Word Outline

2 Open a New Presentation

3 Incorporate the Outline

4 Format the Presentation

NOTE

Organizing the presentation in Word is much like organizing the presentation in PowerPoint itself. The top-level outline headings become slide titles, next-level entries become first-level bullet points, and lower-level entries become successively lower-level bullet points.

NOTE

Check the imported outline carefully. Sometimes PowerPoint does not assign levels that match those in the original Word outline. Use **Tab** and **Shift+Tab** to promote or demote items as necessary.

① Write the Word Outline

Use Word's Outline view to build the outline. As the plan comes together, you can move around major and subordinate points, promote and demote entries, and give yourself a good picture of how the presentation will go.

② Open a New Presentation

In PowerPoint, select **File**, **New Presentation**. Instead of starting with a PowerPoint template, you will build this presentation from the Word outline.

③ Incorporate the Outline

Select **Insert**, **Slides from Outline**. Navigate to the Word outline file, select it, and click **Open**.

The outline is imported into the open PowerPoint presentation. Each top-level heading becomes the title of a new slide. Other headings become bullet points.

④ Format the Presentation

The imported presentation has only a generic format. Select **Format**, **Slide Design** to apply a predesigned slide format, or use the **Format** menu or the **Change Slides** section of the **Formatting Palette** to apply a format of your own.

106 Apply a Slide Master

Before You Begin

✔ **102** Select a Presentation Type

See Also

→ **107** Insert New Text in a Slide

→ **108** Format Bullet Points

A slide *master* sets the style of a presentation. It governs the appearance of every slide in the presentation, ensuring that each slide reflects uniform standards for graphics, type styles, and other aspects of their appearance. Every presentation has a slide master; a presentation without special formatting has a master without special formatting.

You can use a slide master to apply formatting that appears uniformly throughout the presentation. You also can use a slide master to insert elements that should appear on every slide. These might include a corporate logo, page numbers, or a notation about who produced the presentation and when.

The slide master is one of four types of available masters. Others include a separate title master that governs the appearance of the title slide. There are also masters to set the layouts of notes and handouts.

❶ Display the Slide Master

Open the presentation whose slide master you want to change. Select **View**, **Master**, **Slide Master**. The slide master is displayed. Along with it, the **Master** toolbar displays two buttons: one to display a miniature preview of the actual slide and the other to close the master.

❷ Select an Element to Change

You can change nearly every element of the slide master and see the change reflected later in the overall presentation. For example, you can change the typeface in which the slide title appears.

In this example, follow the instruction **Click to edit Master text style**. The text box with that legend is selected. You now can select a new typeface, style, or color.

❸ Select a New Typeface

Select **Format**, **Font**. The **Font** dialog box lets you change the typeface, style, size, and other specifications of the title text for every slide.

In this example, you might want to use a different typeface from the one now in use. Scroll down the **Font** list and select the typeface you want to use. If you want to make any other changes in the type display (such as to font size, color, or effects), make these selections as well. When finished, click **OK**.

❹ Add Footer Information

Three text blocks at the bottom of the slide master suggest they might be used to insert a date, slide numbers, and other information such as the author's name. Nothing appears in these footer areas, though, until you add it.

KEY TERM

Master—A slide design that governs the appearance of elements that appear on every slide in a presentation. PowerPoint uses masters for general slides, title slides, handouts, and notes.

TIP

When you display a slide master, its matching title master is in the Slide 2 position. Press **Page Down** to see the title master. One use of a separate slide master is to include slide numbers on the general slides but to omit the number from the title slide.

TIP

Even at the same point size, some typefaces appear smaller than others in the completed slide. After you make your selection, select **Slide Miniature** in the **Master** toolbar to see how an actual slide will look.

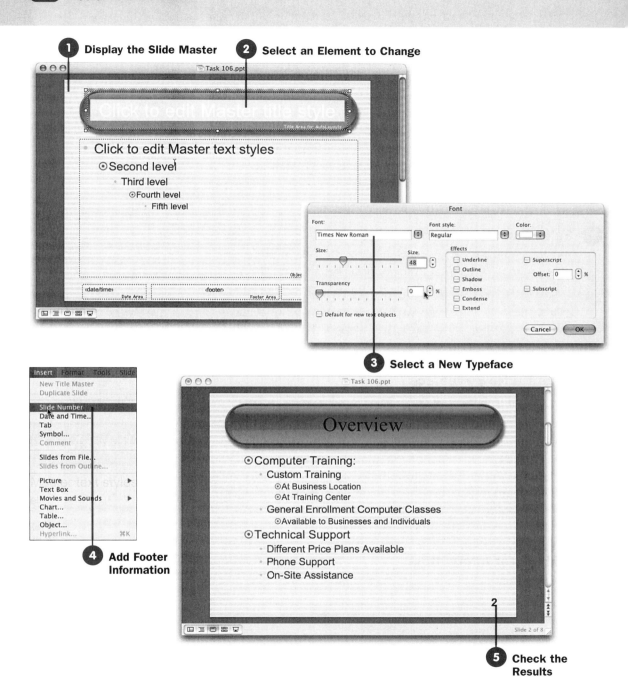

1 Display the Slide Master

2 Select an Element to Change

3 Select a New Typeface

4 Add Footer Information

5 Check the Results

For example, you can click in the lower-right corner box where there is room for a slide number. Then select **Insert**, **Slide Number**. This choice displays consecutive numbers in that position on individual slides. If you later rearrange the slides, the slide numbers are updated automatically.

To add information to either of the other footer text boxes, click in the box and type the information. What you type here appears on every slide (except the title slide) in the presentation.

 TIP

The position of the text box initially determines the alignment of the text. For example, a left text box contains flush left text. If you want to change this, you can use the **Alignment and Spacing** settings of the **Formatting Palette**.

⑤ Check the Results

The changes are reflected in the new master. To return to the presentation, select **Close** in the **Master** toolbar.

107 Insert New Text in a Slide

You can use the PowerPoint outline to add, delete, and rearrange text, but sometimes it is easier just to edit the text in the slide itself. In that case, the process is fairly simple: just click and type.

Before You Begin

✔ **103** Develop a Presentation from Scratch

See Also

→ **108** Format Bullet Points

① Pick a Spot

Open the presentation. Use the up or down arrow keys to move to the slide you want to edit. Click at the spot where you want the new text to go.

If you want to start on a new line, press **Return**. You can use **Tab** or **Shift+Tab** to demote or promote the new line within the bullet-point hierarchy.

② Type the Text

Type the text you want to add. It appears in the format established by the slide *master*.

That's it. About the only other thing you might want to do is to display the outline in Normal or Outline view and confirm that your new entry also appears there.

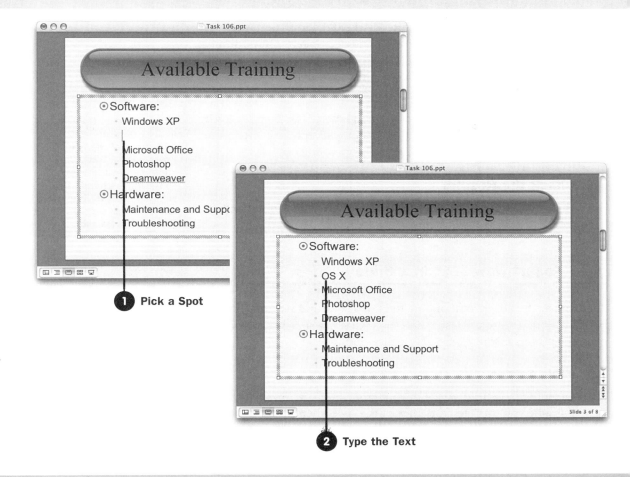

1 Pick a Spot

2 Type the Text

108 Format Bullet Points

Bullet points are a staple of PowerPoint presentations. During a good presentation, they cue the speaker about the points to be made and the order in which to make them. Afterward, when printed in handouts, they serve as reminders to the members of the audience.

Bullet points are so called because they are commonly punctuated with bullet-like dots at the beginning of each point. There's also a subtle suggestion of a speaker who can hit each point like a firing-range target. (In the case of the speaker mentioned at the start of this chapter, that would be automatic weapons fire.)

Despite their tradition, bullets do not have to be the traditional round bullet or limited to those variations provided by some of the standard slide designs. There are other options—many other options.

1 Select a Bullet Level

Open a presentation, and select its slide master. Follow the instruction to **Click to edit Master text styles**.

Make sure the insertion point is in the example of the level you want to customize. For example, if you want to add a different bullet character to first-level bullet points, be sure you have clicked the text at that level. If you are working with a text *master*, the first level is labeled **Master Text Style**.

2 Display Bullet Options

Select **Format, Bullets and Numbering**. The **Bullets and Numbering** dialog box opens. Make sure that the **Bulleted** tab is selected.

This page displays several types of bullet points. If you see something you like, select it and click **OK**. The selection is applied to the bullets, and you need do nothing more. If you'd like to explore other options, click the **Character** button.

Before You Begin

✔ **107** Insert New Text in a Slide

See Also

→ **110** Insert Artwork into a Presentation

 NOTE

To display a slide master for the currently open presentation, select **View, Master, Slide Master**.

 NOTE

Although there's nothing wrong with applying numbers to your points, if the objective is to use a different type of bullet point, make sure that the **Bulleted** tab is displayed in the **Bullets and Numbering** dialog box.

1 **Select a Bullet Level**

2 **Display Bullet Options**

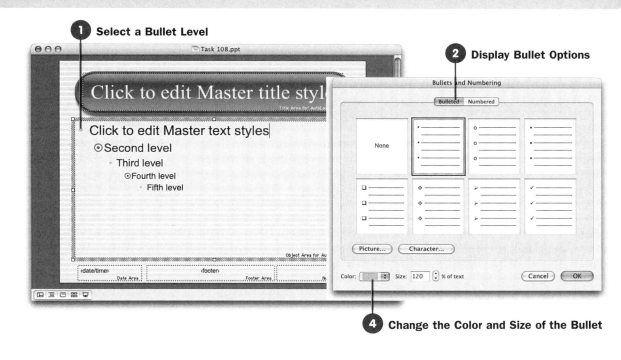

4 **Change the Color and Size of the Bullet**

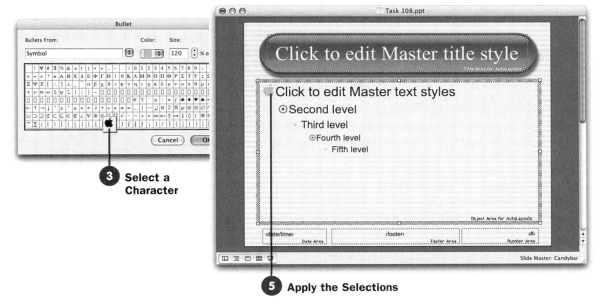

3 **Select a Character**

5 **Apply the Selections**

3 Select a Character

When you click the **Character** button in the **Bullets and Numbering** dialog box, the **Bullet** dialog box opens to display characters from the type font currently in use. The font might include a few characters you can use as bullets, but remember that it is primarily a text font. You'll find better selections in all-symbol fonts such as **Symbol**, **Wingdings**, or **Zapf Dingbats**.

From the drop-down list in the upper-left corner of the window, select a font. If you see a symbol that looks interesting, click it to see an enlarged view.

4 Change the Color and Size of the Bullet

In the **Bullet** dialog box or in the **Bullets and Numbering** dialog box, you also can select a different color and set the size of the bullet relative to the text.

5 Apply the Selections

Click **OK** to close the **Bullet** dialog box; click **OK** again to close the **Bullets and Numbering** dialog box. The new bullet character appears in the slide master. In the presentation itself, all slides with text on that level now have that type of bullet character.

TIPS

There are other bulleting options as well. If you select **None**, no bullet is applied to text on that level. In the slide master, you might remove the bullet for a low bullet point level so you can use it as unbulleted body text.

The **Picture** button lets you select a graphics file from your hard disk and use it as a bullet. Make sure that the graphic you pick is a suitable size for the purpose.

109 Insert an Excel Table

Picture this: You're a creative professional about to make a presentation to a client. There's a lot of competition for this job, so you want to make the lowest bid you can and still cover expenses.

You work up an Excel spreadsheet and include it in a PowerPoint presentation. You're about ready to make the presentation, when you get some good news. Your supplier of inkjet printing paper has just sharply reduced its prices. Your expenses will be less, and you can reduce your bid accordingly.

No problem if you have embedded the Excel data into the presentation. Plug the new figures into Excel, and the PowerPoint presentation is immediately updated. You're ready to go.

Before You Begin

✔ **106** Apply a Slide Master

See Also

→ **107** Insert New Text in a Slide

→ **110** Insert Artwork into a Presentation

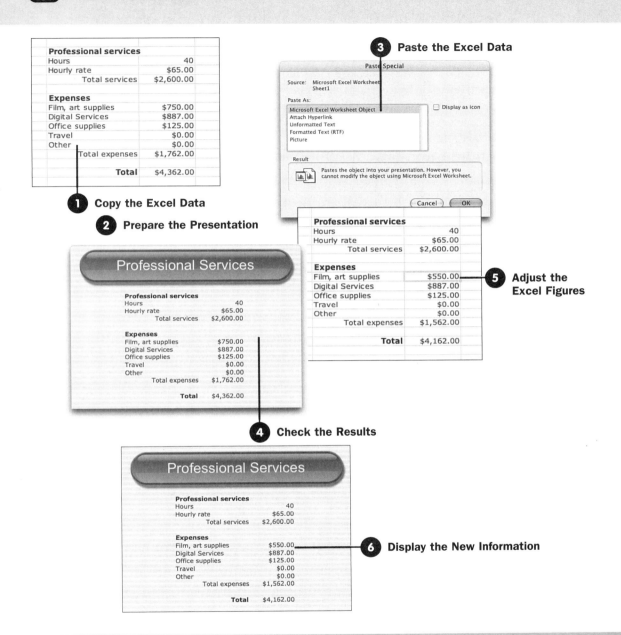

1 Copy the Excel Data

2 Prepare the Presentation

3 Paste the Excel Data

4 Check the Results

5 Adjust the Excel Figures

6 Display the New Information

① Copy the Excel Data

You can start with worksheet data, as we do in this example, or you can choose to import a completed chart. Either select the chart (click in the background of the chart) or drag to select the range in the worksheet, then select **Edit**, **Copy** or press the keyboard short-cut ⌘-**C**.

② Prepare the Presentation

Open the PowerPoint slide where you want to insert the Excel data. Place the insertion point where you want the data to appear.

③ Paste the Excel Data

With the slide open onscreen, select **Edit**, **Paste Special**. The **Paste Special** dialog box should identify the **Source** material you copied as part of an Excel worksheet.

At this point, you have a choice. The **Paste As** list offers several options. Select **Microsoft Excel Worksheet Object**.

④ Check the Results

Click **OK**. The **Paste Special** dialog box closes, and the Excel data is placed in the PowerPoint slide. Because the Excel data is in the form of a graphic, you can use the adjustment handles surround-ing the graphic so its size and position fit properly into the area on the slide.

⑤ Adjust the Excel Figures

If you receive word of a cost change (for example, that your paper supplier has dropped its prices), you'll want to adjust the data in the presentation slide as well as in your original Excel worksheet. Double-click the Excel data in the PowerPoint presentation.

The Excel worksheet opens, and you can make the necessary changes to the data there.

TIP

You might want to build a slide in which the Excel data appears on the left side of the slide with bullet points to the right, or the reverse. If so, apply one of the slide styles that calls for a picture and text in separate columns. Click the picture column and execute the **Paste Special** com-mand. The Excel data appears in the picture col-umn with room for text on the opposite side.

6 Display the New Information

When finished with the Excel worksheet, select **File**, **Close and Return to Presentation**. (This menu item also includes the name of the PowerPoint presentation file.) Excel closes and you return to the slide you double-clicked in step 5. The presentation displays the updated figures.

110 Insert Artwork into a Presentation

Before You Begin

✔ **102** Select a Presentation Type

✔ **103** Develop a Presentation from Scratch

See Also

→ **107** Insert New Text in a Slide

→ **112** Animate a Chart

NOTE

When you add art from an outside source, be sure you have the right to use it in your presentation. Copyright law protects *everything*, and you can use someone else's creation only if that someone has provided written permission for you to do so.

TIP

There is also an **Insert Clip Art** icon in the **Add Objects** section of the **Formatting Palette**. Click it to open the **Clip Gallery**.

A PowerPoint presentation is a visual medium, but it can't be very visual if all it displays is text. Even simple clip art can add visual interest and effectiveness to a slide. You can go further and add photos and other artwork as well. The main requirement is that the art be available somewhere—on your hard disk, on a Web site, or from some other legitimate source.

1 Prepare the Slide

In the **Formatting Palette**, open the **Add Objects** section. Select the **Slides** icon and scroll down to one of the slide layouts that combines a picture and clip art. These provide placeholders for both text and art.

If you want to add a picture to an existing text slide, select **Format**, **Slide Layout** and select a layout that provides for both clip art and text.

2 Select a Picture

Double-click the art placeholder. The **Clip Gallery** opens with a selection of clip art and other pictures. From the **Category** list on the left side of the screen, select a category to see thumbnails of related artwork.

You also can enter a search term in the **Search** window of the **Clip Gallery**. For example, to illustrate a slide advertising a health product, you might search for the term *health* or *medical*.

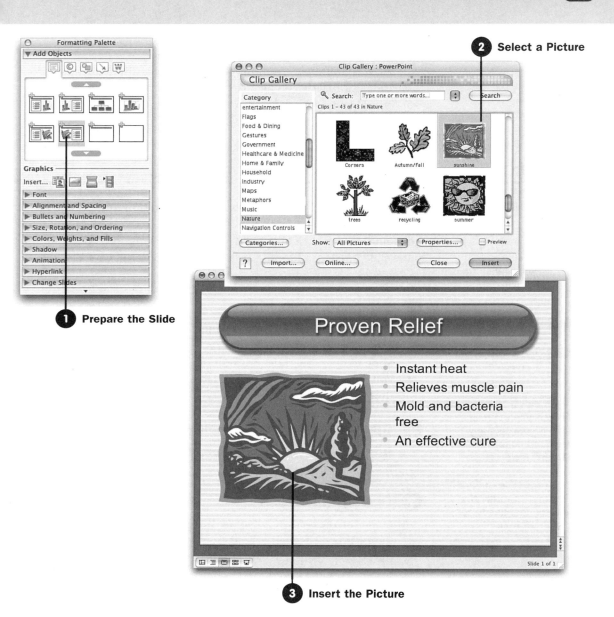

2 Select a Picture

1 Prepare the Slide

3 Insert the Picture

③ Insert the Picture

Select a thumbnail from the right side of the **Clip Gallery** window and click **Insert**. The picture you selected is added to the slide. Initially, the picture adapts to the size of its placeholder. You can select the picture and use its adjustment handles to resize it.

111 Add a New Background

Before You Begin

✔ **102** Select a Presentation Type

✔ **103** Develop a Presentation from Scratch

See Also

→ **106** Apply a Slide Master

→ **110** Insert Artwork into a Presentation

NOTES

When you apply a background, it conceals any background color the slide might now have.

If you use a slide master, don't forget to make the necessary changes to the title slide as well.

TIP

Feel free to explore. The **Background** dialog box has several tabbed pages that offer selections of other background textures and patterns. In addition, an **Other Texture** button lets you apply an existing graphic file as a background.

Sometimes you don't need to reformat a presentation. Just adding a more interesting background can help. You can add a background to an individual slide, or (usually a better choice) you can add a background to the slide *master* so that the entire presentation displays the same background.

① Select the Slide

Open the slide you want to change. If you want to apply the background to the entire presentation, select **View**, **Master**, **Master Slide** to open the slide master for the presentation. Any change you make to the master is applied to every slide in the presentation.

② Open the Background Dialog Box

From the main menu, select **Format**, **Slide Background**. The **Background** dialog box opens.

③ Display Fill Effects

Open the drop-down list under the **Background fill** pane in the dialog box. Select **Fill Effects** from the list. When the **Fill Effects** dialog box opens, click the **Texture** tab. Thumbnails of sample textures are displayed.

④ Select a Texture

Scroll down the texture display and make a selection. Click **OK** to close the **Fill Effects** dialog box.

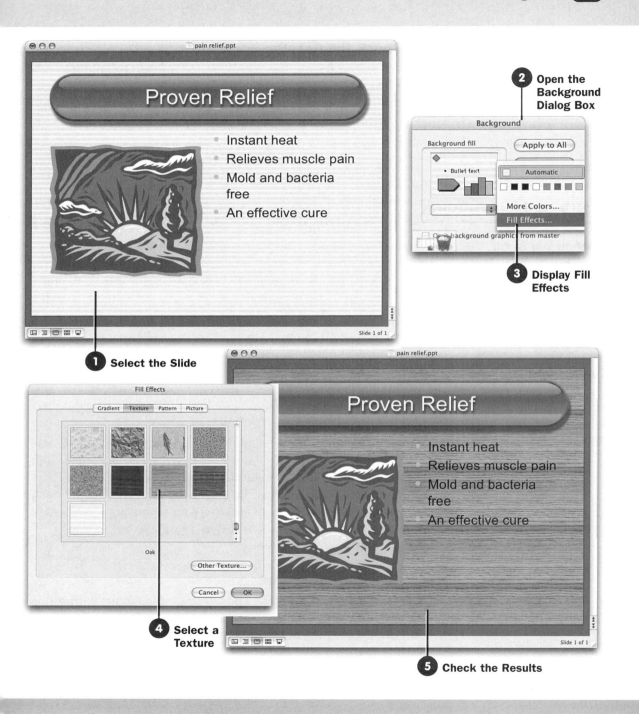

5 **Check the Results**

The chosen background is displayed in the **Background fill** pane in the **Background** dialog box. To apply the change to the current slide, click the **Apply** button. To apply the change to the entire presentation, click **Apply to All**.

The background is applied to the slide master. To see the final effect, select **View**, **Slide** to open the slide in Slide view.

112 Animate a Chart

Before You Begin

✔ **110** Insert Artwork into a Presentation

See Also

➜ **116** Apply Transitions

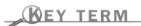

Animation effects—
Advanced transition effects applied to slides or to elements such as graphs.

The initial display shows a vertical bar or column chart. You can click buttons in an upper toolbar to display a different chart type. Using Microsoft Chart is much like creating a chart in Excel, but Excel offers a greater variety of chart type and formatting options.

When a dramatic star takes the stage, she does not just walk on—she makes an *entrance*. If you want your graphs to make a similar impression, you can apply ***animation effects*** to spice up the way they come onto the screen. They can slide in from one direction or another, appear from between blinds, or just appear.

It's not quite correct to say the possibilities are endless, but with about 50 animation effects to choose from, it certainly can seem that way. In most ways, the animation effects are an extended list of the ***transition*** effects you can apply as one slide replaces another in a slideshow. There is one difference: You can apply animation effects to charts, graphics, and other slide elements as well as to entire slides.

Suppose you want to display a graph and discuss each of its data sets separately. The chart might show several months' revenue results from particular activities such as publication design, Web design, and consulting. You could animate the chart so the monthly results from publication design first appear by themselves. After discussing those figures, you could add the results for Web design. Finally, you could add the consulting figures to the screen.

1 **Generate the Chart**

Create a new slide. In the **Add Objects** section of the **Formatting Palette**, select the **Add Chart** design or one of the chart and text designs. Double-click the chart placeholder. The **Microsoft Chart** auxiliary program opens. It displays a sample data sheet plus a graph generated from the sample data.

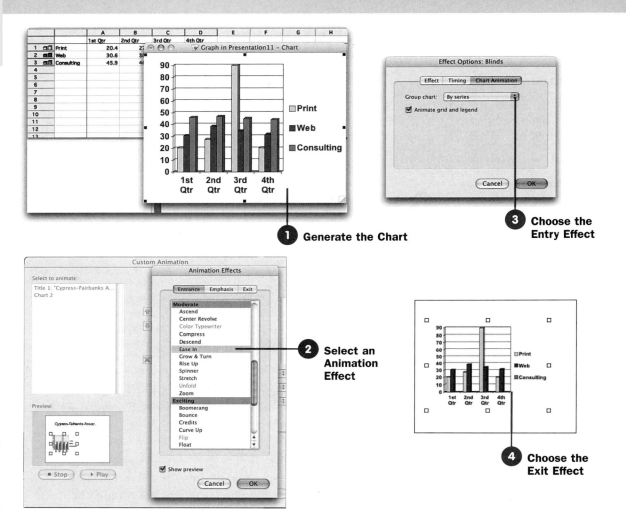

1 Generate the Chart

2 Select an Animation Effect

3 Choose the Entry Effect

4 Choose the Exit Effect

In the worksheet, delete the sample data and enter your own data. As you work, a sample graph displays the results. When you're finished, close Microsoft Chart. The graph is automatically displayed in the slide.

TIP

The **Custom Animation** dialog box is the gateway to a multitude of options. This task can describe only a few of these options. Feel free to experiment and then test the results in the **Preview** window. If you don't like the results, click **Cancel** and start over.

TIP

You normally won't want to animate the grid and legend of the chart, so disable that check box in the **Effect Options** dialog box.

② Select an Animation Effect

From the main menu, select **Slide Show**, **Custom Animation**. The **Custom Animation** dialog box opens.

In the **Select to animate** window, make sure that the chart is selected. Click the **Add Effect** button. All 50 animation effects appear in an extended list; scroll down and select an effect. As you do, the action is demonstrated in the **Preview** window. When you're satisfied with the selected effect, click **OK**.

③ Select Effect Options

You probably will want the individual chart bars to appear on your command as you proceed through the narration of your presentation. If so, make sure the **Start** window reads **On Click**. Then click **Effect Options**.

The **Effect Options** dialog box opens. It includes tabbed pages on which you can add sound and lighting effects and fine-tune the timing of the transition. The **Chart Animation** page contains options for a sequential chart display.

Open the **Group Chart** drop-down list and make a selection. If you want to display the results for one activity at a time, select **By series**. If you want to display each month's results at one time, select **By category**. You also can choose to display individual chart elements in either series or category order. Make a choice; the menu closes. Click **OK**.

You return to the **Custom Animation** dialog box. Under the **Preview** window, click **Play** to see how the bars appear in sequence. If you're satisfied, click **OK**.

④ Display the Chart

You return to the presentation. Click the **Slide Show** button in the lower-left corner of the window.

The slide opens as it would during a slideshow. None of the graph bars are displayed. Click the slide once to add the first set of bars. Click a second time to add the second set; click again to display all three sets.

16

Presenting the Presentation

IN THIS CHAPTER:

In the familiar words of a raffle ticket, you need not be present to win. Adapting that idea to PowerPoint, you need not actually be present to make a presentation.

The most familiar use of PowerPoint, of course, is to project bullet-pointed slides to illustrate an in-person presentation. That's still an important use, but don't limit yourself to that picture. You also can set up a self-running show or even a kiosk-style presentation the viewers can run themselves.

Even when you are there in person, you can do many things to make a presentation more interesting—and thus more effective. You can apply transition effects, make sure that the timing is right, and print handouts for the audience to remember you by.

PowerPoint has a reputation for producing boring presentations. With a little imagination, you can keep yours from falling into that stereotype.

113 Print Your Notes

Before You Begin

✔ **107** Insert New Text in a Slide

See Also

→ **114** Print Handouts

→ **118** Time a Presentation

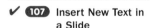

KEY TERM

Notes—A PowerPoint feature with which you can write notes or a narration to accompany each slide in your presentation.

NOTE

A small notes pane is also available in **Normal** and **Outline** views, but the **Notes Page** view gives you more room to work.

PowerPoint has a *Notes* feature that is primarily intended for the benefit of the presenter. It's a place where you can write the narration you plan to deliver with each slide. A companion feature, **handouts**, is intended to produce thumbnails of each slide for delivery to members of the audience. But you might want to do more, such as share copies of your notes with the audience.

PowerPoint envisions a verbal presentation to a room full of supposedly interested people. That's not always the case. The atmosphere might be noisy, there might be distractions, or you might be in an area where people wander in and out. In cases like these, you can distribute printed versions of your notes.

❶ Open the Presentation

Open the presentation in PowerPoint. From the main menu, select **View**, **Notes**. The Notes view opens. Below each slide is a block marked **Click to add text**. You can literally do that. Click the legend, and the **Notes** panel opens so that you can type in it.

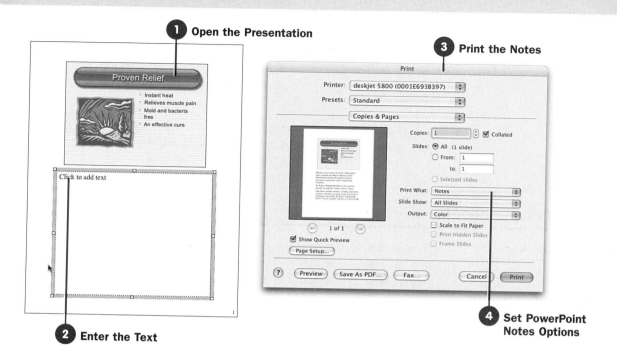

1 Open the Presentation

3 Print the Notes

2 Enter the Text

4 Set PowerPoint Notes Options

2 Enter the Text

Enter the narration you want to use along with this slide. Repeat for the other slides in the presentation.

If you want, you can format the text for printing. Select **Format**, **Font** or use the **Formatting Palette** to select a typeface and size for the text.

3 Print the Notes

When you are done typing the notes or narration for your slides, select **File**, **Print**. When the **Print** dialog box opens, select **Microsoft PowerPoint** from the drop-down list that initially is labeled **Copies and Pages**. The page that opens contains options specific to PowerPoint.

NOTE

Every printer's dialog box looks different, so yours will almost certainly look different from the one shown here. Most printers, though, have a similar list of functions.

4 **Set PowerPoint Notes Options**

From the **Print What** list, select **Notes**. Select any other printing options you want, such as the number of copies. When ready, click the **Print** button. The notes are printed along with copies of each slide.

If the notes run too long for a single sheet, you can enable the **Scale to Fit Paper** check box. You can save paper at the possible expense of legibility while delivering the presentation.

114 Print Handouts

Before You Begin

✔ **113** Print Your Notes

See Also

→ **106** Apply a Slide Master

 TIP

The value of your handouts is directly related to the quality of your slides. If the slides are a well-organized outline of the presentation, the handouts will be the same.

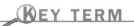 **KEY TERM**

Handouts—A PowerPoint feature that prints thumbnails of each slide in a presentation for distribution to the audience.

 NOTE

The three-slide master is distinct from the other layouts. It leaves room next to the slides for audience members to write their own notes.

An audience would be disappointed if you did not leave them some kind of carry-out reminder of what you had to say—even if they never read it. More to the point, no one's memory is good enough to remember everything you had to say. Accordingly, PowerPoint provides a way to print miniature versions of your slides.

The layout of the printed notes is governed by a handout master, which provides a template for the *handouts* much like a *slide master* provides a template for the slides. Use the handout master to set the number of slides on a printed page and add elements such as page numbers that appear on every page.

1 **Open the Handout Master**

With the presentation open, select **View**, **Master**, **Handout Master**. A diagram of the handout page is displayed along with a pair of toolbars. One toolbar provides tools for working with the handout master in particular; the other has tools for working with masters in general.

2 **Select the Slides per Page**

From the **Handout master** toolbar, select a layout based on the number of slides you want to show on a page. You can choose as many as nine or as few as two slides per page.

1 Open the Handout Master

2 Select the Slides per Page

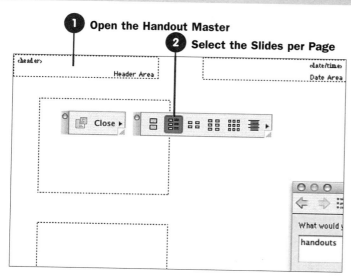

3 Complete the Header and Footer

4 Print the Handouts

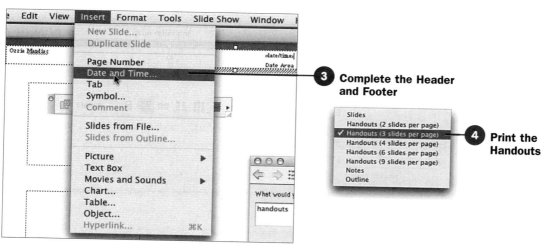

3 Complete the Header and Footer

As with other printed documents, you can add headers and footers with information such as the presentation title and page numbers. The master handout has header and footer placeholders in each of the four corners. Click one of the placeholders and type the header

or footer information you want to appear on each page of the printed handout.

If you want to include text such as your name or the presentation title, click in the header or footer placeholder and type the text you want. If you want to add "codes" for the date or consecutive page numbers (these codes are replaced when the slides are printed), click in the placeholder and open the **Insert** menu. Select the type of entry you want to insert. For example, select **Insert**, **Date and Time**. In the dialog box that opens, select a format for the display of the date and time information.

When you have finished adding information to the headers and footers, click **Close** in the **Master** toolbar. The master handout closes, and you return to the presentation.

④ Print the Handouts

When you are ready to print the handouts, select **File**, **Print**. The **Print** dialog box opens. From the list that is initially titled **Copies and Pages**, select **Microsoft PowerPoint**. A page of PowerPoint-specific options is displayed (for some printers, these options might be in the main dialog box instead of on a separate page, as they are for the printer shown here). Open the **Print what** list and select the **Handouts** option that duplicates the number of pages you selected in step 2. Click **Print**. The handouts are printed.

NOTE

Make sure that the number of pages you print matches the number of pages you selected in step 2. If the number of pages differ, the printer settings take control.

115 Add Sound to the Picture

Before You Begin

 ✔ **103** Develop a Presentation from Scratch

See Also

 → **120** Make a Presentation Run Itself

 → **121** Make a Movie of the Presentation

Would a little background music add interest to a presentation? Probably not if you plan to be speaking; added sound would be too much of a distraction. But if this is to be a free-standing presentation, a musical soundtrack could be a worthwhile addition. A recorded narration might be even more worthwhile. And even in an in-person presentation, you might want to add sound to title slides or other slides that are not specifically part of your talk.

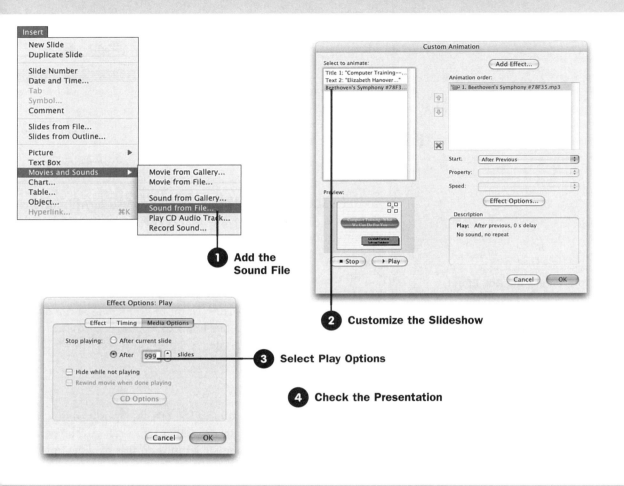

Add the Sound File

Customize the Slideshow

Select Play Options

Check the Presentation

1 Add the Sound File

Open the presentation and display the slide where you want the soundtrack to begin. If you want to run the sound continuously throughout the presentation, open the presentation to the first slide.

Select **Insert, Movies and Sounds, Sound from File**. Navigate to the folder that holds the sound file you want to use. Select the file and then click **Insert**.

NOTE

PowerPoint can use most common sound file formats, including MP3. Be aware, though, that popular music downloads are protected by copyright, and the music industry has been very aggressive in enforcing its rights. Using a copyrighted song in your PowerPoint presentation can be a violation of federal copyright law.

PowerPoint asks whether you want the sound to play automatically when the current slide appears. If so, click **Yes**. Otherwise, you have to start the sound manually.

A sound icon (a speaker horn) appears on the slide to indicate that the sound has been added to it.

② Customize the Slideshow

Now that the sound file has been added to the presentation, you can specify the details of how it is played.

Select **Slide Show**, **Custom Animations**. The **Custom Animations** dialog box opens, which provides options for setting the timing of the sound track.

TIP

You can use the **Add Effect** button in the upper-right corner of the dialog box to add effects that do not now appear in the **Select to animate** list.

The **Select to animate** window in the upper-left corner displays a list of all the text, sound, and other elements on the selected slide. Select the element that represents the sound file you just added. It is added to the **Animation order** list on the right side of the dialog box. If you apply more than one effect to a slide, you can move them up and down in this list box to govern the order in which they appear.

③ Select Play Options

Click the **Effect Options** button. In the **Effects Options** dialog box, select the **Media Options** page (the other pages govern the behavior of text and graphic elements). Settings on this page let you determine when the sound stops playing.

One option is to stop the sound after the first slide. You might select this option if you want the sound to play only while a title slide is on the screen.

TIP

If you want to ensure that the sound plays continuously through the entire presentation, enter **999** as the number of slides. To make the slideshow itself loop continuously, see **120** **Make a Presentation Run Itself.**

If you want the sound to play continuously, in the **Stop Playing** group, select the **After** radio button and enter a number equal to or greater than the number of slides in the presentation (for example, if you have 25 slides in your presentation, enter at least 25).

If you enable the **Hide while not playing** check box, PowerPoint conceals the sound icon on the title slide.

When you're finished specifying the playback options for the sound file, click **OK**.

4 **Check the Presentation**

Select **View, Slide Show**. Click each slide in turn to move through the presentation and check the sound.

116 **Apply Transitions**

When you change from one slide to the next, the normal *transition* occurs like this: One slide disappears, and another takes its place. Applying different kinds of transitions can make the presentation more interesting and perhaps help keep the audience awake.

You can spice up the transition from one slide to another in many ways. You can emulate those ballpark-style billboards that look like changing blinds. Slides can fade in or out, or they can drop down on top of one another. In all, the menu of possible slide effects covers more than the space available on your screen.

1 **Select a Basic Transition**

Display the slide to which you want to apply the transition. The transition takes effect when the chosen slide comes on the screen.

Select **Slide Show, Slide Transition**. The **Slide Transition** dialog box opens. It provides options for the visual transition, accompanying sound effects, and a choice of manual or automatic slide timing.

Open the drop-down list that initially is labeled **No Transition**. The list of effects from which you can choose is lengthy, so scroll to see every possibility. Click the transition effect you want. The graphic to the left of the list displays a preview of the chosen effect.

2 **Set the Timing**

Select one of the three timing options—**Slow, Medium**, or **Fast**. Again, the graphic on the left side of the dialog box provides a preview of the effect.

Before You Begin

✔ **103** Develop a Presentation from Scratch

See Also

→ **112** Animate a Chart

→ **118** Time a Presentation

→ **119** Put Your Presentation on the Web

→ **121** Make a Movie of the Presentation

 KEY TERM

Transition—The onscreen changeover from one PowerPoint slide to another. Also the visual effect, such as a blinds or checkerboard effect, that accompanies the changeover.

TIP

Although slide transitions can add interest to a presentation, be careful that they don't add *too* much interest. You don't want the slideshow to distract people from your message.

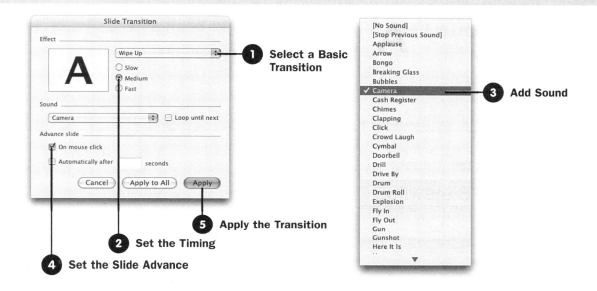

1 Select a Basic Transition

3 Add Sound

5 Apply the Transition

2 Set the Timing

4 Set the Slide Advance

If you go to the main menu and select **Slide Show**, the **Custom Animations** and **Preset Animations** selections provide an advanced transition you can apply to individual slide elements as well as to the slides themselves.

Unless you are a very good speaker, you should use a manual advance (the **On mouse click** option) when you are delivering a verbal presentation. You don't want to find yourself rushing to keep up with the clock or stalling to wait for the next slide. A timed advance (the **Automatically after** option) is the normal choice for an unstaffed presentation.

3 **Add Sound**

From the **Sound** drop-down list, select a sound to accompany the transition, if you want. If you don't want any sound effect to accompany the transition (for example, if you have already assigned a sound file to play during the presentation, as described in **115** **Add Sound to the Picture**), select (**No Sound**).

4 **Set the Slide Advance**

You can call for a manual slide advance by enabling the **On mouse click** check box, or you can set the slide to advance automatically after a certain number of seconds by enabling the **Automatically after** check box and specifying a length of time (in seconds) to wait before advancing to the next slide. A good general rule is to allow 2–3 minutes per slide.

5 **Apply the Transition**

Click **Apply** to close the dialog box and apply the transition to the current slide. Click **Apply to All** to apply this same transition to all the slides in your presentation. If you later want to change the transition for a single slide in the presentation, select that slide and repeat steps 1–4 to change the transition.

You can test the effect of your transition choices by selecting **View**, **Slide Show**.

117 Put Controls on the Slides

In addition to the conventional speaker-delivered presentation, PowerPoint provides several opportunities for interactive shows. These include Web pages, self-running presentations, and PowerPoint movies.

When you allow the audience to manipulate a presentation, you have a pair of conflicting concerns. On one hand, you want to provide the maximum opportunity for the viewer to explore your information. On the other hand, you want to minimize the opportunities for clumsy users to foul things up.

One way to grant control while maintaining it is to provide *action buttons* users can click to advance to other slides in the presentation. The available buttons are animated so when a user clicks them, they appear to be pressed in.

1 **Select the Slide**

Select the slide where you want to apply the buttons. If you select a single slide, the buttons are applied to only that slide. If you select a slide master, the buttons are applied to every slide based on that master.

2 **Select a Button**

Select **Slide Show**, **Action Buttons**. A menu of button types opens. Each can be used for a particular action such as moving to the next slide, going back to the beginning, or playing a movie. Select a button type from that list.

Before You Begin

✔ **116** Apply Transitions

See Also

→ **106** Apply a Slide Master

→ **119** Put Your Presentation on the Web

→ **120** Make a Presentation Run Itself

→ **121** Make a Movie of the Presentation

KEY TERM

Action buttons— Directional buttons that let users interactively switch between slides in a PowerPoint presentation.

NOTE

If a presentation uses more than one slide master, such as a separate title page master, apply the buttons separately to each master where you want them to appear.

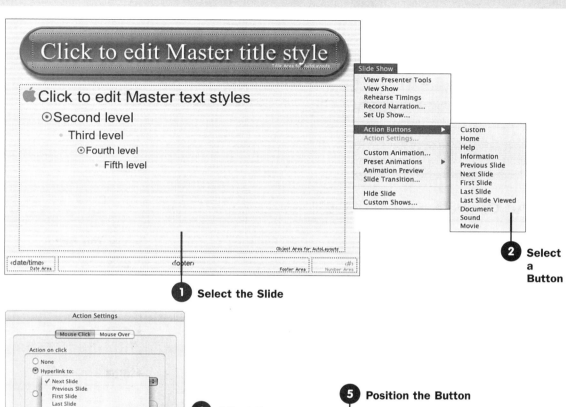

1 Select the Slide

2 Select a Button

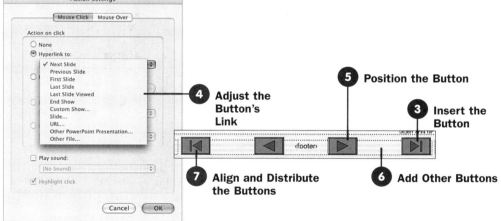

4 Adjust the Button's Link

5 Position the Button

3 Insert the Button

7 Align and Distribute the Buttons

6 Add Other Buttons

NOTE

The **Custom** button selection lets you place a plain button on the slide. You can use its **Action Settings** dialog box to define the destination to which it is linked.

You return to the slide screen, and the mouse pointer is in the shape of a small cross.

3 Insert the Button

Click the spot in the slide where you want the button to appear. The button is placed in that position.

4 **Adjust the Button's Link**

Unless you chose the **Custom button** option in step 2, the button is prelinked to a particular slide in the presentation. For example, the **First slide** button is linked to the first slide in the presentation.

However, each button has an **Action Settings** dialog box that provides a way to change that link. This dialog box opens when you place the button in the slide. You can open the action settings for an existing button by **Ctrl**-clicking the button and selecting **Action Settings**. From the **Hyperlink to** drop-down list, select one of the available links to other slides, Web pages, or external programs.

Change the link if you want; then click **OK**.

5 **Position the Button**

An action button is a graphic object you can move and resize to suit your needs. Click the center of the button and drag to move it. Use the adjustment handles to resize the button.

6 **Add Other Buttons**

Add other buttons as desired. For example, you might want buttons that link to the next and previous slides and to the first and last slides of the presentation. Resize and align them so that they appear as you want them. You can fine-tune the distribution later.

7 **Align and Distribute the Buttons**

Because each button is a separate graphic, you can use drawing tools to line them up and distribute them evenly. Press **Shift** and click each button to select them all. Then select **View**, **Toolbars**, **Drawing**. The **Drawing** toolbar opens.

Click the first graphic in the **Drawing** toolbar. From the menu that opens, select **Align or Distribute**. Then select an alignment method. For example, if you have a row of buttons lined up across the bottom of the screen, **Align Bottom** might be a good selection.

Reopen the **Drawing** toolbar's menu and select **Align or Distribute** again. This time, select a distribution method. For example, **Distribute Horizontally** places equal distances between the buttons in a horizontal row.

Close the toolbar and save the presentation.

 TIP

Press **Shift** while dragging an adjustment handle to resize the button while retaining its original proportions.

118 Time a Presentation

TIP

This rehearsal can be valuable even if you plan to advance the slides manually during the presentation. As you rehearse, a timer records the duration of each slide, and you can check it for times that are too short or too long. At the end of the rehearsal, reject the timings to stay with a manual advance.

Bob Hope's success as a comedian was often attributed to his sense of timing. He could not only tell the right joke, but he could deliver the punchline at precisely the right moment.

Good timing also makes a good presentation. As an audience member, it's hard to remember a slide when it flashes by so briefly you have too little time to read it all. Maybe even more memorable is the slide that stays on the screen f-o-r-e-v-e-r while the speaker drones on through endless points.

As you polish a nearly completed presentation, you should rehearse it. In addition to polishing your delivery, try to get a picture of how long each slide remains on the screen. This is particularly important if you plan to use automatic timing, in which each slide changes after a set interval. With manual timing, you control when the slide changes, but rehearsing your timing is a good idea even then (see **116** **Apply Transitions** for more about the slide-advance options).

PowerPoint has a **Rehearse Timing** feature you can use to get the timing of your presentation just right. Show the first slide, and talk as you normally would while that slide is on the screen. Switch to the next slide and repeat, moving through the entire presentation. PowerPoint records the time each slide was on the screen and sets the automatic timing accordingly. At the end, you have a choice of accepting the timings or trying again.

1 Start the Rehearsal

Open the presentation and display the first slide. From the main menu, select **Slide Show**, **Rehearse Timings**. The slideshow begins, and a timer in one corner of the screen logs the time each slide has been on the screen.

Deliver the presentation as you would before an audience. When you finish your speech for one slide, click to advance to the next. The timer makes a fresh start with each slide.

2 Complete the Presentation

Repeat for each slide in the presentation. Do your best to deliver the talk at the same pace you would use before an audience.

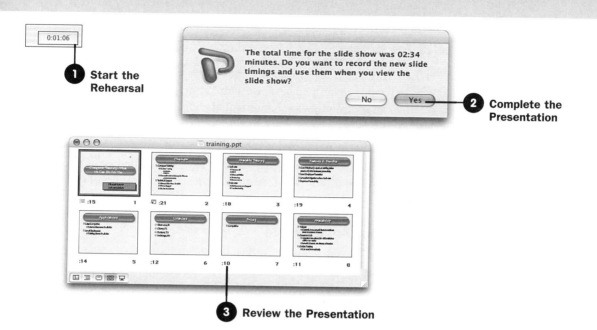

1 Start the
Rehearsal

2 Complete the
Presentation

3 Review the Presentation

At the end of the presentation, PowerPoint reports the total time
and asks whether you want to accept this timing. If you click **Yes**,
the program attaches automatic timing to each slide, using the
time each was on the screen during the rehearsal. If you want to
retain manual timing, click **No**.

3 Review the Presentation

If you accepted the automatic timings, you are asked whether you
want to review the show in **Slide Sorter** view. Click **Yes** to review
the presentation. In **Slide Sorter** view, you can move the slides to
change the order of the presentation. You can also check the time
given each slide.

TIP

If you want to change the
timing of any slide, select it
and then select **Slide
Show, Slide Transition**. You
can change the timing for
the selected slide in the
Slide Transition dialog box.

119 Put Your Presentation on the Web

Before You Begin

✔ **117** Put Controls on the Slides

See Also

→ **120** Make a Presentation Run Itself

→ **121** Make a Movie of the Presentation

Is there any business application these days that does not include some way to produce Web pages? PowerPoint is no exception, and its slide-oriented structure makes it better suited than most for developing a Web site.

When you save a PowerPoint presentation for the Web, each slide becomes a new Web page. Furthermore, each slide title becomes a navigational button in a separate outline panel. You can expand that outline to include the subordinate points as well.

① Name the Web File

Open the presentation and then select **File**, **Save as Web Page**. In the dialog box that opens, specify a filename and a destination. Make sure that the **Format** drop-down list reads **Web Page (HTML)**. Then click the **Web Options** button.

② Select a Page Title

The page title appears in the title bar when the presentation is displayed in a Web browser. Search engines will also be looking for this name. You probably don't want to use the cryptic name PowerPoint initially assigns to the Web file you are creating.

On the **General** page of the **Web Options** dialog box, enter a new page title. Make it something that both people and search engines can relate to.

③ Set Appearance Options

Click the **Appearance** tab in the **Web Options** dialog box to see a page of display options. You can display the completed Web pages in a **Normal** view that includes the navigation aids and outline or in a **Full Screen** view that uses **Forward** and **Back** navigation buttons. The **Default view** options let you choose which of these is displayed when the page first appears in a browser.

If you want your slide notes to appear with the Web pages, enable the **Include slide notes** check box.

TIP

In **Normal** view, other icons along the bottom of the screen display or hide the navigation items, the full outline, and your slide notes.

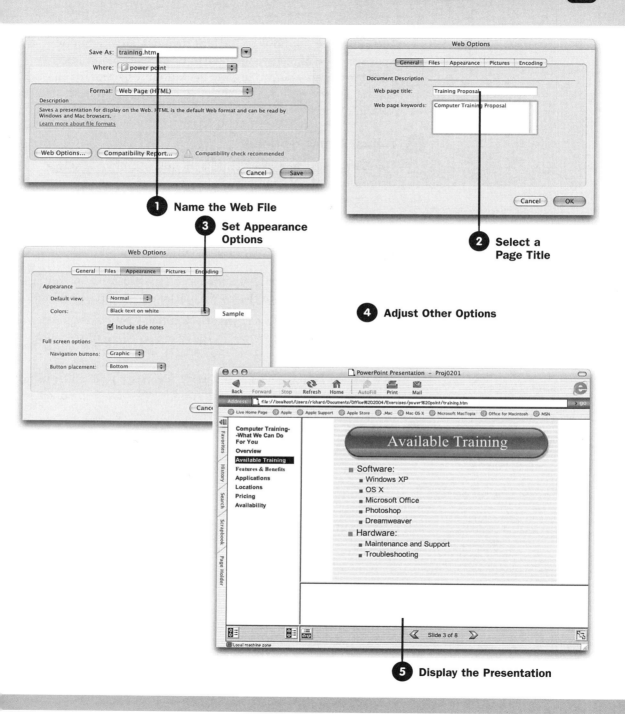

1 Name the Web File

3 Set Appearance Options

2 Select a Page Title

4 Adjust Other Options

5 Display the Presentation

The **Full screen options** define how the navigational buttons appear in **Full Screen** view. These buttons direct readers from screen to screen. You can display the buttons as either graphics or text labels. You also can specify whether they appear at the top or bottom of the screen or in a floating box.

④ Adjust Other Options

The **Files** page contains several file-handling options. These options include the ability to adapt your work to browsers other than Internet Explorer.

The **Pictures** page lets you specify a screen size to adapt to different monitors and decide whether to use the relatively new PNG graphics format.

The **Encoding** page provides advanced language options. You use these options to present the Web pages in non-English languages.

When you're finished specifying the options for the Web pages you are creating, click **OK**. When the **Save** dialog box reopens, click the **Save** button.

The presentation is saved as an HTML file. A separate folder using the presentation's filename holds various Web page components.

⑤ Display the Presentation

In your Web browser, select **File**, **Open** or an equivalent command, and go to the folder where you stored the Web presentation. Select the presentation's HTML file.

The file is displayed in the default view you selected in step 3. Click the icon in the lower-right corner to switch to an alternative view.

To go to another slide, select from the navigational list or use the directional buttons at the bottom of the page.

NOTE

If you used special characters for bullet points in the presentation, they might not appear in the Web page; they might appear as boxes instead. Picking bullets that *do* reproduce on the Web is a trial-and-error process. Save a short Web page to test your chosen characters (and perhaps preview the page on a different computer) before you commit to a large presentation.

---

120 **Make a Presentation Run Itself**

Before You Begin

✔ **116** Apply Transitions

See Also

→ **118** Time a Presentation

You don't have to be present to run a PowerPoint presentation. If you plan to run the presentation at a trade show booth, for example, you could set up a *self-running presentation*.

You could completely automate the presentation so that it runs and repeats itself without action on anyone's part. Or you could make it an interactive demonstration in which viewers can repeat a slide or jump to a new slide of their choice.

If you decide to include interactive controls, be selective about it. Give visitors enough controls to find their way around but not so many that they can cause damage. Let the venue be your guide. If it is an unattended display or kiosk, you probably should provide few (if any) manual controls. If someone will be on hand to guide the process, you can include more manual options.

❶ Open the Set Up Show Dialog Box

Open the presentation if necessary, and select **Slide Show, Set Up Show**. The **Set Up Show** dialog box opens.

❷ Select a Type of Show

Start by selecting the type of show you will present. This can be a live speech by an on-scene presenter, an interactive show browsed by individuals, or a fully automated kiosk presentation that can run in an unattended booth.

❸ Set Show Options

Depending on the type of show you selected, you can select options from other sections of the dialog box. In the **Show options** group, for example, you can enable continuous looping and include or exclude animation or narration. See **112** **Animate a Chart** and **115** **Add Sound to the Picture** for more on adding these features to your presentation.

The **Annotation pen color** option is available only in speaker-led presentations. You can use it during a presentation to make markings on the slide with your mouse, such as circling a key point. It is sometimes called the John Madden tool, after the use of a similar device in televised football games.

❹ Choose Slides to Display

You also can designate one or all of the slides to be presented in the display. For example, a live presentation might have a slide that urges people to contact you after the presentation. You could leave that slide out of an unstaffed show.

KEY TERM

Self-running presentation—A presentation set with automatic timings and limited controls so that it can run without human intervention.

NOTE

A self-running presentation automatically restarts when it is finished. If someone uses a manual control, the presentation restarts after it has been idle for more than 5 minutes.

NOTE

The type of show you select determines several other selections in the **Set Up Show** dialog box. For example, if you select **Browsed at a kiosk (full screen)**, the **Loop continuously until "Esc"** option is enabled as well.

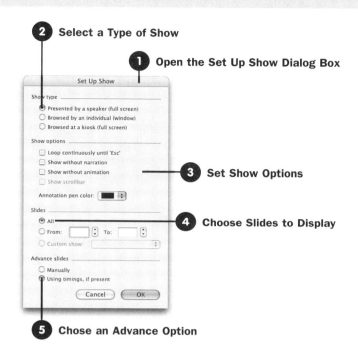

2 Select a Type of Show

1 Open the Set Up Show Dialog Box

3 Set Show Options

4 Choose Slides to Display

5 Chose an Advance Option

A custom show gives you more flexibility; you can show different sets of slides to different audiences. For example, you could include the see-me slide in a live presentation and instead put a see-our-Web-site slide in the kiosk version of the presentation.

To create a custom show, select **Slide Show**, **Custom Shows** from the main menu. A dialog box lets you select individual slides to be included or omitted; you then can save this combination as a named custom show. Then in the **Set Up Show** dialog box, you can select the custom show and its slide selections.

5 Choose an Advance Option

If you want the show to run by itself or allow presenters or viewers to advance through the slides at their own pace, enable the **Manually** option. If you want the slides in the presentation to advance by themselves, enable the **Using timings, if present** option.

When you're finished selecting show options, click **OK**. You can check the results by selecting **Slide Show**, **View Show**. For example, if you have set up an unstaffed kiosk show, the presentation should proceed at preset timing intervals and should restart itself when it reaches the last slide.

⓶⓶ Make a Movie of the Presentation

Want to give a PowerPoint presentation without PowerPoint? Make it a movie, instead.

A PowerPoint movie is much like a self-running presentation, but there is one difference. The movie runs under QuickTime instead of using the PowerPoint program.

Because QuickTime is an advanced animation program available on most computers, making your presentation into a movie can be a worthwhile option if you want to distribute a presentation to a large list of users. For example, you could distribute an online portfolio to prospective clients, and they could play it without the risk that they would alter the slides in the presentation.

However, QuickTime is a bit more particular than PowerPoint about what goes into its shows. You are limited in the use of action settings, animations, and sound settings. Careful preparation in advance is vital to ensuring that the presentation works as expected in the QuickTime movie.

Before You Begin

✔ ⓲⓲ Put Controls on the Slides

See Also

→ ⓵⓴⓺ Apply a Slide Master

→ ⓵⓶⓪ Make a Presentation Run Itself

❶ Prepare the Presentation

Make sure that the presentation is suitable for QuickTime use. Here is a short list of points to check before you can use your presentation as a QuickTime movie:

- Use only a single slide master or, more specifically, a single pairing of a slide and title master.

- Provide navigation buttons, but limit them to the basic functions of going to the next or previous slide and the beginning and end of the presentation. Avoid more advanced links such as those to other presentations or programs.

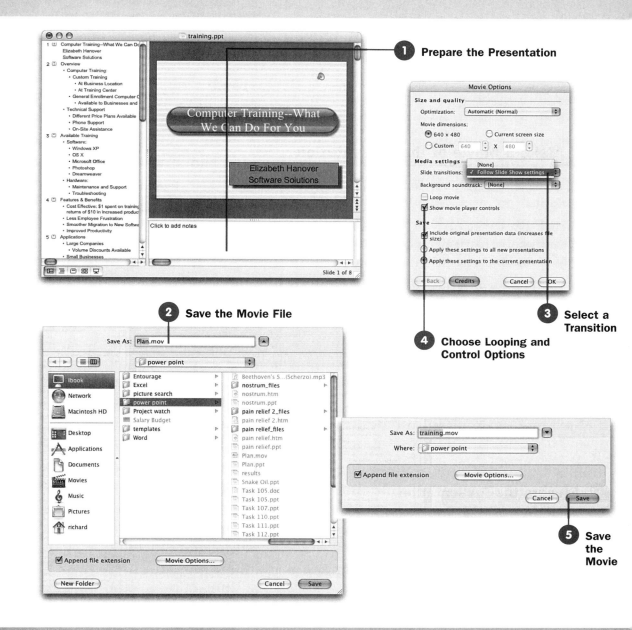

1 Prepare the Presentation

2 Save the Movie File

3 Select a Transition

4 Choose Looping and Control Options

5 Save the Movie

- Many PowerPoint transitions do not work as expected in QuickTime. Instead, QuickTime inserts a similar transition it can execute.

② Save the Movie File

Select **File**, **Make Movie**. Enter or select a filename and a folder in which to store the QuickTime movie file you are creating. Click the **Movie Options** button. The **Movie Options** dialog box opens.

③ Select a Transition

The most important options in the **Movie Options** dialog box are in the **Media settings** section. Because transitions created in PowerPoint might be problematic for QuickTime, you can elect to follow the slideshow settings (including the QuickTime substitute transitions, described in step 1), or to use no transition effects at all.

④ Choose Looping and Control Options

Also in the **Media settings** section of the **Movie Options** dialog box, you can enable the **Loop movie** check box to automatically repeat the movie and the **Show movie player controls** check box to include interactive controls.

The **Size and quality** and **Save** options should normally not be changed unless you have a particular reason to do so.

When you have finished selecting options, click **OK**. You return to the **Save** dialog box for the movie.

⑤ Save the Movie

Back in the **Save** dialog box, the **Use current settings** option is now selected.

If the movie is to run on Windows computers as well as Macs, make sure that the **Append file extension** check box is selected. Click **Save**.

You now can run the presentation as a QuickTime movie.

NOTE

Click the **Credits** button to open a dialog box where you can enter the names of a producer, a director, and performers and include copyright information.

PART V

Entourage 2004

IN THIS PART:

17

Project Management

IN THIS CHAPTER:

NOTE

Entourage also includes the **Project Center** with which you can assemble diverse resources into a single project that then is available to all Office applications. The **Project Center** is described in **1** Display the Project Center.

Entourage is a multifaceted program designed to serve as a personal information manager. In this role, it helps you organize personal information and communicate with friends and co-workers using email. The communication and organizational components of Entourage include email, a calendar, a contact list, a notepad, and a task list.

122 Change Your Identity

See Also

→ **125** Add a Contact

→ **126** Enter Tasks and Notes

KEY TERM

Identity—An Entourage designation that stores the computer settings, email account information, and other individualized information for a particular person.

NOTE

An Entourage identity is not a security feature. An identity simply displays a personalized view of your messages, appointments, and other Entourage items. Identities have no passwords or other means to keep someone else from assuming your identity. For security, count on the logon ID and password with which you signed on to the computer.

When you install Office, an *identity* is established for you, using information you supply during the installation process. Your identity includes information about your email provider account. Using your identity, you can display your personal email, excluding messages addressed to other users of the same computer. Your identity also provides personalized displays of your calendar items, notes, and tasks. Just as your logon ID and password provide access to the Mac system, your identity provides access to Entourage.

If you normally are the same user of the same computer all the time, an identity is of little value. If more than one person uses the same computer, each can establish an individual identity, and each will see only his messages. By the same token, if you use different computers, you can establish the same identity on each; in fact, you can copy an identity from one computer to the other. The identity files are in your **Documents** folder in the **Microsoft User Data/Office 2004 Identities** folder.

If you established an identity during the setup process, it is initially known as **Main Identity**. You can change this title to something more personal, switch to a different identity, or create a new one.

1 Call for a New ID

You access most identity management procedures from the **Switch Identity** command. This is the entry point not only for switching to a different identity, but also for renaming an existing identity or creating a new one.

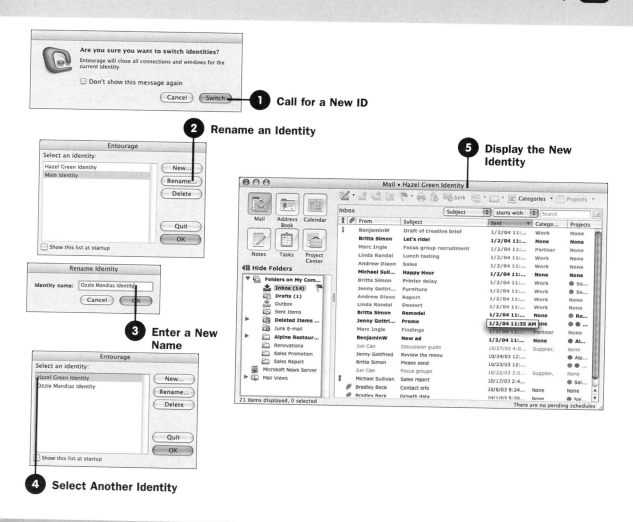

① Call for a New ID

② Rename an Identity

⑤ Display the New Identity

③ Enter a New Name

④ Select Another Identity

Open the **Entourage** menu and select **Switch Identity**. A dialog box asks you to confirm your decision. It also warns you that Entourage will close all windows and network connections associated with the identity you are leaving. If you are prepared to proceed, click the **Switch** button. A dialog box opens with an Entourage title.

NOTE

If another Office application is open, you are asked to close the application and then select the **Switch Identity** command again.

TIP

You can also use this dialog box to establish a new identity. When you click the **New** button, a wizard opens (actually, it's a serial dialog box) to collect personal information and preferences, including your email address.

TIP

There is nothing except your good judgment to keep you from assuming any identity on the list. Although the operating system might keep you from seeing other users' files, it still is best to keep peace with your colleagues by avoiding misuse of their identities. By the same token, protect your own files by properly using the system's logon procedure.

② Rename an Identity

If you now hold the **Main Identity**, you probably can think of a better name. The installation process provided an opportunity to choose another name; if you didn't do so then, you still can rename any existing identity with these instructions.

In the dialog box, select the identity you want to rename and click the **Rename** button. The **Rename Identity** dialog box opens.

③ Enter a New Name

In the **Identity name** text box, enter the new name and click **OK**. The main dialog box displays the identity under its new name.

④ Select Another Identity

From the list in the dialog box, select the identity you want to display. This can be an identity you have just renamed or a different identity that displays your own email, calendar, and other resources. Click **OK** to assume the new identity.

⑤ Display the New Identity

Entourage displays the new identity with the email messages and other resources associated with that identity.

---

123 **Assign Categories**

See Also

→ **②** Set Up a Project

TIP

You can also assign a folder to a category. Select the folder. Then from the main menu, select **Edit**, **Categories** and select an existing category. If no category is available, create one as described in step 1 of this task.

Entourage has enough organizational tools to make it possible to become a little *too* organized. Nevertheless, all the tools have value, whether they're used alone or in combination.

The ability to assign items to categories is a prime example. You can categorize messages, calendar events, and contacts. If you want to distinguish between work and personal items, you can assign items to the **Work** and **Personal** categories, two of several categories already built in to Entourage. You also can create your own category such as one for items related to an art show.

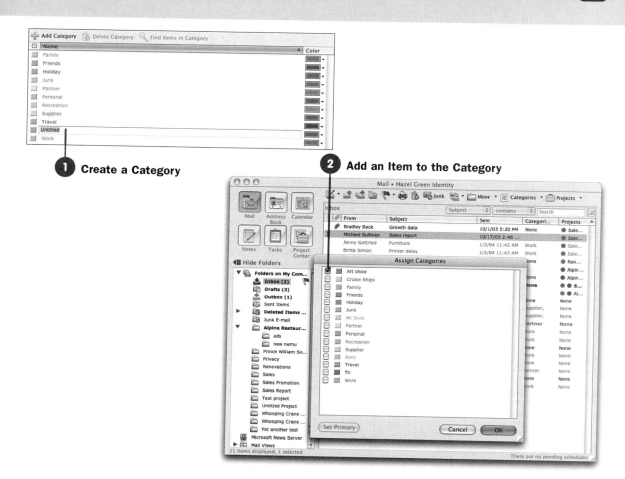

1 Create a Category

2 Add an Item to the Category

1 Create a Category

In the Entourage toolbar, click the drop-down arrow next to the **Categories** button. From the menu that opens, select **Edit Categories**. The **Categories** dialog box opens.

In the toolbar for this dialog box, click the **Add Category** button. A new **Untitled** category opens. The categories are displayed in alphabetical order, so this new entry appears near the bottom of the list.

TIP

Items assigned to the new category are color-coded to identify the category. If you don't like the assigned color, click the arrow in the **Color** column for this item. You then can select a different color.

NOTE

If you add an Address Book contact to a category, all messages from that individual are automatically assigned to the same category.

Select the **Untitled** label and type a new name. If you want to categorize items related to an art show, for example, **Art show** might be a fitting title.

❷ Add an Item to the Category

Any Entourage item can be assigned to a category. Items include email messages, address book contents, events, notes, and tasks. If you are working in the **Project Center**, you also can categorize Scrapbook clippings and Office documents. See **❸ Share Project Resources**.

Select the item. Click the **Categories** button in the Entourage toolbar to open a list of categories. Enable the check box for one or more categories to which you want to assign the item. If you select more than one category, click the **Set Primary** button and identify one of the chosen categories as the primary category. The item then appears in the color of the primary category.

---

124 Set Your Preferences

Before You Begin

✔ **122** Change Your Identity

See Also

→ **123** Assign Categories

NOTE

There are many options on the pages in the Entourage **Preferences** dialog box; this task describes only a few of them. Feel free to experiment with the options on these pages. If you do something that doesn't work out right, go back and reset the option.

As do other Office components, Entourage lets you set your own preferences for how it looks and works. You can do things such as make room for a longer folder list, automatically add your area code to telephone numbers, ensure that Windows users can read your messages, and condense your email replies.

❶ Display the Preferences Dialog Box

Open the **Entourage** menu and select **Preferences** to open the **Preferences** dialog box. You have a lot of flexibility here; the **Preferences** dialog box contains several pages. These pages are listed on the left side of the dialog box and are grouped into **General** and **Mail and News** preferences.

❷ Display a Longer Folder List

Over time, you might create an extensive list of email folders and want more room to display them. If so, you can condense the display of navigation buttons in the upper-left corner of the Entourage window to leave more room for a folder display.

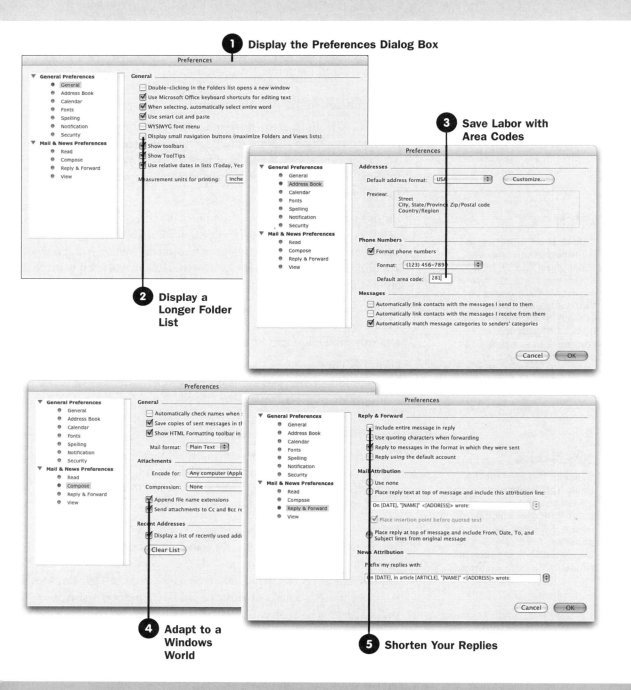

1 Display the Preferences Dialog Box

2 Display a Longer Folder List

3 Save Labor with Area Codes

4 Adapt to a Windows World

5 Shorten Your Replies

In the **Preferences** window, select the **General** page. Enable the **Display small navigation buttons** option. Smaller buttons are displayed, and the folder list is expanded.

③ Save Labor with Area Codes

Some metropolitan areas have more than one area code. Nevertheless, there still are many localities where only a single area code is in effect. If you are in such a locality, you might find that the bulk of the telephone numbers in your address book bear the same area code.

In that case, you can set this area code as the default standard for newly entered phone numbers. The default area code appears whenever you enter a new telephone number, saving you a few keystrokes every time you make a new local entry. If you want to enter a different area code, you still can type over it.

In the **Preferences** dialog box, select the **Address Book** page. In the **Phone Numbers** section, enter the preferred area code in the **Default area code** text box.

From the **Format** drop-down list in this section, you can select the punctuation—parentheses, dashes, or spaces—with which you want phone numbers to appear.

④ Adapt to a Windows World

Mac users as a group have a brand loyalty exceeded only by that of some pickup truck owners. Nevertheless, it's a Windows-centered world out there, and we often have to ensure that our Mac files are compatible with those on other folks' systems.

Office files can readily cross the Mac-Windows divide as long as you remember one thing: *The filenames must include the period-and-three-letter extensions such as .xls, .doc, and .ppt that identify their source programs (Excel, Word, and PowerPoint, respectively).* The Mac can take the extensions or leave them, but Windows insists that the extensions be there.

You might trust your memory always to do this, but if you're like me, that's a bad idea. Instead, you can set Entourage to check for extensions on any filename it dispatches as an email attachment.

NOTE

Default is an unfortunate contribution to computer vocabulary. The Word Thesaurus suggests synonyms that are heavy on terms such as *nonpayment*, *evasion*, and other implications of negligence. In computer use, a *default* is simply the option that takes effect if you do not make a choice yourself.

NOTE

Consider the files for this book. They were written on a Mac but backed up on an older Windows machine whose enduring asset is a generous hard disk. It was important that the files be readable on both systems.

In the **Preferences** dialog box, under **Mail and News Preferences**, select the **Compose** page. In the **Attachments** section, enable the **Append file name extensions** check box. This option ensures that outgoing attachments will carry Windows-acceptable filenames.

⑤ Shorten Your Replies

Normally, when you reply to an email message, the text of the original message appears below your reply. This "reply with history" feature can often be useful. It reminds the recipient of what was in the original message, and it provides a complete record of the correspondence.

A continued exchange, though, can build up a long string of attached previous messages. If you and the other party have repeatedly corresponded on this subject, you probably no longer need the reminders anyway. In that case, you can cut your messages short by excluding the previous messages.

In the **Preferences** dialog box, select the **Reply & Forward** page. Disable the **Include entire message in reply** check box. Now, you can send only your replies, not everything that came before.

There are several other options in this section. The **Use quoting characters when forwarding** option adds angle brackets at the beginning of each line of previous messages. If the previous messages are in HTML format, the messages are indented instead.

The **Reply to messages in the format in which they were sent** option formats your reply to match the previous message, either as plain text or as formatted HTML.

The **Reply using the default account** option sends the reply using the email account set up for your *identity*. If you have more than one account, disabling this option sends replies using the account through which you received the message.

 NOTE

Beware changing the **Encode for** option in the **Attachments** section. The preselected **Any computer** option is almost always the wise choice. The other settings are for special configurations that probably do not match your own.

 TIP

This is not an irrevocable choice. You can enable the **Include entire message in reply** option any time you want.

125 Add a Contact

Before You Begin

✔ **122** Change Your
Identity

See Also

→ **52** Use an Address
Book List As the
Data Source

→ **136** Personalize Your
Address Book with
Pictures

 TIP

There is room for several pages of both business and personal information about the contact. Don't feel you have to complete every blank on these forms. Enter what you know or what you feel will be useful.

 NOTE

If you don't want to display the **Preview** pane, you can conceal it. From the main menu, select **View**, **Preview Pane**. Select this menu command again to display the **Preview** pane again.

The **Address Book** is a place to store names, street and email addresses, telephone numbers, and other information about your personal and business contacts.

The **Address Book** shares its contents with other functions and applications. For example, if you want to address an email message, you can select the recipient's name from the **Address Book**. The message then is addressed to the selected recipient.

Entourage also shares the **Address Book** with other applications. For example, you can use names, titles, and street addresses from the **Address Book** to address a merged form letter in Word. That process is described in **52** **Use an Address Book List As the Data Source**.

As you make new contacts, you can enter their information in the **Address Book**.

1 **Open the Address Book**

With Entourage open, click the **Address Book** icon in the upper-left corner. When the **Address Book** opens, it displays a list of contacts in the upper part of the window. A **Preview** pane at the bottom shows details of the currently selected contact.

Whereas the **Navigation** pane of the **Mail** window displays folders, in the **Address Book** it displays views. A view displays selected contents of the **Address Book**. The program has assembled some initial views, but you can add your own. For example, if you want to add a view that displays only employees of a particular company, you can do so. In the main menu, select **View**, **Custom View**. Give the view a name, and select the condition that the **Company** column contain the firm whose employees' names you want to display.

2 **Add a Contact**

In the Entourage toolbar, click the **New** button. The **Create Contact** dialog box asks for information about the new contact. Fill in the information you want to record about this contact.

1 Open the Address Book

2 Add a Contact

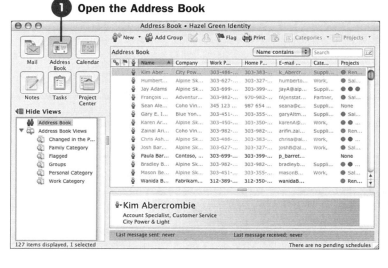

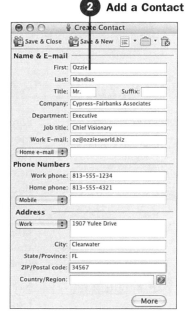

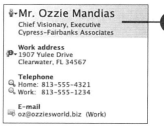

3 Display the Record

When finished, click the **Save & Close** button at the top of the dialog box. If you want to add another contact, click the **Save & New** button instead.

3 **Display the Record**

When you finish adding contacts, you return to the **Address Book** window. Find the new contact in the list and click it to display it in the **Preview** window.

Icons next to the entries in the **Preview** window let you perform various kinds of actions with this information. For example, you can click the icon next to a street address to go to the Internet to find a map or driving directions. Click the icon next to a telephone

 NOTE

If the contact has an overseas address, you can use the **Customize Address Format** button in the lower-right corner to select an address format appropriate to the location. The **More** button opens new windows where you can add more information about this contact if you want. Several new pages provide room for a wide range of information from the contact's home address to her astrological sign.

number to magnify the number to make it easier to see while you're dialing. Click the icon next to an email address to initiate a message to that address.

126 Enter Tasks and Notes

Before You Begin

✔ **122** Change Your Identity

See Also

→ **2** Set Up a Project

KEY TERM

Link—A connection between two Entourage items such as a task and a note or an event and an **Address Book** listing. When you open a linked item, you can use the link to go directly to its companion.

Sometimes life seems like an endless succession of to-do lists. Some are more complicated than others. Watering a plant is a single task, but planning and conducting an art show involves multiple tasks such as arranging for a site, recruiting judges, assigning display booths, and dozens of other chores. The term *multitasking* did not originate here, but it could have.

Entourage cannot make the tasks any easier to perform, but it can make them easier to keep track of. You can make a note of a task, set a deadline and a priority, and issue a reminder when the task is nearly due.

Notes are similar to tasks, but they are more freeform—sort of an electronic sticky note. You might want to write a note about a task you have entered. Then you can *link* the task with the note so that you can use the task or the note to go directly to its linked partner.

1 Display Your Tasks

In the Entourage window's **Navigation** pane, click the **Tasks** icon. The **Tasks** window displays your current task list. You can sort the tasks by their due dates, their assigned categories, or their assigned projects by clicking the column heading on which you want to sort.

Several columns to the left of the task titles use icons to indicate the status of each task. In left-to-right order, a chain icon indicates a linked task; a checked box indicates a completed task; an exclamation point and a down-facing arrow indicate high or low priority; an arrow indicates a recurring task; and an alarm clock indicates that a reminder has been set.

The lower-left part of the **Navigation** pane displays task views that display selected lists of the tasks to be done.

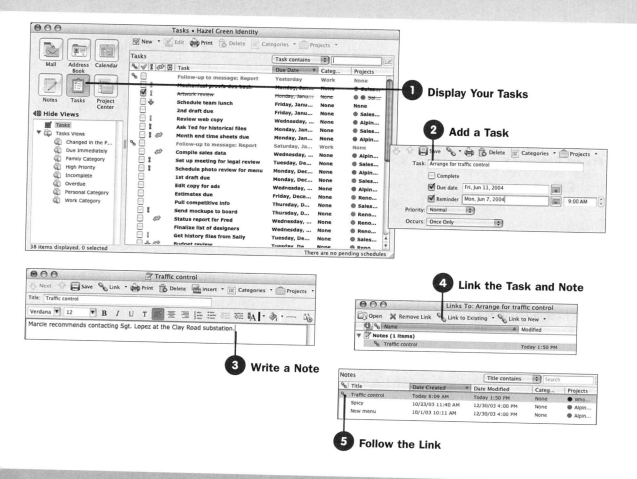

1 Display Your Tasks

2 Add a Task

3 Write a Note

4 Link the Task and Note

5 Follow the Link

2 Add a Task

If you are in charge of a project such as an art show, you will have
an ever-growing list of things to do and always have new things to
add to your task list. For example, you will probably need to
arrange for police officers to direct traffic around the show site.

In the **Tasks** toolbar, click the **New** button. A dialog box asks for
details of the task. The only thing you really have to do here is to
describe the task by giving it a name. (The only thing you'd really
like to do for this task is to check the **Complete** box—which you
can do as soon as you complete the task.)

The other entries in the dialog box are optional. You can assign a due date and call for a reminder in time to meet that deadline. Click the calendar icons to select due and reminder dates directly from a calendar.

TIP

You also can link tasks to projects (see **3** **Share Project Resources**) and assign them to categories (see **123** **Assign Categories**).

You also can open the **Priority** drop-down list to assign a priority; the priority you assign is represented by a flag in the task list. If this is not a one-time task, you can open the **Occurs** drop-down list to select an interval at which the task repeats itself.

When you're finished defining the task, click the **Save** button at the top of the dialog box. The task is added to the task list display; close the dialog box.

NOTE

The **Priority** and **Occurs** entries are similar to those you would make to schedule an event in the Calendar, as described in **141** **Note a Recurring Event**.

3 **Write a Note**

Now that you've created a task to remind you to arrange for traffic control for your art show, how do you actually arrange for traffic control? Fortunately, your predecessor has left a file folder of written notes on her experience with previous shows. They include the name of the contact with whom she made these arrangements last year.

You can enter this reference in an Entourage note so that the information is there with the rest of your art show information. Furthermore, you can link the note to the traffic control task. Like a sticky note, the Entourage note is there to remind you of whom you should call.

Click the **Notes** button in the **Navigation** pane and then click the **New** button at the top of the screen.

TIP

If you are still in the **Task** view, you can click the down arrow next to the **New** button and select **Note**. You can use this method to create any type of entry from any Entourage view.

In the dialog box that opens, enter a title to describe the note; then enter the text you want to include. Click the **Insert** button at the top of the screen to add pictures, sound clips, or even movies to the note. Use the **Formatting** toolbar to access a variety of text formatting options. For most purposes, though, it will probably be enough just to jot down the note (if using a keyboard can be considered "jotting").

When you're finished writing the note, click the **Save** button. The note is added to the **Notes** window.

④ Link the Task and Note

Because the task you created in step 2 and the note you created in step 3 are related to each other, you can link the two. Then when you open either the note or the task, you can jump quickly to the other item. For example, you could open the traffic control task and jump to the note about the person to call.

If the note is still open, you can start from there. Otherwise, display the **Notes** window and double-click the note you want to link to a task.

In the toolbar at the top of the dialog box, click the **Link** button. A **Links To** dialog box opens. Click the **Link to Existing** button. From the menu that opens, select the type of item to which you want to link. If you are setting up a link to the task, select the **Task** option. A list of tasks open. Select the task, and then click the **Link** button. The two items are now linked.

⑤ Follow the Link

It's time to complete the task of arranging for traffic control. But who was that sergeant they worked with last year? To find out, open the task and go to the linked note.

In the **Navigation** pane, click the **Tasks** button. In the task list, find the traffic control task. (If you have trouble finding the task, use the **Task Contains** search feature near the top of the window.)

Click the link symbol next to the traffic control task (it's the chain link symbol in the left column). From the menu that opens, select **Open Links**. The **Links To** dialog box displays all links to that task. Because you are looking for a note, click the arrow next to the **Notes** heading to display any linked notes.

Double-click the note you want to read. The note opens, and you can check the sergeant's name.

TIPS

This process works just as well in reverse. You could open the task and establish a link to the note. You also could use the **Link to New** button to create a new item at the same time you establish a link to it.

You can go even further: Add a contact listing for the police sergeant and then link it to the task and the note. That way, after finding his name in the note, you could immediately look up his phone number. If you have set up the art show as a project, you can make these items part of that project. You also can assign the related items to a category, such as **Logistics**. All these options are available using buttons in the toolbar for the item you are working with.

18

Managing Your Mail

IN THIS CHAPTER:

Email is only one of six Entourage components, but it still is first among equals. Entourage is all about communication and working together, and email has become a ubiquitous form of communication.

At its essence, sending and receiving email is a simple process. Enter an address, a subject line, and a message and then click **Send Now**. Receiving a message is even simpler. Open Entourage mail, and there it is.

Nevertheless, from these simple beginnings, things can get complicated in a hurry. For example, you might be pecking away at your portable computer in some off-network location where you have no connection to your email system. While there, you might write an email message that you must stash in an **Outbox** until you can reach a connection. Or you might start a letter only to find you need more information before you can complete it. Until you can do that, this message must be stored as a **Draft**.

Then there seems to be dozens of ways to classify email messages, put them in categories, tie them to other pieces of information, and combine the whole thing into a project. All these email features are intended to make life easier, and for the most part that's exactly what they do. Even so, the sheer variety of options can make the process seem intimidating.

No dog of any age can learn a whole bunch of tricks all at the same time. So be selective. Work with the features that seem most valuable to you. As you become comfortable with them, try a few more things. Entourage email can lead you to many valuable options for organizing your work and your life. Just don't try to take every path at once.

127 Set Up an Email Account

See Also

→ **129** Organize Your Email

→ **131** Receive "Executive Summaries" of Your Messages

Before you can use email, you must get connected. Even if you're a non-technical type, you must brush at least gently against the technology of communication. Before you can send or receive email, you must have an *email account*. This is both as simple and as difficult as signing up for telephone service or cable TV.

In the case of email, the counterpart to the phone or cable company is an *Internet service provider*. Known by the inevitable acronym ISP, this is the entity that connects you to the Internet and the email system. If you are connected to an employer's network, the network administrator

probably has set up an ISP account; to use it, you need only be connected to the network. Microsoft's corporate email server product is called Exchange; it is popular but not universal. Your network administrator can provide the details of what your organization uses.

You can set up more than one account. If you have an email account for your work, you might want to set up a second account for personal messages. Set up one account for the office, specifying the ISP or network connection used there. Set up another account that uses your personal ISP for home use.

The ISP or the network administrator should be able to provide the technical information you need to set up an email account. If you don't have this information, ask.

❶ Collect the Information

Before you start to set up the Entourage account, your connection with the ISP must already exist. From the ISP, make sure that you have the information you will need to establish the Entourage account. This information includes:

- **Your email address**—This can be your name or some version of it, an @ sign, and a domain name. The domain name is assigned by the organization or ISP, for example, **outernet.com**. You might be free to pick your own name such as **wizard** or **moondoggie**. Or your organization might use its own protocols for assigning email names and addresses.

- **Your account type**—This is the *protocol* the account uses when you receive or send messages. Usually, the protocol for incoming messages is either Post Office Protocol (POP) or Internet Message Access Protocol (IMAP). Your outgoing messages usually use Simple Mail Transfer Protocol (SMTP).

- **The server address for receiving your mail**—This usually is in a form such as **pop.outernet.com** or **mail.outernet.com**.

- **The separate server address for sending your mail**—A typical address has the form **smtp.outernet.com**.

- **Your password**—This is the password Entourage relays to the server when you want to open your email.

KEY TERMS

Email account—In Entourage, stored information that identifies your email service and the communication settings for making contact.

Internet service provider (ISP)—A commercial service that provides connection to the Internet.

NOTE

An email account is only distantly related to an identity as described in **122** **Change Your Identity**. An *identity* is the role in which you sign onto Entourage. In that identity, you then can establish one or more email accounts.

KEY TERM

Protocol—A form of language computers use when communicating with each other.

 TIP

Use an email password that is different from the one you use to log on to your system. Email passwords travel in an insecure world; if yours is compromised, it will affect only your email; the rest of your system will still be secure.

1 Collect the Information

2 Open the Account Assistant

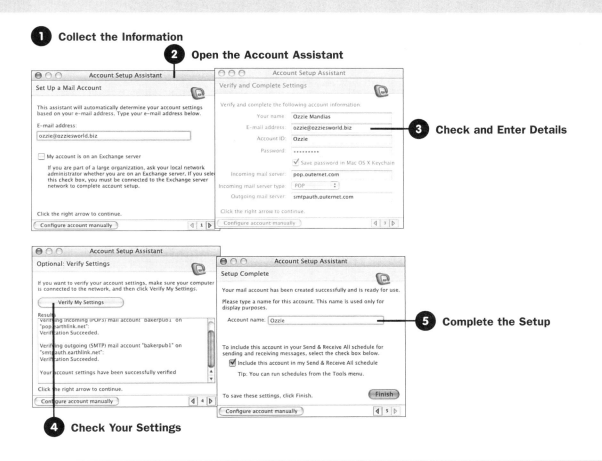

3 Check and Enter Details

5 Complete the Setup

4 Check Your Settings

If you connect to the Internet through a local network, you can sign on to Entourage using only your network user ID, domain name, and password. The network administrator takes care of the rest. (Now, we tell you.)

2 ## Open the Account Assistant

From the main menu, select **File**, **New**, **Email account**. The **Account Setup Assistant** opens. Enter your email address and click the right arrow at the bottom of the window.

This action continues the step-by-step process of using the Assistant. If you prefer, you can click the **Configure account**

manually button to enter your account information in a single dialog box. If your account is on an Exchange server, click the **Configure account manually** button and enter your ID, password, and domain name.

③ Check and Enter Details

The Assistant's second page reports whether Entourage has identified your ISP and entered the server information. If not, you can go back to the first page of the Assistant and reenter your email address (you might have typed it incorrectly the first time), or you can enter the information manually. When you are ready, click the right arrow.

Page 3 asks you to verify and complete your account information. Check and, if necessary, correct any information Entourage has entered for you. Enter any missing information. When finished, click the right arrow.

④ Check Your Settings

Page 4 provides an opportunity to check your entries by using them to connect with your email server. Click the **Verify My Settings** button. The program uses the settings you supplied on page 3 to connect with your email server. After a few minutes, the program either reports success or displays an error message pointing to possible errors in your settings.

If necessary, use the left arrow to go back to page 3 and change your settings. Then try the verification again. After the program makes successful contact with the email server, click the right arrow.

⑤ Complete the Setup

On page 5, complete the process by entering a name for the account. This account name is for your own use and is only for display purposes. Then click **Finish**. Your Entourage account is established.

TIP

Entourage keeps track of the protocols and server names used by major ISPs. If your ISP is one of these, its information is entered automatically. Still, it is wise to obtain this information in advance so that you can verify that Entourage has made the correct entries.

NOTE

You can bypass verification by clicking the right arrow as soon as page 4 opens. If you do so, however, a reminder asks you to confirm that you do not want to verify the settings.

128 Automate Your Inbox

Before You Begin

✔ **127** Set Up an Email Account

See Also

→ **123** Assign Categories

→ **129** Organize Your Email

KEY TERM

Rule—An instruction that helps manage incoming email messages by sorting them into folders, color-coding them, or sending automatic replies.

TIP

If you're unsure what type of account you have, select **Tools, Accounts** and then click the **Mail** tab. The type of email account you have is displayed along with its name.

It's not unusual to open your email and be hit with a cascade of new messages. Unwanted spam might account for some of this, of course, but many of us receive huge amounts of email that is entirely legitimate. Some might be work-related, and some might be personal. Some require immediate action, and some can be put off until later.

With a high volume of email, culling out the good stuff can be time-consuming. To cut through the clutter, you can instruct Entourage to make those decisions for you. You can write a *rule* that assigns particular types of messages to particular email folders. You can assign messages from the boss to a **Work** folder. Messages from clients can be assigned to their own folder or to a *category*. (See **123** **Assign Categories**.) Those messages from the most important clients can be color-coded to get your immediate attention.

① Call for a New Rule

From the main menu in Entourage, select **Tools**, **Rules**. The **Rules** dialog box opens. Click the **Mail** tab for the type of email account you have. Then click the **New** button. The **Edit Rule** dialog box opens.

② Set the Conditions

Let's say Virginia Dale is a key member of the committee planning an art show. You want to write a rule that places all messages from her into an art show folder and in addition assigns those messages to an **Art Show** category.

First, enter a rule name that describes the rule you are going to create. This name is for your benefit in case you have to change or remove it later. In this case, a simple **Ginny** might do.

Then set the conditions or criteria under which the rule will apply. These criteria are stated in the **If** section of the dialog box. Open the list that initially reads **All Messages**. An extended list of selection criteria opens. Because you want to apply this rule to messages from Virginia Dale, select **From**. This condition instructs the program to look in the email address section that identifies the sender of incoming messages.

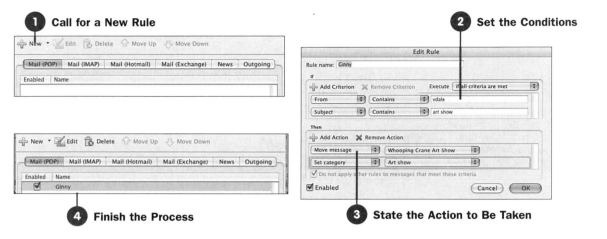

1 Call for a New Rule

2 Set the Conditions

4 Finish the Process

3 State the Action to Be Taken

Additional selection windows are added to the dialog box. If the second window does not read **Contains**, open the list and select that condition.

In the third box, type a condition that identifies Virginia Dale. A message from her might bear the email address **vdale@ozziesworld.biz**. If so, you can enter **vdale**. You don't need the entire address, just enough text to reliably identify the sender.

The completed criteria statement reads, in effect, that the rule applies to any message whose **From** line **Contains** the text **vdale**.

3 **State the Action to Be Taken**

If a message meets the conditions, what then? The rule must also specify one or more actions to take.

The **Then** section of the dialog box has room for two actions, and as you can with the **If** criteria, you can add other actions. In this case, you want to assign the message to both a category and a folder.

Open the first list in the **If** section and select **Move message**. This action instructs the program to move the message to a particular folder. Then open the list to the right, select **Choose folder**, and select the destination folder where you want to store the incoming

NOTE

The **Add Criterion** button adds an additional condition. You could use it to specify two criteria: that this rule would apply only to mail from Virginia Dale *and* that the subject line contains the words **Art Show**. Then you could open the **Execute** list and select whether the rule should apply when all the criteria are met or when only one of them is true.

mail message. In this case, it would be the **Whooping Crane Art Show** folder. (For information on creating folders, see **Organize Your Email**.)

In the second row of action definitions, select **Set category** from the first list if it is not already selected. Open the next list and select the **Art show** category.

④ Finish the Process

Check the **Enabled** check box to apply the rule to future messages; then click **OK**. The rule is applied and appears in the **Rules** dialog box. If you want to edit or remove it later, you can select **Tools**, **Rules** and do so. To temporarily disable the rule, remove the check mark from the box in front of the rule in the **Rules** dialog box.

 Organize Your Email

Before You Begin

✔ **127** Set Up an Email Account

See Also

→ **123** Assign Categories

NOTE

If the **Mail** function is not displayed, click the **Mail** navigation button in the upper-left corner of the window.

When you open Entourage, the window normally displays the contents of the email inbox for your *identity*.

When an email message arrives, it appears as an item in your **Inbox**. The **Inbox** is one of several folders listed in a **Navigation** pane on the left side of the window. In the main window, messages you have not yet read appear in bold-faced type. An icon to the left of the message heading also indicates its status. A sealed envelope indicates an unread message; an open envelope indicates you have read it.

You can move a newly received message to any of the displayed folders, including those you create yourself. For example, if the message is part of a continued exchange between yourself and a client, you can make a new folder for this exchange.

① Display a Preview Window

The message window displays an array of information about each message, including the sender, subject, and time and date it was sent. Entourage displays messages addressed to the current identity. If the sender attached a high priority to the message, a colored exclamation mark appears in the **Priority** column. A yellow mark indicates a high priority; a red mark the highest priority. Other columns indicate whether the message has been assigned to a category or a project.

TIP

If you're bothered by spam from one particular source, you can use this technique to direct email from this source to the **Deleted Items** or **Junk Email** folder.

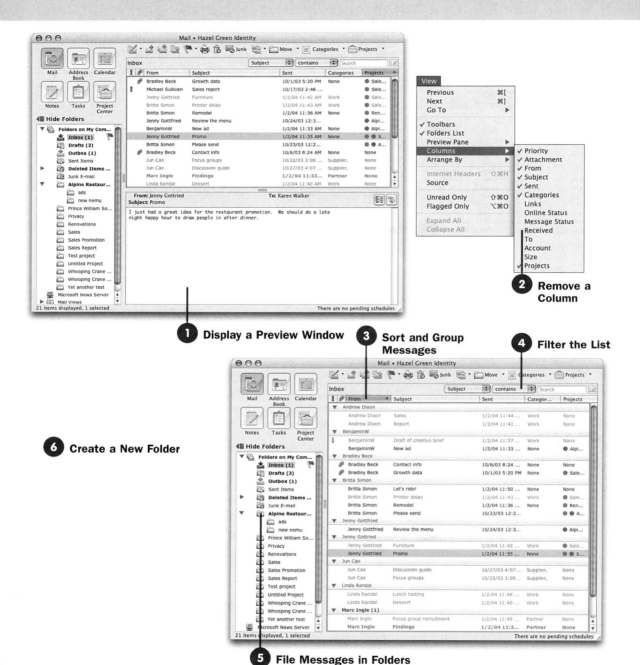

① Display a Preview Window

② Remove a Column

③ Sort and Group Messages

④ Filter the List

⑥ Create a New Folder

⑤ File Messages in Folders

You can double-click a message to display its full contents in a separate window. You can also elect to add a preview window to the display. Single-click a message from the main window, and its contents appear in the preview window. Buttons in the heading of the preview window allow you to change the type size and reset the word wrap of the message display.

To display or change the location of the preview window, select **View**, **Preview Pane** from the main menu. A submenu gives you the choice of displaying the preview window to the right of the email window, below the window, or not at all.

NOTE

There are many icons you might see to the left of each message heading. In addition to the message-read and priority icons, you might also see a paper clip indicating that a file has been attached to the message or a chain link indicating that you have associated the message with an item in the task list. A red flag symbol indicates you have flagged the item for future attention (see **126** **Enter Tasks and Notes**).

NOTE

Projects are described in **2** **Set Up a Project**. Categories are described in **123** **Assign Categories**.

❷ Remove a Column

In its initial form, the message window might tell you more than you really want to know. The messages appear in table format with a row for each message and a column for each type of information such as the sender, message header, and time it was sent. Entourage also initially displays columns for priority flags, attachment notices, and any categories or projects to which the message is assigned.

You can remove columns that are not of value to you right now, or you can add columns with information such as the message size and the time you received it. You can display as many as 14 columns with this kind of information.

To expand or contract the column display, select **View**, **Columns** from the main menu. A submenu displays the available column headings; those currently in use are checked. You can click each heading to add or remove it from the display.

❸ Sort and Group Messages

One advantage to displaying a particular column is that you can sort and group messages by the column's contents. For example, if you want to display messages in the order they were sent, click the **Sent** column heading. To reverse the order (and display the newest messages on top), click the heading again.

You can also display messages in groups. You can group all messages received today, for example, or all messages from a particular sender. To sort by sender, sort the messages on the **From**

column. Then from the main menu, select **View**, **Arrange By**, **Show in Groups**.

All messages from the same sender are grouped together. Use the arrows on the left side of the group headings to collapse or expand the display of individual messages. The bold-faced numbers—such as (2)—after some groups indicate the number of unread messages each group contains.

④ Filter the List

You can filter the message list to display only the messages you want to see right now. Suppose that you want to review all the messages in the **Inbox** that deal with sales. If so, you can apply a *custom filter* that displays only messages whose subject lines include the word *sales*.

Use the selection lists in the upper-right corner of the window. Open the first list and select the column heading on which you want to filter. Selections are **Subject**, **From**, **To**, **Category is**, and **Project is**.

Open the second list and select a comparison operator. The available comparisons depend on the column heading you have selected. If you selected **Subject**, you can ask for subjects that either begin with a particular term or contain it somewhere. If you selected **Category is** or **Project is**, the comparison is already selected, so the second list is not available.

In the third box, type the selection criteria. If you are looking for messages that involve sales, you could type **Sales**.

The filter is applied without doing anything further on your part. Only messages that meet the search criteria are displayed. To remove the filter and display the full list again, click the **Clear** button to the right of the filter criteria boxes.

⑤ File Messages in Folders

Another way to organize email messages, particularly older ones, is to place them in folders. Entourage includes some built-in folders to which it automatically assigns messages. The **Inbox** that holds your incoming messages is a folder; so are folders for uncompleted **Draft** messages and for messages you have **Sent** or deleted. There

TIP

You might be familiar with the *threaded* messages used in Internet discussion groups. Messages and responses are grouped by subject, and you can read the discussion of a particular subject in order. You can emulate the same thing by grouping your **Inbox**. Messages on the same subject often have similar subject lines such as **Re: Art Show**. If you group the display by subject, all messages with this subject line appear together.

KEY TERM

Custom filter—A filter applied to email messages in Entourage that meet certain selection criteria such as a similar subject, the same sender, or a common criteria assignment.

TIP

If you just want to display your unread messages, you can make a quick search. From the main menu, select **View**, **Unread Only**.

NOTE

The folders list includes triangular arrows you can click to conceal or display the list.

is also a **Junk E-mail** folder for messages you consider to be junk mail.

To place a message in a folder, drag the message from the main window to the folder.

⑥ Create a New Folder

You can create your own folders. Suppose that you want to establish a folder for sales-related messages. In the Entourage toolbar, click the arrow next to the **New** button. From the menu that opens, select **Folder**. (If you want to create a subfolder of an existing folder, select the parent folder; then click the **New** button and select **Subfolder**.)

The untitled folder appears in the folders list. Select the name and type **Sales** or some other title you want to give to the folder.

130 Receive "Executive Summaries" of Your Messages

Before You Begin

✔ **127** Set Up an Email Account

See Also

→ **129** Organize Your Email

Who says executive summaries are only for executives? There are times when anyone might want to see only a summary of a longer document. One of those times might be in a hotel room at the end of a tiring day. A long message comes creeping through a dial-up connection. You wait for it to download only to find you didn't really need to see it—at least not right now. At the very least, it could have waited until you got back to the broadband connection at the office.

There's a solution. Set up your email account so that it abbreviates messages of more than a certain size, say 20 kilobytes (KB). That's enough to identify the sender and subject and to display the first few lines of the message. If it's something you want to deal with right now, you can reconnect and download the entire message. Otherwise, you can either delete the message from the server or leave it there so that you can deal with it later.

① Select the Account

From the main Entourage menu, select **Tools**, **Accounts**. When the **Accounts** dialog box open, click the **Mail** tab. Double-click the account you want to modify. The **Edit Account** dialog box opens.

1 Select the Account

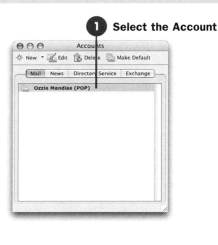

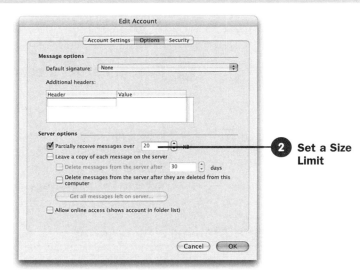

2 Set a Size Limit

3 Read a Partial Message

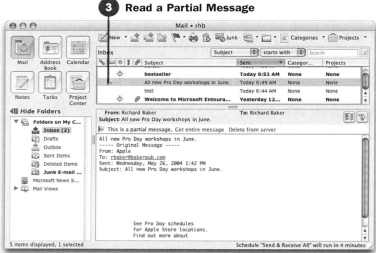

2 Set a Size Limit

Select the **Options** page. In the **Server options** section, enable the **Partially receive messages over** check box. This feature is initially set to truncate messages longer than 20KB. You can retain that

 TIP

Start with the standard setting of 20KB and see how it works. If you find the messages coming in are too short or still too long, follow these steps again to adjust the size value.

setting or select a longer or shorter length by typing a new size value in the text box.

③ Read a Partial Message

When an incoming message exceeds the size limit, it appears in the message window with a **Partial Message** symbol.

When you open the message, only the partial message is displayed; the full message remains on the server. If you want to read the full message, click the **Partial Message** symbol and select **Receive Entire Message** from the menu that pops up.

131 Address a Message to a Group

See Also

➜ **132** Sign Your Work

➜ **133** Email an Excel Worksheet

If you are setting up a meeting in the **Calendar** section of Entourage, you can use the group to address the meeting invitations.

If the member is a frequent correspondent, the program translates a partially typed entry into a complete one. You also can drag names from the **Address Book** window into the group dialog box, but this requires that the windows be carefully sized and positioned. Otherwise, the windows tend to obscure each other at critical moments.

Sometimes you want to send messages to more than one person. If several of you are engaged in a common effort, such as planning an art show, you might find yourself sending several messages to the same group. If so, you can add all the recipients to a group. The group then becomes an email address in its own right, and any message you send to the group automatically goes to all the members.

① Establish the Group

Display the **Address Book**. In the **Address Book** toolbar, click the **Add Group** button. A group dialog box opens. Enter a group name, such as **Art show committee**. The dialog box takes on that name.

② Add Members

In the toolbar at the top of the group dialog box, click the **Add** button (the large plus sign). If the member is in the **Address Book**, start typing the member's name. The program suggests a completed entry. If it is correct, press **Return**. The name is added to the list of group members.

To add the email address of someone who is not in the **Address Book**, click the **Add** button and type the member's email address.

3 Select Options

1 Establish the Group

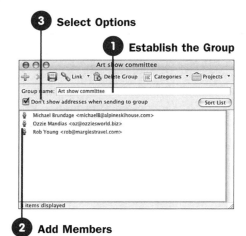

4 Address a Message to the Group

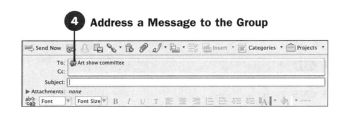

2 Add Members

3 Select Options

The group dialog box provides several options you can select if you want. If you don't want the full group to see who else is receiving the message, enable the **Don't show addresses when sending to group** check box.

You can use the dialog box's toolbar options to link other Entourage items to the group or assign the group to categories or projects.

When you're finished setting up the group, click the **Save Group** icon in the toolbar (it looks like a floppy disk, although Macs no longer have floppy disks). Then close the dialog box.

4 Address a Message to the Group

Open a new mail message. In the **To** field, type the name of the group. The message is addressed to every member, although you won't see the individual members' names. If you have enabled the **Don't show addresses** option, the recipient sees your address in both the **To** and **From** lines and any replies come directly to you.

132 Sign Your Work

Before You Begin

✔ **127** Set Up an Email
       Account

See Also

→ **131** Address a Message
       to a Group

→ **133** Email an Excel
       Worksheet

EY TERM

Signature—Standard
information added to email
text. It can include the
sender's name, title,
address, a graphic, and
similar information.

TIP

Click the **Use HTML** button
at the left end of the toolbar to activate formatting
features such as selecting
a typeface and size.
Otherwise, the signature is
formatted as plain text. If
you insert an HTML signa-
ture into a plain text message, the added formatting
is ignored. For more on
message text options, see
133 **Email an Excel
Worksheet**.

When you send an email message, the system sends your name and
email address as part of the header information of the email message.
This helps recipients recognize the source and makes it easy for them to
send you a reply. But you might want to include more than that: your
title, company, mailing address, or phone number—or all this information. If so, you can create a *signature* that automatically appends this
information to the text of the message. You can also include a corporate
logo or other graphic information.

A signature is not limited to the conventional identifying information.
Perhaps your organization requires that each message include standard
text such as a slogan or a notice to treat the contents as confidential
material. This information can also be included in a signature. If you
send your mail in HTML format, which permits graphics, you can go
further and include your picture or a company logo. (Note that, even if
you can send graphics, not all your recipients will have email programs
that allow them to view the graphics.)

You can create as many signatures as you like, perhaps one for business
use and another for personal messages. If you really want to entertain
your recipients, you can write several signatures and instruct Entourage
to apply them at random.

1 **Create a Signature**

From the Entourage main menu, select **Tools**, **Signatures**. In the
Signatures dialog box, click the **New** button. A dialog box for the
new signature opens.

In the **Name** box, give the signature a name. Apply a name you
can associate with the contents of the signature you are about to
create when that name appears later in the **Signatures** dialog box.

In the main window, type the text of the signature you want to
appear in each message. The first line includes a pair of dashes to
separate the signature from the text. This is a conventional format, but it is not required. You can leave this line blank or insert a
row of asterisks or other characters of your choice. Then start the
signature on the next line.

PART V: Entourage 2004

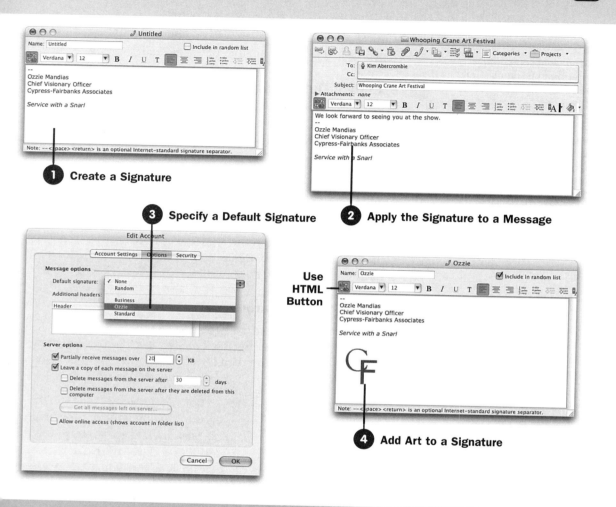

① **Create a Signature**

③ **Specify a Default Signature**

② **Apply the Signature to a Message**

④ **Add Art to a Signature**

When you're finished creating your signature text, close the dialog box. You are asked whether you want to save the signature. Select **Yes**.

② Apply the Signature to a Message

Write a new email message or open an existing one. When you are finished, place the insertion point at the bottom of the email message. In the message toolbar, click the **Signature** button.

TIP

If you want to be mildly entertaining, you can set Entourage to display several versions of your signature in random order. Select **Tools**, **Signatures**. When the **Signatures** dialog box opens, select each signature in turn; then click the **Edit** button. Enable the **Include in random list** check box. Then, when applying a signature, select **Random** from the signature list.

A list of saved signatures opens. Select the signature you want to apply. It is added to the bottom of the message.

3 **Specify a Default Signature**

If you maintain separate business and personal email accounts, you might want to use a different signature for each of them: formal for the business account and friendly for the personal account.

From the Entourage main menu, select **Tools**, **Accounts**. A list of Entourage accounts is displayed. Select the account for which you want to specify a default signature. The **Edit Account** dialog box opens.

Select the **Options** tab. In the **Message options** section, open the **Default signature** list and select the signature you want to use with this account. Click **OK**.

4 **Add Art to a Signature**

If you want to add a company logo—or your own picture—to a signature, you can do so in HTML mode. Select **Tools**, **Signatures** from the main menu and then select the signature to which you want to add the art. The selected signature is opened.

 TIP

You also can use the method outlined in step 4 to insert sound or movie files to be played when the message is opened.

Make sure that the **Use HTML** option is selected. Click inside the signature at the place where you want to apply the graphic. From the Entourage main menu, select **Message**, **Insert**, **Picture**. Use the **Finder** to locate the picture. Select it and click **Insert**. The picture appears in the signature. Click **OK** to close the dialog box. When prompted to save the signature, click **Save**.

133 Email an Excel Worksheet

See Also

→ **28** Insert an Excel Worksheet

You can create and send an email message in either of two formats. *Plain text* is what its name implies: It sends a text message with no attempt at added formatting. The advantages to this format is that it is quick and easy and all your recipients can read it.

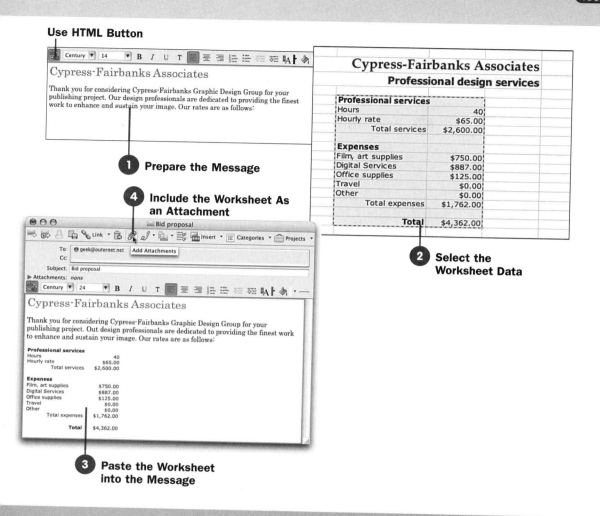

Use HTML Button

1 Prepare the Message

4 Include the Worksheet As an Attachment

2 Select the Worksheet Data

3 Paste the Worksheet into the Message

HTML format uses the language of the World Wide Web to add formatting that makes your message stand out. You can select type faces, styles, and colors, and you can insert graphics, sound, and movies. Often, including this kind of information might be overkill for a recipient who wants only quick facts. In fact, some email recipients might turn off the HTML feature. But sometimes HTML format can be as useful as it is decorative.

NOTE

You can turn HTML formatting on or off for messages you send, but it is always on for messages you receive.

NOTE

This process does not use the type of linking that that can place an editable Excel worksheet into a Word document (see **28** **Insert an Excel Worksheet** for instruction on editable linking). You probably do not want that capability anyway in an email message to be sent immediately. Nevertheless, you can insert the worksheet into the email message while retaining its contents and formatting.

NOTE

Other options on the **Paste Special** submenu are **Paste As Quotation** and **Paste As Plain Text**. Both insert the Excel data in text form; **Paste As Quotation** applies somewhat more formatting than the **Paste As Plain Text** alternative.

You might encounter such an opportunity if you are a design professional who wants to submit a bid by email. If you have worked up the bid amount in an Excel worksheet, you can incorporate that worksheet into the email message.

❶ Prepare the Message

Open a new or existing email message. Make sure that the **Use HTML** button is selected (the button is at the left end of the message toolbar).

❷ Select the Worksheet Data

In the Excel worksheet, select the range of cells that contain the information you want to insert in the email message. Select **Edit**, **Copy**.

❸ Paste the Worksheet into the Message

Return to the message window. From the main Entourage menu, select **Edit**, **Paste Special**. From the submenu that opens, select **Paste As Picture**. The Excel data is pasted into the message as a graphic that retains the original appearance and formatting. You can complete the message and send it.

❹ Include the Worksheet As an Attachment

If the worksheet contains too much data to include in the email message, you can send the entire workbook file as an attachment to this email message—indeed, you can send any other file as an attachment. To attach a file to an email message, click the **Add Attachments** button (the paper clip) in the toolbar at the top of the message window. In the **Finder** window that opens, locate and select the file you want to attach.

(134) Manage Email on Two Computers

Computers are like potato chips: You're seldom satisfied with just one. You might have one at work, another at home, plus a laptop or hand-held computer for those times in between. Perhaps you even have a wireless network to connect them all.

But how do you manage email across all those computers? Suppose that you receive a personal message at the office. Common sense, and likely company policy, dictates that when you reply to it, you should do so that night from home. That means you might have a problem: The message you want to respond to at home now is only on the computer at work.

There is a way to prevent this problem. When you receive an email message, it normally is stored on the computer that receives it. You can set up the program, though, so that the message remains on the server. Then you can retrieve it on any—or all—of your several computers.

This solution requires that you have access to the company network from your home computer. Whether you can do so, and on what terms, depends on the policies of your IT department. An alternative is to forward the message you receive on the work computer to the email address of your home system.

1 Open the Account

From the Entourage main menu, select **Tools**, **Accounts**. The **Accounts** dialog box opens. Click the **Mail** tab if that page is not already open. Double-click the account you want to change. The **Edit Accounts** dialog box opens.

2 Select the Server Option

Click the **Options** tab. On the **Server options** section, enable the **Leave a copy of each message on the server** check box.

3 Select a Deletion Option

Although your messages will now remain on the server, don't plan to leave them there indefinitely. The server's proprietors probably have limits on how many messages you can leave there and for how long. It's best to stay ahead of them.

Before You Begin

✔ (127) Set Up an Email Account

See Also

→ (130) Receive "Executive Summaries" of Your Messages

NOTE

The problem of email messages being located on a single computer's hard drive occurs only for accounts that use Post Office Protocol (POP). Most other protocols automatically keep messages on the servers. POP accounts, however, are the most common.

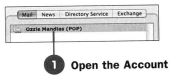

1 Open the Account

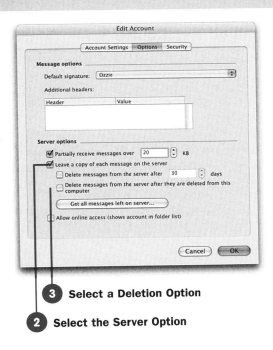

3 Select a Deletion Option

2 Select the Server Option

After selecting the **Leave a copy of each message on the server** option, you can select a way to maintain your server storage. You can delete the server messages after a fixed period of time; initially that interval is set at 30 days, but you can change it. You can delete messages from the server when you delete them from the computer. Or you can click the **Get all messages left on server** button. A list of messages appears, and you can delete them individually.

135 Put Email on a Schedule

See Also

→ **130** Receive "Executive Summaries" of Your Messages

If you have a full-time Internet connection (as you would with an Exchange network or broadband service), the Entourage email service is also full-time. You can expect to receive new email messages automatically throughout the day—and throughout the night, for that matter.

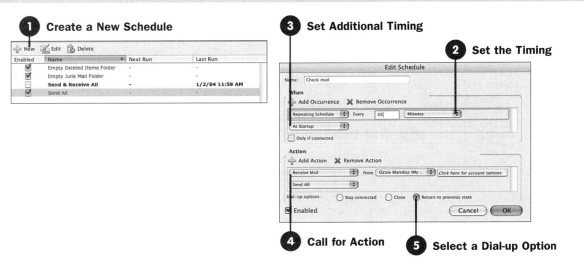

1 Create a New Schedule

3 Set Additional Timing

2 Set the Timing

4 Call for Action

5 Select a Dial-up Option

But if you have a dial-up service, retrieving email is more of a manual process. When you want to read your new email, you must specifically tell the program to dial the connection and download your messages. You must specifically take time to do it, and it's easy to forget.

Especially if you have a dial-up Internet service, it pays to put Entourage on a schedule. You can set the program to retrieve your mail at regular intervals throughout the day. You can use schedules in other ways, too. You can also write a schedule to empty your **Deleted Items** folder once a month or at some other interval. You can do the same with your **Junk Email** folder. You can write a new schedule, or you can edit one of the built-in schedules Entourage provides.

For these steps, suppose that you want the schedule to check for new email every 30 minutes and to send any outgoing messages at the same time. After you write them and click **Send**, outgoing messages are stored in the **Outbox** folder until they can be sent. This is also the storage folder for messages that are not sent because they have inaccurate addresses or other problems. You can open these unsent messages and correct them.

 NOTE

Scheduled activities can be set most easily by editing an existing schedule. This activity starts with a fresh schedule to demonstrate the entire scheduling process.

① Create a New Schedule

From the Entourage main menu, select **Tools, Schedules**. A list of existing schedules is displayed. You can enable the check boxes for those you want to run or remove the check marks from those you do not. Click the **New** button to create a new schedule.

② Set the Timing

The **Edit Schedule** dialog box opens. In the **Name** box, enter a title for the schedule you are about to create, such as **Check mail**.

The rest of the dialog box is divided into two sections. In the **When** section, you specify the time interval at which to run the schedule, such as every 30 minutes. In the **Action** section, you direct the actions to be taken at those times: receiving and sending the mail.

In the **When** section, open the first drop-down list (the occurrence option) and select **Repeating Schedule**. This is the best choice when the schedule is to be run every so many minutes, hours, or days. In the **Every** text box, enter **30** and select **Minutes** from the last drop-down list.

③ Set Additional Timing

There's one problem with this every-30-minutes schedule. When you first start Entourage, you might have to wait half an hour before the system retrieves your mail. You probably would like quicker initial service. You can add a condition that Entourage also check your mail when you first start the program.

Click the **Add Occurrence** button. A new line is added to the **When** section. It might already read **At Startup**. If not, open the drop-down list and select that occurrence option. This is the only entry necessary on that line.

④ Call for Action

In the **Action** section, open the first drop-down list and select **Receive Mail** as the action to happen. From the next drop-down list, select your email address. The **Click here for account options** button presents a single option: to limit the size of messages as described in **130** **Receive "Executive Summaries" of Your Messages**.

You can also add the action of sending mail. As often as Entourage checks for mail (as specified in the **When** section), it also sends any mail waiting in the **Outbox** folder. Click the **Add Action** button and, in the new row, select **Send All** from the action drop-down list. This option needs no further entries.

5 Select a Dial-up Option

If you are using a dial-up connection, you also must tell the program what to do after the action is complete. The options include staying connected or closing the connection. The **Return to previous state** option is often the best choice. It restores the connection status that was in effect before the schedule was run. Thus, if you were using the connection for something else when the schedule was run, you won't find yourself suddenly cut off when the action is completed.

 NOTE

If you want the schedule to run as you have set it up, make sure that the **Enabled** box is checked. You also can enable or disable schedules in the **Schedules** dialog box by placing or removing check marks in the boxes next to the schedule names.

136 Personalize Your Address Book with Pictures

The **Address Book** can hold a massive amount of information about your contacts: their addresses, ages, spouses' names, and even astrological signs. You can do one more thing to personalize a contact's record even further. You can add the person's picture.

See Also

→ **123** Assign Categories

→ **137** Import Contacts from Windows

1 Open the Contact's Window

In the **Navigation** pane, click the **Address Book** icon. In the list of contacts that appears, double-click the name of the contact whose picture you want to add.

When the contact's window opens, click the **Personal** page.

2 Drag the Photo from the Finder

The picture you want to use in this contact's page in the **Address Book** must be a graphics file available on your hard disk or network. Use the **Finder** to navigate to the picture file. Click the file and drag it into the image box of the **Address Book** listing.

NOTE

If you enter the contact's birth date on the **Personal** page of the **Address Book** record, Entourage automatically calculates his astrological sign.

① **Open the Contact's Window**

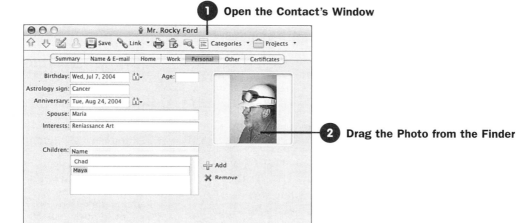

② **Drag the Photo from the Finder**

⒈⒊⒎ Import Contacts from Windows

Before You Begin

✔ **127** Set Up an Email Account

See Also

→ **138** Synchronize Two Address Books

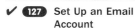

Delimited text file—A text file arranged to be imported into an Entourage **Address Book** or another database program. Within the text file, the columns are delimited by tabs or commas.

Many Mac users are recent migrants from Windows systems. If you are among that number, chances are you left behind an Outlook or Outlook Express address book that includes an extensive list of contacts. Retyping all these names and details into Entourage looks like a daunting experience. That's because it *is* a daunting experience.

It also is unnecessary. On the Windows side, you can export your contact information in the form of a *delimited text file*. This is a type of database file whose columns are delimited by either tabs or commas. You then can import that file into Entourage.

① Export Outlook Express Contacts

On the Windows computer, open Outlook Express. From the main menu, select **File**, **Export**, **Address Book**. The **Address Book Export Tool** opens.

Select the **Text File (Comma Separated Values)** option from the list of options and click the **Export** button. The **CSV Export** dialog box opens. In the **Save exported file as** text box, enter the name of the folder—or use the **Browse** button to select the folder—where you want to store the exported text file. Click **Next**.

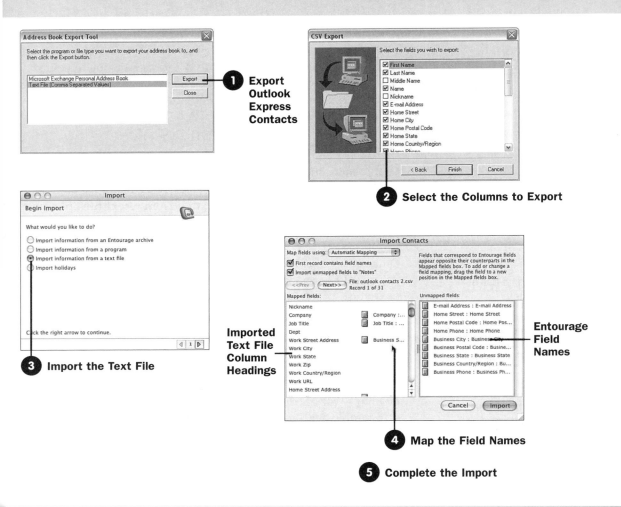

① **Export Outlook Express Contacts**

② **Select the Columns to Export**

③ **Import the Text File**

Imported Text File Column Headings

Entourage Field Names

④ **Map the Field Names**

⑤ **Complete the Import**

② **Select the Columns to Export**

The next page of the **CSV Export** dialog box displays a selection of columns you can export. The column headings you check here appear when you import the text file into Entourage. Enable the check boxes for the columns you want to export; disable the check boxes for those you do not want. Click **Finish**.

The file is saved in the specified destination folder. If you are on a network, you can save the file directly to a Macintosh folder, or

NOTE

If you are exporting from Outlook rather than Outlook Express, the commands are slightly different. Select **File**, **Import and Export**; then select **Export to a file**. You then can specify a tab-separated file and a destination folder.

you can copy it to your Mac after saving the file. If you have no network connection between the Windows machine and your Mac, consider sending an email from the Windows machine to your Mac, with the exported address book file as an attachment. On the Mac, open the email message in Entourage and save the attached file to a folder or the desktop.

3 Import the Text File

On the Mac, open Entourage. From the main menu, select **File**, **Import**. The **Import** dialog box opens. On the first page of the dialog box, select the **Import information from a text file** option and click the right arrow at the bottom of the dialog box to display page 2.

On page 2, select the **Import contacts from a tab- or comma-delimited file** option and click the right arrow to advance to the next page. In the **Import Text File** window, navigate to the folder where you saved the text file in step 2 and click **Import**.

4 Map the Field Names

Outlook and Entourage use different column headings, also called *field names*. For example, the imported file might use the column headings **Work Street Address**, **Work City**, and **Work State**. The comparable fields in Entourage are titled **Business Street**, **Business City**, and **Business State**. The field names in the imported file must be *mapped* to the field names in Entourage.

After you import the file, its fields are displayed in the left column of the **Import Contacts** dialog box. If the program was able to match the imported field name with an Entourage field name, the Entourage names are displayed in the center column.

The right column in the **Unmapped fields** window contains the Entourage fields that have not been successfully mapped to fields in the imported file.

To correct that, drag each unmapped field to the center column opposite the imported field to which you want to map it. For example, you can drag the **Business Street** field to a position opposite the **Work Street Address** field. When you're finished mapping the Entourage fields to the imported column headings, click **Import**.

KEY TERM

Map—To match the column headings in an imported data file with the column headings in the file that will accept the import.

NOTE

At the top of the **Import Contacts** dialog box, the **First record contains field names** option creates a record that contains the field names; the first contact thus becomes record 2, and this record is displayed in the **Unmapped fields** column. The **Address Book** imported for this exercise contains real names, so the field names in record 1 are displayed in the illustration. The **Import unmapped fields to "Notes"** option provides a place to put data that neither you nor the program could map. This information is appended to a note that appears when you display the contact's record.

5 Complete the Import

Before the import is completed, you are asked whether you want to save the mapping settings. If you do so, you can retrieve them later if you want to apply the same mapping to a different file. Make your choice, and click **Import**. The import is completed, and the contacts appear in the Entourage **Address Book**.

138 Synchronize Two Address Books

If you use Entourage in conjunction with an Exchange email server (as is likely in a corporate setting), the two programs regularly synchronize information about **Address Book** listings. If you make a change in your **Address Book**—entering a new contact, for example, or updating a contact's telephone number—Entourage and Exchange synchronize their records as necessary so that both contain the latest information.

This might sound like a good thing, but that's not always the case. For example, your **Address Book** might contain some personal contacts. For any of several good reasons, you might not want these contacts to appear on the company's Exchange server.

You can use categories to selectively choose which contacts are or are not synchronized. You can specify, for example, that contacts in a **No Sync** category should not be synchronized or that all items in a **Sync** category should be included in the synchronization.

1 Assign a Category

Assign the contacts to a category you want to either include or exclude from synchronization with the Exchange server.

In the **Address Book**, double-click the name of the contact you want to categorize. The contact's record is displayed. From the main Entourage menu, select **Edit**, **Categories**. A list of available categories is displayed. Click to place a check mark next to the categories in which you want to place the contact. If the contact is a family member you want to exclude from synchronization, select the **No Sync** category. If you want to include this contact as a work-related contact, select the **Sync** category. You can place a contact in more than one category. The family member could also be in a **Family** category, and the work contact could also be categorized as a **Customer** or **Supplier**.

Before You Begin

✔ **123** Assign Categories

See Also

→ **129** Organize Your Email

NOTE

You can use this method to synchronize Mail and Calendar items as well as individual **Address Book** contacts.

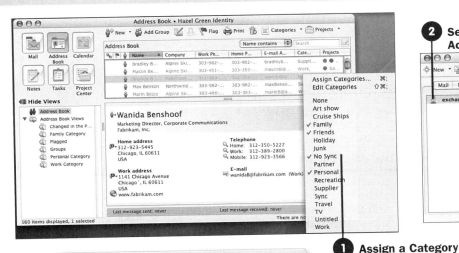

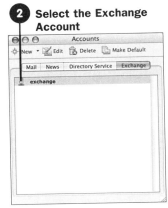

2 Select the Exchange
Account

1 Assign a Category

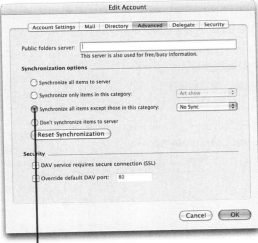

3 Set Synchronization Options

TIP

To create a new category for synchronization purposes, select **Edit**, **Categories**, **Edit Categories**. Click the **Add Category** button and type a category name—**Sync**, for example—and press **Return**.

When you're finished assigning this contact to categories, click **OK**. The contact is assigned to the selected categories.

2 Select the Exchange Account

From the main menu, select **Tools**, **Accounts**. In the **Accounts** dialog box, click the **Exchange** tab to open that page. The names of

one or more Exchange accounts are displayed. Select the account for which you want to set synchronization.

3 Set Synchronization Options

Click the **Edit** button at the top of the **Accounts** dialog box. When the **Edit Account** dialog box opens, click the **Advanced** tab to open that page.

In the **Synchronization options** section, you have four choices. You can choose to synchronize all or none of the **Address Book** records, you can choose to synchronize only the records within a certain category, or you can exclude a category from synchronization.

For example, to synchronize all items in the **Work** category, select **Synchronize only items in this category**; then select **Work** from the drop-down list on that line.

Click **OK**. When asked to verify the action, click **OK** again. Your synchronization options now are in effect.

 TIP

You can assign records to more than one category, so you can use a **Sync** or **No Sync** category *in addition to* any other category assignments.

19

Keeping Track of Times, Dates, and Schedules

IN THIS CHAPTER:

The Calendar module of Entourage is a planner and schedule that helps you keep track of what Microsoft calls *events*. As we all know, of course, most of these events are actually meetings.

Entourage gives other people the ability to schedule meetings and invite you to attend. Entourage gives you a *quid pro quo*: You can schedule your own meetings and issue your own invitations.

The Entourage Calendar can display your schedule for a month, a week, or a day, depending on your choice. You can use the Entourage Calendar to schedule events—both one-time events and recurring events. You can issue invitations by email and instruct Entourage to post a timely reminder notice. You even can set the Calendar to provide enough advance notice to allow for travel time.

139 Enter an Event

See Also

→ **140** Enter a Reminder

→ **141** Note a Recurring Event

→ **142** Keep Track of Time Zones

 NOTE

The author disclaims responsibility for the model schedule used in this chapter; it was prepared by Microsoft for use in training manuals like this book. The schedulers seem to be of the mind that meetings consume too much valuable working time, so they often must be held after hours. No doubt the weekly Friday night sessions on this calendar are wildly popular.

The Calendar has three main components. On the left side of the window is the **Navigation** pane that displays selected items from your schedule. Also, a small calendar appears at the bottom of the left column; select a date on that calendar to display the schedule for that day.

In the center of the window is the Calendar itself. It displays your schedule for the current month, week, or day, depending on the time period you have selected. To the right is a **Task** list that displays pending tasks.

① **Display the Calendar**

In the upper-left corner of the Entourage window, click the **Calendar** button. The **Calendar** window opens and displays your schedule for the current month, week, or day, depending on the time period you have selected most recently.

You can select a different time span from the toolbar across the top of the display. In a weekly view, you can display the work week or the full week including weekends. You also have the option of displaying events in list form rather than as a calendar (to do this, select **View**, **List** from the menu). Another option is to click the **View Date** button in the toolbar and then type the date you want to see.

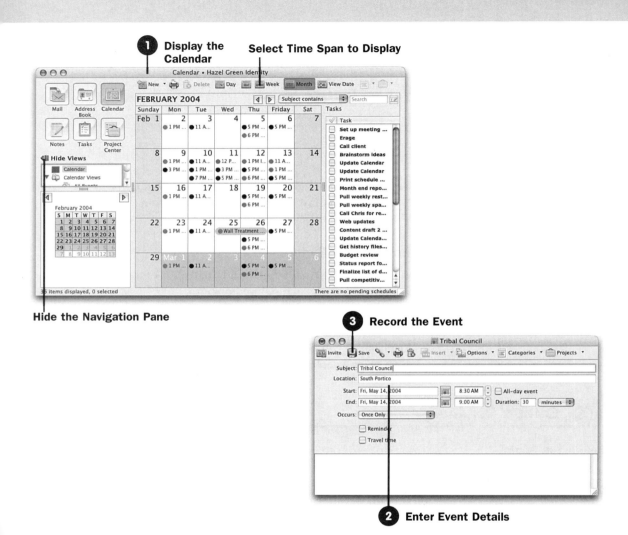

① Display the Calendar

Select Time Span to Display

Hide the Navigation Pane

③ Record the Event

② Enter Event Details

You can hide the **Navigation** pane and gain more room for the Calendar by clicking the **Hide Views** arrow in the middle of the left column. You can hide the **Task** list by opening the **Calendar** menu and removing the check mark next to the **Task List** option.

2 **Enter Event Details**

To schedule a new event on your Calendar, click the **New** button in the Calendar toolbar. A dialog box provides the means to enter details of the event.

In the **Subject** text box, type a name that identifies the event. In the **Location** box, enter the place where the event will be held. On the next line, set the date and the starting time.

On the next line, you can set either the finishing time or the duration of the meeting. The two are linked, so changes in one are automatically reflected in the other.

3 **Record the Event**

When you have finished entering the details of the event, click the **Save** button on the dialog box toolbar. The event is now listed in the Calendar.

If you want to remind yourself of this event, see **140** **Enter a Reminder**. If you want to notify other people of the event, see **143** **Invite People to the Event**.

140 Enter a Reminder

Before You Begin

✔ **139** Enter an Event

See Also

➔ **143** Invite People to the Event

You wouldn't want to be late for your own event, would you? If you want a wake-up call in time to get to the event, enable the **Reminder** check box and select the advance warning you want. At the appointed hour, an Office Notification appears on the screen.

That notice is the product of the Microsoft Office Notifications feature. You might say that this feature helps you manage your time by displaying timely reminders that an event is due. Well, you might say that. You also could say that this feature is an intrusive reminder that there is something else you should be doing right now. You'll probably have both reactions from time to time.

Office Notifications is installed when you install Office, and it is always running unless you turn it off—even if you are running no Office programs. If a reminder is scheduled while your computer is turned off, you receive the reminder when you turn the system back on.

2 **Set the Reminder**

1 **Open the Event**

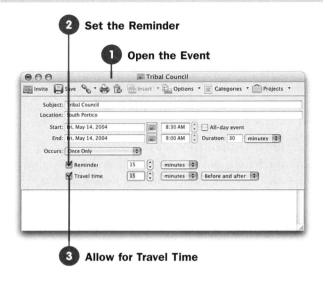

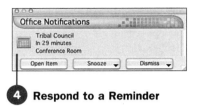

4 **Respond to a Reminder**

5 **Turn Off Office Notifications**

3 **Allow for Travel Time**

---

1 **Open the Event**

If you are planning the event, you can set the reminder at the same time you schedule the event. If you already have added the event to the Calendar, double-click the event to open the dialog box for it.

2 **Set the Reminder**

Enable the **Reminder** check box. In the fields to the right of this option, set the amount of advance notice you want to have. The program initially suggests 15 minutes. You can call for an advance notice of several hours or even days if you want.

3 **Allow for Travel Time**

If the event is farther away than down the hall, you might want the Calendar to allow for travel by blocking out a longer period of time for the event. If so, enable the **Travel time** check box. Enter the time it will take you to travel to the event and specify whether you want the Calendar to allow this time for travel to the event, from the event, or both.

NOTE

You can use Office Notifications in any Office program. For example, you could set a reminder that a Word document is due or that a colleague has asked for a copy of an Excel workbook. In the program's Standard toolbar, click the **Flag for Follow-Up** button. Then enter the date and time you want to receive the reminder.

4 Respond to a Reminder

When a reminder is due, a note pops up on your screen. At this point, you can do several things with it:

- **Close the reminder permanently**—If you are prepared to respond to the reminder right now, click **Dismiss**. The reminder will not be seen again.

- **Close the reminder temporarily**—If you click the **Snooze** button, the reminder disappears for 5 minutes. To snooze for a longer time, click **Snooze**, hold down the mouse button, and make a selection from the pop-up menu.

- **Open the event**—Click **Open Item** to display details of the event.

You also can call for a notification before a task is due or before the deadline for acting on a file you have flagged for follow-up. If so, you might also have these options:

- **Open a file you have flagged for follow-up**—Click the name of the file.

- Mark a task as complete—Click **Complete**.

5 Turn Off Office Notifications

If the Office Notifications feature becomes too intrusive, you can turn it off. Open the **Entourage** menu and select **Turn Off Office Notifications**. Repeat the procedure to turn on Office Notifications again.

NOTE

Office Notifications can be sent and received from any Office program—even if you don't have Entourage installed. To open a flagged file or to mark a task as complete, however, Entourage must be installed on your computer.

TIP

You can also turn Office Notifications on and off using the Finder. Go to the **Microsoft Office 2004** folder. Open the **Office** subfolder, and select **Microsoft Office Notifications**. When the program starts, open the **Office Notifications** menu and exercise the menu option to turn notifications on or off.

---

141 Note a Recurring Event

Before You Begin

✔ **139** Enter an Event

Some events might be all-day or multiday events (such as open houses, seminars, or training sessions). For these types of events, you can enable the **All-day event** check box in the event window and then complete only the date entries. For a three-day training session, for example, set only the starting and ending dates.

1 Open the Event

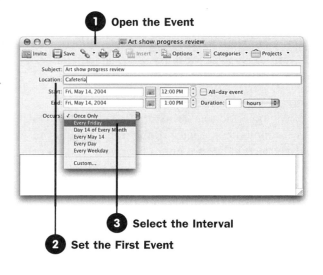

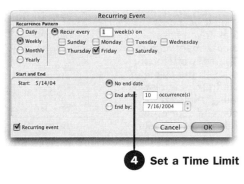

4 Set a Time Limit

3 Select the Interval

2 Set the First Event

Other events such as weekly staff meetings or monthly strategy sessions are **Recurring** events. For these kinds of events, you can set up the event only once and add each subsequent occurrence to the Calendar by selecting an option from the **Occurs** list.

1 **Open the Event**

If the event dialog box is not open, double-click the event in the Calendar listing.

2 **Set the First Event**

Set up the first occurrence of the event in the sequence of recurring events. Assume initially that the occurrence is a one-time event. For example, if you are planning to meet over lunch every Friday, set up an event for the first Friday you plan to meet.

3 **Select the Interval**

From the **Occurs** drop-down list, select an interval such as **Every Day**, **Every Thursday**, or **Day 23 of Each Month**. Each occurrence of the event is added to the Calendar. If you are scheduling a weekly event, the event appears in the Calendar every week for an indefinite period.

NOTE

When you first set a recurring event, it becomes perpetual. If you have scheduled a meeting for every Thursday afternoon, you can open the calendar 20 years from now, display that week's Thursday schedule, and your event will be there. So will your reminder setting if you have set one.

 Set a Time Limit

You might not want your event to recur indefinitely into the future. Perhaps you will want to reconsider the meeting schedule after a certain date or after you have held a certain number of these events.

Open the event dialog box and select **Custom** from the **Occurs** list. The **Recurring Event** dialog box opens. In the upper part of the dialog box, you can select additional options for recurring events, such as setting an annual occurrence. In the lower part of the dialog box, you can set the recurring event to stop after a certain number of occurrences or after a particular date.

For example, you might want to reconsider a weekly meeting schedule after 12 meetings. As an alternative, you could set the meetings to end after a particular date.

Select an interval and then click **OK**. After that interval, you can opt to continue the schedule for a few more months, or you can change the schedule. Either way, open the event listing and make the changes you want.

142 Keep Track of Time Zones

Before You Begin

✔ **139** Enter an Event

See Also

→ **143** Invite People to the Event

Sometimes, meetings are held down the hall or on the second floor. At other times, they are held in different time zones. You could schedule a conference call or an online chat from your office in Denver with a supplier in Philadelphia and a customer in Seattle. Entourage can readily adjust the Calendar display so that it displays the proper time in your time zone.

For the most part, Entourage automatically adjusts for events held in different time zones. For example, if a West Coast customer invites you to join a conference call, the customer probably will issue the invitation in Pacific time. Entourage can automatically adjust the time so it appears correctly on your computer for your time zone. Nevertheless, there are times when you must make manual adjustments, such as when you are scheduling a meeting while you are traveling outside your local time zone.

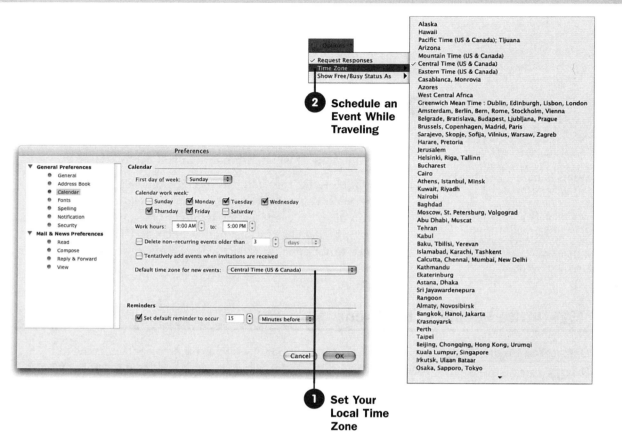

2 Schedule an Event While Traveling

1 Set Your Local Time Zone

1 Set Your Local Time Zone

Entourage is manufactured in the Pacific time zone, so it installs on your computer set for that time zone. Unless you live on the West Coast, you must first reset the program to your local time.

To do that, open the **Entourage** menu and select **Preferences**. In the **Preferences** dialog box, select the **Calendar** page. Open the list labeled **Default time zone for new events** and select your time zone.

 NOTE

The time zone you set for the Entourage Calendar is separate from the time zone you set for your system clock. When scheduling an event, though, Entourage compares the time zone settings and notifies you of any mismatch. You then can follow step 2 of these instructions to reset the time zone for the event.

This dialog box has several other Calendar preferences you can adjust. For example, if your standard week is something other than Monday through Friday, 9 to 5, you can change your work hours here.

② Schedule an Event While Traveling

TIP

Traveling overseas? You can set the time zone for events in dozens of cities throughout the world. Select Amsterdam, Baghdad, Bejing, or any other major international city, and its time zone is automatically set for the selected event.

Perhaps instead of a teleconference, you want to set up a meeting at the customer's Seattle office. If you enter the time according to your time zone, it will be wrong when you get to Seattle.

For situations like this, you can specify a different time zone for a single event. You can do this while you are creating the event, or you can open the event and do it later. In the toolbar of the event dialog box, click the **Options** button and select **Time Zone** from the menu that appears. Click the time zone in which the event will occur.

143 Invite People to the Event

Before You Begin

✔ **139** Enter an Event

See Also

➜ **140** Enter a Reminder
➜ **142** Keep Track of Time Zones

A meeting is not a meeting unless you can get people to come to it. In one snack food commercial, a leader gets people to a meeting by serving the sponsor's product in the conference room. You probably can get by with less devious means. After you've scheduled a meeting as a Calendar event, one way to get attendance is to send email invitations.

① Address Invitations

The label *invitations* makes the meeting sound like a social event, but it actually refers to an email procedure. If you have just scheduled the event, leave its dialog box open on the screen. Otherwise, double-click the event in the Calendar to open the event dialog box.

In the toolbar of the dialog box, click the **Invite** button. In the email form that opens, type the email address of the first person you want to invite. If that person is listed in the **Address Book**, you can drag or type her name and the email address is automatically filled in. Click **Add** to invite another participant; click **Remove** to take a name off the list.

1 Address Invitations

2 Send the Invitations

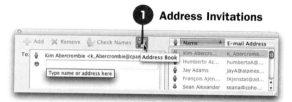

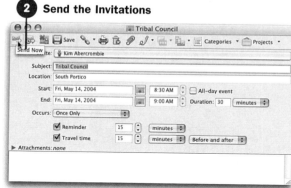

You also can click the **Address Book** button to open a list of names from the **Address Book**. Double-click a name to invite that participant to the open event. Use the **Check Names** button to ensure that the invitation list is made up of valid email addresses.

2 Send the Invitations

When you're finished, close the email message. In the dialog box for the event, click the **Send Now** button at the left end of the toolbar. The invitations are sent along with instructions to respond by return email.

If you do not have a full-time network connection, click the **Send Later** button instead. The invitations will be sent the next time you connect to the network.

NOTE

If you are connected to an Exchange server, there is a **Scheduling** page tab you can select to check the participants' schedules for available free time. It's somewhat common, though, for those with Exchange Calendars to schedule themselves for phantom events at times they do not want to be disturbed.

Index

Symbols

Numbers

A

B

How can we make this index more useful? Email us at indexes@samspublishing.com

409

D

E

How can we make this index more useful? Email us at indexes@samspublishing.com

411

F

How can we make this index more useful? Email us at indexes@samspublishing.com

413

G

H

I

J-L

How can we make this index more useful? Email us at indexes@samspublishing.com

415

M

How can we make this index more useful? Email us at indexes@samspublishing.com

417

Save

How can we make this index more useful? Email us at indexes@samspublishing.com

421

T

U-V

W

How can we make this index more useful? Email us at indexes@samspublishing.com

423

X-Z

Your Guide
to Computer
Technology

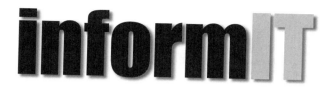

Key Terms

Don't let unfamiliar terms discourage you from learning all you can about Microsoft Office 2004. If you don't completely understand what one of these words means, flip to the indicated page, read the full definition there, and find techniques related to that term.